Work Under Capitalism

New Perspectives in Sociology

CHARLES TILLY AND SCOTT MCNALL, SERIES EDITORS

Work Under Capitalism

Chris Tilly
University of Massachusetts at Lowell

Charles Tilly
Columbia University

 WestviewPress
A Division of HarperCollinsPublishers

To Charlotte, Christopher, Abigail, and Jamie—
the next generation of workers

New Perspectives in Sociology

Copyright © 1998 by Westview Press, A Division of HarperCollins Publishers, Inc.

Published in 1998 in the United States of America by Westview Press, 5500 Central Avenue, Boulder, Colorado 80301-2877, and in the United Kingdom by Westview Press, 12 Hid's Copse Road, Cumnor Hill, Oxford OX2 9JJ

Library of Congress Cataloging-in-Publication Data
Tilly, Chris.
   Work under capitalism / Chris Tilly and Charles Tilly.
      p.   cm.—(New perspectives in sociology)
   Includes bibliographical references and index.
   ISBN 0-8133-2278-2 (hardcover).—ISBN 0-8133-2274-X (pbk.)
   1. Labor.   2. Labor market.   3. Economics—Sociological aspects.
I. Tilly, Charles.   II. Title.   III. Series: New perspectives in
sociology (Boulder, Colo.)
HD4901.T54   1998
331—dc21   97-29016
                                                                            CIP

10   9   8   7   6   5   4   3   2   1

Contents

Illustrations

Figures

Photo Credits

1
How to Work Things Out

Lessons from a Life of Hard Work

Rural French worker Marie-Catherine Gardez, born in 1891 in the Nord region, worked hard for all of her long life (Grafteaux 1985). Although she received four years of schooling, at the age of nine she began plying a loom with the rest of her family in the basement of their house. They wove cloth in a putting-out system, in which an agent provided them with thread and then paid them by the piece for cloth. Since automated, factory-based power looms had swept the French textile industry decades earlier, their hand looms and home-based labor represented a disappearing style of work.

During the growing season, the family migrated to Normandy, where they toiled on a farm owned by a large Parisian company, here receiving a combination of piece rates—40 sous per plot weeded, 3 sous per row of sugar beets thinned, and so on—and day rates for spreading fertilizer or working in the farmyard or house. At the harvest they gathered sheaves of wheat, in the early years following strapping young men with scythes, later following a mechanized harvester. Meanwhile, young Marie-Catherine helped her family with household tasks, such as cooking, cleaning, and laundry, and "stole" thread from her parents to weave handkerchiefs for a trousseau.

When Marie-Catherine married Auguste Santerre, they continued weaving and doing seasonal farmwork. At the farm, she moved on to helping with cooking and housework at the farmhouse, while he helped to run the farm's sugar refinery—both now earning fixed salaries. Marie-Catherine continued to cook and clean in her own household and soon was raising a son; Auguste made fuel bricks and kept a garden for their own use, and also joined the volunteer fire department.

Their son, Auguste junior, apprenticed to a local barber, then took a barber's assistant job (found for him by a cousin) in a distant town in the Paris region, working for wages plus tips. He supplemented his income by loading bricks at a factory. When the barbershop closed down, he opened his own small barbershop for business on weekends when the factory was closed, renting space from an acquaintance of his parents, a woman originally from the same village in the Nord. Marie-Catherine and Auguste senior then joined him in his town, finding work on another farm owned by the same Paris-based company. During the turbulent 1930s, Auguste père joined a union and went on strike. The union, with some help from France's Social-

With permission of the Russell Sage Foundation, we have adapted some material in this book from our "Capitalist Work and Labor Markets," in Neil J. Smelser and Richard Swedberg, eds., *The Handbook of Economic Sociology* (Princeton and New York: Princeton University Press and Russell Sage Foundation, 1994). We are grateful to Alex Julca for research assistance, to Paula Maher and Hong Xu for library assistance, to Cheryl Seleski for help with manuscript preparation, and to Jennifer Swearingen for copy editing.

ist-led government, won the right to permanent rather than seasonal jobs. During World War II, the farm and its sugar refinery came under German military rule, and food and other necessities were rationed. When Marie-Catherine and Auguste finally retired, he cultivated their garden and those of neighbors; she continued to do housework and knit socks for neighbors, and the neighbors offered help in return. Even at a hospital and rest home in her mid-eighties, Marie-Catherine knit for the women in her ward.

What can we learn from this arduous curriculum vitae (other than heaving a sigh of relief that we no longer face the twelve-hour workdays and seven-day workweeks that the Santerres experienced in their paid employment)? For one thing, work for an employer with the power to hire and fire at a determinate rate of compensation—that is, work in a labor market—only represents one of many forms of work in the Santerres' lives. Volunteer work, favors for neighbors, self-employment, housework, and even children's unpaid work at the loom (since the parents received the pay) fall outside this model.

In addition, the incentives and rewards for the Santerres' work varied widely. In some cases, they received material compensation, including cash (whether piece rate, hourly wage, tip, or proprietor's income) or other rewards (such as training in the son's apprenticeship or the thread Marie-Catherine and her sisters "stole" from their parents). For much of the work, the main incentive was commitment to a family unit or community. Coercion, which played some role even in these more benign cases, came to the fore under German occupation. We will return frequently to the triad of compensation, commitment, and coercion throughout this book.

The Santerres even performed the same work both inside and outside a labor market, under different incentive systems. Marie-Catherine prepared food, cleaned, and laundered for pay in the farmhouse, then went home and performed the same tasks without compensation for her family. Auguste the elder tended the company's crops, but also worked his own garden. The younger Auguste barbered as apprentice, wage-laborer, and proprietor.

A number of larger forces shaped the Santerres' work lives. Capitalist firms—the farm, the cloth merchant, the brick factory—exerted the largest single influence, but their power was tempered by worker organization, by state intervention, and by workers' alternative sources of subsistence. Technological change drove down the price of the family's weaving services, and altered the pace and work environment of the wheat harvest. The family's own history stamped the location and nature of their toil, as did France's productive history. Finally, a dense set of social relations surrounded the Santerres' work. This is clearly true for the work not mediated by markets, but it holds as well for their interaction with the labor market. They migrated and found jobs through networks of kin and acquaintances. They performed work at times as a family unit, at other times among coworkers whose shared norms formed the basis for unionization.

Getting to Work

The saga of Marie-Catherine and Auguste anticipates many of this book's major themes. In contemporary industrial countries, what people call "going to work" typically means leaving home, traveling for a while, and arriving at a place someone else owns to expend effort for pay under someone else's orders; it means holding a job of some kind. Waged work of this kind has certainly become much more prevalent in the industrial world over the last century. Measured by total effort expended, nevertheless, a large share of work still takes place outside the ambit of jobs and labor markets: not only family business, fiction-writing, professional consulting for fees, commission sales, recital-giving, services for tips, and criminal enterprises, but also child care, domestic food preparation, home repairs, and schoolwork. Our book takes a large view of work in order to place the contemporary operation of jobs and labor markets in comparative perspective. It also takes a long view in order to promote understanding of the constant change that occurs within the world of work.

While concentrating on paid work and labor markets in the United States and other sites of industrial capitalism, the book frequently sweeps its gaze farther afield. Combating technological, market, and cultural determinisms, it argues that

- work does not issue from the efforts of isolated individuals who respond to market cues but from social relations among workers, employers, and consumers;
- labor markets are not natural, universal phenomena, but historically contingent products of struggles for control over the conditions of work;
- histories embedded in law, memory, prevailing beliefs, accumulated knowledge, and existing social relations strongly constrain paths of change in productive organization;
- employers, workers, and entrepreneurs create new productive organizations as mosaics of previously existing social structure and thereby unwittingly commit themselves to the established connections of that social structure;
- new technologies enter the organization of work chiefly as instruments of profit-seeking capitalists, always within stringent limits set by shared understandings and existing social relations;
- workers, employers, and supervisors often use their specialized knowledge of productive technologies as means of struggle;
- outcomes of struggles themselves reshape shared understandings, laws, governmental action, and beliefs of all parties concerning what organizations of work are proper or possible.

Above all, we reject efforts to derive work, labor markets, and professions directly from the timeless logics of individual interests, technology, market forces, or ideology.

Although we blast away at rival theories from time to time, however, our book does not concentrate on destruction or deconstruction of bad ideas. Instead, we do our best to construct a culturally grounded, historically informed account of work and labor markets as social interaction rather than as summations or resultants of individual action. In so doing, we seek to advance a program of transactional analysis that dates back to Adam Smith and Karl Marx, but has recently been gaining strength in economics and adjacent social sciences after a long period of inattention.

Assaying the Competition

Three broad views of labor dominate the theoretical landscape in both economics and sociology. In economics, the three perspectives go by the names of *neoclassical, Marxist,* and *institutionalist* theories. Sociologists most commonly call their close cousins rational-actor, Marxist, and structural theories. Within sociology, Weberian and functional analyses of economic phenomena (which explain social processes quite differently from rational-actor, Marxist, and structural approaches) have sometimes prevailed, but at present they have almost nothing distinctive to say about work and labor markets. Although more sociologists than economists pursue neo-Marxist or institutionalist analyses of economic structures and processes, the three perspectives cut across disciplinary boundaries.

Neoclassical Theories

Neoclassical theorists approach work with a startling degree of naturalism. According to this view, *homo sapiens* is *homo economicus*. Rational maximizing economic behavior has been characteristic throughout history. In particular, the trade-off between labor and leisure is eternal. Humans have always had to decide how to divide their time between work (with the consumption goods it brings) and nonwork, regardless of who is in charge. "In a perfectly competitive market," according to Paul Samuelson (1957: 894), "it really doesn't matter who hires whom: so have labor hire 'capital.'" A corollary of Samuelson's theorem is that self-employment generates the same results as other-employment. Even the invention of labor markets, by this view, did not mark a dramatic break in the history of work.

In this naturalistic framework, what propels economic history? The neoclassical view emphasizes the role of technological change and population growth, as formalized in the Solow growth model (Solow 1970). Other historical changes leave little or no trace. Of course, neoclassical analysts readily acknowledge that people modify labor markets with a variety of coercive or consensual structures. But the impact of these structures is transitory; once coercion is lifted, employers and workers soon revert to the same behavior they would have followed in the absence of coercion. And, in any case, *explaining* these changes is not part of the neoclassical agenda. "Often the economist takes as data," Samuelson remarked in another work, "certain traditionally noneconomic variables such as technology, tastes, social and institutional conditions, etc.; although to the students of other disciplines these are processes to be explained and analyzed, and are not merely history" (1983: 318–319).

Most neoclassical theorists, furthermore, see modern Western capitalism as free of such modifying structures, even if Milton Friedman (1962) and Hernando de Soto (1989), among others, argue that it should be made freer still. Where institutionalists see a thicket of labor market institutions rooted in custom, neoclassical labor economists such as Edward Lazear and Joseph Stiglitz see profit-maximizing solutions to efficiency problems. Neoclassical theorists allow limited exceptions to the view that "history is neutral." For instance, macroeconomists note that worker and firm expectations of future inflation depend on past experience with inflation, with the result that once a level of inflation has arrived it tends to persist. Similarly, elevated unemployment may self-perpetuate in a process of "hysteresis" (Blanchard & Summers 1986). But these exceptions are few and short-term in their historical scope.

Neoclassical thinking spotlights *individual preferences.* Persons exist as independent, self-motivating actors. Each person acts in a rational, self-interested way to maximize his or her (inherently unmeasurable) utility. Not only is the individual the unit of analysis, but indeed—given certain plausible axioms about the nature of utility—one cannot meaningfully aggregate from individuals up to a group or social utility function, as Kenneth Arrow (1950) demonstrated with his Impossibility Theorem.

Neoclassical scholars assume that the tastes or preferences that make up a person's utility function are relatively stable and logically consistent. They take for granted certain patterns of preference: More goods are better, leisure is preferred to labor, marginal utility diminishes (that is, each additional unit of a good brings less utility to a consumer than the previous unit). Although a neoclassical framework does not altogether rule out altruism or envy (either of which implies that an individual's utility is affected by the utility levels of others), the framework does presuppose that narrowly focused self-seeking dominates in the aggregate. Thus, for example, if many people preferred an austere lifestyle to an abundance of consumer goods, or if the typical worker's choice of job and degree of effort exerted on the job were shaped primarily by affection or loyalty to employers rather than wages and working conditions, standard neoclassical models of work would go awry.

Neoclassical theory holds that preferences are determined outside the economy, and thus outside of the world of work. Indeed, according to

George Stigler and Gary Becker (1977), sufficiently little variation in tastes prevails that such variation is unlikely to have much economic significance. Meanwhile, the neoclassical firm—the key economic unit other than individual consumers or workers—acts single-mindedly to maximize the owner's or stockholders' profits. Again, neoclassical theorists do not deny that individual businesses may espouse world peace, environmental sustainability, or the promotion of a Christian lifestyle, nor that some managers may hold false or outdated beliefs about the way the economy works. But to the extent that any of these beliefs interfere with profitability, says the neoclassical doctrine, harderheaded maximizers will shoulder aside these owners and managers within their firms, and/or the firms will be displaced by more practical competitors.

Although this individualistic, rational model of economic activity has long characterized neoclassical descriptions of the *microeconomic* world of individual markets, until recently neoclassical *macroeconomics* left more space for the power of broadly held beliefs. In explaining why wages are "sticky" (failing to fall even when unemployment expands), John Maynard Keynes (1964) argued that workers strenuously resist any attempts to reduce their wages *relative to those of other workers*. He added, however, that due to "money illusion," they do not perceive the erosion of real wages by inflation as a wage cut. In short, he described workers more attentive to their *relative* than *absolute* well-being—a description quite at odds with mainstream microeconomics.

Gary Becker sounded the battle cry of a new generation of neoclassical economists when he proclaimed (1976: 5) that "the combined assumptions of maximizing behavior, market equilibrium, and stable preferences, used relentlessly and unflinchingly, form the heart of the economic approach as I see it." In the early 1980s, the rational expectations revolution (Begg 1982) swept Anglo-American macroeconomics, as theorists not only posited that all economic actors act rationally, but assumed as part of any economic model that all economic actors understand fully how the model works.

Neoclassical theorists look at the world of work and see symmetry of power. When a worker sells labor services to a capitalist (or, for that matter, directly to a consumer), both parties equally enjoy what could be called *Walrasian power*—the power to do business with someone else instead. (This sort of power bears the name of Léon Walras, the nineteenth-century Belgian economist who theorized that a bidding process brings supply and demand into balance.) Since "it really doesn't matter who hires whom," workers and capitalists make their contracts symmetrically. Such symmetry depends on a labor market that acts as if it were made up of many small units (individual workers and small employers).

Although actual economies manifest a mix of large and small units—18 percent of U.S. workers are represented by unions and 50 percent work in establishments employing 500 people or more—neoclassical economists argue that Walrasian impulses undermine market power and concerted economic action in all its forms. Workers' ability to migrate erodes the employer's power in a company town. Defectors, undercutters, and free riders jeopardize union attempts to extract rents as well as employer cartels' endeavors to depress wages. Employers who discriminate on the basis of race, gender, or any other characteristic not linked to productivity will profit less than nondiscriminators and will eventually be driven out of the market. Government policies that seek to overrule the market generate underground economies, informal sectors, black markets. Thus—at least tendentially—power remains atomized, and the power of workers and owners remains symmetrical. Of course such reasoning follows a circular path, first assuming that workers and employers each pursue individual ends independently, then concluding that workers and employers act individualistically. But that circularity gives the argument an agreeable coherence.

Corresponding to Walrasian atomization in the market is ostensible pluralism within organizations and the polity. Elton Mayo, one of the founders of industrial psychology, denounced the supposition of power imbalances in no uncertain terms:

> Management is capable, trained, and objective. Management uses scientific knowledge, particularly engineering knowledge, for making decisions. Political issues are illusions created by evil men. Society's true problems are engineering problems. (Mayo, quoted in P. Thompson 1983: 27)

In this sense, neoclassical theory has an impressively egalitarian cast.

Neoclassical theory thus solves the problem of distribution between workers and capitalists *and* the problem of varying wage levels among workers at a single stroke: Each person gets paid the value of the marginal product of the input (labor, capital, land) they provide. Human capital theory (Becker 1964; Willis 1986) and the theory of compensating differentials (Rosen 1986) extend the basic model, positing that in equilibrium workers must be rewarded for costly investments in their own productivity (through means such as education, training, and health care) and must be compensated for hardships and threats on the job (such as dirt, noise, or danger).

Marxist Theories

Karl Marx and Friedrich Engels declared that the history of all hitherto existing society is the history of class struggles" (Marx & Engels 1958: 34). But within Marxism, even within Marx's own works, a dispute has long raged between *teleological* and *contingent* views of how these class struggles have unfolded. Marxists emphasize that labor markets are a recent historical phenomenon, displacing work organized on the basis of feudal ties, slavery, and other bonds of obligation or direct coercion. The creation of labor markets depended not only on achieving a particular level of technological development, but also on the initial accumulation of wealth and productive resources by capitalists, as well as the proletarianization of large groups of people.

From this starting point, however, teleological and contingent Marxist views diverge. The teleological perspective, much like the neoclassical one, views technology as the mainspring of economic development: "The hand mill gives you society with the feudal lord; the steam mill gives you society with the industrial capitalist" (Marx 1976: 166). Although Marx never fully committed himself to so invariant a trajectory (see Hobsbawm in Marx 1964), Engels (1978) described an inexorable sequence leading from primitive communism to slavery, feudalism, capitalism, and then socialism, with change in the forces of production driving changes in relations of production. In a similar spirit, Harry Braverman (1974) portrayed ceaseless efforts by capitalists to deskill workers through an ever-finer division of labor. On the other hand, Marxists since Marx in the "Eighteenth Brumaire" (Marx 1958) have stressed the indeterminacy of political and economic struggles. Recently, for example, the French *régulation* school and their non-French emulators have argued that capitalism forms a series of regulatory regimes, with the nature of each successive regime depending on contingent historical circumstance (Aglietta 1976; Boyer & Mistral 1978; Gordon, Edwards & Reich 1982; Piore & Sabel 1984).

Marxists emphasize asymmetry of power and the *exploitation* of workers by capitalists. As Marx turned from commodity exchange to labor exchange, he described the two main actors:

> He, who before was the money-owner, now strides in front as the capitalist; the possessor of labor-power follows as his laborer. The one with an air of importance, smirking, intent on business; the other, timid and holding back, like one who is bringing his own hide to market and has nothing to expect but—a hiding. (Marx 1976: 176)

Beginning with Marx, Marxists point to three reasons for this imbalance. First, workers have no alternative to working in the capitalist labor market; they have nothing to sell but their "hides." Second, capitalism in its normal functioning generates persistent unemployment. The reserve army of labor bids down wages, minimizing workers' bargaining power. Third, the state bolsters capitalist economic power. To be sure, Marxists have hotly debated whether capitalist influence over the state is direct or indirect, instrumental or structural (see Jessop 1972 for a useful summary). Furthermore, although employers have the upper hand, the actual balance of power at a given time and place depends on the class struggle.

Beyond this central fault line of power running through the workplace, economy, and society, Marxists—at least since the influence of the New Left—attempt to theorize patterns of alliance and enmity, privilege and exclusion among and between groups of workers and employers. Marxists argue, for example, that worker attempts to gain more favored positions have coupled with capitalist interests in keeping workers divided to create or reinforce distinctions by race, gender, and nationality.

In contrast with the neoclassical notion of individual preferences, Marxists stress *class consciousness*—collective consciousness of a class's interests. In a Marxian model, class consciousness grows more or less naturally out of the social relations of production. Capitalists, aware of their minority status, work together to defend their economic and political interests. Working class consciousness springs from a twofold socialization of labor: the growth of large establishments with a detailed division of labor and, more broadly, the growing economic interdependence (via exchange) of workers in all industries. The actual institutions that express and propagate class consciousness may vary widely: political parties, unions and employer associations, clubs, secret societies, bars, sporting or musical events, schools, and so on. Moreover, consciousness has a decisive influence in the class struggle that structures work relations.

Once more diverging from neoclassical thought, Marxists hold that ideology is rooted in the economy: One's consciousness is shaped by one's material situation. Just as Marxists have divided over teleological versus contingent views of history, they have quarreled over *deterministic* versus *interactive* views of the relationship between base and superstructure, economy and consciousness. Although most present-day scholars of Marxist and associated structuralist schools distance themselves from the mechanical formulation that the economic base dictates the world of ideas, they still generally hold that *people's perceived interests are greatly molded by their structural economic contexts*. Thus, for example, workers' experiences of the working world constrain and channel their aspirations and preferences (Cohen & Rogers 1983; Burawoy 1979, 1985; Dunk 1992; Steinberg 1991).

This claim offers Marxists some leverage on an important problem in their worldview: Proletarian consciousness has generally fallen short of Marxist expectations. A strong case *can* be made for the power of capitalist class consciousness—although this consciousness is hardly consensual, as evidenced by comparison of the *Wall Street Journal* and *Business Week*, or of contrasting views among the Council for Economic Development, the Business Roundtable, and the National Association of Manufacturers. But although historians such as E. P. Thompson (1963) and Alan Dawley (1976) demonstrate the vitality of working class ideology in particular times and places, overall working class consciousness in Western capitalism has been fragmented and sporadic.

Marxists reject the technological determinism implicit in the neoclassical model of wage-setting. They argue instead that a combination of class struggle and custom set the overall wage level at "the cost of existence and reproduction of the worker" (Marx 1978: 206). As for variations in wage levels among workers, Marx himself espoused a variant of human capital theory *avant la lettre*, but neo-Marxists tend to view wage differences in terms of privilege and power. According to Samuel Bowles and Herbert Gintis (1976), the most important function of education under capitalism is not to enhance worker productivity, but to socialize and prepare the different classes for their roles in the hierarchy of production.

Institutional Theories

Much like Marxists, institutionalists have oscillated between naturalism and contingency. For every Selig Perlman arguing for a "natural" form of unionism or John Dunlop claiming that postwar U.S. industrial relations represented a predictable outgrowth of industrial society, there has been a Thorstein Veblen commenting on the "opaque," blind drift of history (Dente 1977) or a Michael Piore suggesting that alternative ways of organizing work under capitalism are possible. The institutionalist emphasis on custom builds a certain amount of contingency into models of the labor market. For, as Marc Bloch points out in the context of feudalism, customs are powerful shapers of behavior, but are also themselves constantly undergoing change (Bloch 1970: 113–116). Alfred Chandler (who identifies himself as an evolutionary theorist rather than an institutionalist but retains many affinities with institutionalism) goes so far as to argue that far from acting as simple vehicles of market forces, firms make, shape, and use markets to their own advantage or detriment (Chandler 1992; Teece 1993).

Institutionalists portray pluralism as the typical configuration of power in capitalist work relations. While acknowledging some of the asymmetries posed by Marx, they identify a set of forces blunting capitalist power. Organized labor and the welfare state represent "countervailing powers," in J. K. Galbraith's phrase. Workers with long-term jobs possess job-specific knowledge that is of great value to their current employer and of little or no value to other employers. A bargaining process over wages and other terms of employment results, with no economically determinate outcome. Institutionalist analysis thus dissolves the division between capitalist and working classes into a set of smaller relationships shaped by product demand conditions, technology, custom, and a variety of institutions. For example, workers and capitalists in the capital-intensive "core" of an economy may have more interests in common than obtains between workers in core industries and those in peripheral industries; in any case, there are marked and systematic differences between jobs in the two sectors.

Where neoclassical theorists speak of individual preferences, and Marxists of class consciousness, institutionalists emphasize *group norms*. Arthur Ross's (1948) "orbits of coercive comparison" or John Dunlop's (1957) "wage contours," for instance, echoed Keynes by placing relative wages and notions of fairness at the center of wage determination theory. Contrary to Stigler and Becker, institutionalists argue that different people view the world quite differently and that understanding these differences constitutes an important objective of economic theory (Piore 1979a). Of course, worldviews do not always remain static, as James March (1972) notes in his call for a "theory of goal-finding" (he also terms it a theory of "sensible foolishness") that would explain how people move from one view to another.

Like Marxists, institutionalists see ideologies constantly regenerated and reshaped by the functioning of the economy. But institutionalists more often point to the independent power of ideas. All social institutions are *inventions*—"humanly devised constraints"—holds Douglass North (1991: 97). But inventions such as concepts and measures, once coined, color the perceptions of employers, workers, and policymakers: For example, Fred Block (1985, 1990) and Michael Best (1990) describe how outmoded accounting systems and productivity measures have steered the attention of U.S. firms and government officials to cutting labor costs—even though competitive advantage has increasingly shifted to other grounds.

Institutionalists remain ambivalent on the question of *individualism*—the extent to which independent, self-motivated actors with preestablished interests and preferences make the decisions that drive the world of work. Implicitly rejecting John R. Commons's call for an economics beginning with transactions rather than individuals, for example, Oliver Williamson holds closely to a neoclassical conception of rationally maximizing actors and beams his theoretical energy at constraints within which rational action takes place. Economic institutionalists, on the whole, temper individualism chiefly by insisting on collective influences and limits to rationality. Indeed, institutionalists differ from *both* Marxists and neoclassical theorists in entertaining the possibility that the "bounded rationality" of managers (to use Herbert Simon's [1976] term) may be so narrowly bounded as to be essentially nonrational. Instead of an ordered pursuit of profit, institutionalists often point to managerial behavior decisively shaped by customs, by—in some cases obsolete or inaccurate—beliefs, and even by the arbitrary experimentation that Tom Juravich (1985) describes as "chaos on the shop floor."

Institutionalists direct attention toward actual practices of wage-setting within firms. Wage-setting criteria include comparisons with other firms, internal equity and custom, seniority, productivity, and firm performance—but the particular combination and weights of these criteria vary greatly across industries, nations, and time periods, institutionalists observe. *Labor market segmentation* offers one way of conceptualizing the differences that occur within a single national economy—indeed, often within an individual industry or even firm (Doeringer & Piore 1971; R. Edwards 1979; Gordon, Edwards & Reich 1982; Osterman 1987). For most jobs in the United States, training is relatively brief and takes place on the job, so that education serves more as a way to screen for trainability than as a way to augment productivity (Spence 1973; Thurow 1975).

The Trouble(s) with Neoclassical Accounts

To the extent that we wax polemical in this review, we primarily target neoclassical conceptions of work. Although we surely have already betrayed our sympathies, let us spell out broadly the weaknesses we see in the neoclassical approach. First of all, we view as misguided neoclassical scholars' heroic attempts to strip away the social context of work, leaving only market relations characterized by their impersonality (Lazonick 1991). In Amartya Sen's words (1982: 99), neoclassical economics' hyper-individualistic *homo economicus* "is close to being a social moron." In reality, social context and social connections envelop the world of work, as readily demonstrated by a quick closer look at any of the major elements of social and economic organization: businesses themselves, family and community, and government.

Most transactions in modern economies occur *within* businesses and other economic organizations structured by coercion and commitment rather than Walrasian exchange. This holds even on the terrain of international trade: In 1987, 92 percent of U.S. exports and 72 percent of U.S. imports took place *within* multinational corporations (Mahini 1990; see also Marcusen 1995). Furthermore, successful innovation and competition in the world market increasingly requires that firms build nonmarket, cooperative relationships with other firms—as evidenced by the success stories of manufacturing industries in Japan and the Third Italy (Piore & Sabel 1984; Best 1990; Lazonick 1991).

Turning to family and community, a majority of American working adults heard about their job through someone they know, and more than one-third got help from a friend or relative in obtaining the job (Corcoran, Datcher & Duncan 1980). Studies of poor communities commonly find that a person's probability of being jobless, engaging in crime, receiving welfare, and so on, are correlated with the incidence of these activities among family, friends, and neighbors (see Case & Katz 1991; Van Haitsma 1989; and Massey, Gross & Shibuya 1994; as well as reviews by McLanahan, Garfinkel & Watson 1987 and Jencks & Mayer 1989).

Government, as well, lays a heavy nonmarket hand on work and labor markets, as employer, buyer, and regulator. Government purchases in Western industrialized countries account for about one-fifth to one-quarter of all output, and governments of those countries employ a similar proportion of the workforce (U.S. Council of Economic Advisors 1991; Organization for Economic Cooperation and Development 1980). One illustration of the impact of government regulation even in the comparatively deregulated United States: In 1984, when the minimum wage in real terms was at its lowest level in years, it nonetheless constituted a wage floor for 11 percent of hourly wageworkers and a much higher percentage in low-wage regions of the country.

Social context and connections are particularly crucial for understanding differences in work across time and space. It is, to say the least, implausible that the nature of work in certain industries could have remained essentially invariant as work organization passed from production based on various forms of mutual obligation, to petty commodity production, to putting out, to factory production with foremen serving as contractors, to Taylorized factory work under management despotism, to unionized forms of Taylorism, to factories organized around continuous improvement, total quality management, and profit sharing! Likewise, differences in work among first-world, third-world, and socialist or formerly socialist countries command attention (Burawoy 1985).

Even within capitalist western Europe, the structure of work differs markedly across borders and among regions. Marc Maurice and colleagues (1984), seeking to understand why earnings inequality was greater in France than in Germany, compared twelve matched factories in France and Germany. They discovered that the two sets of factories had totally different management hierarchies, which resulted in turn from the different articulation of educational institutions with the workplace and different industrial relations systems in the two countries. The newly industrializing countries (NICs), which confound the distinction between first and third world, also exhibit "anomalous" labor markets: Alice Amsden (1990) notes the meteoric rise of Korean wages—possibly more rapid than in any other industrialization to date, in spite of an elastic labor supply and anti-union repression—and explains it via unique institutional features of late industrialization.

In addition to objecting to the de-contextualization of work in neoclassical theory, we find the core of the neoclassical approach to labor—the marginal productivity theory of compensation and human capital models—wanting. Theoretically, marginal product may be indeterminate, as with the Leontief (fixed coefficients) production function (Leontief 1951) or reswitching (Robinson 1953–54). In the case of increasing or decreasing returns to scale, even though marginal product is well-defined, it cannot serve as the basis for compensation (Thurow 1983). (With increasing returns, for example, marginal product exceeds average product—product per head—so that there is not enough output to pay every factor its marginal product.)

Neoclassical scholars have shrugged off these special cases, arguing that they have limited applicability to real-world economies. This logic can be turned against them, however, for empirically individual marginal product is unmeasurable in most work settings. Indeed, Herbert Simon (1991) points out that measurability problems are inherent in the rationale for forming firms: The activities most advantageous to consolidate within a firm (rather than to organize through markets), are precisely those requiring the greatest interdependence among actors. Empirically, in any case, wages within firms turn out to change and vary in patterns that marginal productivity alone cannot come close to explaining (Baker & Holmstrom 1995; Lazear 1995).

Employers themselves do not appear to set wages based on some notion of marginal product. Rather, employers think of wage levels—and particularly relative wage levels—as one factor in *eliciting* productivity, by increasing motivation and/or attracting better workers. Furthermore, as Doeringer and Piore (1971) note, long-term attachment of a worker to an employer eliminates any reason for wage to equal marginal product in any particular period or even any particular job. Because of limited information, employers' interests in assuring future worker performance, and worker collective action, nothing like moment-to-moment Walrasian markets ever form.

The standard human capital model, similarly, displays theoretical and empirical weaknesses. "The traits and characteristics of the investor matter in human-capital investments and they do not matter in physical investments," points out Lester Thurow (1983: 178); this divergence raises a host of theoretical difficulties. Moreover, human capital theory can, at best, serve as a model of expected lifetime earnings (people will invest only if they expect to recoup the investment over a lifetime), *not* current wage. Empirically, education and experience only explain a small percentage of variation in wages. The payoff to education varies by race and gender. Although some jobs reward education, others offer essentially no pay premium (Dickens & Lang 1985). Whereas on-the-job training (OJT) is the most important source of job skills, there appear to be no markets for OJT. More fundamentally, the credibility of human capital theory rests on the *assertion* that wage equals marginal product. In the absence of direct measures of individual productivity, strong tests of human capital models are impossible.

The status of neoclassical thinking within the analysis of work, and specifically within labor economics, has fluctuated over time. Over the last forty years, the dominant position in labor economics has shifted from institutionalists to neoclassical economists who dismissed institutions, to economists who seek to explain institutions with little or no institutionalism. At midcentury, labor economics was the province of institutionalists such as John Dunlop, Lloyd Reynolds, and Albert Rees. Some view that era with distaste: Sherwin Rosen (1992: 157) described the labor economics of the time as "far outside the mainstream of economics." Others value the old institutionalism as "an old dog that still has new tricks to teach us all" (Jacoby 1990: 340). In any case, neoclassical labor economics raised a sharp challenge to institutionalism in the 1960s, with Gary Becker (in the realm of theory) and Jacob Mincer (in the realm of empirical research) leading the charge. The combination of elegant theoretical models and the new opportunity to use computers to analyze large data sets proved irresistible; neoclassical perspectives swept the field.

The institutionally sparse approach of Becker and company, however, left many institutional peculiarities of labor markets unexplained. In the late 1970s neoclassically trained economists such as Joseph Stiglitz and Edward

Lazear led the field in a new direction, using concepts such as information costs, incomplete contracts, and principal-agent problems to model institutions. Stiglitz (1991: 15) complained that neoclassical economists had "relegated the study of organizations to business schools, or worse still, to sociologists," and set out to remedy the omission. Advocates call their new approach the "New Economics of Personnel" (Jacoby & Mitchell 1990), the "New Information Economics" (Stiglitz 1984), the "New Institutional Economics" (England 1992), and even the "New Efficiency-Oriented Institutional Labor Economics" (Jacoby 1990).

Whatever we call the approach, it clearly holds the current initiative in labor economics. Efficiency wage models have been its greatest triumph (Akerlof & Yellen 1986). Its leaders have also created models purporting to explain, among other things, mandatory retirement and pensions (Lazear 1979, 1990), pay increases tied to seniority (Lazear 1981; Topel 1991), wide executive pay differences (Lazear & Rosen 1981), and the use of layoffs rather than wage reductions in response to declines in demand (Rosen 1985). Despite the new labor economics' renewed attention to institutions, the models are driven by efficiency considerations and the pursuit of self-interest by rational individuals. Like older neoclassical models, they leave little space for power, history, or culture. In the rest of this book, we do our best to reclaim that space.

The Work Before Us

A satisfactory general theory of work and labor markets would have these characteristics:

- It would deal with variation in the organization of work over all its many forms.
- It would specify when and where labor markets appear, as well as when and where the organization of work takes forms other than labor markets.
- Within the world of labor markets, it would account for a wide range of phenomena, including the segregation of jobs by race, ethnicity, or gender; differential compensation of jobs and categories of workers; how people find jobs; how jobs find people; people's work histories; and the use of different incentive systems for workers.
- It would specify verifiable causal mechanisms for its effects.
- It would be consistent, parsimonious, and accurate.

No existing theory scores well in all these regards. Neoclassical theories have the advantages of broad scope, parsimony, and relative consistency, although their users have accomplished all three, to some degree, by means of special pleading in the form of such devices as retrospective readjustments to imputed preferences, for example preference for workers of a certain race, gender, or ethnic category. Neoclassical theories do not provide a believable analysis of nonmarket work, a compelling account of the conditions under which labor markets appear, a valid treatment of changing forms of inequality, a persuasive and verified specification of causal mechanisms, or an explanation of the many circumstances in which work involves open conflict, coercion, and deceit.

Marxists have fashioned more fruitful models of conflict, coercion, and deceit than neoclassicists or institutionalists. But they have not produced an adequate theory when it comes to such matters as job finding, careers, and inequality by gender, race, or ethnicity. Institutionalists, for their part, have not worked out anything like the range of applications that neoclassical analysts have proposed and have assumed the validity of neoclassical accounts in many respects. We stand a long way from definitive confrontation among the three clusters of theory.

Figure 1.1 represents the conceptions of work and labor markets prevailing in neoclassical, Marxist, and institutionalist writings. For neoclassical analysts, rationally motivated exchange dominates economic life. The great bulk of work in all times and places therefore conforms to models of competitive markets; such zealots as Gary Becker claim, indeed, that market models can, with appropriate specifications, encompass all of human behavior through endless time. Hence two dimensions define the basic space of work: the amount of human capital required (from capacities that many people have to highly trained specialties) and the degree of competition (from nonmarket to monopoly to highly competitive). Thus professions involve substantial human capital but also some restraints on competition, whereas an unskilled labor pool falls into a corner defined by high competition but relatively little human capital. In such a view, every economy features a labor market that—within limits set by the degree of competition—offers higher prices for labor embodying extensive human capital.

Marxists, in sharp contrast, consider each mode of production to have its own rationale, each one (except the yet-to-be communist) drawing its dynamics from some form of exploitation; genuine labor markets belong clearly and uniquely to the capitalist mode of production. For Marxists, two fundamental dimensions are the proportion of all labor power offered for sale (from the nonmarket relations of precapitalist economies to the extensive wage work of both capitalism and socialism) and the extent of producer control over labor processes (increasingly low for capitalism, according to the standard theory, increasingly high for socialism). The historic evolution of capitalism, then, runs from the lower right corner toward the upper left corner: from high producer control with little commoditization of labor to high commoditization and little or no producer control.

FIGURE 1.1   Neoclassical, Marxist, and institutionalist maps of work

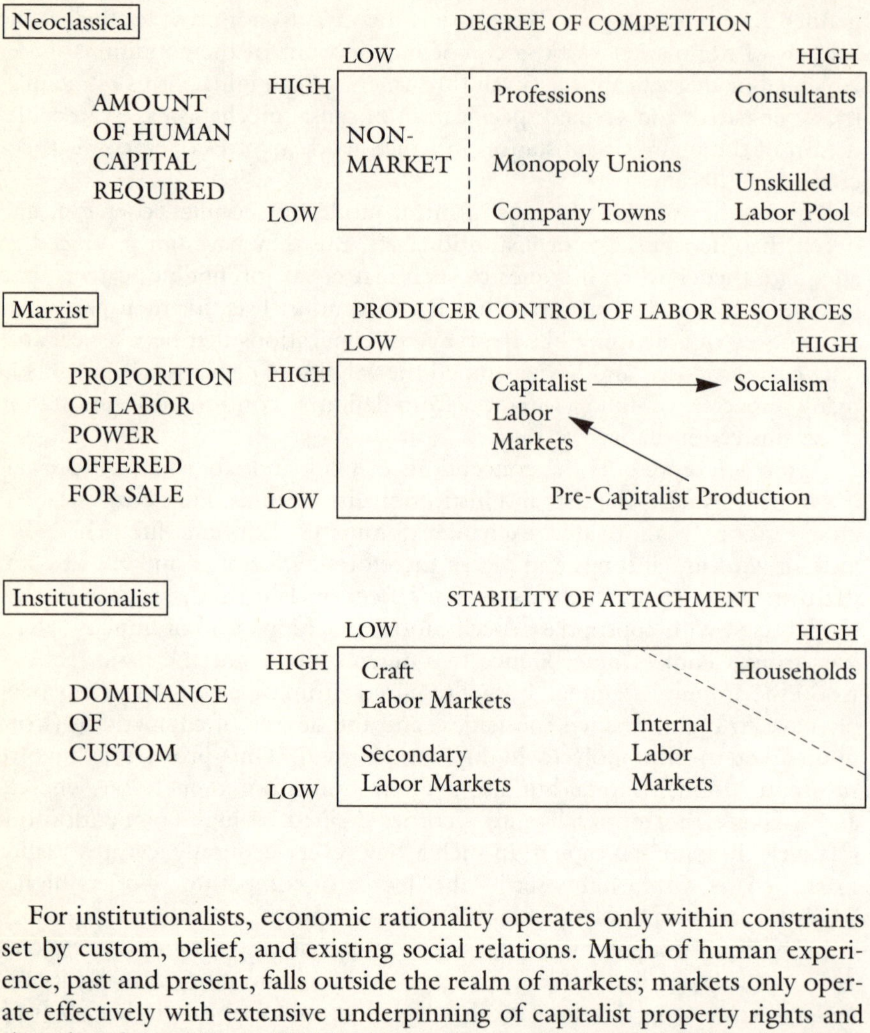

Neoclassical   DEGREE OF COMPETITION

		LOW		HIGH
AMOUNT	HIGH		Professions	Consultants
OF HUMAN		NON-		
CAPITAL		MARKET	Monopoly Unions	
REQUIRED				Unskilled
	LOW		Company Towns	Labor Pool

Marxist   PRODUCER CONTROL OF LABOR RESOURCES

		LOW	HIGH
PROPORTION	HIGH		
OF LABOR		Capitalist ———→ Socialism	
POWER		Labor	
OFFERED		Markets	
FOR SALE	LOW	Pre-Capitalist Production	

Institutionalist   STABILITY OF ATTACHMENT

		LOW	HIGH
	HIGH	Craft	Households
DOMINANCE		Labor Markets	
OF			Internal
CUSTOM		Secondary	Labor
	LOW	Labor Markets	Markets

For institutionalists, economic rationality operates only within constraints set by custom, belief, and existing social relations. Much of human experience, past and present, falls outside the realm of markets; markets only operate effectively with extensive underpinning of capitalist property rights and shared understandings. Within that realm, furthermore, significantly different institutions and regularities characterize competitive markets, internal labor markets, and specialized markets such as those created by organized crafts. Two salient dimensions therefore become the dominance of custom and the stability of workers' attachment to their work; institutionalist models of households, for example, portray them as sites not only of stable attachment but also of customary work arrangements, the opposite of secondary labor markets with their dependence on mobile workers and constantly reorganized production.

When we place analysts neatly in neoclassical, Marxist, and institutionalist camps, we are of course drawing arbitrarily sharp lines in a continuous space. George Akerlof's "institutionalist" analysis of efficiency wages assumes much of the neoclassical paradigm, whereas Douglass North's institutionalism makes transaction costs and implicit contracts central to the entire enterprise of economic analysis. Jon Elster fashions a rational-actor version of Marxism, while James Coleman pushes rational action far into the zone of norms and institutions. We reify the three "schools" only to clarify theoretical choices confronting today's analysts of work, labor markets, and professions.

What vision, then, do we hold of work and labor markets? At the center of our analysis stands an image of a worker and an employer, each involved in extensive social networks that connect them not only with each other but with many others inside or outside the place of employment. The worker and employer are bargaining out the terms of work, using the material and organizational resources (including existing and available technologies) at their disposal. They draw on previously existing social relations—both work-generated and otherwise—in seeking their advantages. In the process, they generate new agreements, understandings, and social ties, which in turn constrain subsequent interaction. They interact within strong limits set by their shared culture and by the previous history of the productive organization at hand.

We recurrently complicate the image, for example by adding such actors as governments and labor-supplying households. We extend it far beyond the bounds of labor markets as conventionally understood, arguing that labor markets constitute only one of many different historical organizations of work. The image does not constitute a precise model, but it does signal a line of thought. It challenges future investigators and theorists of work, labor markets, and professions to take history, power, and culture more seriously than they generally have in the past.

We have a straightforward plan for amplifying and focusing the image. In Chapter 2 we offer a preliminary map of what must be explained. Chapter 3 sketches the histories of cotton textile production, coal mining, and health care in Great Britain and the United States, for a more detailed illustration of change and variation in work's organization. Chapter 4, the book's densest and most demanding section, lays out the analytical tools for a treatment of work and labor markets as social interaction. Chapter 5 follows up by proposing a model of employer decisionmaking and action, and Chapter 6 sketches similar models for the behavior of workers, families, and states—the other major actors in work and labor markets. The form and organization of work changed dramatically as capitalism arose and matured, and they continue to change in smaller ways: Chapter 7 applies our framework to these changes. In Chapters 8 through 11, we narrow our attention to the very important special case of work within labor markets. We start in Chapter 8 by

2
Worlds of Work

What Works?

Meg Luxton studied three generations of women who worked at home in Flin Flon, a metal-mining town in northern Manitoba. Worked? One of the women Luxton interviewed had this to say about what she was doing:

> It's looking after your family, and what could be more important? You don't have anyone standing over you so you get to do what you want, sort of. But you don't get paid, so you're dependent on your husband, and you have to be there all the time, and there's always something needs doing. I feel so confused because it could be so good and it never is. (Luxton 1980: 12)

Another Flin Flon woman took a more collective view:

> When I think about what I do every day–I cook meals for my family, I make cereal for breakfast and sandwiches for lunch and meat and potatoes for supper. Nothing unusual about that. But when I think about all those thousands of other women all doing the same thing, then I realize I'm not just making porridge. I'm part of a whole army of women who are feeding the country. (Luxton 1980: 13)

Neither woman was collecting wages for her effort, but both were working hard. Any conception of work that excludes their daily toil—as many market-oriented conceptions of work do—misrepresents work's many worlds.

Work includes any human effort adding use value to goods and services. However much their performers may enjoy or loathe the effort, conversation, song, decoration, pornography, table-setting, gardening, housecleaning, and repair of broken toys, all involve work to the extent that they increase satisfactions their consumers gain from them. Prior to the twentieth century, a vast majority of the world's workers performed the bulk of their work in other settings than salaried jobs as we know them today. Even today, over the world as a whole, most work takes place outside of regular jobs. Only a prejudice bred by Western capitalism and its industrial labor markets fixes on strenuous effort expended for money payment outside the home as "real work," relegating other efforts to amusement, crime, and mere housekeeping.

Over human history, most work has taken place in one of three settings: household enterprises, such as farms or workshops; local communities, such as hunting bands or villages; and larger organizations, such as plantations and armies, run by specialists in extraction and coercion. In none of these settings does a labor market operate in any strong sense of the word. Even today a large share of all work—certainly a majority, in terms of labor-time expended—still goes on outside of labor markets: unpaid domestic labor, self-help, barter, petty commodity production, and more.

Despite the rise of takeouts, fast foods, and restaurant eating, unpaid preparation of meals probably constitutes the largest single block of time among all the types of work, paid or unpaid, that today's Americans do. As "caring" work, ironically, its proper execution requires camouflage as something else: entertainment or devotion (DeVault 1991; di Leonardo 1987). According to a parallel logic, payment of a stipulated cash sum by one partner to another at the time of sexual relations marks the relationship as prostitution—hence market work—rather than friendship, love, marriage, or adventure. In forcing recognition of the genuine work women do outside the market, feminist scholars have in recent years drawn attention to the large portion of all work that women, men, and children all actually perform outside the world of wages, indeed outside the world of direct pecuniary compensation (Siegel 1994).

Classifications of the labor force—active population as employed people plus people looking for employment—express the market prejudice. Employment for wages becomes the criterion of work, with the logically peculiar term "self-employment" spread like a fig leaf to cover the conceptual embarrassment occasioned by unsalaried workers who strive for profit, rent, or some other form of income. As the constantly changing line between goods and services that are/are not commercially available indicates, however, no intrinsic difference sets off "real work" from the rest. Why should conversation, song, decoration, and so on count as work when performed as commercial services but not when carried on for the benefit of friends and relatives?

To be sure, not all effort qualifies as work; purely destructive, expressive, or consumptive acts lie outside the bound; in so far as they reduce transferable use value, we might think of them as antiwork. To the degree that effort adds use value to goods and services that are available, at least in principle, to others, we consider the effort work. We adopt a generous criterion of "use value": a good or service that could sustain any activity carried on by a person other than its producer—whether or not we approve of the activity—has use value. To the extent, then, that (a) effort adds to the capacity of a good or service to sustain activities of other persons than its producers, and (b) those others could under specifiable circumstances lay claim to the good or service, the effort qualifies as work. This definitional strategy has an ironic result: Where standard criteria exclude nonmarket efforts from the world of work, ours exclude nonsocial efforts; solitary weight lifting pursued solely for personal gratification does not qualify, whereas weight lifting for the pleasure of sports fans qualifies.

All work involves **labor processes**: allocations of various intensities and qualities of effort among different aspects of production within specific technical conditions. On the whole, similar labor processes yield similar products, whereas dissimilar labor processes produce different products. Given similar raw materials, settings, talents, and knowledge, two potters produce different urns because they employ different labor processes, perhaps with one of them working quickly by using high-tech machinery, the other working slowly by time-honored hand methods. Now and then, however, a hobbyist automobile maker reproduces by hand a classic car that in its time the manufacturer used big machines and assembly lines to build; in such cases, different labor processes occasionally produce indistinguishable results. Innovations in work consist of alterations in labor processes: changing intensities and qualities of effort, changing allocations of effort among different aspects of production, and changing technical conditions. Minor adjustments in labor processes go on incessantly even in highly standardized forms of production, as workers maneuver between their own propensities and job requirements, and as workers, employers, and consumers renegotiate their agreements and disagreements about what to produce and how.

Labor Markets

Work is a means of acquiring goods for use, possession, or bestowal. If you want to consume or purvey a certain good beyond your current stock of the good you have four choices, singly or in combination: (1) produce it yourself (perhaps in collaboration with others), (2) seize it, (3) buy it, (4) make someone else produce it. Labor markets proliferate when numbers 3 (for consumers) and 4 (for purveyors) become the dominant options. Labor markets have formed chiefly under capitalism, the system of production in which holders of capital, backed by law and state power, make the crucial decisions concerning the character and allocation of work. Because they are thinking of capitalist markets and taking the capitalist's perspective, economists commonly narrow the available choices to two: *make* (which typically means persuading someone else to produce) or *buy*.

Labor markets divide work into enduring *jobs* within competing *firms* whose owners and managers hire and fire the holders of those jobs, negotiate with them over the conditions of their employment, pay them, supervise their work, and appropriate their products. Labor markets range from (a) the simple shape-up, in which workers gather at a designated location each morning in hopes that someone will give them jobs for the day, to (b) the rule-encrusted civil service systems that govern public employment, to (c) the elaborate ballet by which architects move from project to project and shop to shop. Labor markets involve not only jobs and firms but these other elements:

workers who are formally free to enter and leave different kinds of employment;

employers who are formally free to engage, assign, and discharge workers;

hiring, transactions in which, within stipulated limits, workers concede control over their labor power to employers in return for payment stipulated in advance of receiving assignment to specific jobs;

employment networks, lines of communication that link many potential occupants of jobs in multiple firms with employers who make decisions to fill those jobs. (Although they ultimately articulate and even merge, we can conveniently distinguish between **recruitment** networks defined from the starting point of employers and **supply** networks defined from the starting point of workers.)

contracts, agreements (explicit or implicit) regarding the tasks, level of effort, working conditions, and form, frequency, and amount of payment.

In combination, workers, employers, firms, jobs, hiring, employment networks, and contracts constitute labor markets. Historically these elements have rarely coincided. Industrial capitalism brought them together. Although labor markets thrive under capitalism, however, attenuated versions now sometimes appear in nonindustrial and socialist economies as well.

In the process of forging industrial capitalism, capitalists became creators, managers, and advocates of labor markets. Labor markets have become the standard organization of employment for wages under industrial capitalism. Firms producing related goods create labor markets by means of two activities: (a) by recruiting workers from overlapping labor pools and (b) by their managers' communication to each other of appropriate prices and working conditions for labor. But labor markets also operate within firms, as employers recruit candidates for certain jobs from among those who already hold other jobs in the same firm; promotion ladders represent a familiar feature of labor markets inside firms. Hence, a rough distinction exists between **external** and **internal labor markets**, labor markets among and within firms. Industries vary enormously in their relative reliance on external and internal labor markets: visual arts, moviemaking, construction, and publishing, for example, have only skeletal internal labor markets. Military services and major churches, in sharp contrast, do very little external recruiting except at entry level; they operate vast internal labor markets. Continuous-process manufacturing firms follow a third option, typically relying on external labor markets for some classes of workers (usually those who are more easily replaced) and on internal labor markets for others (especially those they recruit to middle and top management).

A **job** is the set of rights and obligations that connects a given worker with other members of the same firm. It centers on a relation to an employer in which the employee cedes limited control over his/her time and effort on condition that the employer pay a specified remuneration and respect known limits to that control. Where exactly we draw the distinction between personal obligation and jobholding, on one side, or between individual entrepreneurship and jobholding, on the other, remains theoretically arbitrary and practically contestable. Demands that unpaid housewives receive a wage, for example, rest precisely on the argument that unpaid provision of sexual, emotional, and domestic services constitutes an unrecognized, insufficiently compensated form of employment rather than voluntary fulfillment of a personal obligation. American lawyers have sometimes persuaded juries that cast-off lovers deserved "palimony" payments on parallel grounds. Similarly, the generally successful international drive for family allowances treated it explicitly as an alternative to a wage.

Despite the illusions of census occupational statistics and economic theory, all real labor markets segment radically; any firm maintains effective access to only a fraction of the workers who could, in principle, fill its jobs, while any potential worker maintains effective access to only a fraction of the jobs she could, in principle, fill. Newspaper advertising, employment agencies, and school placement offices mitigate the particularism of labor markets, but fall far short of eliminating the central importance of prior contacts, direct or indirect, between employers and potential workers. Hiring within restricted existing networks theoretically diminishes the efficiency of markets in matching people (or the "human capital" they embody) with jobs. However, it also reduces the cost of collecting information on either side, speeds up the spread of news about openings, expands the tacit knowledge shared by fellow workers, permits exchanges of favors that will serve future opportunities, and provides some guarantees to both parties that the other will meet commitments implied by the hiring. Indeed, many of the same factors that lead firms to organize internal labor markets encourage employers and workers to segment external labor markets.

Occupations

The formation of labor markets shapes the idea and practice of **occupations:** sets of jobs in different firms that employers and government officials consider equivalent, building them into organizational rosters, censuses, labor market interventions, and vocational education. Whereas in actuality, jobs always involve multiple rights and obligations vis-à-vis other persons than the employer, the aggregation of jobs into occupations emphasizes obligations to the employer. To say that two people belong to the "same" occupation means that their employers have equivalent claims on them, not that they perform their work in the same manner or maintain the same relations with their fellow workers and people outside their firm.

Two centuries ago, few people had "occupations" in the contemporary specialized sense of the word. When asked their social positions, people more often called themselves bourgeois, householder, or day worker than offering anything that their twentieth-century counterparts would recognize as an occupational title; none of these titles specified a strong set of obligations to a particular employer or firm. Retrospective attempts to assimilate these titles to occupational hierarchies and to argue that such categories as "peasant" evolved by specialization into such categories as "berry picker" or "tractor driver" miss the whole point; these earlier identifications existed independently of jobs, occupations, and labor markets.

Before the twentieth century, nevertheless, labor markets themselves operated most fully at the level of occupations, reinforcing the job categories—hence the forms of exclusion by gender, race, ethnicity, class, or citizenship—managers and privileged workers had established. Very few so-called occupations had the connecting social structure of crafts such as tanning and glassmaking. Yet as labor markets spread, workers in general began to describe themselves in occupational terms. They told census takers that they were machinists, cooks, laborers, or something else rather occupational.

Not all work crystallized into occupations: Thus cash-crop farming, street peddling, screenplay writing, retail-store ownership, mugging, private speculation in securities, baby-sitting, sculpture, hustling for tips, lawn mowing, casual prostitution, collection of deposit bottles for redemption, and running for public office all involve work for remuneration, but still take place mostly outside the world of labor markets, jobs, and occupations. Nevertheless, even those who work in distinctly informal settings now often view their roles in occupational terms. Women who "sell lines" in New York bingo halls—run their own illegal game of secondary bets on the numbers that come up in the main game's drawings—often treat it as a full-time occupation and make substantial money doing so (Lesieur & Shelley 1987). In a 1987 survey, street children in Paraguay's capital city of Asunción reported "occupations" including vending, selling newspapers, shining shoes, minding cars, carrying, and cleaning windshields (International Labour Office 1992: 16).

Craft labor markets institutionalize occupations, with members of a trade admitting and certifying those who are allegedly competent to practice it (Jackson 1984). Such markets fit neatly with subcontracting, in which a foreman, household head, or *padrone* hires workers with an employer's authorization, supervises their production, and essentially sells their collective product to the employer, taking a profit from the difference between the amount received from the employer and the amount paid to workers. (Because they worked for their colonels or generals rather than for the kings in whose names they fought, mercenary armies long fought on just such a subcontracting principle, which helps account for the frequency with which they mutinied or plundered when unpaid. [Caferro 1994; Casparis 1982; Ingrao 1987; Mallett 1974; Redlich 1964–65; J. Thomson 1994]).

Subcontracting arrangements reached a peak as capitalists, who had previously operated primarily as merchants for goods produced at their command but not under their close supervision, began to regroup different categories of workers in centrally directed shops and factories. They frequently relied on subcontractors for that regrouping. Subcontractors, in turn, often drew their workers from migration chains: particular ties between nearby workers and others at some distant source of labor who stayed in touch and migrated in one direction or the other in response to relative opportunities at the two ends. Ethnic enclaves often grew up at the destination in precisely this way. In a sense, almost all large-scale manufacturing once took place via subcontracting; merchants who actually sold goods contracted directly with household heads or craftsmen who produced goods at a stipulated price using labor of which they disposed—journeymen, apprentices, day laborers, servants, or members of their own households. In those circumstances, capitalists exercised little or no direct control over who performed what productive task or how. Instead, they exercised control by setting minimum standards for the quality of goods they would accept from subcontractors at the stipulated price.

Subcontracting's golden age arrived with the nineteenth-century concentration of fixed capital and the concomitant grouping of workers into large shops. Employers then frequently relied on subcontractors in two distinct ways: (1) organizing segments of their firms as if they were almost separate firms, paying a foreman, master, or senior worker for the goods produced as a function of quality and relying on the intermediary to recruit, organize, discipline, and pay his or her labor force; (2) actually farming out some portion of manufacturing (e.g., the dyeing of textiles) to outside households or shops at a stipulated price for quality. Craft labor markets incorporated weak versions of subcontracting, with representatives of the craft substituting to some extent for the foreman (Jackson 1984). Those arrangements lost their prominence in the United States during the twentieth century as large firms began to internalize their labor processes, create centralized hiring, and reduce the autonomy of middlemen. Only around World War I did top management of large American firms generally create personnel departments and direct top-to-bottom, beginning-to-end surveillance of production. Before the introduction of what many historians call Fordism (for Henry Ford's assembly-line production), attenuated variants of craft organization and subcontracting predominated in labor markets.

Throughout our contemporary world, workers in the huge "informal sector" of individual entrepreneurship and semi-legal enterprise still thrive on subcontracting (Portes, Castells & Benton 1989). Direct-sales and franchising firms rely heavily on various forms of subcontracting. And in recent years even very large establishments, souring on the merits of vertical integration, have turned increasingly to (a) "outsourcing" of components previously produced within the firm, (b) contracting for services previously performed by directly supervised employees and (c) commission sales or other devices to avoid the legal, moral, political, and economic burdens imposed by full-time, long-term salaried workers. With almost all forms of subcontracting, recruitment of workers becomes highly selective, even more dependent on existing relations of kinship and friendship than in direct hiring by labor-incorporating firms, since subcontractors are less likely to wield the formal recruiting and selection apparatus of larger firms. If so, we should expect the current renaissance of subcontracting to increase inequalities of employment and rewards for work by race, national origin, and gender. Subcontracting, chain migration, segmented labor markets, and job monopolies reinforce each other.

Professions

Similar but stronger monopolies operate in professional hiring. **Professions** consist of those exceptional labor markets in which workers, collaborating with governmental authorities, exercise collective control not only over employment but also over dispensation and consumption of a whole class of goods and services. Governments permit only licensed practitioners—persons who have received collective approval by existing members of the profession—to purvey the relevant goods and services. Professions thereby obscure the distinction between internal and external labor markets, not to mention the line between employers and workers. Although professionals commonly hire nonprofessionals to do their dirty work, within professions the line between capital and labor blurs, since membership in the profession itself constitutes a jealously guarded sort of capital.

Thus a capitalist country's architects and their collaborators in the government not only decide which people can call themselves architects and regulate the training of prospective architects but also limit stringently the conditions under which nonarchitects can design, build, or modify structures in which people work or live. Again, even though outside the United States most of the world's physicians now work for wages in government-controlled facilities, physicians everywhere collectively retain strong influence over who has a right to deliver or receive paid medical treatment, indeed any medical treatment at all (Frenk & Durán-Arenas 1993). Restaurateurs, cinema operators, and prostitutes exercise nothing like that exclusive power over the delivery and receipt of their specialized services. Professions thus follow a particular strategy to render demand for their labor inelastic (by barring substitutes), meanwhile restricting supply, so that they can reap rents. If labor markets are a special way of organizing work, professions are a special way of organizing labor markets.

As Andrew Abbott has shown, professionalization usually occurs when two or more distinct groups of practitioners compete for the same clientele, and at least one enlists government support in securing a monopoly over some version of the service and some portion of the clientele (Abbott 1988; see also Goebel 1994). The struggle ends with either a division of the territory among different kinds of practitioners (all now professionally certified to some degree) or the condemnation of some unfortunate practitioners as quacks and incompetents. As Chapter 3 will show, physicians adopted this course of action in the United States, subordinating, segregating, co-opting, or disqualifying other healing groups. For decades, they also fought threats to fee-for-service compensation, such as health maintenance organizations. Physicians were so successful in building a monopoly that other professions proliferated within health care, emulating the M.D. model. In the last two decades, the market power of American physicians has finally faced serious challenges. But, as Paul Starr points out, the challenges have not come from the market itself (i.e., from consumers or competitors) but from governments and managers of hospitals and managed care organizations (Starr 1982).

These days state agencies regulate the commercial practice of medicine, nursing, psychological counseling, dentistry, social work, law, pharmacy, accounting, engineering, schoolteaching, architecture, city planning, cosmetology, and so on through the list of specialties that have erected legally sanctioned collective controls over the production and sale of their services. Representatives of professions uniformly argue for special protection on grounds of the dangers that malpractice would otherwise bring the public. It is not obvious, however, that professionalized occupations offer a greater threat in this regard than barkeeps, bicycle messengers, building contractors, bus drivers, drug dealers, gamblers, herb sellers, hit men, hockey players, loggers, palm readers, pimps, police officers, public utility employees, speedboat operators, spies, street preachers, or thieves, none of whom enjoy the legally protected collective control over labor and commodity markets exercised by their professional cousins.

Varieties of Work

Figure 2.1 represents our own initial mapping of work's diverse forms. Once again we reduce a complex set of variations to just two dimensions: short-term monetization of work and imposition of time-discipline over its execution. ("Short-term monetization" means the extent to which workers invest effort, or fail to do so, contingent on the prospect of monetary compensation in the immediate future—say within a month or less. "Time-discipline" means the extent to which other persons decide the disposition of a worker's effort within the working day.) Each separate position within the diagram implies a somewhat different organization of labor processes, a different combination of technical conditions with allocations of varying qualities and quantities of effort among various aspects of production. Each distinctive labor process, in turn, entails somewhat different relations to fellow workers, employers, consumers, and other people. Variation of work in these regards therefore involves important variations in social relations as well.

FIGURE 2.1   Organizations of work within capitalist economies

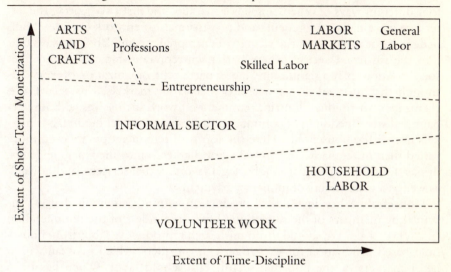

Over the last three hundred years, work in Western countries has moved massively toward the diagram's upper right corner, toward short-term monetization and extensive time-discipline. The space's upper right contains the world of labor markets, jobs, and occupations. With the frequent intervention of state agencies, households, and organizations such as trade associations and labor unions, capitalists and workers today create labor markets where workers deliver a high proportion of all work for monetary compensation at the scale of the transaction, the piece, the hour, the day, or the week, and producers yield control of their time and effort to others, at least for the paid workday's duration. Even today, considerable paid work occurs outside that corner: In the zone of extensive monetization but little time-discipline, for instance, we still find arts and crafts epitomized by a street musician's performance for quarters, a comedian's paid appearance on a television talk show, or a potter's turning of a bowl for immediate sale.

Some boundaries remain porous. At the frontier between jobholding and entrepreneurship, for example, in 1984 five percent of the American labor force worked in direct sale organizations such as Amway or Tupperware, selling almost entirely on commission with only the slightest day-to-day supervision (Biggart 1989: 2); those five percent tested the limits of "jobs." The payment of remuneration fixed a priori in return for stipulated effort nevertheless sets a rough boundary to jobs, differentiating them approximately from work performed chiefly for tips, bribes, praise, affection, self-satisfaction, prestige, influence, experience, credentialing, or unspecified future favors.

General labor, skilled labor, entrepreneurship, and professions identify four different ways of organizing labor markets, the first two central, the latter two marginal; entrepreneurs and professionals often work outside of full-fledged labor markets. In the vicinity of entrepreneurship, labor markets blur into the **informal sector**, where barter, entrepreneurship, and nonmarket social relations play a significantly larger part in the organization of work. Although the informal sector overlaps with labor markets, this sector also claims its own residual domain: remunerated work such as casual house repairs and street peddling of contraband that takes place neither in labor markets nor within households. Here the forms of remuneration are even more varied than in regularly constituted labor markets, since they include drugs, drinks, food, stolen property, jobs, legal favors, sexual services, and housing as well as a wide variety of monetary payments.

Household labor includes all production within households that is consumed by members of the same households, regardless of the remuneration (if any) received. We should distinguish such reproductive labor from household-based production for exchange with outsiders, which may fall within labor markets or the informal sector. Household labor, which has been largely unpaid in Western countries since the huge twentieth-century decline of domestic service, occupies a distinct niche in the organization of work. Within households, producer control ranges from considerable autonomy on the part of different family members (high) to centralized patriarchal authority in the presence of servants, baby-sitters, and others working for room, board, and experience alone (low).

Finally, **volunteer work** constitutes unpaid effort provided to parties to whom the worker owes no contractual, familial, or friendship obligation. This is another invisible but substantial realm. As of the late 1980s, 80 million Americans—some 45 percent of all Americans over 18 years old—were "engaged in some kind of voluntary caring activity" (Wuthnow 1991: 5). Slightly more men than women reported volunteering; 23 percent of adults reported devoting 6 or more hours per week to voluntary caring for others (Independent Sector 1986: 25). Volunteer work ranges in degree of producer control from lowly soup kitchen helpers to powerful chairs on volunteer boards of directors. Despite the professionalization of many social-movement organizations into something like pressure groups, it also includes much of politics, social movements, and popular collective action, where millions work for causes without pay. Between personal helping and social activism, a majority of adult Americans engage in volunteer work.

Elsewhere

We have described a capitalist world in which a high proportion of all production occurs within labor markets characterized by capital-directed firms, jobs, time-discipline, and short-term monetization. Zones of industrial socialism have so far differed from that world chiefly in vesting much more ownership in states, allowing much less retention of profits within producing units, offering a much wider state-mandated range of benefits to producers' households, therefore displaying different mixes and connections of arts and crafts, labor markets, informal sectors, household labor, and volunteer work. Still, work in capitalist and socialist industrial economies has many family resemblances resulting from the logics of industrial production as such and from the mutual influence of those economies. The largest differences in our contemporary world separate poor, labor-repressive agrarian economies such as those of Haiti and Cambodia from industrial economies, capitalist or socialist.

If we reserve the term "industrial" for those economies where a substantial proportion of all work transforms goods into other goods rather than drawing goods directly from the earth, then until recently most economies have been nonindustrial. Nonindustrial economies vary enormously, from hunting and gathering, pastoral, and slash-and-burn agriculture to labor-repressive estate and plantation systems; aside from saying that on the average such economies operate at smaller scales of coordination, lower per capita expenditures of nonhuman energy, and lower per capita incomes than industrial economies, any generalization about the nonindustrial world requires many qualifications and exceptions. Nor can we infer the nonindustrial past from the decreasing number of economies that today remain largely nonindustrial, since those economies now form part of a global division of labor dominated by industrial economies. In contemporary India, for example, farm households not only draw significant shares of their income from wage-labor but cushion shocks to farm income less by shifting agricultural production than by taking on additional outside employment (Kochar 1995).

The world of industry displays greater uniformity because it has taken shape in a connected worldwide process; the same capital has moved from continent to continent, the same firms have established new plants in distant lands, and firms in one country have emulated firms in another. Industrialization—increase in the proportion of goods-into-goods production—has generally featured large expansions in the scope and volume of waged employment. On the whole, that transformation has occurred under the auspices of one variant or another of capitalism. Under capitalism, owners of capital exercise great autonomy and power in the organization of work and the disposition of labor, with the state generally guaranteeing their property rights, whereas wageworkers enjoy relatively little power, individual or collective.

At the expense of widespread inequality, exploitation, and waste, capitalism has proved a powerful vehicle of industrialization. Nevertheless, some economies have industrialized through socialism, a system of production in which some central authority exerts strong control over capital in the name of workers, directs production toward politically defined ends, and commits

TABLE 2.1   Differences Between Capitalist and Socialist Economies

Capitalist	*Socialist*
private ownership of capital	public ownership of capital
contingent relationship of capital to state	priority of government over capital
autonomy of capital in production decisions	restraint of capital in production decisions
production for profit measured against capital	production for some set of use values
priority of markets for commodities and capital	political process selects prior use values
subordination of labor markets	autonomy of labor markets
vulnerability to shortages of demand	vulnerability to shortages of commodities
retention of profits by capital	redistribution of profits for collective goods or reinvestment

a significant share of production to the provision of some minimum of welfare among the general population. The disintegration of the Soviet Union and its associated socialist economies has not created capitalism but, rather, the negation of socialism's features: collapse of constraints over capital, decline of political direction for production, and decay of welfare systems throughout the region. Before that disintegration, most of those states had undergone significant industrialization through socialist means. Recent capitalist self-congratulation has obscured the enormous success socialist regimes have had in transforming miserably poor and unequal agrarian economies into semi-industrial economies with a minimum of welfare for almost everyone. These days, among large countries only China hews to a form of socialism, and even there the state has either promoted or tolerated the development of quasi-capitalist conditions in a growing number of enclaves.

Schematically, differences between capitalist and socialist economies look something like Table 2.1. The largest differences spring from private ownership of capital under capitalism versus public ownership of capital under socialism, a distinction which arose from the very origins of socialism as a critique of autonomous capital's consequences and a political seizure of control over capital. Variations among socialist systems, indeed, result largely from their varying approaches to capital, from extensive collaboration in Scandinavian social democracies to once-stark state control in Albania.

The "government" in question under socialism varies from party cell to central committee to workers' collective. Nevertheless, in general, socialist systems embed much more decisionmaking concerning the organization of work in political processes. Under capitalism, governments certainly intervene in the organization of work by such means as corporate taxes, minimum wages, regulation of working conditions, licensing of professions, sub-sidies to agriculture, promotion of exports, enforcement of union-manage-ment contracts, coordination and insurance of capital markets, supervision of pensions, and administration of unemployment benefits, but they inter-vene more indirectly, intermittently, and contingently than under socialism. We call capitalist labor markets' networks and contracts "contingent" be-cause they result from asymmetrical bargaining and improvisation more than from central planning.

Although from time to time we will undertake comparisons with socialist or nonindustrial organizations of production, in this book we are concen-trating on capitalist transformations and processes in Western economies. Contingent, asymmetrical, improvised, and variable capitalist contracts for work figure crucially in the analyses to come.

3
Cotton, Coal, and Clinics

Contrasting Trajectories of Industrial Change

Despite the factory's proliferation after 1800 and the bureaucratized office's spread after 1900, no single organizational form ever dominated production in the United States, much less in the capitalist world as a whole. Although capitalization, commercialization, and mechanization touched a wide range of work, each industry followed its own trajectory. Within large-scale manufacturing, for example, organization of work varied widely. Let us disregard earlier steam-driven road vehicles and arbitrarily date the automobile's "invention" in 1886, at Karl Benz's and Gottlieb Daimler's separate production of four- and three-wheeled vehicles powered by internal combustion engines. Within two decades of that invention manufacturers were beginning to organize production around assembly lines, around the continuous movement of vehicles-in-the-making from one specialized worker to the next. Despite occasional efforts to "enrich" work by creation of teams and sharing of jobs, the industry has never abandoned that continuous-flow organization.

Even when they grow enormous, on the other hand, chemical plants generally organize around a spatial division of labor, different products and processes in different parts of the plant. Electronics firms segregate production even more, with multiple firms making different components for machines that other firms assemble and sell. The stories people tell about such differences generally stress technological necessities. Technological stories predominate because they identify rapid breakthroughs in which entrepreneurs have the upper hand in reorganizing production and because they fit so neatly with the assumption that efficiency drives economic change. But technology explains only some of the variation. Major organizational changes such as corporate takeovers, state-led alterations of property law, and entries of labor unions into nonunion fields periodically recast the character of work without significant shifts in technology. Indeed, such changes frequently *drive* technological change, as when employers respond to unionization by investing in labor-displacing machines. More incrementally, an industry's historical development, the accumulation of culture within it, and everyday struggles for power all strongly affect what technologies its firms adopt, in what order. Technology, in any case, includes production routines and modes of supervision as well as machines and mechanized techniques. Any story of change and variation in work that features only capitalists and mechanical devices grossly distorts economic history.

Although it occasionally recounts particular transformations of work and draws examples of work's variable organization from historical experience, most of this book organizes not around long-term industrial changes but around explanatory problems: why different industries feature contrasting systems of authority and compensation, why employment segregates so sharply by gender and race, why some kinds of workers move within well-defined job ladders while others shift incessantly from employer to employer, and so on. All the more reason, then, to begin with an overview of industrial change. This chapter provides such an overview; Chapter 7 elaborates and analyzes the process of change in more detail.

Instead of trying to generalize about all industries, however, let us start by considering changes in a few rather different cases. Cotton textiles, coal mining, and health care—our three main cases—each cover a wide range of productive organization and distinctly different paths of change. For simplicity's sake, we will concentrate on developments in Great Britain and the United States. (The story of cotton textiles, for example, sounds quite different when told from the perspective of India, where through both economic competition and political intervention the British drove a thriving industry into deep decline.) In order to provide raw material for the analyses in later chapters, this chapter will concentrate on descriptions rather than explanations. Our sketches are therefore cartoons, smoothing out leads, lags, and variations *within* each industry. Still they serve to specify what sorts of change and variation we have to explain.

Cotton Textiles

For centuries before the eighteenth-century British mechanization of cotton production, Europeans had been producing fustian, a rough fabric woven of cotton and linen yarn, with cotton grown around the Mediterranean. Households and small shops spun yarn and wove the fabric by hand under the guidance of merchants who knew how to get the stuff to market. English merchants imported finished fustian cloth from southern Germany, Sicily, Spain, and Turkey beginning in the thirteenth century or earlier. Protestant refugees probably introduced fustian manufacturing—still by hand, and chiefly through putting out—into England during the sixteenth century; they also seem to have imported the making of bombazine, a mixture of cotton and silk. Not until the eighteenth century, however, did English and Scottish merchants follow their continental counterparts in organizing the production of pure cotton goods on any scale. Although some raw cotton still arrived from older sources in India and the Mediterranean, by then cotton was coming to Great Britain chiefly from its Caribbean colonies, especially Jamaica and Barbados. Spinning and weaving raw cotton into relatively cheap, standardized fabrics, Britain's highly productive cotton industry set a standard for the entire world.

Before the late eighteenth century, the European cotton industry produced mainly through putting out. Historians of cottage industry often distinguish between the "purchase system" (*Verkaufssystem,* in which merchants buy finished products from manufacturing households) and the "putting-out system" (*Verlagssystem,* in which a merchant, a *Verleger,* buys raw materials and feeds them through successive rounds of household or small-shop processing before marketing the finished goods). In the purchase system, capitalists exercised control over production chiefly through their ability to set prices and specify qualities. Depending on their other activities—which frequently involved subsistence agriculture, market gardening, and/or seasonal wage-labor in capitalist agriculture—households in the purchase system retained some ability to organize their own work and bargain with competing merchants. Putting out, on the average, proletarianized its labor force more completely, with not only raw materials but also means of production such as looms often belonging to the merchants rather than to their users. It made living conditions of workers depend heavily on the textile market's booms and busts.

Because they could grow their own flax, or at least buy it from neighbors, local producers could sometimes make linen goods for sale on their own accounts. Locally raised sheep also sometimes supported a producer-run woolen industry. But for western European workers, silk and cotton always arrived through merchants who exercised substantial control over access to both raw materials and markets for finished cloth. By the eighteenth century, cotton textiles operated almost entirely on putting out (Dewerpe 1985; Gutmann 1988; Kriedte 1983; Kriedte, Medick & Schlumbohm 1992). Merchants who knew how to market cotton cloth imported raw cotton and farmed it out to successive groups of workers (ordinarily working as households and at home for payment by the piece) who carded, spun, twisted, wove, bleached, dyed, and performed all other essential steps between raw cotton and finished cloth. One person (most often an adult male) generally contracted and received payment for a whole household's work. Rural and small-town households commonly raised some of their own food on garden plots attached to their houses and sometimes worked seasonally for others in agriculture, but the more intense their production the more they depended on markets for food, hence the more devastating either rises in food prices or downturns in the textile trade. Subsistence crises, textile depressions, or both at once, came frequently and aggravated each other's effects. With little or no technological change, seventeenth- and early eighteenth-century expansion of cottage textile production—not only cotton, to be sure, but also silk, linen, and wool—industrialized and proletarianized vast regions of the European countryside.

After 1740, nevertheless, a momentous mechanization of cotton production began with spinning machines, soon followed by mechanical carders, twisters, and other machines (for more nuanced histories of cotton textiles in Great Britain and the United States than the following sketch, see Berg 1985; Berg, Hudson & Sonenscher 1983; Bolin-Hort 1989; Dublin 1994; Gullickson 1986; Hareven 1982; Landes 1969; Scranton 1983, 1989; Wadsworth & Mann 1931; Wallace 1978). Between 1740 and 1800, three major strands of invention intertwined: (1) improvement of means for a single operator's processing of many threads, (2) integration of previously separate operations (for example, carding and spinning) into a connected set of routines and mechanisms, (3) a shift from human to animal or water power, then eventually to coal-generated steam power, as the operation's motive force.

From 1770 onward entrepreneurs incorporated the new technologies into large mills devoted to the production of finished thread for weaving. At Derbyshire-born Samuel Slater's first mill, established in Pawtucket, Rhode Island, during 1791:

> manufacturing cotton yarn began outside the mills, among outlying "pickers" who opened and picked clean the raw cotton. Next—again as in Derbyshire— the cleaned cotton was taken inside the factory and fed into carding engines whose water-driven, teeth-covered cylinders turned out strands of cotton called slivers. Slivers were then fed into the "drawing frames," which rendered their strands more even and parallel, and then into "roving" machines, which introduced a slight twist to the fibers. Finally, the bunched, attenuated slivers were attached to water frames, whose rapidly turning bobbins completed the process of twisting by turning the strands tightly around one another. (Prude 1983: 42)

With weaving relatively unmechanized and special orders often produced by hand, warehouses (bases for putting out of weaving and specialized spinning) multiplied along with factories (Lloyd-Jones & Lewis 1988). Aided by improved shuttles, hand-loom weaving throve for another half-century until after the Napoleonic Wars the perfection of power looms facilitated the mechanization of that branch of cotton production as well. Thereafter standardization of machines throughout the industry facilitated movement of workers from one mill to another, but also made workers more substitutable, therefore more vulnerable to firing for insubordination or unsatisfactory performance. In the process, firms capitalized, the ratio of fixed to circulating capital rose, and employers imposed time-discipline on their workers as they took increasing control over step-by-step planning of production. Thus, merchants turned into manufacturers. In the same process, labor markets, unemployment, workers' organizations, collective bargaining, and strikes all became more extensive.

Despite their closely connected origins and similar technologies, British and American cotton textile production subsequently organized in different ways (Freifeld 1986; Lazonick 1990). The difference appears dramatically in mule spinning. A mechanical mule operates many spindles simultaneously. Workers themselves supplied motive power for mules' hand prototypes, called spinning jennies, which served them in household production. But as mechanics and inventors created improvements over the decades after 1780, water- or steam-powered mules became capable of running hundreds of spindles and of twisting the resulting yarn as well, which invited their incorporation into large mills. Throughout the nineteenth century, factory mule spinning still occupied the attentions of experienced workers who could adjust the machine for varying thicknesses and qualities of yarn, repair frequent breaks in the yarn, fix the mechanism when it broke down, carry on preventive maintenance, and supervise the children or adolescents who ordinarily helped them spin.

In Britain, mule spinners brought subcontracting into mills from household enterprises and small shops. As a result, they retained considerable influence over the production process well into the twentieth century. U.S. cotton manufacturers, in contrast, generally built their mills in areas where little or no cottage cotton production had prevailed and faced labor shortages that drove wages up. They moved more rapidly than their British counterparts toward labor-saving technologies, notably the use of higher-grade cotton. As William Lazonick sums it up:

> The structure of social power that determined the relation between effort and pay in the U.S. mills constrained American managers to make their choice of technique (cotton quality) on the basis of a relatively capital-intensive range of factor combinations that substituted effort-saving material inputs for labor effort, while the structure of social power prevailing in British mills constrained British managers to choose their technique within a relatively labor-intensive range of alternatives. (Lazonick 1990: 18)

American manufacturers likewise moved massively toward ring spinning, which eliminated mule spinners entirely. As a result, even experienced British workers who emigrated to work in American textile mills were unable to establish the sort of shop-floor power mule spinners commonly enjoyed in Great Britain (Cohen 1985a,b). In a fast-growing country with shortages of skilled labor, American capitalists turned more readily than their British counterparts to labor-saving and labor-subordinating production routines, but American workers enjoyed the opportunity to escape undesirable employment by moving frequently from job to job.

In both countries, nevertheless, mixed systems of payment long survived. Task work, piecework, and time-payment crisscrossed textile mills. Periodically, representatives of management and of pieceworkers bargained out a price list—often printed and posted—for production of different goods. In a residue of subcontracting, senior spinners and weavers typically worked at these collectively negotiated piece rates and received payment for their assistants, whom they then paid at daily rates. Maintenance workers likewise received daily wages. Except when working as independent contractors, specialists such as dyers—until well into the twentieth century, experienced dyers rather than their bosses generally guarded the secrets of mixing colors on command—commonly collected weekly wages and year-end bonuses. Managers who were not also owners (and therefore recipients of shares in profits) received wages by the week, month, or year.

Thus time-payment prevailed at the hierarchy's top and bottom, with loyalty instilling perquisites for privileged employees and closely supervised routine labor for the rest. In large mills, jobs typically segregated sharply by age, sex, ethnic origin, as hiring for different departments drew from distinct recruitment networks. As of 1915, for example, recent male immigrants were displacing young American-born women in the cotton mills of Pawtucket, Rhode Island:

> Throughout the carding and combing department in the Lorraine Mill a number of the unskilled jobs (such as lap carriers, can boy, oiler, scrubber, and sweeper) were held by males (probably young boys) with Italian, Polish, Portuguese, and occasional Irish or English surnames. These jobs paid the least in the department, between $5.00 and $8.25 (per week). With the exception of the supervisors (the overseers and two second hands who were Irish or English males), recent immigrant men (probably both older married men and young boys) worked with young unmarried women of the more established immigrant groups (English, Irish, and French-Canadians). Young unmarried Portuguese, Italian, or Polish youths had the lowest-paying unskilled jobs, and men from the same ethnic groups were the pickers and carders and also tended some of the ribbon lap machines, the combing machines, the slubbers, and the intermediate roving frames. (Lamphere 1987: 344)

Small masters often saved expenses by offering room and board to their workmen, deducting charges for those services from wages. In company towns, firms also used housing, truck, and various collective benefits to enforce work discipline. Even as company towns and blatantly paternalistic practices disappeared, employers continued to seek the creation and retention of a reliable labor force. With the shift to such labor-simplifying technologies as ring spinning, they drew that labor force decreasingly from men and unmarried women, increasingly from older married women. Although computerized control and automation eventually altered textile production, the main lines of nineteenth-century cotton textile organization endured through most of the twentieth century.

Coal Mining

At first glance, coal mining seems less attractive work than spinning or weaving: dirtier, darker, more dangerous, more taxing physically, more threatening to health. Yet in most forms of mining underground workers have enjoyed freedoms and strategic advantages their textile cousins never dreamed. Mining requires detailed knowledge of particular sites, exhausts its raw materials, requires constant moving to new places less well known than the old, and goes through cycles of productivity generated by the dialectic of increasing local knowledge on one side with the exhaustion of seams and the rising cost of transporting coal to the surface from more distant locations on the other. The big question is who obtains the critical knowledge. So long as mines operated through the opening of a central shaft or tunnel flanked by side channels each dug out by a small group of workers, their productivity depended heavily on the miners' personal expertise and their knowledge of the particular seams they were working. Costs of surveillance and point-by-point instruction made anything like a drive system inconceivable. Miners at the coalface worked quite independently for payment by the ton, the carload, or the unit volume.

For the duration of a given field's productivity, furthermore, coal production typically supported relatively isolated single-industry communities. Five consequences followed from all these circumstances:

1. Until the recent spread of capital-intensive methods such as strip mining, managers made little serious effort to impose centralized time-discipline on the workers who directly extracted coal from the earth, settling instead for hard bargaining over perquisites, fees, and piecework. For much of coal mining's history, operators essentially subcontracted with miners who hired their own helpers.
2. Operators capitalized, imposed time-discipline, and moved to payment for time instead of results in surface and auxiliary activities— hauling, ventilating, sorting, cleaning, and so on—much earlier and more extensively than they did in underground extraction.
3. Workers at the rock face therefore retained considerable discretion and autonomy with respect to the effort, method, and timing of their work.
4. The industry remained fragmented, with repeated opportunities for new operators and mobile workers as a field developed.
5. Mining communities, and especially their underground workers, long maintained considerable capacity to stop production and act collectively.

Coal mining was never a worker's paradise, but for several centuries it generated some of labor's most sustained solidarity and collective action (Ashworth 1986; Church 1986; Cohn 1993; Dix 1977; Feldman & Tenfelde 1990; Flinn 1984; Levine & Wrightson 1991; Lewis 1987; Long 1989; Metcalfe 1988; Supple 1987).

Coal began its commercial career as heating fuel. Driven by urban growth, population growth, and shrinking forests, England shifted massively from wood to waterborne coal during the century after 1550. Industrial uses of coal expanded as well: "It was used extensively in lime-burning, smithying, and metalworking, in salt- and soap-boiling, starch- and candle-making, malting and brewing, food processing and sugar-refining, textile finishing, smelting, brick- and tile-making, and in glassworks, as well as in the manufacture of alum, copperas, saltpetre, and gunpowder" (Levine & Wrightson 1991: 8; "copperas" is a kind of ferrous sulfate used in fertilizer and ink). For the most part, landlords or their leaseholders supplied capital, contracted with miners (more precisely, with hewers, haulers, and banksmen) to extract, move, process, and sell their coal, employed stewards to run their mines from day to day, and financed the enterprise from its own profits.

Unlike silk, spices, or even cotton, coal fetches a low price per unit volume or weight; transport costs strongly affect its commercial viability. As a consequence, railways, waterways, mines, and miners grew up in intimate connection long before the steam age. In Newcastle's coal-bearing hinterland, woodshod wagonways began spanning the distance from mines to rivers as early as 1620; Newcastle gained its early commercial advantage in the industry because its boats could easily work their way down the North Sea coast to London (Levine & Wrightson 1991). Within mines as well, hewers laid track as they penetrated into the mine's depth, and mules or human beasts of burden long dragged coalcars through the labyrinth on rails leading to the elevators or (in horizontally cut mines) the exits.

Hewers occupied central and peculiar positions in the mine—central because their pace determined the mine's overall delivery of coal, peculiar because their work included not only cutting and loading but also timbering, laying rails, pushing loaded cars to and from the main track, not to mention getting to and from the coalface, for all of which they typically received no direct remuneration. (With the spread of explosives, their work also came to include drilling and blasting. In each of these regards, safe procedures usually cost them money in the short run, but in the long run unsafe procedures cost mine owners money and workers injuries or deaths; such arrangements offered ample grounds for dispute and recrimination.) From early on, the crucial hewers generally received substantially higher wages and greater autonomy than all but the loftiest supervisors; they typically gained their wages according to the volume and quality of coal delivered, less often by the task, almost never by time expended. Other employees, including members of hewers' families or gangs, commonly received time payments by the day, week, fortnight, month, quarter, or year. Subcontracting and sub-subcontracting prevailed, so that many mine owners paid only a minority of their putative employees directly.

In labor-short Scotland, coal barons and their kin established a version of serfdom in coal mines, but undermined their own system by competing ruthlessly for workers (Hatcher 1993: 310–313). Through the late eighteenth century, Scottish mines recruited a substantial minority of female workers, especially daughters of hewers, for work both underground and at the pithead (Flinn 1984: 333–336). Elsewhere, female and child mineworkers likewise came chiefly from mining families and frequently worked for their own relatives; valued by operators for their small size and low cost, girl and boy miners remained numerous in Great Britain through the first five or six decades of the nineteenth century.

The sort of mining organization established in the sixteenth and seventeenth centuries carried over into the great expansion of coal production that (literally) fueled steam-powered industrialization during the eighteenth and nineteenth centuries. Stationary steam engines pumped water from mines and raised coal to the surface long before coal-generated steam powered the mobile engines that in the nineteenth century began to transport coal where waterways did not run. For a century or so, coal drove industrialization through much of the West (Wright 1990).

During the century after 1850, a division opened up between variants of **pillar-and-room** production, in which a single miner or a pair worked an alcove ten to thirty feet wide and increasingly long, separated from other alcoves by columns of coal left standing to support the ceilings at least until their excavation during the alcove's abandonment, and **long-wall** production, in which substantial groups of miners, sometimes on double or triple shifts, dug all the accessible coal from a seam, filling in the emptied space with rubble to support the ceilings as they abandoned it.

On the whole, pillar-and-room production (which long prevailed in the United States) lent itself to subcontracting, team-paid piecework, and simple underground administration, whereas long-wall production (much more common in western Europe) generated a more extensive underground division of labor, more complex payment systems, bulkier administrations, and eventually wider opportunities for machine hewing. In Great Britain, long-wall production gained ground steadily after 1850.

In either system, however, coal operators developed an interest in stabilizing their workforces, especially in retaining the local knowledge that experienced workers acquired. To that end, they not only maintained the higher wages received by hewers—who after all set the pace of production for the mine as a whole—but also offered bonuses for high yields, built company housing whose occupancy depended on acceptable work and political subordination, created truck systems that kept workers in debt, and colluded with other operators in denying work to troublemakers who left their jobs too freely or organized resistance to management's demands on the part of their fellow workers.

Despite the introduction of explosives, improved lighting, and better transportation, hewing itself remained individualized handwork in most mines until halfway through the twentieth century. Often bent over or lying on wet ground, hewers did filthy, strenuous, risky work. Gas, fire, and falling rock incessantly threatened life and limb. In 1842, government commissioner Thomas Tancred described what he saw in western Scotland:

> In whichever way the coal is worked the labour of the collier is the hardest with
> which I am acquainted. The thickness of the seam affords him more space to

work in than is the case in the general yet he seldom stands to his work. The ordinary posture is leg doubled beneath him, and the other foot resting against, reclining his body to one side so as often nearly to touch the shoulder; he digs his pick with both hands into the lower part of the coal, or into a stratum of fire-clay, or some other softer material beneath the coal. In this way he picks out an excavation often for a considerable distance under a mass of coal, beneath which he half lies to work. When he has after two or three hours' labour undermined as much as he judges it prudent to attempt, he inserts iron wedges by means of a heavy hammer between the coal and the roof above it, by which, and by the weight of the ground above, the mass of the coal is detached and falls. The cramped posture, the closeness of the subterranean atmosphere loaded with coal dust, and the smoke of his lamp, and at times with sulphurous exhalations, together with the bodily exertion, cannot fail to be very exhausting. (Church 1986: 201)

The hewers Tancred described were ordinarily men, but well into the nineteenth century workers who carted away their booty were often women or children.

Nevertheless, mining masculinized underground, and to some extent at the surface as well, during the nineteenth century. It also became more of an adult occupation. Plenty of children worked in early nineteenth-century mines; the 1841 census for Great Britain suggests that 31 percent of the male mining labor force was under 20 years old, many of them having started work at 8 or 10 years of age (Church 1986: 199). Indeed, nineteenth-century miners' lore said that no one who started much older would ever master the craft of hewing. Despite the lore, from the legislation of 1842 onward the numbers of both women and children sank steadily; although the more restrictive Act of 1872 still permitted children between 12 and 16 to work up to 54 hours per week underground, miners were beginning to withdraw their own families, especially wives and children, from work in the mines. As a result, mining communities came increasingly to consist of males (often in father-son teams) who worked in the pits, women who worked in shops or at home, and children who attended school while helping in family enterprises (Friedlander 1973).

In both Britain and the United States, coal mining depended overwhelmingly on handwork into the 1930s. In Britain, "throughout the pre-nationalization era coal mining continued to be an extremely labour-intensive process, hand-cut coal accounting for 90 per cent of production in 1913 and greater than 50 per cent until the late 1930s. The conveyance of coal was even less mechanized" (Church 1990: 15).

Before the 1930s, large changes in the organization of mining work in Great Britain—the virtual elimination of women and children, the shortening of working hours, the growth of larger firms, the specialization of surface workforces, and so on—resulted chiefly not from technological innovation but from bargaining between miners' unions and owners, negotiations between owners and financiers, direct state intervention in labor processes and benefits, or some combination of the three. In the face of competition with oil and with overseas coalfields, British workers lost some of their day-to-day leverage, but miners' ability to cripple a still coal-dependent economy if they could sustain regional or national strikes often brought the state in on their side. Indeed, the increased demand for coal during the labor shortage of World War II gave miners great strategic advantages and contributed to the state's nationalization of the decreasingly profitable industry in 1946.

By that time, however, mechanization of coal cutting and hauling were proceeding apace. The hewer's hegemony and autonomy then declined as his wages rose and his working conditions improved. During the nineteenth century, underground management had taken a form that would have astonished any operator of an overground manufacturing plant in the same size range: A single foreman, or perhaps a foreman and an assistant, monitored all the underground workers, walking from room to room checking out complaints and problems, but rarely telling miners how to do their work. The later twentieth-century system increased the intensity of surveillance and supervision. Mining as a whole probably did not deskill in Great Britain, since engineers and technicians occupied increasing shares of the mining workforce. (The man who became grandfather and great-grandfather of this book's authors worked as an engine operator in the South Wales coalfield before the coal crisis of the 1920s impelled his migration to the United States, where he became chief mechanic of a food factory; his older brother, who had left Wales and the mines earlier to become a locomotive engineer for the Northwestern Railroad, facilitated his junior's transatlantic move.) Still, time-discipline and various forms of payment by time expanded greatly at the expense of once-prevalent systems of subcontracting and payment by quantity of coal produced. To that extent, British miners' experience became more similar to work in capital-intensive manufacturing industries.

Unimportant as a coal source at midcentury, by 1900 the United States had become the world's greatest producer of coal. North America's iron and steel industries grew up on coal. English, Scottish, and Irish immigrants dominated the industry's skilled workforce during most of the nineteenth century. Yet in the United States, pillar-and-room production predominated much longer than in Great Britain. Unlike their counterparts in cotton textiles, American coal operators opted for the more labor-intensive, less capital-intensive method. Historians of the industry (e.g., Dix 1977: 7) explain the American preference for pillar-and-room production by means of geological conditions, but it seems likely that labor organization and labor supply played important parts. Before the 1930s, chronic overproduction, consequent price competition, and fragmentation of ownership (with one firm for every two or three mines in bituminous coal) also set barriers to capital-intensive methods. Capital's fragmentation cannot explain everything, however, even in anthracite, where big, heavily capitalized railroads owned a significant share of mining capacity, pillar-and-room mining long prevailed.

Whatever the cause and effect, hewers remained predominant both numerically and organizationally within American mines; as of 1890, for example, 90 percent of Pennsylvania's bituminous workforce consisted of tonnage miners, only 10 percent being "company men" paid by the day. As late as 1930, tonnage miners still constituted more than 75 percent of that workforce (Montgomery 1987: 334). American miners pressed for craft organization of the labor process: collective control over hiring and job assignment, worker-monitored weighing of output, equal access of hewers to transport for their coal, self-scheduling of worktime, pay for underground travel, minimization of "deadwork" (nonremunerative tasks such as cleanups), free movement within the mine, and defense of the "stint" (a fair day's production) against rate-busters and management pressure.

Intense conflict centered on the supply of empty cars to the coal face because hewers spent more time loading than in any other task, because once coal lay on the mine floor the absence of a car left the hewer (or both the hewer and the loader, where the loading job was separate) idle, and because earnings depended ultimately on the quantity and quality of coal loaded into cars. The "free turn," in which foremen's favorites got an extra car, recurrently infuriated disfavored workers. In anthracite, where tonnage miners commonly hired laborers by the day and big subcontractors who did not themselves mine often stood between hewers and management, competition for cars became a bitter issue (Montgomery 1987: 334). In addition to the all-important schedule of payments for different qualities of coal, strikes and day-to-day struggles in the mines generally concerned these work-control questions (Brody 1990; Dix 1977; Goodrich 1925; Long 1989).

In these circumstances, mine managers frequently combated craft control not only by direct repression but also by indirect measures such as hiring black workers and immigrants below the prevailing wage or in place of strikers. Although black slaves had worked Virginia mines before the American Revolution, and black convicts were providing a significant share of cheap mine labor in Georgia and Alabama by the 1880s, the hiring of blacks as substitutes for higher-waged whites accelerated after 1880. Only in West Virginia did black and white miners work on something like terms of economic equality (Lewis 1987).

Managers also adopted technologies that enhanced their control. For example, "blowing the coal off the solid"—drilling and blasting without preparatory undercutting—actually produced inferior coal and fouled the mine, but did not require experienced hewers; in 1898, it accounted for 75 percent of all Illinois coal production (Long 1989: 135). The undercutting machine, which began to spread shortly after that date, did raise productivity without sacrificing coal quality. Still, it likewise appealed to managers because it reduced the need for skilled, autonomous hewers.

The arrival of thousands of young immigrants during coal's expansive years before World War I broke the age grading and family succession that had characterized the later nineteenth century: the sons who entered mines very young as their fathers' helpers before working their way up to skilled jobs, the underground division among child trappers, adolescent muleteers, and adult miners. Yet families (emphatically including their women) remained intensely involved in mining life. In both Britain and America, wives of miners bore exceptional numbers of children (Haines 1975). In contrast with Britain, however, few women ever worked in American mines, especially underground.

Yet women's work figured importantly in American mining towns, not just because feeding, washing, nursing, and cleaning up after miners demanded long days, but also for a series of other reasons:

- the sheer number of children to be cared for;
- the fact that sons often followed their fathers into mines at 10 or 12 years of age and therefore required extra care as well;
- responsibilities that devolved onto women when their men died or sustained injuries at work;
- frequent generation of family income from boarders who also had to be tended;
- encounters of wives with company stores that often ran as monopolies at a profit to the firm;
- maintenance of households through the hardships of strikes and unemployment.

Mine women often joined their men in collective action concerning issues of work and livelihood. Great strikes and demonstrations became family affairs.

They often occurred. For most of the last 120 years, coal mining has produced the highest strike participation of any major American industry. In the average year from 1881 through 1905, for example, 74.7 workers struck for each thousand employees in all American industries; in mining, the figure was 196 strikers per thousand employees, almost twice the 100 strikers of its closest competitor, tobacco (Edwards 1981: 106). The solidarity of mining communities showed up in deep and sometimes violent confrontations with mine managers, private police in the mines' employ, and sometimes state or federal military forces. A famous strike against the Colorado Fuel and Iron Company (a Rockefeller property) in 1913–1914 centered on these demands:

recognition of the union and its grievance committees, removal of armed guards, abolition of company scrip and of obligatory trading at company stores, enforcement of safety regulations, the right of miners to choose boardinghouses and doctors for themselves, the eight-hour day and elected checkweighmen as provided by law, and a 10 percent increase in wages. (Montgomery 1987: 345)

In Ludlow, lethal battles with company guards induced Governor Ammons to dispatch the Colorado National Guard, whose units attacked a miners' tent city on April 20, 1914. "All told, 66 people were killed between September 1913 and April 29, 1914: 18 strikers, 10 guards, 19 scabs, 2 militiamen, 3 noncombatants, 2 women, and 12 children. On April 30, federal troops arrived on orders from President Woodrow Wilson. The fighting stopped, but the strike continued" (Montgomery 1987: 347). This much violence rarely occurred, yet miners' strikes remained rough affairs into the 1940s.

Although technological change came slowly to the American mining industry, saturation of the market plus competition from oil and other fuels began to squeeze miners badly after World War I. The Depression brought immense suffering to coal miners, but government support helped John L. Lewis and his United Mine Workers to fashion agreements with mine operators. The new contracts brought those workers who retained their jobs in a fast-shrinking industry relative prosperity from the later 1930s through the 1950s. High-priced labor and industrial consolidation, however, promoted a pronounced shift toward mechanization, time-discipline, and time-payment. By the 1960s large public utilities had become the chief customers for coal; more so than railroads, metalworking industries, and domestic consumers, they bid for the cheapest coal available, thus pushing firms to economize on labor. The rise of highly mechanized strip mining, steady concentration of mine ownership, introduction of continuous machine-based mining underground, a movement toward long-wall production, and competition from oil and natural gas all hastened the collapse of miners' unions and the disappearance of experienced hewers from the mining scene. The trajectories of British and American coal miners converged.

Health Care

Unlike cotton textile production and coal mining, health care has existed for millennia as both specialized work and generalized social activity. Healers enjoy special—often supernatural—cachet in all cultures. In the West, such specialists as physicians, surgeons, and midwives have long played important parts in the human drama. Yet ordinary people have always given advice and help on problems of bodily health to others around them. Even today, drug stores thrive on the health treatment nonspecialists give themselves and each other. (In Europe, indeed, pharmacists commonly dispense not only medicine but authoritative advice for the treatment of minor ailments; in the United States, organized physicians have made pharmacists fear to infringe on the medical profession's prerogatives.) The nineteenth- and twentieth-century growth of the health care industry consisted largely of the commercialization, capitalization, professionalization, and reorganization of age-old human activities.

Health care deserves attention for its impact on daily life, but also for its contribution to our understanding of work and labor markets. Despite widely shared beliefs and knowledge concerning health, health care comes in multiple forms: competing organizations within the same country, substantially different organizations from country to country. Variations include loci of health care (home, work, hospital, other), agents (doctors of various sorts, nurses of various kinds, midwives, attendants, technicians, counselors, others), technologies (from talking cures to immense machines), capitalization (from unpaid ministrations by family members to dispensation of treatment or drugs by large firms), and relation to state power (from illegal practitioner to licensed professional to state employee). Moreover, participants and observers offer wildly different explanations of its variation and change: massively technological accounts (the inexorable march of science), tales of supernatural intervention (spirits heal), histories of heroic individuals (great doctors and nurses), and largely political accounts (medicine as oppression, exploitation, or liberation). Here we make sense of health care chiefly by recognizing it as a field of work where from highly diverse crafts, most of them noncommercial, a relatively connected commercial industry arose in Britain and America during the nineteenth and twentieth centuries.

Few full-time specialists in health care worked in eighteenth-century Great Britain: a small number of licensed physicians who ministered to the ruling classes; a larger set of surgeons and bonesetters who bled, cut boils, fixed broken limbs, and carried on similar interventions in human tissue; a tiny corps of specialized dentists (most dentistry being practiced as a medical sideline or by such laymen as blacksmiths); an unknown quantity of midwives; a continuum of apothecaries, chemists, druggists, herbalists, and patent-medicine vendors; and those many servants who tended the ill, the incompetent, and the insane. If we included in health care what the nineteenth century began to call psychiatry, public health, and nutrition, to be sure, we could find thousands of other "medical specialists" in eighteenth-century Britain among the era's parsons, wisewomen, asylum keepers, and cooks. But the number of persons plying remunerated full-time public trades as acknowledged medical practitioners remained very small as compared with workers in cotton textile production or coal mining.

Still, some professionalization was occurring. After centuries during which obstetrics and gynecology (as later generations called them) belonged almost entirely to women, elite male surgeon-apothecaries were beginning to attend births and to introduce such instruments as the British-invented forceps into birthing procedures. Despite concerted resistance from physicians who preferred to maintain their separation from vulgar tradesmen, surgery was acquiring new dignity. The professionalization of elite medical practice appears in moves from the Barber Surgeons' Company to the Company of Surgeons (1745), then the Royal College of Surgeons (1800), which joined the Royal College of Physicians and the Society of Apothecaries in licensing and representing medical specialists at a national scale.

As sites for intensive treatment of acute medical conditions, hospitals did not exist in Great Britain before the eighteenth century. Their closest equivalents were charity hostels, leprosaria, asylums, and poorhouses. As of 1817, the workhouse of St. Martin in the Fields had

> separate wards for men and women who were ill, who were aged and infirm, and who could work. Pregnant women had their own ward, as well as a lying-in ward. Mothers and their nursing infants had a separate ward. There were "itch and foul" wards—one, perhaps, a "casual" ward for women and children, and one for women only. There were lock-up wards for women . . . a ward for men accompanied by boys, and two general dorms for healthy men; two wards for sick women, one of which dealt with very serious illnesses; another two sick wards, similarly arranged, for sick men; a ward for men and women who were or who had been married, the former householders; a ward for children too young to work . . . and live-in school wards for boys and girls. (MacKay 1995: 215)

Clearly, St. Martin's authorities had created a facility not for the sick as such but for the dependent poor.

Eighteenth-century medical care generally took place at home, with practitioners traveling to sites of illness or injury. Rare exceptions included religious orders and military organizations, which had little choice but to incorporate health care into their routines. Over the eighteenth century, nevertheless, the situation began to change, with the creation of 40 or 50 general hospitals, having a total capacity of about 4,000 beds, in London and the provinces (Berridge 1990: 204–205). Private madhouses likewise proliferated as the eighteenth century proceeded. The increase of such institutions directly paralleled the substitution of poorhouses for at-home parish relief and the decline of year-round live-in servants in agriculture (Digby 1978; Kussmaul 1981).

In company with rapid construction of insane asylums and enormous increase in the number of people identified as suffering from insanity, psychiatry took shape as a recognized profession during the nineteenth century. Even more so than other medical specialties, however, British psychiatry depended on state guarantees of its growing monopoly over a branch of illness:

> Psychiatry was to find that its fate was bound up with the burgeoning growth of an administrative state. At every turn, its practitioners discovered that they were dependent upon state approval, supervision, and sponsorship. The overwhelming majority of their nominal clientele could not afford to pay for the services

they offered; the cost of confinement in an asylum was prohibitive for all but
the most well-to-do segments of the population so the network of asylums for
paupers was necessarily constructed and maintained by taxpayers. A major segment of the profession consequently consisted of salaried employees in the public sector and direct dependents of the state apparatus, broadly defined. (Scull,
Mackenzie & Hervey 1996: 7)

Nevertheless, as the century wore on psychiatrists moved away from the
treatment of insanity as a distinctive, unitary disease for which incarceration
was the necessary therapy toward a much closer integration into an ascen-
dant medical profession. That move included the substitution for asylums of
psychiatric hospitals drawing on a wide range of medical practitioners and
much more greatly resembling their nonpsychiatric counterparts.

Technically speaking, health care changed very slowly until 1850 or so,
then entered a period of increasingly rapid transformation. If in 1800 a
physician relied largely on his unassisted senses for diagnosis and on such interventions as cupping, bleeding, purging, and administering emetics for
treatment, by century's end stethoscope, ophthalmoscope, blood-pressure
cuff, and fever thermometer had become standard diagnostic equipment,
anesthesia and asepsis commonly accompanied surgery, X-ray machines were
coming into use, microscopes and microtomes functioned in every re-
spectable medical laboratory, and bacteriology was revolutionizing both theory and practice with respect to disease. In general, nineteenth-century shifts
in technology and ideology moved health care away from whole-body treatments toward localization of attention in specific organs and disease sites.

Most of the period's technological changes promoted the capital-intensity
of health care and increased the advantages of pooled medical facilities such
as laboratories and hospitals. As hospitals metamorphosed from havens of
charity to science-based curative institutions, physicians began to take over
hospital management from lay trustees. These changes increased the power
of men (who monopolized essential knowledge and resources) in a field
whose actual personnel continued to be overwhelmingly female and whose
actual work, measured in hours of effort, continued to consist overwhelmingly of bodily care.

On the demand side, two superficially contradictory trends promoted the
expansion of paid health care in Great Britain. The first was the flowering of
a middle class with the means to command the sort of medical attention previously confined to the aristocracy and gentry. The other was the proletarianization of the population as a whole—the movement into wage-labor on
other people's premises—which exposed workers to new health hazards
while it reduced their access to health-mending relatives and neighbors. In
response, Britain reorganized medical education as licensed, university-based
professional training; from its founding in 1826, for example, University

College London maintained faculties for law, engineering, and medicine. Hospitals multiplied as they shifted from long-term incarceration to intensive short-term treatment, including treatment of outpatients. Growing demand for medical services blurred the previous distinctions among physicians, surgeons, and apothecaries; the latter two groups increasingly entered general medical practice. (The label "general practitioner" then described precisely that merger of previously segregated specialties. By default, it later designated those physicians who declined to take up licensed specialties, now ironically including surgery and drug-centered activities such as anesthesiology.) In response to pressure from leading professionals, Britain's parliament set up a regulatory system for physicians and their education in 1858.

About the same time, Florence Nightingale (who nursed heroically during the Crimean War, 1853–1856, and who drew some of her ideas concerning disciplined nursing from continental religious orders) began to organize British nurses and their training. In contrast to the domestic servants who had heretofore provided the bulk of day-to-day medical care, Nightingale recruited educated women into disciplined nursing. As distinguished from other health specialists, professional nurses combined three attributes: (1) commitment to bodily and emotional care of sick and injured persons, (2) application of available medical knowledge to that care, (3) mediation between sick persons and other medical institutions, especially physicians and hospitals. The relative weights of the three activities became contentious issues then and thereafter. Nightingale and her sometime enemies in the British Nursing Association (who divided over just such issues as well as Nightingale's imperious style) established nurses as a distinct profession shielded in part from control by medical doctors. From that point until well into the twentieth century, hospitals served as training sites for student nurses who after graduation generally moved into private service—sometimes including temporary return to hospitals for care of individual private patients. An influential minority created the special field of public health nursing, which operated chiefly in streets, homes, and schools rather than hospitals. Only after World War I did registered nurses concentrate in hospitals.

Despite pressure from the state and competition from physicians, midwives took a long time to professionalize in Great Britain. Physicians, nurses, local wisewomen, and officially designated midwives all attended births well into the twentieth century. Class differences were sharp: "Nearly all women from the ranks of shopkeepers' wives and up the social scale," reports Ellen Ross, "used private physicians as their childbirth attendants and had been doing so throughout the nineteenth century, but among the rest of the female population, at least until the commencement of national health insurance in 1911, private doctors were the one kind of practitioner not used" (Ross 1993: 118). Working-class people often preferred midwives to physicians, since midwives were likely not only to be known local women but also to help with household tasks that physicians disdained. In 1917, licensed midwives handled 78 percent of all births in Liverpool, 65 percent in Oldham, 70 percent in London's Shoreditch (Ross 1993: 121). Yet even in childbirth the trend ran toward physicians and hospitals.

As hospitals multiplied in Great Britain, so did medical specialties and complementary occupations: laboratory technicians, anesthetists, dishwashers, file clerks, hospital administrators, and many more. In the course of that expansion, specialized physicians (so-called consultants) came to dominate hospital medicine, whereas general practitioners stayed on their own private premises. Increasing reliance on expensive equipment and large organizations intersected with the creation of bureaucracies, internal labor markets, specialized professional societies, and associated government agencies. Under Liberal and Labour political influence, the British state greatly expanded the licensing, inspection, and promotion of health services from the early twentieth century to the 1970s. Britain's 1911 National Health Insurance Act guaranteed medical care for low-income workers (although not their families), stabilized the position of approved insurance providers, and led to collaboration between hospitals and general practitioners, who acquired crucial roles in certifying illness and referring clients to specialized medical services. The spread of Friendly Societies providing health insurance for workers reinforced these shifts.

During the interwar years, central government intervention in medical care and insurance increased somewhat, but most organized health care remained in private and municipal hands. Increased controls over public health services during World War II helped open the way to establishment of a National Health Service—still guaranteeing considerable power and fee-for-service compensation rather than salaries for most doctors—between 1946 and 1949. Subsequent reorganizations have redistributed power among hospitals, physicians, government, and patients, but left a government-coordinated health system in place. In Britain, an interventionist state allied with a collaborationist medical establishment to produce a paternalistic industry.

Although they drew on a common fund of medical knowledge and belief, the health care industries of Great Britain and the United States developed in significantly different directions. During the eighteenth century, American health professionals resembled their British counterparts, except that no centers dominated elite practice in the way that Edinburgh, Glasgow, and especially London prevailed in Great Britain. In Boston, New York, Philadelphia, and other older cities, sons of wealthy families commonly went to college before taking up medicine, often studied in Europe, regularly apprenticed themselves to hospitals for years without pay, and later competed for prestigious but unpaid appointments in charity hospitals. Even in those cities, well-born physicians comprised only a small share of all health-care specialists. Elsewhere most medical men learned their craft on the job,

in apprenticeship to more experienced practitioners, then exercised it outside of hospitals, in other people's homes or their own.

With American independence, the country's political fragmentation undermined all legal supports for medical monopolies; during much of the
nineteenth century, specialties, doctrines, and forms of practice competed in
wonderful profusion. State and local governments generally resisted licensing and restricting medical treatment or the dispensation of drugs. Physicians and surgeons as a whole enjoyed little prestige and less income. Their
variety nevertheless resembled that of clergy in our own time: Just as American clerics run from Episcopalian bishops to part-time street preachers, medical specialists ranged from Benjamin Rush, signer of the Declaration of Independence, to itinerant herb sellers.

The parallel with clergy extends to doctrine and practice. As Paul Starr describes the American medical situation:

> More than a qualified analogy links religious and medical sects; they often over-
> lap. The Mormons favored Thomsonian medicine and the Millerites hydropa-
> thy. The Swedenborgians were inclined toward homeopathic medicine. And the
> Christian Scientists originated in concerns that were medical as well as religious.
> In America various religious sects still make active efforts to cure the sick, while
> the dominant churches are more or less reconciled to the claims of the medical
> profession and have abandoned healing as part of pastoral care. (Starr 1982: 95)

Various medical persuasions warred with each other for a century. Winners
became "the profession," whereas losers remained "sects."

Intellectual and organizational fragmentation in medicine permitted medical schools to multiply and a great variety of practitioners to hang out their
shingles. Elite physicians bemoaned their loss of standing, so much so that
Dr. Benjamin Joy Jeffries titled his 1888 annual address to the Massachusetts
Medical Society "Re-establishment of the Medical Profession" (Vogel 1980:
59). The profession's reestablishment took a major political effort, but it occurred. The effort intertwined with importation from Europe of the new
"scientific medicine" characterized by antisepsis, bacteriology, X-rays, and
the coupling of clinical practice to research. Formation of Johns Hopkins's
medical school in 1893 signaled the new commitment to science and to consolidation of control over medical education. In 1901 the previously ineffec-
tual American Medical Association reorganized with the declared intention
to "foster scientific medicine and . . . make the medical profession a power in
the social and political life of the republic" (Numbers 1985: 191).

Nevertheless, only during the early twentieth century did the "orthodox"
majority of physicians form state-by-state alliances that licensed medical
practice, excluded practitioners from outside their coalition as quacks, and
limited the number of medical schools. Echoing Jeffries's 1888 call for "re-
establishment," the elite among physicians struggled to reshape the medical

profession in their own image. Central to this effort was a famous report on medical education by Abraham Flexner (1910), which accelerated and justified the dissolution of the proprietary medical schools that had multiplied with rising demand for professional health services during the nineteenth century. The American College of Surgeons (founded in 1910 as the Clinical Congress of Surgeons) established a rating system for hospitals that promoted scientific medicine and physician control. Modeling their organization on hotels rather than prisons or asylums, hospital managers and their boards turned away from their previous orientation to charity for poor people and began active recruitment of well-off patients who had been receiving treatment at home. About the same time, neurologists began (less successfully than their internist cousins) to create "psychopathic hospitals" centered on identification, diagnosis, and treatment of the curable insane by the best scientific means (Rothman 1980: 324–335).

In a similar spirit, the American Medical Association battled with major drug manufacturers and the U.S. government, eventually working out standards and agreements giving physicians substantial control over dispensation of medicines, a set of moves that considerably diminished the autonomy, scope, and authority of American pharmacists. Doctors became major actors in the financially crucial definition, diagnosis, and treatment of work-related disorders such as telegraphist's cramp, noise-induced hearing loss, and the lung ailments of coal miners and textile workers (Dembe 1996); Charles Tilly still remembers his indignation at suffering acute shortness of breath after shoveling barley in a factory, going to the family doctor who was also the factory's company physician, and hearing the troubled physician declare that the disorder resulted from allergies that had nothing to do with the job.) Doctors shouldered their way into the administration of hospitals where trustees, lay administrators, and superintending nurses had previously held sway; within hospital hierarchies, men displaced women. Although chiropractors, psychologists, optometrists, osteopaths, physical therapists, sellers of patent medicine, and a variety of other healers continued to attract patients, a relatively unitary medical establishment, headed by male M.D.'s, came to dominate public policy.

Nevertheless, physicians faced a dilemma: how to take advantage of the new facilities without becoming their captives. For decades they maintained autonomy by means of a triple strategy:

> first, the use of doctors in training (interns and residents) in the operation of hospitals; second, the encouragement of a kind of responsible professionalism among the higher ranks of subordinate health workers; and third, the employment in these auxiliary roles of women who, though professionally trained, would not challenge the authority or economic position of the doctor. (Starr 1982: 220–221)

The mystique of science and service made it easier for dominant doctors to build loyalty systems integrating subordinate would-be professionals and their helpers into the ethos, if not the financial rewards, of the medical profession. Nursing, for example, developed in a dialectic with physicians' hegemony. American nursing professionalized through a system in which students learned their craft in hospital-based schools. They thereby supplied the bulk of patients' personal care under intense time-discipline at very low cost. From only 3 in 1873, the number of nurses' training schools in hospitals increased to about 1,600 by World War I (Baer 1990: 462). Registered nurses then went out to serve contract by contract in private homes or, more rarely, as public health employees or private-duty nurses for affluent hospital patients. Thus with the collaboration of a few supervising registered nurses, hospital administrators drew on a cheap, compliant, and committed labor force.

In the course of these changes, physicians became prosperous, doctors turned much more frequently to surgery for internal ailments such as appendicitis and tonsillitis, medical practice capitalized, insurance companies began intervening directly in medical care and policy, and hospitals became central as loci of treatment for the wealthy as well as the poor. Other practitioners became marginal or subordinate. For instance, midwives lost their place due to vigorous (some would say vicious) competition from medical doctors; having attended roughly half of all American births in 1900, by 1930 midwives accounted for only 15 percent of births. That trend continued: By 1973, midwives delivered far fewer than 1 percent of babies (Litoff 1978: 27, 58, 114; see also Kobrin 1985). By that time, a double transformation of childbirth was well under way: Not only were physicians taking over the supervision of childbearing, but women were increasingly giving birth in hospitals. For decades, physicians' strategy worked extremely well, gaining them high incomes, extensive autonomy, and considerable political power.

The depression of the 1930s, however, introduced new dynamics into U.S. health care that eventually evolved to threaten that strategy, expanding the role of the state and large insurers. The temporary collapse of U.S. capitalism led to new public welfare programs that in some cases paid poor people's medical costs as part of welfare. The Depression and war years also provided a favorable milieu for hospital-based insurance plans, notably Blue Cross. Registered nurses moved out of private households into the expanding hospitals, establishing niches of professional control including command of practical nurses, aides, orderlies, and students. With the end of World War II, the powerful Veterans Administration centered its medical benefits on government-built hospitals. The American Medical Association blocked national health insurance, called for by unions and others, but under the alternative legislation adopted, generous government funding subsidized the construction of community hospitals (and, later, other local health facilities) throughout the country.

In the National Institutes of Health (created in 1930 but greatly expanded in 1946 on the model of wartime research efforts concerning malaria, dysentery, gonorrhea, and other military health problems), postwar governments created a growing medical presence where researchers rather than practicing physicians held the upper hand. Meanwhile major nonprofit organizations such as the National Cancer Society pressed harder for capital-intensive research than for changes in medical service. Perhaps the largest changes in medical care as such occurred with the emotionally disturbed; the United States moved dramatically away from long-term incarceration in asylums toward intensive short-term intervention by such means as electroshock, community mental health clinics, extensive outpatient services, placement of elderly disturbed persons in nursing homes, and stabilization of patients' behavior through drugs.

Both big-business management and organized labor (sometimes independently, sometimes in reluctant collaboration) involved themselves in providing workers with health insurance; John L. Lewis's United Mine Workers often led the way. In 1965, establishment of Medicare (for recipients of Social Security benefits) and Medicaid (for recipients of public welfare) brought the government massively and sometimes directly into payment for medical services. Despite the American Medical Association's strenuous efforts to preserve fee-for-service arrangements with direct payments from consumers to physicians, the combination of organizational and financial shifts eventually weakened the position of independent doctors as it strengthened cooperation between government and medical capital. In the 1970s, indeed, a long-protective U.S. government began taking antitrust action against organized physicians. In a 1987 finding of conspiracy by physicians against chiropractors, U.S. district judge Susan Getzendanner ruled that

> under the Sherman Act, every combination or conspiracy in restraint of trade is illegal. The court has held that the conduct of the AMA and its members constituted a conspiracy in restraint of trade based on the following facts: The purpose of the boycott was to eliminate chiropractic; chiropractors are in competition with some medical physicians; the boycott had substantial anti-competitive effects; and the plaintiffs were injured as a result of the conduct. (Wolinsky 1993: 20)

Although in the same ruling Judge Getzendanner indicated the AMA could defend itself by proving that it acted out of honest concern for the health of patients, these words broke sharply with the friendly tone of a half century's governmental conversation with physicians.

The concentration of medical capital was rendering group practice and hospital affiliation more attractive to physicians not only for their financial benefits but also as bases for collective action; as their professional association lost national leverage, physicians banded together for local bargaining. Even there, doctors faced competition: In recent decades hospital administrators (whether M.D.'s or not) have acted vigorously to restrict the autonomy and power of staff physicians. Through direct competition and financial leverage, rapidly growing health maintenance organizations (HMOs), in their turn, have placed great pressure on hospitals to cut costs, ration treatment, and discipline their staffs.

The struggle continues. Physicians divide increasingly between those who are starting to organize as workers (however privileged their working conditions) and those who trust in classic professional controls over the supply of their services. Some M.D.'s employed by health maintenance organizations are beginning to join nurses and other medical professionals in unionizing through the Federation of Physicians and Dentists; in 1996, physicians at the Thomas-Davis Medical Centers in Tucson, Arizona, became the first such employees of a profit-making HMO to form their own union local (Adelson 1997: 35). But professional organizations are also moving in the opposite direction. Commenting on organizing among managed-care doctors, the AMA's general counsel conveyed the association's disapproval: "We would defend them if they were challenged. You do not need a union to do that. Once you do, you run the risk that professional values are going to be perceived as not the goal" (Adelson 1997: 36).

Faced during the 1990s with stagnating individual incomes for physicians, the American Medical Association began speaking of an "oversupply" of doctors and recommending that the U.S. government reduce its support for medical residencies, especially those occupied by physicians trained overseas (Holden 1997: 1571).

Not that physicians are disappearing or facing poverty. In 1990, physicians and surgeons still comprised about 547,000 —some 5.6 percent—of the 9.7 million workers in the health services industry. Americans still insist on seeing doctors frequently: 715 million office visits to physicians per year in 1991 and 1992—2.9 visits each year per person in the United States, according to a recent estimate (Schappert 1995: 3; during the same period, Americans made an additional 62.5 million visits to hospital outpatient departments [Lipkind 1995]). Translated into visits per hundred persons per year, the figures by specialty ran as follows (Schappert 1995):

general and family practice	76.8	general surgery	9.1
internal medicine	40.6	otolaryngology	8.4
pediatrics	34.1	psychiatry	7.1
obstetrics and gynecology	25.0	urological surgery	5.5
ophthalmology	17.5	cardiovascular disease	5.3
orthopedic surgery	14.8	neurology	2.9
dermatology	11.7	all other specialties	27.3
all visits	286.3		

The bulk of these physicians continued to collect fees for services rendered, although they collected them increasingly from insurance companies and health maintenance organizations.

American health care resembled American coal mining in one important regard. Just as hewers long held on to their autonomy, retaining pillar-and-room extraction, payment by volume, and substantial control over work routines while the rest of the industry proletarianized massively, American doctors prospered and retained fee-for-service arrangements while health care as a whole moved toward heavily capitalized organizations in which most workers labored for low pay under strong time-discipline. The bulk of the medical labor force, after all, has long consisted not of doctors but of cleaners, nurses' aides, students, clerks, cooks, porters, food servers, launderers, guards, and other subordinate workers. Medical work had a crucial difference from coal mining: Just as it bypassed agriculture, American labor-rights legislation of the 1930s generally excluded health care workers. In hospitals, the multiplicity of job ladders and the high proportion of easily replaceable workers further dimmed prospects for unionization and collective action.

Even professionalized nurses and technicians, for the most part, found themselves relegated to fixed inferior salaries and subjection to doctors' authority. Through the twentieth century, nurses—not only graduates of hospital nursing schools and university programs but also practical nurses and nurses' aides—have actually delivered the bulk of direct commercial health care. Nurses' work centers on ministration to sick bodies: feeding, cleaning, monitoring, administering medicine, managing complaints, providing moral support, and tending their deaths. Despite the rise of paperwork and high-technology treatment, physical caring for the human body remains the center of nursing. For nurses, the great twentieth-century changes concerned not technology but conditions of employment. First, around World War II began a major shift of registered nurses from job-by-job contracts (so-called "private duty," whether in homes or hospitals) to direct employment in hospitals; prior to that time, nursing students had done the major part of general in-hospital nursing. Second, nursing differentiated into multiple levels and specialties, with registered nurses serving as bosses and intermediaries among patients, physicians, subordinate workers, and hospital management. Third, nursing work itself incorporated more and more machine tending and record keeping. The generality of nursing skills, thus the replaceability of one nurse by another, declined dramatically.

Only gradually did nurses translate this increase of organizational leverage into pay and power. A nurse in California's Santa Clara Valley reviewed her history:

I started in 1951 at St. Mary's in San Francisco. Back then you didn't even ask about the pay. I had no benefits. I think I was getting about $155 a month and no social security. After I got divorced in 1960, I had two kids to take care of and I was making $320 a month—only $90 more than the nurses' aide. We had no overtime pay and no holiday pay. We'd get one weekend out of six or seven off. And we had no respect at all. We were there to serve, and we were in the service. I remember getting wrote up because I didn't get up to give a doctor my chair. Then we got our first contract in 1965, and that's when things started to change. (Johnston 1994: 117–118)

In the great health-care expansion of the 1960s and thereafter, nurses and other hospital workers began to organize and strike after decades of political passivity. The movement of hospitals, nursing homes, and other medical facilities from nonprofit charitable organizations to big business spurred their organization. For nurses and other medical professionals, the transformation has opened up a division between public and private sectors, with public employees more likely to organize in concert with other public employees regardless of specialty and private-sector workers more inclined to organize within their specialized across-firm labor markets.

Meanwhile, pharmacy reorganized dramatically. Large drug companies and biogenetic firms became major actors on the medical scene, with government sanctioning of drugs for the treatment of AIDS or cancer making significant differences to their profitability. Chains displaced or absorbed thousands of small-business pharmacies. The previous balance between retail pharmacists (overwhelmingly male, frequently owner-operators, and enjoying considerable autonomy in their work) and hospital pharmacists (more often female but strictly subordinated to physicians) shifted as retail pharmacy feminized rapidly, prepackaged drugs increasingly dominated sales, more and more pharmacists became employees of large stores, and hospitals became the bastions of high-technology drug preparation (Higby & Gallagher 1990; Tanner & Cockerill 1996).

In recent years, hospitals have likewise undergone major changes. Hospitals and health care have become big business: National medical expenditures rose from $250 billion in 1980 to an amazing $650 billion in 1990 (Light 1993: 74). Profit-making hospital corporations occupy a larger and larger part of the scene, as both insurance companies and the federal government (especially via Medicare and Medicaid) place pressure for cost cutting. Over the last few decades, as Table 3.1 indicates, American hospitals have been reducing in number and in total beds but have expanded their employment; in 1975, the average hospital responding to the American Hospital Association survey reported the full-time equivalent of 435 workers including trainees (2 half-time employees = 1 full-time equivalent); by 1990, the figure had risen to 624. An increasing share of those "full-time equivalents" consisted of part-time workers: 25 percent of hospital workers in 1979, 29.4 percent in 1990 (USDHHS 1993: 8). Because low-benefit part-time work-

TABLE 3.1 U.S. Hospitals and Hospital Employment, 1975–1990

	Number of:			Full-Time Equivalent Personnel:			
Year	Hospitals	Beds	Physicians, Dentists	Registered Nurses	Licensed Practical Nurses	Other Salaried Personnel	Total Personnel
1975	7,156	1,465,828	54,712	510,118	239,949	2,217,818	3,022,597
1982	6,915	1,359,783	53,968	744,304	267,535	2,892,864	3,958,671
1990	6,649	1,213,327	63,775	895,324	197,843	2,906,346	4,063,288

SOURCE: Data from American Hospital Association, *Hospital Statistics*, 1979, 1983, and 1991–92 editions (Chicago: American Hospital Association).

ers cost less, because hospital administrators turned increasingly to contracting for such items as food service, and because equipment costs spiraled, the share of hospital budgets spent on labor declined over the same period (USDHHS 1993: 8).

Hospitals continued nevertheless to increase their professional personnel—especially their registered nurses—as they shifted from long-term care to acute treatment. The ratio of registered nurses to physicians and dentists rose from 9:1 in 1975 to 14:1 in 1990, at the same time as educational requirements for nursing rose. Nurses acquired widened responsibilities and powers while hospitals saved money by shifting work from physicians to nurses. At the same time, professional distinctions sharpened between registered nurses and lower-ranking providers of nursing care such as practical nurses, who typically differed in race, ethnicity, and/or nationality from registered nurses (Glazer 1991). However, as managed care takes health care by storm, it seems likely that pressures to economize will offset, and sooner or later reverse, the trend toward increasing professional employment. One step in this direction is hospitals' apparent increased readiness to dismiss or demote senior doctors and nurses (Rosenthal 1997). Age discrimination complaints to the U.S. Equal Employment Opportunity Commission from health care workers doubled from about 500 in 1989 to close to 1,000 in 1994, 1995, and 1996, and anecdotes of dismissals on thin pretexts abound. In the context of a cost squeeze, salary comparisons make such dismissals easy to understand: Although senior nurses can earn over $75,000 a year, freshly minted registered nurses make only half that much.

With their increasingly capitalist orientation, American hospitals retain distinct properties in international perspective. As Rosemary Stevens remarks:

> When I arrived in the United States in the 1960s, I was struck by the incongruities of the American hospital and health-care system compared with that of my native country, Britain. There most hospitals are owned and operated as government institutions within an organized national health service, and services are available to all irrespective of income and are generally free of fees. In Britain, too, there is far less overt emphasis on medical technology and a willingness to wait for services that would not be tolerated by Americans. In the United States, in contrast, general hospitals are run under a variety of auspices. Seen through British eyes, they are luxuriously, even extravagantly, built and equipped. Much of hospital administration appears to revolve around patient-billing procedures and business offices. However, oddly enough, hospital volunteers are much more in evidence in the United States than in Britain. (Stevens 1989: 5)

Stevens had moved from the mildly socialized European medical system to the quintessentially capitalist realm of American medicine.

Trends and Contrasts

Table 3.2 pins down recent trends in the work forces of cotton, mining, and health care. Available U.S. numbers for "mining" now include roughly one-third coal miners and two-thirds workers in oil or natural gas, and "textiles" includes all fabrics, not just cotton. Even so, by 1990, health care occupied more than ten times as many workers as the dwindling labor force in mining, not to mention twelve times more workers than textiles. Mining and textiles, once major American industries, are shedding employees as they increase their capital-intensiveness and as imports displace domestic production. Still, the three industries retain distinctive occupational profiles. In mining, craft and transport workers are diminishing as managers, sales, and technical workers (the latter reflecting the growing dominance of oil and natural gas more than fundamental changes in coal extraction) increase. Even in 1990, however, craft workers comprised more than a quarter of all persons employed in mining. While managers likewise increased their share in textiles, operatives (especially textile machine operators) continued to constitute a full majority of all the industry's workers.

The largest recent changes have occurred in health care, both hospital-based and outside: a considerable increase in managers, continued multiplication of professional and technical workers, declines in service workers, and minor drops in administrative support as information systems automate. More detailed tabulations show a marked displacement of licensed practical nurses by registered nurses and a much more rapid increase of nurses than of physicians. Both in hospitals and in such nondiagnostic facilities as nursing homes or home health care, registered nurses are becoming the increasingly central category of health workers. So far few men have entered nursing. As a result, the health industry as a whole has feminized considerably over recent decades. Nevertheless, the sprawling industry now embraces a remarkable variety of workers. The 5.2 million hospital workers of 1990, for example, included 17,124 computer specialists, 7,554 biological and life scientists, 59,446 respiratory therapists, 17,514 occupational therapists, 38,465 physical therapists, 5,756 librarians, 54,188 social workers, 36,207 guards and police, 51,827 cooks, 63,097 janitors, 836 writers, 144 musicians and composers, 1,844 photographers, 1,338 lawyers, 1,058 public relations specialists, 2,664 economists, 1,345 statisticians, and a mere 80 sociologists (1990 Census of Population SSTF–14, Occupation and Industry).

Cotton textiles, coal mining, and health care since 1800 cover a wide range of work; they describe a field of variation across activities, products, space, and time. Their histories display very different principles of organization, from the familial production of cottage textiles to the professionalization of twentieth-century nurses. In each case, we observe strong historical effects, with the organization of work at one point in time circumscribing

TABLE 3.2 Occupations of Employed Persons in Mining, Textiles, and Health Care, United States, 1980 and 1990 (percentages)

Occupation	Mining		Textiles		Health Care	
	1980	1990	1980	1990	1980	1990
Managers	8.78	10.04	5.21	6.75	4.79	7.61
Professionals	7.10	6.93	1.67	2.12	30.05	33.35
Technical	3.22	15.44	1.47	2.10	12.50	12.95
Sales	1.00	11.40	1.51	1.91	0.37	0.48
Admin. support	10.55	8.59	9.61	9.77	17.04	16.32
Service	1.71	1.52	2.74	2.35	31.42	26.06
Farming, etc.	0.07	0.08	0.06	0.07	0.13	0.11
Craft	41.37	26.04	15.01	14.27	1.98	1.71
Operative	4.52	3.78	52.60	51.53	1.18	0.85
Transport	15.50	12.81	2.77	2.65	0.31	0.36
Labor	6.18	3.39	7.34	6.47	0.23	0.19
Total	100.00	100.00	100.00	100.00	100.00	100.00
Number employed	1,028,178	891,406	946,423	780,784	7,250,465	9,677,355

SOURCE: Data from U.S. Bureau of the Census, Occupation and Industry, SSTF-14. CD-ROM, 1990 Census of Population, 1995.

possibilities for the next point in time; once American physicians managed to get state backing for their monopoly, for example, their defense of high incomes, autonomy, and fee-for-service treatment shaped medical treatment for decades. Although technological change certainly figures in all three stories—power looms, undercutting machines, and bacteriology made enormous differences in cotton, coal, and health care respectively—the histories show us incessant strategic interaction over the adoption, use, and organizational ramifications of available technologies.

Our three industries cover a wide range of capital-intensiveness, with cotton textile undergoing an early burst of investment in plant and machinery followed by relative stability, coal mining (especially its underground segments) remaining labor-intensive until recent moves into strip mining and earth-moving machinery, health care retaining to this day an emphasis on human labor despite the arrival of CT scans and diagnostic computer programs. They therefore help define what variations in work we have to explain: dramatic differences among the organizations in which production typically takes place, very different systems of incentive and control for various groups of producers, great variety in the recruitment and retention of workers, from the family inheritance that once characterized coal mining to the professional schooling and bureaucratic allocation of jobs that prevails in the health industry's higher reaches. Cotton, coal, and health set two challenges for this book's remaining chapters: first to specify what sorts of differences we have to explain, then to provide convincing explanations of change and variation in the organization of work.

4
An Analytical Frame

What's the Problem?

As the histories of cotton textiles, coal mining, and health care suggest, an adequate theory of capitalist work and labor markets should provide consistent, plausible, verifiable, parsimonious, and determinate answers to questions of the following sort:

1. Why do workers devote variable degrees of their available effort, knowledge, and care to work?
2. In a given work setting, what determines the relative predominance of (a) use of labor markets, as opposed to household production, other petty commodity production, and the informal economy? (b) hiring via internal versus external labor markets? (c) different systems of supervision and reward? (d) purchase, subcontracting, and supervised production?
3. What factors shape the scope, definition, and remuneration of particular jobs?
4. What produces categorically selective hiring, promotion, and separation? What produces boundaries in segmented labor markets? Does the same process account for both?
5. What sets the wages and other rewards of different workers? Why do whole categories of workers (especially categories of age, sex, race, and ethnicity) differ substantially in rewards from work?
6. What explains the varied individual voyages in work careers?
7. How and why have these relationships and patterns changed over time?

Despite several generations of theory and research, no existing theory provides satisfactory answers to this full range of questions. By and large, available answers—neoclassical, institutional, or Marxist—err in one of two ways. On the one hand, many models opt for radical individualism; in competing terms, they analyze the confrontation of a single decision-making employer with a single decision-making worker, then compound from there. That intellectual strategy enlists neatness in its favor but inhibits serious consideration of networks, organizational structure, culture, history, and collective action. On the other hand, theories that offer dense social analysis usually narrow their focus to small areas of inquiry, conceding to methodological individualism the prerogative of theorizing a full range of work-related phenomena.

In contrast to individualist theories, we begin by examining social interaction, then compound it into variable structures of social life. We also formulate a model that is sufficiently broad to characterize and explain much, if not all, of the world of work. Because previous theorists have not worked

FIGURE 4.1   Units of work relationships

	TRANSACTION	CONTRACT	ROLE	NETWORK	ORGANIZATION
(Share of All Transactions Work ↑)	Work Transaction	Work Contract	Job	Hierarchy	Firm
					Trade Association
				Market	
					Union
				Industry	Work Community
			Exchange Nexus		
	Exchange Transaction	Exchange Contract		Coalition	
					Household
	Social Interaction	Social Tie	Family Membership	Neighborhood	
				Friendship	
					State
				Kinship	

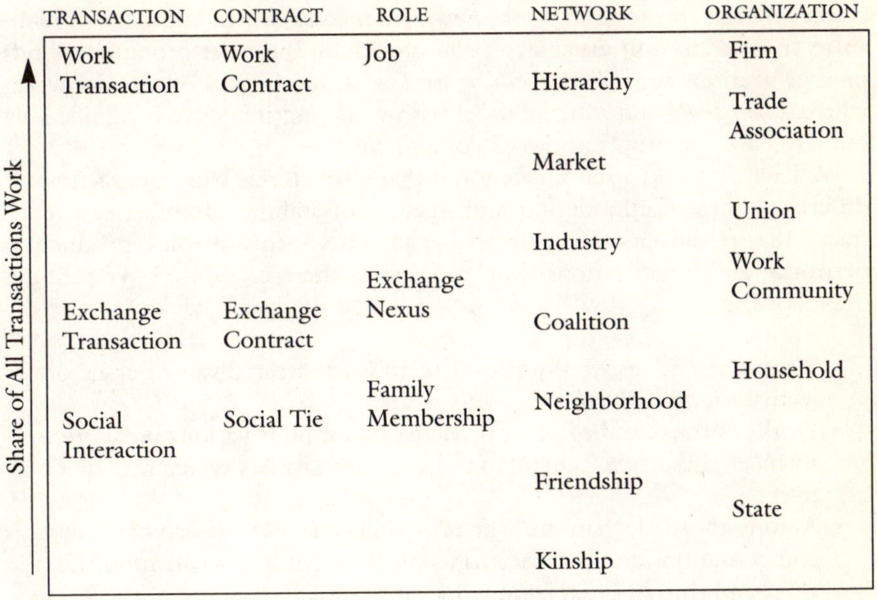

out the full implications of an interactional approach, this chapter pours much of its energy into definitions, arguments, conceptual schemes, and lists of relevant factors. That way, later chapters can proceed without constant interruption for new definitions and analytic schemes.

The chapter contains two narratives: a survey of the key units of work relationships, from small to large (Figure 4.1), and a discussion of work's analytic characteristics, including causes of variation in these characteristics (Figure 4.2). Our survey of units of analysis focuses sharply on relationships. We begin with the *transaction,* the fundamental relationship that links producer and recipient of use value; transactions outside of work we call simply social interactions. Work contracts are organized cumulations of transactions; their nonwork equivalents are social ties, which likewise always have some element of contract, however informal. Workers and recipients of value bundle contracts, in turn, into *roles,* most notably into those packages known as jobs. Similarly, the role known as *family membership* bundles together contracts, in this case typically concerning both work and nonwork transactions.

Work contracts compound into *networks,* of which the most prominent work-based versions are *markets* and *hierarchies. Industries* designate connected work networks and organizations maintaining similar relations to upstream and downstream markets. *Coalitions* sprawl across the boundary of work and nonwork, whereas *kinship, friendship,* and *neighborhood* concatenate social ties in different ways outside the world of work. *Organizations* are bounded networks in which some agents have the power to act for the whole. Within the zone of work, *firms, trade associations,* and *work communities* (e.g., crafts and organized professions) are the most prominent kinds of organizations we will deal with; *unions* bridge from work to nonwork, whereas *household* and *state* intersect with work and influence it significantly but also have important nonwork components.

We have sketched a set of categories that characterize work interactions at different scales of cumulation and degrees of stability: transactions, contracts, the special sets of contracts that take the forms of roles, production networks, and organizations. But what drives these categories? We propose the following:

- Producers and, especially, recipients of work-created value pursue objectives of *quality, efficiency,* and *power.*
- Work contracts and production networks embody various *mechanisms* to meet these requirements in a way that satisfies recipients' objectives.
- Among those mechanisms, the provision of *incentives*—commitment, compensation, and/or coercion—plays a central part in motivating work and thus in organizing work more broadly.
- Demands of recipients for quality, efficiency, and power constrain the availability of alternative mechanisms and thus shape the resulting contracts and organizations.

The configuration of any contract at any point in time, however, is not a determinate outcome of short-run demands for quality, power, and efficiency but rather depends on a historically contingent *bargaining* process set within a *cultural* framework.

Figure 4.2 schematizes this dense set of propositions. Let us begin to unpack them. Return to the elementary work contract linking a single producer to a single recipient and the basic question: How does the immediate recipient (R) of work's product get useful effort from the producer (P)? From R's viewpoint, P must have the propensity and capacity to perform or to learn the task in question, as well as the material means to do so. From P's viewpoint, R must supply information about what task to perform and how to perform it, as well as incentives to do so. With variable specificity, the work contract between P and R provides answers to these elements of the question *how.*

Think of Figure 4.2 as outlining the plot of the causal story we tell in answer to that question: History shapes past social relations and culture; past social relations and culture affect objectives and labor mechanisms; bargaining mediates the relation between culture and labor mechanisms but also

FIGURE 4.2   Characteristics of work and causes of variation

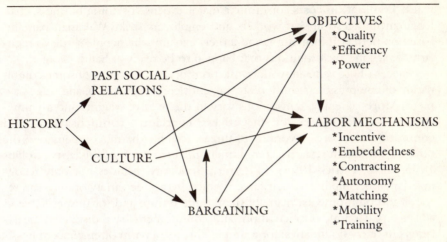

leads directly to the adoption of certain labor mechanisms rather than others; objectives affect labor mechanisms but are also themselves affected by bargaining. As we reviewed the histories of cotton textile manufacturing, coal mining, and health care, we sketched three versions of this story without stopping to point out its elements. Now it is time to be self-conscious about how the pieces operate and fit together. Contract by contract, job by job, network by network, the rest of this book tells variants of the causal story over and over.

Units of Work Relationships

Work Transactions and Their Incentives

Although solitary workers certainly exist, in general work depends on **transactions** among parties, notably between producers and immediate recipients of use value added by work. Transactions consist of interpersonal transfers of information and/or goods of which the parties are aware; they become work transactions when the effort of at least one party adds value to the element transferred. (The recipient in one transaction, of course, often becomes a producer in the next, and producers and recipients often participate simultaneously in more than one transaction.) As institutional economists have insisted, every transaction costs something, and different types of transactions cost variable amounts depending on their intrinsic character and their relation to the context; familiar transactions, to take the most obvious example, generally take less learning, meet less resistance, and pass more information than unfamiliar ones which in principle could accomplish exactly the same work. **Transaction costs** constitute a major expense of doing business, challenge any suggestion that workers and employers strike Walrasian bargains based on perfect information, and largely explain why people settle so regularly for second-best solutions that happen to be ready at hand.

Transfer of use value in work transactions occurs as a result of some combination of compulsion, stealth, bestowal, entitlement, purchase, and wage payment. More generally, transactions vary in the relative weights and asymmetries of three classes of incentives: **coercion**, **compensation**, and **commitment**. Coercion consists of threats to inflict harm, compensation the offer of contingent rewards, commitment the invocation of solidarity (Collins 1975, ch. 6; Patrick 1995). In its turn, solidarity includes not only recognized membership in a valued category but also a wide variety of long-run rewards and punishments, many of them quite diffuse and/or unspecifiable in advance. Coercion, compensation, and commitment have distinctive heartlands but fuzzy boundaries; for example, threats of harm often concern possible withdrawals of contingent rewards, whereas long-term threats and rewards shade over into invocations of solidarity. Behind "Do a fair day's work and you'll get a fair day's pay" or "Doing good work will bring honor to your family's name" lurk implicit threats: "If you don't do a fair day's work, you'll be fired" or "If you do poor work, your parents will know about it."

We have seen combinations of coercion, compensation, and commitment at work in hospitals. The student nurses who provided much of hospitals' direct bodily care between 1900 and World War I performed under close supervision for little or no money (compensation) within an ethos of service and solidarity (commitment) but ran the risk of dismissal, hence of bars to any career (coercion) if they failed to meet local expectations. The registered nurses who took over control of bodily care thereafter enjoyed greater autonomy, received from miserable to modest compensation depending on their setting, and built up an immense web of professional commitment; if they displayed due deference to physicians, they ran little risk of coercion. Elsewhere in hospitals, compensation, coercion, and commitment took other combinations, from the high-flying brain surgeon to the newly hired orderly.

Compensation, commitment, and coercion thread through every aspect of the world of work. Indeed, the central questions regarding work are why people perform work in the settings that they do and why they exert effort. The question of incentives arises with particular force in capitalist labor markets, but it also matters in the home, in the underground economy, or in precapitalist work settings. And although a first glance at capitalist labor markets suggests a single answer to the incentive question—compensation— a closer look suggests far greater complexity. Business schools, after all, build whole departments of management on the proposition that it takes much more than a job definition and a wage to induce workers to perform as desired. In the course of our discussion, we will return again and again to the trade-offs and complementarities among different kinds of incentives, among compensation, commitment, and coercion. We will also show how they operate differently depending on the history, culture, and social relations of their settings.

Work Contracts

Organized, durable transactions cluster into implicit or explicit **work contracts** stipulating parties, rights, obligations, and sanctions to the transactions in question. Work contracts differ from mere accumulations of work transactions in featuring enforceable agreements that govern durations, limits, enforcement mechanisms, and relations among transactions. They differ from nonwork contracts, which deal with exchange or consumption alone. A bank loan, for example, rests on a repayment contract that in itself entails no work, in the sense of value-adding effort. Work contracts govern the expenditure of human effort that adds or transfers use value. The difference between work and nonwork contracts is a continuum rather than a sharp boundary: The sharecropper's obligation to deliver crops regulates labor as strictly as the slave's obligation to perform tasks; many African-Americans discovered as much in the postbellum South.

Like the transactions they incorporate, work contracts cost something. They entail not only the costs of transfer but also costs of monitoring and enforcement. Although in theory we might imagine an exploitative manager imposing continuous surveillance and tyrannical discipline, the costs of such arrangements usually exceed their gain, a condition which promotes the multiplication of threats, the organization of espionage, the creation of intermittent surveillance, and the striking of implicit bargains with subordinates. Familiar contracts have enough advantages in these regards as well as with respect to learning and overcoming resistance that employers and workers commonly borrow existing models instead of searching for the contract which, in the absence of transaction costs, would most efficiently accomplish the work at hand.

The most elementary work contract involves just two parties: a **producer** and a **recipient**. The producer generates an increase in use value and transfers whatever embodies that increase to a recipient. (In the limiting case, Robinson Crusoe before Friday's appearance, the producer simply stores the embodiment of increased use value—the mashed papaya, the improvised shovel—for his own later consumption.) Even the elementary work contract sets the general problem of work: How does R (recipient) get useful effort from P (producer)? Specific work contracts state various answers to that question.

Work contracts typically set limits to the time, place, quality, and quantity of effort and/or product involved. They set limits, but by no means do they specify all contingencies; indeed, complex contracts normally include provisions for negotiated responses to unanticipated problems, thereby refashioning the agreement. Nor do they usually involve perfectly symmetrical understandings of what the worker must do. As Julian Orr points out in his revealing ethnography of men and women who service copy machines, "The activities defined by management are those which one worker will do, and work as the relationship of employment is discussed in terms of a single worker's relationship to the corporation" (Orr 1996: 10). But, as Orr documents tellingly, effective service work always involves negotiation of relations among parent corporation, machines, customers, and fellow service workers; daily practices and incessant conversations about them center on how to negotiate those relations even when they involve deep technical knowledge of how machines operate.

All work contracts also involve trust: a relation in which at least one party exposes valued assets to a risk that the other will seize, misuse, or damage them. Low-trust contracts (for example, a tacit agreement between shoeblack and customer that (a) the shoeblack will polish the customer's shoes without damaging shoes, feet, or trousers and (b) the customer will pay a standard fee without abuse) often proceeds with cash on the spot and simple enforcement. A high-trust contract (for example, the relation between hospital and a patient who enters for brain surgery) typically involves elaborate preparation, monitoring, and third-party enforcement. In addition to trust, work contracts also differ in their presumptions of previous training, knowledge of the local scene, outside connections, and many other features of the parties' characteristics and performances. Work contracts therefore vary enormously in scope, substance, stability, and enforceability, ranging among an attorney-crafted agreement between author and publisher, the exchange of a traveler's tip for a redcap's luggage-handling, and wage-benefit arrangements connecting a team of bus drivers to their local transit authority.

Work contracts definitely cover transactions within households, neighborhood arrangements for the pooling and barter of goods or services, deployments of work in the underground economy, and voluntary contributions of time and effort, just so long as those arrangements involve human effort, production or transfer of use value, and durable, mutual recognition of rights, obligations, and limits. The baby-sitting cooperative, the long-term arrangement about which parent cooks dinner, the division of labor in a drug distribution ring, or the implicit commitment by parent-teacher association members to attend monthly meetings qualify just as surely as the 200-page union contract. Such contracts establish mutual obligations and rights among two or more social units.

Work contracts do not necessarily link single individuals. Two firms can create such a contract, with one a producer and the other a recipient of added value. Before the spread of extensive labor markets, merchants often contracted for the labor of whole households—women, men, children, and even servants. Employers have frequently acquired goods by means of subcontracts in which whole work teams produced under their own supervision and essentially sold their products to the employer; even within apparently hierarchical factories, subcontracting occurred widely until the early twentieth century (Buttrick 1952; Clawson 1980). Hewers and their teams produced coal on subcontract until the recent past. At times, the California farmworkers' union grew strong enough to take over hiring for lettuce growers; thus the union effectively became a subcontractor. More generally, labor unions specialize in negotiating collective work contracts with employers and acquiring legal guarantees for those contracts.

Most work contracts engage third parties, permitting or requiring other workers, bosses, beneficiaries, risk takers, or outside authorities to intervene in the production and transfer of use values, as when construction contracts include legally enforceable penalties for faulty performance. The greater the trust involved, in general, the more extensive the engagement of third parties. Work contracts, furthermore, need not link producers and recipients directly. In more complex cases, when the contracting parties are organizations, the persons actually performing the work usually have little or no involvement in fashioning the agreement. These contracts shade from "pure" work contracts to contracts that mix work and exchange: agreements to provide security guards, to cater meals, and to deliver fertilizer as needed span part of this spectrum.

Like the transactions within them, work contracts differ significantly in the relative weights and asymmetries of compensation, commitment, and coercion. Slavery involves a great deal of asymmetrical coercion but little compensation or commitment on either side. An independent artisan relates to her customers through some combination of compensation and commitment but not much coercion. A teacher-pupil relation ordinarily produces work from the student without compensation through a blend of commitment with mild, asymmetrical coercion. As the teacher-pupil example suggests, in complex organizations most producers also serve as recipients within the same or other work contracts, and most people participate in several contracts at a time. If from a pupil's viewpoint a teacher acts chiefly as a recipient, from a school principal's viewpoint the same teacher acts chiefly as a producer. A child's achievement or misbehavior, moreover, affects the teacher's production record, just as a principal's intervention affects the teacher's performance as a recipient. In this way simultaneous, connected work contracts influence each other.

Work contracts connect to other work contracts. An injection molding machine operator, for example, turns plastic parts, products of her own work, over to a packager, who contributes further work by placing the parts in boxes and passes on the joint product to a worker in the shipping department. A mother pieces together child care based on commitments from her mother, her spouse, and a paid baby-sitter. Surgeons rely for their own work on the contracts that bind them to anesthetists, nurses, and orderlies.

Work contracts link, as well, to nonwork contracts involving exchange or consumption alone. Plastic comes to the molding machine operator's factory from a series of low-bid suppliers (resulting in variable quality and character-istics, which in turn generate different troubleshooting requirements); the parts go to a major appliance manufacturer in a just-in-time system, again structuring and pacing the operative's job. The mother's web of child care arrangements is part of a larger skein of family obligations, many of which do not involve work per se, but rather love, loyalty, and deference.

Networks

Social networks in general are sets of relations among persons, organiza-tions, communities, or other social units. Most commonly we think of a sin-gle network as the set of relations among specified actors of a given type de-fined by a certain kind of tie: for example, the interlocking of corporate boards of directors or shared involvement among supporters of a social movement. A **production network** consists simply of a connected set of work contracts linking multiple producers and recipients. The social struc-ture of work centers on concatenated contracts; jobs, occupations, careers, firms, unions, labor markets, discrimination, and inequality all appear as spe-cial cases or outcomes of that concatenation.

To use the notion of production networks in analyzing the actual organi-zation of work, we must draw boundaries around each set of connected con-tracts under examination. Almost all such boundaries are arbitrary, since flows of added or transferred value proliferate in many directions, often crossing the frontiers of firms, households, and trades. Given an arbitrary boundary, however, we can single out the concatenated work contracts that constitute production networks; they form webs of producer-producer, re-cipient-recipient, producer-recipient ties varying in their values of compensa-tion, coercion, and commitment.

Thus a classically hierarchical textile mill contains a differentiated, central-ized network in which commitment plays a significant part within densely connected clumps of contracts, since close coworkers tend to forge implicit understandings about cooperation. But coercion and compensation loom larger in the links among clumps. Relations among architects, on the other hand, form much more decentralized and shifting networks in which com-mitment and compensation produce strong temporary clumping, while co-ercion figures less prominently than in a hierarchical factory. Again, the stan-dard make-or-buy decision pits multiple contracts combining coercion, compensation, and commitment within a firm against producer-recipient contracts centering on compensation that cross a firm's boundary.

We refer to concatenated work contracts, then, as production networks, distinguishing chiefly among hierarchies, markets, industries, and coalitions. Where the network maintains a well-marked boundary and relatively centralized internal authority, we call it an **organization**. If the network has a well-marked boundary but no more than diffuse internal authority (as in many forms of ethnic entrepreneurship), we call it a **categorical network**. Jobs exist at intersections in those networks; a job is a role, a bundle of work contracts, durably occupied by a single person. For example, a beat police officer's job involves her in distinguishable contracts with the sergeant, fellow officers, storekeepers, tow-truck drivers, detectives, and a number of other people, sometimes including drug dealers, informers, or local politicians.

Production networks consist of concatenated work contracts. However, they generate and intersect with **nonproduction networks** featuring ties other than strict producer-producer, producer-recipient, and recipient-recipient transactions: ties of friendship, kinship, religion, ethnicity, class, schooling, informal communication, sexual relations, taste, political affiliation, sports, and shared avocation. (The distinction between production and nonproduction is of course relative; people often work within these sorts of social relations, but the creation of use value dominates them less than it does those we are calling production networks.) Such nonproduction networks vary considerably in their degree of correspondence to production networks, from the friendship group generated directly by daily contacts within a shop to a religious congregation whose members scatter widely across different work sites. As industrial sociologists never tire of documenting, work-generated nonproduction networks significantly affect relations of production; on-the-job friendships, enmities, nepotism, patronage, circuits of gossip all shape the production and transfer of use value.

Economists and sociologists have less often recognized the crucial importance of other nonproduction networks, especially those that extend far beyond the job, in the shaping of work and labor markets. Both managers and organizational analysts commonly think of organizations as abstract designs, conceived of de novo for consistency and efficiency, then corrupted and constrained by the development of informal social structures and external connections. In fact, hardly anyone ever creates a new organization from top to bottom. Unfamiliar organizational elements usually cost more to invent and install than familiar ones since new elements require effort for conception, design, testing, articulation with other elements, education of their occupants, and overcoming of resistance to their use. Sometimes creators of organizations borrow existing overall designs from other organizations. But even more often they combine not only models drawn closely from elements of other organizations, but also concrete social structure, as when a Korean kinship group converts some segment of its membership into the staff of a New York delicatessen, or an established network of Los Angeles Chicano activists form a voluntary association to forward their ends. Over and over, the creators of new organizations build existing categories of gender, race, age, and education into their very structure and with those categories the social relations they entail outside the organization.

Every organization, then, is a mosaic, a composite of clumps of social relations, many of them borrowed from or connected with relations outside the organization. Neither employers nor workers therefore set contracts as untrammeled individuals; they bring to negotiations and to everyday work segments of networks in which they already live out other portions of their lives. Both often use existing networks—their own and other people's—to solve work problems. Thus employers and senior workers build existing network boundaries by race, gender, or ethnicity into distinctions among jobs, while both male and female workers sustain same-sex solidarity by means of jokes, gossip, teasing, and sharing of personal styles on the job.

Much of what passes for prejudice, discrimination, and preferential treatment in an individualistic perspective actually consists of differential connections among relations of production and nonproduction networks that are segregated by gender, race, ethnicity, age, schooling, and neighborhood. For example, the labor supply actually available to any employer depends heavily on the existing social networks of present employees; even in the face of bureaucratized hiring, word of job openings spreads quickly but selectively through socially segregated personal ties. More generally, the implication of producers and recipients in nonwork networks significantly constrains the parties with whom they contract and the kinds of work contracts they form.

For matching purposes, firms create, inherit, or adopt **recruitment networks** that reach out into potential supplies of workers and articulate with **supply networks** through which aspiring workers find jobs. Recruitment networks range from almost entirely internal (as in the case of the Catholic Church's nuns, priests, and monks, but not its sextons or ushers) to almost entirely external (as in the Hollywood movie industry's recruitment of actors). Supply networks commonly form as by-products of friendship, kinship, migration, schooling, neighboring, and other social processes in which work fuses with a number of other activities, but employment agencies, government registries, and other specialized organizations sometimes deliberately form their own supply networks. Recruitment and supply networks articulate in such common routines as current employees spreading word to friends that their firm has job openings and parents finding places for their children within the same mine, mill, or clinic.

Many networks wind through social life with little visibility to their members, much less to outsiders; although the very regularities of social processes disproportionately often produce meetings between "strangers" who have common links to third persons, people continue to be surprised when they discover that an apparent stranger they encounter has strong connections to other people they know. (Surprised, but often delighted, since discovery of a common link usually defines and stabilizes the new relationship; that effect helps account for the frequency with which strangers of similar backgrounds, on meeting, begin their conversations, "Oh, you're from ____. Do you know ____?") Certain networks, however, have publicly visible identities and markers that separate insiders from outsiders; race, ethnicity, gender, and religion provide outstanding examples. Such categorical networks articulate strongly with work contracts because for different reasons both producers and recipients frequently build network boundaries into relations of production.

Categorical networks regularly surface in the organization of factory work. Factories typically combine a small number of contracts based on long-term commitment with a much larger number of contracts based on hour-by-hour supervision, piecework, and similar systems of tight control. That distinction between the few and the many commonly correlates with the difference between **command** and **turnover**: (1) command-and-promotion hierarchies assuring long tenure as well as substantial short-term benefits and (2) pools of jobs involving less training before and after hiring, low promotion ceilings, high turnover, little power, and few benefits. For reasons we will explore later on, employers and current workers often recruit new workers into the two sets of jobs from opposite sides of a category-network boundary, differentiating the two by race, ethnicity, gender, and/or religion. In the contemporary United States, the great bulk of male-female wage differentials result not from differences in job qualifications or wage discrimination within the same jobs, but from just such sex segregation of jobs. Recruitment of such a sort has a strong tendency to reproduce and justify itself. It comes to seem natural, so much so that people on either side of a line construct myths about innate differences among the categories involved: white/black, female/male, ethnic origin, or other socially significant distinctions.

Many analysts of work and labor markets have overlooked the mosaic character of economic organizations and their honeycombing by previously existing networks. Analysts have commonly supposed that each type of organization had its own intrinsic logic, with market-driven organizations going one way, for example, and authority-driven organizations going another (e.g., Sah & Stiglitz 1986). They have also supposed that in economic organizations relations of exchange and production established the basic structure, whereas friendships, hostilities, noneconomic categories, and shared memories merely accumulated like barnacles on the hard armature. Organizational logics do vary enormously, but a significant part of that variation results from the array of preexisting social relations that participants, often inadvertently, build into the structure.

Let us single out for special attention those overlapping networks we call hierarchies, markets, industries, and coalitions:

Hierarchies are networks linked chiefly by command and subordination.

In the networks formed by **markets**, arm's-length, one-shot transactions mediated by price and quality predominate. Market networks have two sorts of boundaries: (1) where the density of transactions declines to intermittent; (2) where the predominant character of transactions shifts from short-term exchange to other types of relation. Labor markets are simply those that link formally designated workers and employers through formal acts of hiring, promotion, and separation within employment networks.

One particular set of market networks consists of **industries**, composed of production networks and organizations maintaining similar relations to upstream and downstream markets.

Coalitions avow interests that are widely shared. They carry out sets of related, long-term contracts based on mutual determination of these shared interests. Examples of coalition structures include clans, professions, old-boy networks, and some religious communities, although in practice such structures generally incorporate elements of hierarchies as well.

Hierarchies, markets, and coalitions sometimes compound into **organizations**: connected, bounded sets of contracts where the occupants (individual or collective) of certain positions defined by intersections of contracts have internally and externally recognized rights to (a) speak authoritatively for the set, (b) allocate the set's collectively held resources. Organizations include firms, trade associations, unions, households, work communities, and states. In classic coal mines, the firm joins hierarchy, market, and coalition: hierarchies encompass the above-ground structures, complex market relations connect hewing teams to weighers and bosses, while coalitions link hewers and their teams together. Organizations linked by trust or shared investments engage in sets of related, long-term contracts while pursuing divergent interests as well as shared ones. Small organizations often nest within larger ones; in other cases organizations overlap. Markets sometimes appear within organizations, but more often cross organizational boundaries.

The word "firm" designates a special sort of organization, one having legal standing as a purveyor of goods or services. In this case we usually call the positions bestowing rights to speak authoritatively and allocate resources "management." Firms come into being, as institutional economists insist, because bounding and managing in certain ways reduce the transaction costs of establishing, coordinating, and effecting connected work contracts. An internal system of movement from job to job, for example, increases workers' firm-specific knowledge—an advantage for both firm and workers to the extent that the firm maintains distinctive forms of production.

We can recast distinctions among markets, hierarchies, and coalitions in terms of the nature and symmetry of incentives. An articulated set of work contracts spanning multiple organizations, in this formulation, constitutes a market in so far as its links emphasize symmetrical compensation. It constitutes a hierarchy to the extent that its links emphasize asymmetrical coercion and commitment. (Although the language sounds very different, Williamson's identification of extensive hierarchy as the situation in which "one or a few agents are responsible for negotiating all contracts" [Williamson 1985: 221] actually conveys a similar notion.) A coalition, finally, links primarily by symmetrical commitments.

Many other sorts of production networks exist: not only mixtures of hierarchies, markets, and coalitions, but also warlike sectors where coercion meets symmetrical coercion, cults matching members' commitment with prophets' coercion, patronage systems in which patrons receive long-term commitment for the short-term dispensation of favors, and so on. Small-scale production networks coexist cheek by jowl. A union representing workers in a particular industry may consist of a coalitional structure attached to a network of hierarchies within a market. In fact, the same individual, and even the same work contract, usually occupies a place within one or more hierarchies, markets, and coalitions simultaneously. A coffee shop counterman answers to his boss within the coffee shop's hierarchy; he changes jobs within a local labor market; and he offers special service and the occasional extra to fellow members of a coalition, a set of friends.

Small-scale production networks, in turn, cumulate into macrostructures, such as the social structure of accumulation (Gordon, Edwards & Reich 1982) or the mode of production. The capitalist mode of production emphasizes market structure, whereas existing (or formerly existing) socialism builds more extensively on hierarchy; the two rely about equally on coalitions as well. Large production networks persist due to inertial, self-sustaining activities. Let us return, however, to the small scale, reviewing in more detail how networks intersect in jobs and how organizations use a variety of mechanisms to structure work to meet recipients' objectives.

Jobs

A **job** is a cumulation of work contracts assigned durably and formally to a single person; it therefore does not constitute a network as such, but a junction of two or more networks. A person may hold more than one job at a time, two persons may have the "same" job, and jobs always entail interaction with other persons, but the basic matching of roles with individuals marks off jobs from other ways of organizing work. A lathe operator in a shop has a job, but a freelance writer does not. An actor typically holds a sequence of jobs punctuated by unemployment, but a street mime has no job. (Another more paradoxical way of putting the same point runs this way: The freelance writer and street mime hold so many jobs—so many fleeting bundles of work contracts—that the term "job" loses its utility in describing their work.)

Later we will discuss the creation, transformation, articulation, and filling of jobs in great detail. For the moment, let us stick to elementals: Employers play the major part in bundling work contracts into jobs, but employers operate within constraints set by industry traditions, ideas of management, previously created jobs and their current occupants, obligations to trade unions and political authorities, systems of compensation, and ties to available workers. Once hired, furthermore, workers themselves modify their work contracts, hence their jobs, through interaction with managers, other workers, unions, and sometimes outside authorities. In thoroughgoing labor markets, almost all work gets done in jobs, most of it within clearly bounded firms.

Characteristics of Work and Causes of Variation

Quality, Efficiency, and Power

Recipients in work contracts have three main objectives or standards for judging the performance of producers: quality, efficiency, and power. Quality, efficiency, and power parallel each other; all of them relate outputs to inputs over multiple combinations and quantities of inputs; to represent them mathematically, we must use not single numbers but whole surfaces of relationships. Figure 4.3 therefore greatly simplifies by presenting them in two-dimensional terms, as relations between pairs of inputs and outputs.

In the case of **quality**, the question is how closely the use values produced by various levels of a worker's effort approximate an ideal configuration of product characteristics. High-quality work approximates that ideal configuration with relatively little effort. Low-quality work deviates greatly from the ideal configuration regardless of workers' efforts. Thus citizens judge a police department's output primarily in terms of the quality of protection it provides, relegating efficiency and power to secondary positions. Similarly, automobile purchasers judge their vehicles by looks, comfort, horsepower, size, prestige, maintenance requirements, and a series of other largely qualitative characteristics. A work process's level of quality depends crucially on past investments in producer knowledge, organization, and physical capital.

Efficiency denotes elimination of waste. The efficiency of a given work contract or cluster of work contracts refers to the schedule of outputs that results from various combinations of inputs; large output for small inputs spells efficiency. Economists often represent the relationships in question as production functions: mathematical expressions summarizing stable joint and individual contributions of major factors of production to total commodity output. Economic actors adopt efficiency criteria for two reasons:

FIGURE 4.3   Quality, efficiency, and power

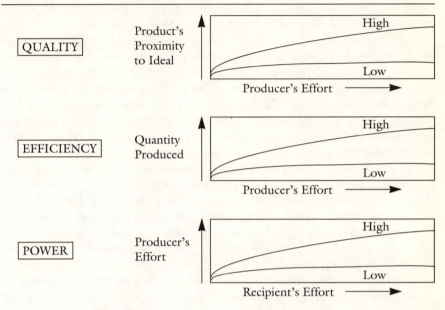

They prefer more output to less, and a competitive selection process permits efficient firms and forms of economic organization to displace inefficient ones—for instance, by selling similar products for lower prices.

Standard neoclassical analysis focuses on **static efficiency**, meaning the allocation of resources in a way that avoids waste at a given point in time. However, three other dimensions of efficiency are salient. **Adaptive efficiency** denotes forms of economic organization that allow parties to adjust to unexpected changes with a minimum of waste (Williamson 1985). **Innovative efficiency**, on the other hand, refers to organization that works out new solutions to problems, altering the environment rather than simply reacting to it (Schumpeter 1947; Lazonick 1991). Finally, **organizational maintenance** sustains the platform on which the other three forms of efficiency are built. Despite appearances, some degree of organizational maintenance occurs even in the most transitory relationships. Although farmers generally maintain no long-term ties with seasonal farmworkers, they do and must keep up ties with labor contractors who supply essential labor. They must also maintain good standing with legal, fiscal, and subsidy-granting branches of the government or run the risk of being forced out of business.

Efficiency interacts with **power**. Power is the schedule of P's effort as a function of R's inputs of commitment, compensation, and coercion; if R gets extensive and/or high-quality effort from P for small inputs of incentives, R exercises great power over P. In a simple view of work as Walrasian exchange, power should not exist. In fact, a clever mix of coercion, commitment, and compensation—such as effective military organizations frequently deploy—produces incredible effort for small inputs of reward.

Timescale presents a problem in evaluating these three objectives: Inputs of effort have different effects instantaneously, in the short run, in the middle run, and in the long run. What do we do with actions achieving short-run efficiency, quality, or power that in the long run destroy the worker, the firm, or the environment? The answer has two obvious components: (1) always specify the timescale of any particular output measure; (2) treat not just the instantaneous effects but the time functions of quality, efficiency, and power as determinants of work contracts' viability. Below some joint threshold of quality, power, and efficiency over some expected period of collaboration, in fact, no work contract (or cluster of connected work contracts) survives; recipients simply turn elsewhere for the use values they are seeking.

The relative salience of quality, power, and efficiency to work contracts also varies dramatically with the relations of contracts to their social environments. A symphonic musician or her orchestra as a whole must produce high-quality sound, although the sheer quantity of sound produced for a given effort and the amount of browbeating it takes from the conductor to produce the sound remain secondary. In price-competitive industries such as fast food, on the other hand, above some minimum of quality, efficiency carries the day, and power serves chiefly as a means to efficiency. Thus a cotton spinner's contract promotes fast, low-cost production rather than artistry or subservience. Finally, in a master-servant relationship, power—the master's ability to elicit work in response to relatively small inputs of commitment, coercion, and compensation—typically matters most. Existing analyses of work most often go wrong by assuming that always and everywhere one of the three objectives—quality, efficiency, or power—has priority, or even exclusive sway, in production. Thus neoclassical accounts generally build on static efficiency, whereas many Marxist accounts stress power—and deplore the sacrifice of quality. In fact, the history and culture of production strongly affect priorities among objectives.

Labor Mechanisms

To meet requirements of quality, efficiency, and power, parties in contracts adopt a set of **labor mechanisms**. Each labor mechanism designates a dimension of variation in work contracts and/or production networks. More precisely, the mechanisms describe variation in (a) stipulated performances of parties to contracts, (b) relations with other work contracts and their parties, (c) location of contracts within larger configurations, or, (d) characteristics of persons assigned to different contracts. Seven mechanisms span major functional areas: incentives, embeddedness, contracting, autonomy, matching, mobility, and training. We could, of course, add many other mechanisms to the list: formalization of work relations, procedures for adjudicating disputes, and much more. Furthermore, parties in work contracts also choose among technological mechanisms as well as social ones—deciding, for example, what capital investments to make. However, we single out these seven mechanisms on these arguments:

- They identify distinctions among work contracts and production networks that producers and recipients themselves treat as substantially different from one another.
- When disputes about work contracts arise, they almost always concern one or more of these mechanisms.
- The mechanisms characterize a wide range of variation in the quality, efficiency, and power relations of work.

Each labor mechanism offers, in principle, a menu of specific ways to organize that functional area. Table 4.1 lays out alternative options corresponding to each mechanism.

The first labor mechanism and no doubt the most central one is the **incentive**, which ties effort to rewards. This connection provides the mainspring of work. We have already referred repeatedly to the three key characteristics of incentive: commitment, compensation, and coercion. Commitment is the invocation of solidarity, which commonly operates through internalization of the goals of the productive organization, be it firm or family. Capitalism displays a wide variety of compensational incentives: tips, piece rates, bonuses, profit sharing, pay for knowledge, pension contributions that only vest after a fixed number of years of service, a wage premium (over other jobs) the worker stands to lose if dismissed for subpar work. Capitalism stands out from other economic systems for its stress not only on compensation relative to commitment and coercion but also on **fungible** forms of compensation: money and similar rewards that easily convert into other goods. Compensation nevertheless extends beyond cash to other sorts of rewards, such as deference. Coercion—in the shape of the foreman, the slave overseer, or the military court-martial—provides a backstop where other incentives do not obtain. The cumulative effect of the three specifies the balance of power between the producer and recipient of labor, which may be symmetrical or asymmetrical. To some extent, incentives employed by a recipient map back to the recipient's objectives. Recipients rely particularly on commitment to elicit quality, on compensation to spur efficiency, and on coercion to buttress power.

More generally, contracts articulate into organizational structures in three ways: through producer-recipient ties, producer-producer ties, and recipient-recipient ties. Ties take the form of repeated transactions, some of them crystallized into other work contracts, some governed by nonwork con-

TABLE 4.1   Different Options for Labor Mechanisms in the Organization
of Work

Labor Mechanism	Options
1) Incentive	Commitment Compensation Coercion
2) Embeddedness	Multiple producers (linked or not) Multiple recipients (linked or not) Nonproduction networks
3) Contracting	Incorporation Sustained contracting Job contracting Purchase
4) Autonomy	Producer control over specification of work process Recipient control over specification of work process
5) Matching	Merit Network Categorical Walk-in
6) Mobility	Promotion Turnover Stagnation
7) Training	Formal education On-the-job training Apprenticeship

tracts, some not contractual. Table 4.2 schematizes the possibilities for contracts, substituting simple dichotomies of presence/absence (+/-) for the actual continua of compensation, coercion, and commitment. It thereby distinguishes 24 sorts of ties differing greatly in their significance, prevalence,
and effectiveness within actual work organizations. For all its schematism,
the table suggests several interesting conclusions: that few work situations
rely on ties organized around only one sort of incentive—even compensation alone; that ties connecting adjacent contracts often differ in incentives
(thus the hospital volunteer toils next to the physician, the intern, and the
prisoner doing community service); that even when joined with other incentives, coercion provides effective incentives to producers only where large
power differentials exist—where the sum of commitment, coercion, and
compensation greatly favors recipients.

Our emphasis on networks brings home that every work contract is **embedded** in a broader set of social relations, including both production and

nonproduction relations. Each of those relations brings its own contribution of accumulated, shared understandings, rights, and obligations to bear on the contract's execution. Within production, multiple producers sometimes tie contractually to a single recipient (as in factories or offices), or multiple recipients link to a single producer (for example, a doctor or lawyer with her clients). Additional ties among multiple producers or recipients (such as unions or professional associations) further shape the relationship. Finally, nonproduction networks harness producers and recipients to additional sources of resources and demands.

Embeddedness is not merely a dimension of variation of work contracts: It shapes and constrains them. Wage levels, for example, depend partly on technology, productivity, and market conditions (efficiency), and on traditions and expectations (culture), but they also depend critically on degree of unionization, state enforcement of a minimum wage or of limitations on wage increases, state use of repression or other forms of pressure against unions and employers, the social organization of biological reproduction, and group commitment to exclude other groups (such as women) from certain jobs. What's more, networks of social relations strongly influence other labor mechanisms such as contracting, matching, and mobility. The key elements in social relations include the state, family structures, production networks (markets, hierarchies, industries, and coalitions, plus organizations such as firms and households), and nonproduction networks.

Contracting and autonomy characterize a work contract at a given moment: They are instantaneous or "snapshot" mechanisms. **Contracting** involves the choice of whether to incorporate work within the hierarchy of a producing organization, subcontract for an intermediate good or service, or simply purchase a finished good or service. Subcontracting, in turn, segments into sustained relationships (such as those forged by Japanese manufacturers) or job-by-job pairings (as in modern Hollywood film production). One critical aspect of contracting is the degree of short-term monetization: To what extent is pecuniary compensation tied to performance in the short term?

Employers and workers also settle on some pattern of **autonomy**. Autonomous routines produce use value through a variety of paths at workers' discretion whereas nonautonomous routines closely follow the recipient's specifications; nonautonomous routines generally call forth intensive short-term supervision. The degree of time-discipline captures one key element of autonomy. Autonomy not only encompasses time (who decides on the pace of work and the time worked?), but also space (who determines where tasks will be performed?), and tasks (at whose discretion does the repertoire of tasks performed vary from one time period to another and at whose discretion?). On the whole, autonomous contracts involve greater trust, at least from management's perspective: more valued assets at risk to the other's performance, greater scope for seizure, damage, or misuse of those assets.

Autonomous contracts therefore commonly depend on prior socialization, long on-the-job training, and extensive commitments to third parties.

Matching, mobility, and training are longitudinal, "movie" characteristics of contracts, laying out laws of motion over time. **Matching** specifies the means of selecting the worker for a task, whether this involves hiring, promotion, contracting, transitory assignment, or some other means. In some instances, an employer (or other user of labor services) selects workers on the basis of merit. In other instances she defines the pool primarily by positions within a network (seniority is a leading example) or by categorical distinctions (gender, race, nationality). Finally, in low-skill, high-turnover jobs, employers are likely to hire whoever walks in or use a subcontracting agency such as a temporary help service. In practice, employers typically combine these mechanisms. Within a hospital, for example, hiring of laundry workers and cleaners typically passes through an employment office (although current workers often ease friends and relatives through the office), whereas professions play major parts in the placement of nurses and physicians. Workers seek both to influence the mechanism selected and, when possible, to exploit their network or categorical status.

Although we have spelled the selection process out in terms of jobs, these categories transfer to other types of work contracts as well. Marriage matches—and thus contracts to exchange certain services—may be made based on attractiveness (merit) or a network or categorical basis (which may range from finding a mate within a social network, such as a high school graduating class, to arranged marriage). Men or women who seek a short-term match are more likely to resort to singles bars or engage a prostitute—or visit a fast-food restaurant, depending on what services they hunger for.

The **mobility** mechanism determines worker movement from job to job. Most commonly, firms divide their workforce into pools characterized by promotion (upwardly mobile management), stagnation (much of middle management, skilled workers), and turnover (unskilled workers). Mobility paths to and from a particular producer position represent one of the sets of links embedding that position. Finally, **training** may take place outside of a workplace through formal education, within the workplace through on-the-job training, or in some combination of the two (of which apprenticeship is a common model). Training interacts with matching: Some recipients of labor services undertake to train producers, whereas others seek producers who come with a complete set of skills.

To recapitulate the repertoire of mechanisms, let us return to the hospital nurse. She (even today the vast majority of nurses are female) provides work effort in response to strong commitment and modest compensation, avoiding coercion by cooperating with physicians and nursing supervisors. Her work contract embeds deeply in social relations within and outside of production: relations with supervisors, fellow nurses, aides, orderlies, technicians, and food handlers, relations with patients, their friends, and their families as well. She works on a direct contract (rather than a subcontract like her private-care predecessors) within a well-defined hierarchy. Her autonomy—her ability to choose the path by which she gets her work done—varies considerably from assignment to assignment: small as operating-room assistant, large as emergency-room supervisor. In her case, matching of worker to job operates through a series of conventions between hospitals and organized nurses, strongly mediated by nursing supervisors. Correspondingly, mobility patterns (a) separate nurses from other workers, (b) produce shallow hierarchies, and (c) encourage lateral movements from service to service or hospital to hospital rather than through a series of promotions. Training takes a highly standardized form, increasingly passing through a college-level degree, supervised clinical experience, and then a good deal of on-the-job learning. Incentives, embeddedness, contracting, autonomy, matching, mobility, and training distinguish nurses sharply from all other hospital workers.

In a hospital, administrators (who report variously to trustees, stockholders, religious superiors, or public officials) and organized professionals bargain out the relevant mechanisms for different work contracts; once in place, of course, they begin to look natural and inevitable. Using criteria of quality, efficiency, and power, administrators and professionals choose the combinations of incentives, contracting, autonomy, embeddedness, matching, mobility, and training that will best meet their requirements, within limits set by the costs of the mechanisms selected.

In principle, hospital administrators and other recipients of use value could combine this set of mechanisms in virtually endless ways. But in practice, recipients never have the opportunity to simply select a set of mechanisms at will. Functional compatibilities and incompatibilities favor some combinations over others. Organizational inertia and imitation privilege familiar, established mechanisms. What's more, consummation of a work contract does not necessarily proceed smoothly and harmoniously. Value recipients, such as employers, are not the only protagonists who struggle to define relevant mechanisms. A capitalist wielding commitment, compensation, and coercion in an attempt to extract effort from workers sometimes faces workers who lengthen their lunch hours and breaks (seeking to win tacit capitalist commitment for this expanded leisure), shift work to others, or mobilize commitment and coercion on their own behalf to prevent coworkers from being rate-busters. Although an employer may have the power to write the rules, enforcing their implementation is something else again.

Indeed, providers of work services and users of those services almost invariably pursue conflicting objectives in some regards. In most circumstances, neither party has the absolute power to impose his or her preferred set of characteristics entirely. As a result, the parties bargain. In **bargaining,** two or more parties exchange rewards, punishments, threats, or promises contingent on agreements with respect to future performance. Moreover, in some cases groups of workers go beyond day-to-day, largely individualized bargaining to organize **contention**—mutual, collective making of claims which, if realized, affect other people's interests. Third parties such as the state often enter the bargaining process, especially when contention takes place.

Thus, employers do not wield anything like absolute control over labor processes. Employers, however, generally have much more control over the choice of mechanisms than do workers. Unequal bargaining under widely varying technical and social conditions creates the enormous variety of organization we have encountered in health care, cotton textiles, and coal mining. The framework laid out in this chapter yields a general sense of how this process unfolds. To understand it in more detail requires moving from broadly conceived analysis of the relations among "producers" and "recipients" to more focused examination of the behavior of employers and workers.

5

Employers at Work

The Worker-Employer Pair

> *EMPLOYEE: Mr. M., I would like to ask you to give me a leave of absence for two months, which I want to spend in attending school.*
>
> *EMPLOYER: What did you say? A leave of absence! In the time when the season starts, in the time when I need you most; no such thing—a leave of absence! What kind of school is it that you want to go to?*
>
> *EMPLOYEE: It is the Bryn Mawr Summer School for Women Workers in Industry.*
>
> *EMPLOYER: Oho! Now I know. You want to attend a school which teaches workers how best to fight bosses.*
>
> *EMPLOYEE: Not at all. This school's aim is to enable workers to think more clearly on problems that they are confronted with.*
>
> *EMPLOYER: I hope you don't intend to become a philosopher. And what will it be if you get so educated there that after you return, you won't want to work any more in a tailor shop?*
>
> *EMPLOYEE: If I did not want to work for you any more, I would not want you to keep the job for me.*
>
> *EMPLOYER: What for do you want education? Can't you stitch coats without having any?*
>
> *Dialogue recounted by a participant in the Bryn Mawr Summer School, 1920s, from the Hilda W. Smith Collection, Schlesinger Library, Radcliffe College, quoted in Kessler-Harris 1982, p.243.*

Employer-employee relations are charged. The foregoing dialogue brims with themes of power and deference, loyalty and fairness, paternalism and rebellion. Next to this bristling interchange, the relatively neutral categories of "producer" and "recipient"—which imply little beyond someone's relative position in the production of value—pale.

We started out our analysis with these neutral terms to make a point: An individual can have multiple statuses—here a recipient, there a producer. This is true within production processes, as in the case of subcontractors, or of the chains of supervision that characterize large firms. Even more widely, individuals occupy multiple statuses across industries: A physician treats a hairstylist one day and has her hair done by him the next; a coal miner is a producer in the mine, but a recipient of his wife's unpaid efforts at home.

But we now narrow our attention to one part of the world of work, labor markets composed of employers and workers. This places the producer-recipient pair in a particular institutional context, in which the transactions, contracts, roles, networks, and organizations that bind the pair together have a particular character. The institutional context in question, of course, is a momentous one in any developed country: Labor markets constitute the largest single claim on the work time and efforts of adults and provide the predominant source of income and the means of subsistence. Precisely because of this preeminence, production relations shaped in the labor market spill over into broader class-shaped social and political relations.

What makes the worker-employer pair—and the labor markets that result from the cumulation of such pairs—distinctive among the many pairings in the universe of work? In Chapter 2, we defined labor markets as the convergence of workers, employers, hiring, employment networks, and contracts. Having introduced the set of labor mechanisms in Chapter 4, we can now specify that labor markets exhibit a distinctive combination of the three mechanisms of incentive, contracting, and embeddedness.

1. In terms of incentive, labor markets run primarily on compensation. Slaves, conscripts, volunteers, and housewives are not workers in the usual sense.

2. In terms of contracting, workers occupy the position of producer in a sustained way. This does not mean that they necessarily have a protracted contract with an individual recipient; workers hired for a day at a time through a shape-up or a temporary agency are workers nonetheless. But it means that workers are, on the whole, proletarianized—they lack other options than to sell their labor.

3. In terms of embeddedness, employer-worker relationships are embedded in hierarchical organizations (firms), which confer authority on the employer. There is a critical distinction between a customer who can take his or her business elsewhere and an employer who can fire a worker. When I buy finished cloth weekly from the same family (meeting the incentive and contracting criteria), I am not considered the family's employer; but when I pay the family members to produce cloth under my direction, I am. Thus, independent professionals, craftspeople, and virtuosi—who each possess their own form of capital—are not workers in this sense. Subcontracting remains a gray area, with relations ranging from crypto-employment to firm-to-firm relations.

In Chapter 7 we will trace in some detail the process of proletarianization, which has shifted more and more work in the direction of compensation-based incentives, creating a workforce of people whose only option is to be producers. The upheaval this process brings can be seen in miniature in the U.S. health care industry today, in which physicians—independent professionals one hundred years ago, powerful subcontractors through most of this century—find themselves becoming employees.

Employers and workers, then, are the two key actors we examine in this chapter and the next. In the next chapter we also, more briefly, examine states, whose involvement in the world of work has typically expanded in tandem with the spread of proletarianization, and families. We pose three main questions about these actors:

- Behavior. What forces drive and shape employer and worker behavior? What about states' and families' behavior with respect to labor markets?
- Bounding. What determines the boundaries of the firm? Secondarily, what determines the boundaries of firms' claims on workers?
- Networks. How do networks shape individual worker and employer behavior? How does such individual behavior compound into the structure and action of networks?

Incentives, contracting, and embeddedness remain central to our inquiry throughout the two chapters. Incentives loom large in the determination of behavior. The question of bounding addresses choices among forms of contracting. And networks give substance to the notion of embeddedness.

Employer Objectives

When we undertake to characterize employer behavior, we do not narrow the focus to profit-seeking, capitalist firms. Employers include households, self-employing individuals, and organizations built around nonmarket goals (governments, churches, or nonprofit organizations, for example) as well. However, we contend that in many ways the behavior of nonmarket organizations resembles that of business organizations. This is true because (1) both groups of organizations seek to optimize—that is, to achieve the most favorable possible outcome in terms of a set of predefined objectives, given the constraints facing them—some mix of quality, efficiency, and power; (2) variation in the composition of that mix of objectives is as great or greater *within* each group of organizations as *between* them; (3) similar social and economic influences structure the particular mix of objectives adopted by a given organization in either group; and (4) despite attempts by both groups to optimize, both also face similar obstacles to optimization.

We emphasize that employer objectives are socially formed. Thus, they do not emerge unproblematically from economic pressures on the organization (as theories of a unitary profit motive imply); nor do they emerge unproblematically from individual preferences developed in isolation (as simple managerial theories imply). The social formation of employer objectives plays out, for instance, in battles for the souls of middle managers. The personnel director of a convenience store chain based in the north central United States told Chris Tilly that among store managers,

> There's always a resistance to keeping people part-time. If things are allowed to go naturally, you get to know a person, you develop confidence in a person, so

if that person wants more hours, you try to satisfy them and make them full-time ... If full-time workers [i.e., store managers and assistant managers] had their way, they would prefer to have more full-time people. The number one thing that keeps them on the job is interaction with a peer group at work. (Chris Tilly 1996: 111)

But the personnel director and other top executives were striving to overcome these tendencies and keep store managers directed toward reducing costs by hiring part-timers, who received lower hourly wages and few benefits.

As this example illustrates, objectives are socially formed based both on organizational structures designed to consolidate particular goals and on social ties that cut across these structures within the firm and in many cases extend beyond the firm. The retail chain's structure of managerial hierarchy impresses store managers with the goal of minimizing costs. But social ties with coworkers forged in the intimate setting of a single convenience store push managers' objectives in another direction. And managers' community, ethnic, kin, and class connections with the blue-collar world so important in this region surely reinforce their presupposition that "part-time people are not as involved," as the personnel director put it.

Capitalist firms and other employers, like any recipients of value, pursue objectives of quality, efficiency, and power. Rarely do they conceptualize the objectives in this clean, tripartite fashion. In general, employers conceptually combine elements from two or more of these canonical objectives. Efficiency goals such as cost reduction explicitly or implicitly incorporate some minimum acceptable quality threshold; quality goals entail some cost target. In addition to aggregating objectives in this way, employers fragment them. Paul Osterman (1988) reported that U.S. managers he surveyed discussed efficiency in terms of three finer—and at times, conflicting—labor objectives: cost minimization, flexibility (both in staffing levels and in the deployment of labor to various tasks within the enterprise), and predictability (the ability to plan on the availability of a labor force with a known set of skills at a known cost). Soviet managers, on the other hand, were legendary for defining efficiency primarily in terms of quantity of output since the central plan's incentive system was pegged to output. And Japanese managers at Toyota use throughput—the rate at which materials move through the production process—as a critical efficiency criterion. Each of these views of efficiency is institutionalized in measurement and incentive systems—constituting the shared understandings and representations of particular industrial cultures. These cultures bear the imprint of the production systems that spawned them but also limit and direct the future evolution of these production systems (as those attempting to reform the Soviet economy, among others, have discovered).

Culture-bound conceptions of efficiency have more invidious effects as well. Owners and managers bring into the workplace understandings of who is fit to perform various types of work. Hospital administrators act on the widespread assumption that doctors are better able to diagnose and recommend treatment than nurses, despite the fact that nurses have far more sustained contact with patients. Employers who make hiring, promotion, and firing decisions draw on stereotypes of African-Americans as hostile, immigrants as industrious, and women as physically weak (or nimble, or submissive), among many others. (Despite elements of truth in some stereotypes, what makes them stereotypes is their overstated nature and generalized application.) They connect these stereotypes to often exaggerated or stylized norms about the charm, energy, brute strength, or dexterity particular jobs require.

Such views strengthen and feed on segregated networks of hiring and interaction within the firm. When conditions of labor supply and demand shift, stereotypes can follow suit, as when clerical work feminized in the early twentieth-century United States. For this reason, it is tempting to categorize these stereotypes as part of the pursuit of power. And indeed, employers do at times discriminate to shore up their own authority or to win the approval of incumbent employees or customers. But typically employers understand stereotypes as actual differences in skill or abilities (Moss & Tilly 1996): Acting on these views constitutes sincere, if misguided, attempts to increase efficiency.

If culture marks efficiency objectives, it even more clearly stamps quality. Quality, after all, consists of a product's approximation to an ideal configuration which changes and varies from group to group. Food production provides one obvious case where national traditions differ enormously, from the well-cooked beef of England to the raw fish on rice of Japan. Definitions of quality vary particularly widely in the service sector. We expect privacy in health care, but conviviality in restaurants—and even these ideals differ across the world. Culture dictates which service workers are expected to be obsequious, which affable, and which authoritative.

Power is particularly invisible, but nonetheless present, in employers' self-described objectives. Stated concerns with efficiency and quality frequently cloak power objectives. Speaking of interviews concerning numerical control (N/C) of machines he conducted with two Connecticut shop managers, David Noble reports:

> Here, as elsewhere, much of the N/C programming is relatively simple, and I asked the men why the operators couldn't do their own programming. At first they dismissed the suggestion as ridiculous, arguing that the operators would have to know how to set feeds and speeds, that is, be industrial engineers. I pointed out that the same people probably set the feeds and speeds on conventional machinery, routinely making adjustments on the process sheet provided by the methods engineers in order to make out. They nodded. They then said that the operators couldn't understand the programming language. This time I pointed out that the operators could often be seen reading the mylar tape—twice-removed information describing the machining being done—in order to know

what was coming (for instance, to anticipate programming errors that could mess things up). Again, they nodded. Finally they looked at each other, smiled, and one of them leaned over and confided, "We don't want them to." Here is the reality behind technological determinism in deployment. (Noble 1979: 38)

The managers' initial diffidence is understandable, and their eventual frankness unusual. Avowing power as a goal has become socially unacceptable in most contexts within modern polities and societies. Even dictators defend their policies in terms of defending order against internal and external enemies. Similarly, employers frame many of their interests in terms of some variant of organizational maintenance. In the name of organizational maintenance, capitalists and other employers typically try to bolster their own authority, enhance the organization's prestige, reduce manifest conflict, reward workers on whom they rely for command, information, ideas, political support and/or deference, and keep good relations with crucial outsiders.

Organizational maintenance blurs power with long-term efficiency. Some investment in organizational maintenance no doubt amounts to sustaining productivity over the long term. Organizational maintenance contributes to predictability, assuring, for example, that competent managers will still be available to drive production ten or twenty years hence. It aids in keeping down costs by reducing turnover and encouraging productivity-enhancing cooperation among employees (or inversely by disrupting cooperation aimed at coordinated shirking or sabotage). But over a considerable range employers trade off short-term efficiency for maintenance. They often fail to recruit the cheapest qualified labor as they rely on recruitment networks mediated by existing employees, reject potential workers whom their present employees would dislike, and give easy jobs to ostensibly overqualified workers with an eye to their subsequent promotion. More importantly, they also forgo long-term efficiency by ignoring or rejecting innovations and alternatives in technology or organization that threaten the established order. Organizational maintenance, as well as the preservation of power relations that implies, becomes an end in itself.

Workers are acutely aware of how management guards its prerogatives. In a recent survey of U.S. workers, Richard Freeman and Joel Rogers (1994) found that large majorities of employees believe that "if more decisions about production and operations were made by employees, instead of managers," their company would be "stronger against its competitors" and "the quality of products or services" would improve (p.7). When asked why, then, management failed to invite more worker participation in these decisions, a majority responded that such participation would threaten managerial power.

Organizational maintenance not only shores up the status quo within the organization but also connects to systems of status and power that extend beyond a particular employer. H. E. Dale's description of the "doctrine of feelings" in *The Higher Civil Service of Great Britain* exemplifies this:

> The doctrine of feelings was expounded to me many years ago by a very eminent civil servant.... He explained that the importance of feelings varies in close correspondence with the importance of the person who feels. If the public interest requires that a junior clerk should be removed from his post, no regard need be paid to his feelings; if it is the case of an assistant secretary, they must be carefully considered, within reason; if it is a permanent secretary, feelings are a principal element in the situation, and only imperative public interest can override their requirements. (Quoted in Goffman 1967: 10)

Distinguishing among quality, efficiency, and power helps to uncover contradictions in the "quality movement" that has swept U.S. manufacturing, inspired by Japanese and European examples. Manufacturers, as well as analysts of this movement, often confuse two quite different processes under the rubric of "quality." One truly represents a movement toward quality: attempts to reduce defects and perfect the product, in many cases via the development of customized products designed to find niche markets. But manufacturers also use the term "quality" to refer to processes simply aimed at boosting efficiency by speeding up production and reducing costs. Furthermore, experience with quality programs has been quite mixed, in large part because U.S. managers resist the loss of managerial power implied by programs that invest workers with greater autonomy and authority.

As we have already suggested, objectives vary not only across employers, but also within them. This is true, first, because most employers bundle a variety of work processes. Thus, hospitals have all along been particularly concerned about the quality of surgeons' work and the efficiency of launderers' work. Second, and very importantly, employers bundle together a variety of actors with differing objectives. By definition, firms unite actors with varying interests and varying definitions of success—owners, various categories of managers, workers. (Although we will consider workers as actors in their own right in the next chapter, in practice it is not possible to cleanly separate "employer behavior" from "worker behavior.") Varying definitions of success spring in part from parties' narrowly defined self-interest, but only in part. Managers clash with stockholders over the managers' self-interested pursuit of large salaries, easy jobs, or comfortable relationships with subordinates. But they also conflict in various cases because owners seek to maximize short-term resale value whereas managers nurture a long-term commitment to manufacturing despite short-term competitive setbacks, because managers care more about their workers' well-being, or because owners are more concerned about environmentally responsible conduct—none of which neatly fits into "self-interest."

Historically forged social relations and culture help to explain the multiple objectives within employers. The trustees of nonprofit hospitals, concerned with quality of care because it enhances their status within the community, contend with budget-constrained managers pursuing efficiency. On the other hand, stockholders of for-profit hospitals, linked to the hospitals only by the desire for profit, push efficiency, whereas managers within the hospitals also seek to preserve their own power within the organizational hierarchy. Within the managerial ranks of either kind of hospital, physicians and nurses, socialized within their professions, stress quality, whereas business-school-educated financial and operational managers favor efficiency.

To a significant extent, we can explain these social relations and cultures themselves in functional terms, as Arthur Stinchcombe (1986, ch. 12) has pointed out. (A social arrangement is functional to the extent that it simultaneously (a) promotes some collective outcome that in turn supports continuing organizational activities and (b) initiates processes that reproduce the social arrangement itself.) Managers, whose chief responsibilities are supervisory, must concern themselves with maintaining power, and the shared understandings that grow up around managing incorporate this concern. Boards of trustees, accountable to investors, donors, and a wider community, must keep other goals in mind. But history enters once more to account for the institutional environment within which the relations are functional. Only historical analysis can tell us why the summit of power in the typical hospital is in some times and places occupied by philanthropic trustees, in others by profit-hungry shareholders, in others by physicians avid for prestige and power, and in still others by a bureaucratic state agency.

Constraints on Employers

Based on their objectives, employers attempt to design and implement mechanisms of hiring, compensation, job mobility, training, and so on. We echo and expand on Paul Osterman (1988) and Susan Christopherson (1988) in suggesting that employers pursue objectives subject to five constraints: (1) the nature of product markets (or in general the preferences of clients outside the producing organization), (2) the nature of the available labor force (including patterns of organization, power, and privilege among workers), (3) physical technology (and particularly the skills involved in jobs), (4) social technology (the set of relations and beliefs within an organization that establish what is feasible, legitimate, or customary), and (5) state policy (comprising laws, regulations, and practices affecting the organization of work).

Like employers' objectives, these constraints are socially constructed. Indeed, the constraints are not tidily separable from the objectives because the constraints themselves mold employer objectives and because objective-guided employers themselves alter the constraints! Consider how a constraint such as the product market shapes employer behavior. It does so by limiting the extent to which employers can achieve their objectives, by altering the objectives of existing employers, and by selecting for employers whose objectives are most consistent with it.

As a result, the relative importance of the three objectives of quality, efficiency, and power varies systematically across employers, shaped in large part by the nature of the product market. Where products are standardized—as in most cotton textile and coal production since the industrial revolution—employers stress efficiency. Luxury or customized production emphasizes quality. Acute health care, because it must be customized to accommodate each patient, targets quality, whereas employers carrying out more standardized public health activities aim for efficiency. Employers are most likely to prioritize power when they enjoy some sort of monopoly status—not because monopolists crave power more than the rest of us, but because the absence of price competition shields them from pressure to adopt efficiency criteria. Thus, churches, armies, and government agencies are particularly likely to steer themselves with power considerations. Family businesses, in which patriarchal power is often paramount, might seem at first glance to be a counterexample. But note that many small family businesses engage in monopolistic competition: They parlay small differences (the location of a corner store or the distinctive ethnic cuisine of a restaurant) into limited but significant market power. Furthermore, the enormous turnover of family businesses testifies that those who prioritize power without the shelter of monopoly often pay the price for doing so.

Product markets themselves, and thus their effects on employer behavior, are sites of change and struggle. In the United States, the third party payers responsible for health care costs have attempted mightily to standardize the provision of acute care. In the 1970s, despite resistance from organized hospitals and physicians, the federal government—the largest purchaser of health care services, through Medicare and Medicaid—created diagnostic related groups, which specify standardized reimbursements for particular diagnoses, pressing health care providers to adopt relatively uniform treatments. Large insurers followed suit. Inexorably, health care organizations have been pushed toward "managed care," which directly mandates restrictions on the treatments provided. The balance of objectives among these employers has tilted from quality toward efficiency.

Take hospital medical directors, the top rank among physicians, as a fixed vantage point in this process. Medical directors who remain committed to quality find that the new financing regime limits their ability to provide heroic levels of care. Other medical directors who once swore a (Hippocratic) oath to quality of care now, for reasons of pragmatism, cognitive dissonance, or simple persuasion, place increased value on efficiency. Within hospitals, on average, medical directors lose power to efficiency-minded financial managers. And in the new funding environment, for-profit hospital chains such as the massive Columbia/HCA Healthcare (with annual revenues of $14.5 billion) grow, absorb struggling nonprofit hospitals, and build new hospitals. All of these changes ripple through the hospital workforce, altering the autonomy and compensation of physicians, nurses, and housekeepers. As one consequence, physicians' median annual earnings dropped in 1994 for the first time since the American Medical Association started keeping records (Narisetti 1995).

Similarly, as energy consumption shifted to oil, natural gas, and remotely generated electricity, coal consumption in the United States became concentrated among electric utilities. These utilities consume large amounts of coal but can readily utilize lower grades. Thus, demand shifted away from higher-quality, lower-efficiency underground mines in the southeastern United States to lower-quality, higher-efficiency open pit mines in the West. Individual coal mine operators bent their operations to the new market realities, but more importantly, the composition of mining activity and employment shifted in the direction of employers who had always pursued a different set of objectives. This wrought dramatic changes in compensation (down), worker safety (up), and the United Mine Workers union (way down).

The same reasoning extends to employers' more fine-grained objectives. For example, firms facing stiff price competition emphasize cost minimization. Those facing large variations in the amount of demand or the mix of products demanded make flexibility a top priority. Businesses experiencing steady growth in demand stress predictability. A single employer, moreover, will shift micro-objectives in response to changes within and without the firm. A manufacturer tilts toward cost minimization when a new competitor aggressively undercuts it, toward flexibility when a recession makes demand more uncertain, and toward organizational maintenance when a union drive or buyout bid unleashes centrifugal forces within the business.

Although constraints grip employers, employers, individually and collectively, constantly engage in concerted action to reshape that constraining grasp. Examples illustrate how they have shifted each of the five constraints:

- U.S. associations of hospitals and physicians lobbied successfully to ward off nationalized or single-payer health care in the 1940s and again in the 1990s, blocking one direction of change in the product market for health care.
- Over the nineteenth century, the U.S. textile industry created and recreated its labor supply by first recruiting Yankee farm daughters, later recruiting one wave after another of immigrants, and simultaneously relocating to the South to tap new labor pools. The garment industry in the twentieth century drew on this same repertoire with the addition of subcontracting, allowing the eventual relocation of portions of the production process to *maquiladora* assembly plants in Mexico, Central America, and the Far East.

- Industries themselves have been the main seedbed of innovation in physical technology, and employer actions such as investment in research and development, deskilling or upskilling of manual work, and employment of technical experts have conditioned the emergence of inventions from the spinning jenny to the artificial heart.
- As for social technology, textile employers responded to social relations but also sculpted them, for example by hiring from different ethnic groups to staff different jobs or to break strikes. In the anonymous New England mill described by Susan DiGiacomo Mulcahy and Robert Faulkner (1979), management designed the physical layout and division of labor to foster a "shop floor ethos [of] individual independence" (p.239), steering workers to blame each other for problems and to seek individualized solutions.
- And when state intervention in areas such as labor relations grew in the United States, as elsewhere in the world, employers weighed in through their associations and lobbies—for example, winning the 1947 Taft-Hartley law's restrictions on union activity following the post-World War II strike wave. (Coal miners, a frequent target of Taft-Hartley injunctions, responded with a sardonic ditty: "Mr. Taft can dig it, Mr. Hartley can haul it, Mr. Truman can supervise the crew.")

As this litany of strategic business interventions highlights, the constraints—and even the degrees to which they pose constraints—are hammered out by historical processes. Consider the least obvious case, physical technology and its impact on efficiency (which we will consider in more detail in Chapter 7). Efficiency and the innovation process itself are highly path-dependent, so that past events favor or discourage current options. This fact can explain technological failures as well as successes. Despite confident predictions that nuclear power would generate electricity "too cheap to meter," by the end of the 1970s U.S. utilities had abandoned that technology as hopelessly costly. Steve Cohn (1990, 1994) argues that the prediction could have become self-fulfilling: a massive commitment to nuclear power in the United States during the 1950s and 1960s could in fact have rendered nuclear power more efficient than a number of other energy sources. The nuclear option would have reaped efficiency benefits from research and development investments, learning curves, economies of scale in production, and investments in complementary energy system infrastructure ("locking in" a commitment to nuclear generation). Absent that commitment, the technology foundered.

Social relations, as well as economic conditions, channel history's impact on technological choices. This is visible in the innovation process itself. For example, innovations in products for sale beget more dense and varied communication among inventors and users than process innovations for one's own use, spurring additional innovation, as Ross Thomson found in studies of patenting patterns. Among nineteenth-century shoe manufacturing inventors and nineteenth- and early twentieth-century innovators of metalworking lathes, those with product patents averaged more than twice as many patents as those with process patents (Thomson 1989, 1991).

More broadly, social relations, power, and culture in the workforce—factors we have classified as the nature of the available labor force, social technology, and state policy—set the frame for efficiency. The efficiency of slavery depends on the legitimacy and state enforcement of property rights to human chattel. The most efficient approach to organizational maintenance depends on patterns of culture and social relations: As Gary Becker (1957) pointed out, racial segregation may be "efficient" if racial antipathies shape people's preferences for workmates. The importance of social constraints on technology helps to explain cross-national variation: British mule spinners' power and mastery of technique made labor-intensive technologies the efficient choice in that country's cotton textile industry for decades after American manufacturers had automated in the name of efficiency. Workforce social patterns also change over time. Two centuries ago, an American textile merchant or garment manufacturer could assume that almost every rural woman knew how to spin, knit, and sew. Today very few American women (and far fewer American men) do any of them well.

Satisficing and Bargaining

Pursuing objectives, hemmed in by constraints, employers do their best to optimize. They generally don't succeed, for two reasons. First, firms lack a clear and detailed assessment of the constraints facing them. That is, employing firms are subject to bounded rationality, in which "behavior is *intendedly* rational, but only *limited* so" (Simon 1976, xxviii). Employers function in complex environments, and information about these environments is costly, limiting how much they can understand the environments. The various actors within the firm act on different knowledge sets. And second, employers, with few exceptions, have multiple objectives rather than a unitary objective. Not only do they not know how to achieve the best outcome, but there is typically disagreement about what that outcome is.

Employers respond to bounded rationality by satisficing, in James March and Herbert Simon's (1958) term. "Organizations focus on targets and distinguish more sharply between success (meeting the target) and failure (not meeting the target) than among gradations in either" (March & Simon 1993: 302). More broadly, they gather only that information that is most critical and/or least costly. In general, this approach dictates "that investment in the quest for understanding be deferred until there is a symptom of trouble to deal with" (Winter 1980: 18). This applies to the various intrafirm actors as well. Whereas the manager of an individual chain store worries about weekly sales and employee scheduling, chain-level operations and personnel executives focus on monthly sales and labor costs, and chief executives and company stockholders dwell on annual sales and profits. Each struggles to understand the information that is key to the other, but only when problems demand it. Satisficing has a powerful inertial component: Businesses and the actors within them continue accustomed practices unless and until alarm bells ring.

When the alarms do go off, employers' repertoires of problem solving draw heavily on repetition, imitation, and manifestation. They repeat solutions or "rules of thumb" that have been developed in the past. They imitate perceived industry leaders and peers. For instance, when midsized companies seek to change a personnel policy provision, personnel officials will typically call up several other companies viewed as comparable to find out what policies they have adopted. A growing empirical literature (reviewed in Scott 1987 and DiMaggio & Powell 1991) documents that such forms of organizational imitation are widespread, often overriding what appear to be more efficient options for action. And when neither repetition nor imitation will serve, managers will often manifest action—in the sense of taking some action, any action, to demonstrate concern and decisiveness to one's superiors and subordinates. Again, none of these three strategies represents optimizing; they are shortcuts. The responses reflect the cost of new information and the cognitive limits on decisionmaking. They also further the objective of self-protection: Repetition and imitation shield managers from criticism since they have followed accepted procedures; manifestation deflects criticism when normal procedures appear inadequate.

Innovation is far less common. As Stinchcombe (1986, ch. 10; see also Scott 1995) points out, the status quo of work arrangements—and particularly organizational forms—has significant advantages aiding its stability. Indeed, constraints of inherent compatibility would operate even if we were designing a new organization from scratch with an entirely new set of managers and workers. But in the real world even new organizations build doubly on old ones: taking previously established organizations in their field as models and actually incorporating chunks of existing organization in the form of management teams, recruitment networks, social categories, and external connections. In so doing, organizers draw on the known array of mechanisms for getting work done, innovating chiefly at the edges. Within operating organizations, the choices are even narrower due to the following:

- The previous history of bargaining within the organization lays down strong constraints on conceivable forms of innovation.

- Selective recruitment and socialization create a web of understandings concerning what is possible, effective, and desirable.
- Multiple parties develop an interest in any particular work mechanism, an interest often fortified with collective rights—at least the right to be consulted in the event of change. Such vested interests often defend the established order against alternative arrangements that have only partly predictable implications for power, autonomy, and resource distribution.
- The same kinds of path-dependent processes that render advantages to incumbent physical technologies—learning curves, lock-in via complementary technologies, and the like—privilege the organizational status quo as well. Transaction costs of invention, experimentation, application, negotiation, and training give the advantage to mechanisms resembling those already in place.

Certainly the histories of the textile, coal mining, and health care industries confirm the durability of established patterns of work: Despite our emphasis in Chapter 3 on change, the central fact in all of these industries is the stability that change punctuates.

Furthermore, organizational innovation itself tends to follow the same well-worn channels as ongoing satisficing behavior. Employers frequently imitate innovations from competitors, high-prestige organizations, or organizations linked via network ties; consultants and the business press fan such imitation into faddism. Armed with simple principles, firms steadfastly pursue innovations well past the point of optimality. Robert Eccles, Nitin Nohria, and James D. Berkley (1992) point out one consequence: Both within organizations and within sets of businesses linked by network ties and other channels of communication, organizational forms cycle back and forth between centralization and decentralization.

Satisficing and related nonoptimizing approaches often work tolerably well. They work less well when employers and their environments are changing rapidly and especially when critical outcomes are difficult to measure. For example, Chris Tilly (1996) argues that U.S. retailers and restaurateurs gradually increased part-time employment to the point where they now systematically overuse it. Retail businesses innovated broader utilization of part-time hours in the 1940s and 1950s, and the practice diffused and escalated in response to the lower benefits, and in some cases lower wages, employers were able to offer part-timers, as well as the ability to match staffing to peak times. However, these employers have for the most part failed to take into account difficult-to-measure productivity losses resulting from higher turnover and lower commitment in this part-time workforce.

In addition to bounded rationality, multiple objectives shape employer behavior. Multiplicity appears in two forms. First, single actors—such as managers—themselves target disparate and sometimes conflicting objectives: quality versus efficiency, productivity versus organizational maintenance, cost minimization versus flexibility. The typical managerial response is, once more, a variant of satisficing. Managers do not simply incorporate these multiple objectives into an algorithm that yields a prediction of profits as a function of the level of each objective achieved. No such algorithm exists. Instead, managers will typically focus on one primary objective at a time, paying less attention to other objectives unless performance on these objectives falls below some threshold of acceptability.

Second, multiple actors within management pursue diverse agendas, leading to bargaining. Employers and workers bargain incessantly, but bargaining also takes place within the employer. Different groups of owners and managers cajole, threaten, compromise, sanction, and exit in pursuit of their objectives. In some cases, employers attempt to plan and structure the bargaining. Large firms often explicitly assign primary responsibility for different objectives to particular management teams—cost minimization to Operations, organizational maintenance to Human Resources, and so forth—who fight for resources, authority, and attention from top executives. But, planned or unplanned, bargaining abounds.

Vicki Smith, in her case study of a California bank whose top executives attempted to rapidly reorganize and speed up production, found that

> [middle managers attempted to] ward off the draconian aspects of the new corporate agenda. In different ways, middle managers circumvented strategic management's demands, their respective organizational latitude shaping their ability to reinterpret or reject them. . . . Middle managers' sense of what best served the corporate interest emphasized practices that could achieve a more gradual turnaround; their goal was to preserve the existing framework of consent, using that framework to achieve new goals and maintain long-term corporate viability. (Smith 1990: 25–27)

A trainer brought in by the bank's strategic management complained that "it's the manager who doesn't see the environment properly, who doesn't expect enough stretch, who doesn't give challenging enough assignments"; a middle manager retorted, "I'd rather quit than extract 'stretch' from my employees through your criteria" (Smith 1990: 80–81 and 54).

The specific forms and patterns of bargaining in a firm will depend on the resources and networks of the bargainers, as well as past patterns of bargaining. Chris Tilly (1996, ch. 6) found middle managers responding in a variety of ways to top management directives about part-time employment—including resistance, obliviousness, compliance, and overzealous implementation. In turn, higher management used browbeating, budgetary and procedural rules, or laissez-faire approaches to communicate and enlist support for their goals.

Within the repertoire of top management instruments of control, budgetary control superficially appears to be a powerful tool. But within the planned economy of the firm, as in other planned economies (Kornai 1992), budget constraints are "soft." Furthermore, like wages, budgets are relatively blunt instruments for regulating behavior. Where budgetary categories themselves are not fungible, managers can alter job descriptions, task assignments, or hours expectations to shift resources from one activity to another. Monitoring a manager's performance is, if anything, more difficult than monitoring the work of a lower-level employee.

Bounded rationality and multiple objectives amplify the importance of social relations in employer decisionmaking. On the one hand, network ties provide ready sources of trusted information. On the other hand, social relations encompass alliances, enmities, obligations, and degrees of autonomy that determine various actors' power to bargain and implement.

"Stupidity" and Competition

This framework posits that employers do "stupid" things (see Brunsson 1985, 1989). Firms do not do everything possible to maximize profits. Firms fail to carry out policies decided at the top, due to managers' divided loyalties. Firms facing identical market conditions and technological options pursue different strategies; firms facing decisively different environments pursue the same strategy due to imitation. Such behavior is, perhaps, understandable in public sector or nonprofit firms. But among profit-seeking firms, in a competitive model of the economy, "stupid" firms should be weeded out, driven from business by sharper competitors. Why doesn't this happen?

Competitive pressure is blunted, first, by the fact that all businesses are in the same boat. All confront bounded rationality and multiple objectives. Indeed, given the power of repetition and imitation, entire industries can pursue ill-advised courses of action.

In addition, large sections of capitalist economies are buffered from competition. Much of big business functions in oligopolistic markets, in which entry by new firms is extremely difficult, and product loyalty and access to distribution networks overwhelm price competition. Large sections of small business engage in monopolistic competition: Small distinctions (a gas station's location, a metalworking shop owner's personal ties to industrial buyers) enable them to carve out a stable market share that is relatively immune to small price differences. What's more, most privately held businesses (those not traded in equity markets) are driven by the ambitions and desires of the owners (above all, the desire for ownership), not by the quest for returns that the stock market would find acceptable. For all these reasons, widely varying prices and profit rates are possible, leaving wide scope for nonoptimal business strategies.

Alternative, potentially more efficient strategies are also often excluded, or at least rendered unattractive, by short time horizons and externalities. Short time horizons—impatience of owners, creditors, or investors—can foreclose business actions that require substantial up-front investments for uncertain future returns. This holds particularly true for actions that flout conventional wisdom. Returning to retailers' use of part-time labor, for example, a key advantage of full-time workers is that they build up more skills on the job because they turn over less quickly and log more on-the-job hours in any given time period. But a retailer who shifted the workforce mix toward more full-timers might have to wait years before reaping the benefits of this shift. Meanwhile, the company would have to endure increased labor costs (higher fringe benefits and in many retail settings higher wages as well), while swimming against the current of retail industry "common sense."

Externalities, unintended spillover effects that one firm's action can have on another, can also block certain firm actions that would otherwise be optimal. Due to externalities, widespread business conformity can make it economically costly for a firm to break ranks. David Levine and Laura D'Andrea Tyson (1990; Levine 1993) point out that worker participation yields the greatest productivity benefits when firms offer employment stability and protections against unjust discharge. But in an economy where few firms offer these things, a firm that does must pay a cost. Providing employment stability costs more when there are wide swings in demand—which are typical of economies where most firms don't guarantee such stability. A lone firm offering protections against firing will suffer from adverse selection, selectively attracting workers whose marginal performance puts them at risk for firing. The high-layoff, no-due-process policies of other firms, willy nilly, impede any firm from adopting these policies.

A similar externality argument applies to training. For many skills, on-the-job training is most effective. But an employer who trains a worker risks having that worker bid away by other employers, thus losing the anticipated benefits of the training. Given this risk, employers will tend to systematically underinvest in training.

Externalities can be viewed as representing coordination problems. If firms could agree to simultaneously alter their layoff and discharge policies, they could all gain higher productivity. If businesses all trained workers, worker mobility would not pose a problem for a firm carrying out training. Arguably, institutions such as Japanese firms' lifetime employment guarantee for a subset of employees and Germany's widespread apprenticeship programs represent solutions to such coordination problems. But in the absence of coordination, collectively optimal alternatives are unattainable. Like short time horizons, externalities of this sort favor small, incremental changes.

For all of these reasons and more, employers persist in diverging from strict economic rationality. This leaves a wide ambit of influence for social context. The same is true for workers and, *a fortiori,* for the state and family, whose links to the workplace depart further from purely economic transactions.

6
Workers and Other Actors

Work to Live, or Live to Work?

In 1995, survey firm Roper Starch Worldwide interviewed adults in 40 countries about the relative importance of work and leisure (Roper Starch Worldwide 1995). They asked respondents to choose between two options: "Work is the important thing—and the purpose of leisure time is to recharge people's batteries so they can do a better job;" or "Leisure time is the important thing—and the purpose of work is to make it possible to have the leisure time to enjoy life and pursue one's interests." (Some respondents volunteered that the two are equally important.)

The results were instructive. Views about work and leisure varied widely across countries. Roughly two-thirds of adults in Brazil, the Philippines, and Saudi Arabia rated work paramount. On the other hand, half or more exalted leisure in Australia, the Czech Republic, Denmark, and Great Britain. (The United States fell somewhere in between, with about 40 percent each choosing work and leisure and the remainder rating them equally important.) But particularly striking is the relationship between attitudes and behavior. Subtract the percent voting for leisure from the percent privileging work, yielding an "importance of work" index ranging from 0.5 in the work-valuing Philippines to –0.3 in leisure-loving Poland. This importance of work index is *negatively* correlated with the labor force participation rates of all adults, men, and women.

In other words, the more people claim to value work for itself, the less they work; the more they work, the less importance they place on work. Why? One explanation is that as countries become more wealthy, two things happen. On the one hand, standards of living rise and consumption is increasingly commoditized, requiring additional income-earning labor (at least for the majority lacking other income-producing assets) to live at a generally accepted standard. On the other hand, more and more labor is alienated: People are more likely to be working for someone else and correspondingly less committed to work for its own sake. So as nations grow richer, their people work more and like it less. Indeed, national wealth (GNP per capita) is positively related to the level of labor force participation and with the proportion of the workforce that toils for wages (a convenient proxy for alienated labor); the proportion working for wages is highly negatively correlated with the importance of work index (Table 6.1). This statistical excursion suggests several important characteristics of attitudes toward work:

- Contrary to labor market theories that view work as simply an instrument to obtain goods, people do value work for its own sake. Even in Poland, where the index of the importance of work is lowest, 40 percent of respondents rated work as equally or more important than leisure; in the United States, 63 percent shared that view.

TABLE 6.1   Correlations Among Index of the Importance of Work and Other
Economic Indicators

	Index of importance of work (Index)	GNP per capita (GNP/C)	Adult labor force participation rate (LFP)	Proportion of workforce that is waged (Waged)
Index	1.00	−0.45	−0.43	−0.69
GNP/C		1.00	0.39	0.61
LFP			1.00	0.23
Waged				1.00

NOTE: Index of importance of work is defined as (% saying work is more important – % saying leisure is more important). Correlations calculated on data from 20 countries (since Roper Starch Worldwide only made data publicly available on these 20). Some countries were missing data for some variables. Details available from the authors upon request.

SOURCES: Data from Roper Starch Worldwide, "The global work ethic? In few parts of the world does work take clear priority over leisure." Press release, 1995; International Labour Organization, *World Labour Report 1993* (Geneva: ILO, 1993); International Labour Office, *World Employment 1995* (Geneva: ILO, 1995).

- Attitudes toward work are far from uniform around the world.
- Work behavior, while certainly affected by people's views about work, is greatly influenced by the broader economic and social structures surrounding work.
- People's attitudes toward work are critically shaped by the social context of work.

Worker Behavior

In seeking to understand worker behavior, these insights serve well. Sociologists and social psychologists have long recognized that workers find intrinsic value in work (see, for example, Miller 1988). This is self-evident for the "labors of love" undertaken by volunteers, hobbyists, and struggling artists (Freidson 1990). Wageworkers at various levels also cherish some aspects of their work: This shines through in Norman Best's (1990) first-person account of highway survey crews outmaneuvering corner-cutting contractors and complicit bureaucrats to build durable roads and Tom Juravich's (1985) tale of semiskilled operatives struggling to keep their machines working despite befuddled management meddling.

Even when labor is coerced, workers often find elements of pride in their work and identification with the work's purposes. Among participants in

U.S. "workfare" programs, compelled to perform public service work in return for their welfare grants, a striking 70 percent indicated satisfaction at receiving benefits tied to a job, rather than simply receiving unconditional benefits (Gueron 1987; on the other hand, an even larger majority believed they were being underpaid for their work). The International Labour Office, discussing ongoing chattel slavery in Mauritania, complained that "many slaves, even when they discover that slavery is illegal, find it difficult to break the mental chains of servitude" (1993: 10). Even in the grimmest outpost of the U.S. apparel industry—a Texas prison factory staffed by death row inmates—one inmate commented that pride, not the limited privileges he receives in return for his work, is the main motivator: "It's mostly to prove something to yourself. We do it to say, 'By God, I showed them I'm not really the threat they think I am'" (Clines 1994: A1).

Thus workers, like employers, pursue multiple objectives. They work for pay, to be sure, but they also toil for pride in a job well done, for the enjoyment of learning, for the appreciation of bosses and coworkers, for continuing access to the social world of the workplace, and for the purpose of fulfilling traditions or the expectations of others. As with employers, this mix of motivations cannot readily be simplified to a simple objective function. Social relations structure the relative importance of varying worker objectives, in similar fashion to the ways that they influence employer objectives. These social relations once more include organizational structures created by management design, other production networks, and networks that extend beyond the workplace.

The chief constraint on a worker is the range of jobs available to him or her. This range is a function of the worker's skills, network resources, membership in privileged or excluded groups, and so on (as we will discuss in more detail in the section on matching in the next chapter). But workers can act to change this range. Such action is perhaps most dramatic in the cases of the formation of professions, as when U.S. physicians consolidated a monopoly on certain healing activities, and of social movements such as the Civil Rights movement that have demanded access to jobs. But more subtly, individual workers reshape the jobs they inhabit as well (Miller 1988: 338–340). Anne Miner found that among nonfaculty university personnel, one to two percent of jobs per year were officially reclassified based on the evolution of incumbents' duties (Miner 1985, cited in Miller 1988: 339). So the constraint is doubly socially determined: created in the first place largely by social relations and modified over time through social interactions large and small.

As workers pursue objectives subject to constraints, their actions once more parallel employers in that they act with bounded rationality. Workers find jobs through networks not only because the network ties make it more likely that employers will hire them but because this is a low-cost, readily accessible source of information about available jobs. Workers satisfice, limiting job search efforts when their current job appears adequate.

We have previously distinguished among compensation, coercion, and commitment as worker incentives. Commitment is important not only because of its independent effects but because it renders compensation and coercion more effective. It is not surprising, then, that managers attempt to orchestrate worker feelings of loyalty and shared identity with the employer—that is, to tune worker objectives. John Van Maanen and Gideon Kunda (1989) described in detail how Disneyland and the company they call High Technology Incorporated nurture corporate cultures through explicit codification of values, careful screening, orientation, and socialization of new hires, promotion of formal and informal interactions among employees, and ongoing monitoring of workers' attitudes and behavior. The textile company towns of the American south were designed in part to extract added surplus through rents and company store purchases, in part to strengthen management's coercive power via the threat of eviction, but in large part to construct a paternalistic system in which company owners won loyalty from their employees by "looking out for" all aspects of their lives. Canvassing door to door in Cannon Mills' wholly owned company town of Kannapolis, North Carolina in 1985, Chris Tilly found many workers and their families nostalgic for the paternalistic regime of "Uncle Charlie" Cannon, which had been displaced by his heirs and later an outside buyer who appeared to view the company as simply an investment. The outside buyer succeeded in repelling a union-organizing drive by invoking the old norms of mutual loyalty.

Of course, the flip side of employer efforts to win commitment are workers' resistance activities. Resistance may be directed at management, at customers, or even at coworkers. Nurses resist speedups from hospital management, shun difficult patients, and attempt to shift unpleasant work onto other classifications of workers (or to prevent other workers from shifting work onto them). Workers who feel they have been treated unfairly draw on a wide and creative repertoire of forms of retaliation (Hodson 1995). In the British merchant marine, for example, R. A. Ramsay reports:

> It was not unusual for members of the catering staff (who were subjected to a stream of "do this, do that, do this, do that" orders from obnoxious second stewards) to feel so fed up they would heave a whole pile of dirty dishes through an open porthole instead of washing them. Stewards who do personal laundry are quite capable of "making a mistake" and burning through a shirt with the iron. When sailors are loading stores and accidentally let a sling load crash on the wharf below, their reaction is usually one of suppressed glee rather than sorrow. Deck crews who are driven too hard can quite calmly paint over oil and water and take a malicious delight in doing so. (Ramsay 1966: 63)

Similarly, Van Maanen and Kunda (1989: 67) enumerate Disneyland ride operators' many methods for dealing with excessively disrespectful patrons: the "seatbelt squeeze," the "break-toss," the "seatbelt slap," the "break-up-the-party" maneuver, the "hatch-cover ploy," and the "sorry-I-didn't-see-your-hand" tactic; we leave the details of these colorfully named actions to the reader's imagination. Beyond such individual and small group acts of sabotage, venting, and getting even, workers engage in more concerted resistance activities as well, regulating effort, building worker organizations, striking, and so on. Coal hewers' efforts to sustain craft control over their work fall into this category, to be addressed more in detail in Chapter 11. Resistance also shades over into the games and diversions that workers devise, individually and collectively, to make dull or degrading work more endurable.

Workers' degree of commitment to their work is socially conditioned; the same can be said about their response to compensation. Ironically, we can learn a great deal about this from labor economists' efforts to estimate the wage elasticity of labor supply—the ratio of percentage change in hours of labor supplied to the percentage change in hourly wage—a concept that attempts precisely to set aside (or control for) social context and isolate workers' response to the wage. Elasticity estimates for the United States and Britain reveal, for example, that gender roles within the family are paramount. Men's labor supply is essentially fixed relative to wages; men respond to higher wages with small reductions in labor supply (presumably because higher wages allow them to achieve earnings targets with fewer hours). Wives, on the other hand, display large, positive responses to wage variations; single mothers' responses are smaller. There also appear to be important national differences: German wives supply considerably more labor in response to higher wages, U.S. and British wives a bit more labor, and among Canadian wives higher wages correlate with fewer hours supplied (as among men). This ordering is inversely related to women's labor force participation rates: The more wives attach to the labor force (that is, the more they act like men in this regard), the less they respond to wage variation. Finally, even within narrowly defined groups elasticity estimates range widely in sign (positive versus negative) and scale, suggesting that economists are missing important contextual variables (Pencavel 1986; Killingsworth & Heckman 1986).

In contextualizing workers' responses to compensation, we can start with the neoclassical labor economist's customary list of factors affecting labor supply:

1. Availability of nonwage income (or other sources of consumption)
2. Family structure (and the earnings potential of other family members)
3. Alternative activities of the worker or potential worker (such as child rearing or enrollment in school)

Each item on this list affects not only whether (and how many hours) a person will work but the importance of wages to that person. And in each of these areas, historically formed social structures reverberate. The degree of access to common grazing lands, the generosity and terms of public income support programs, the relative frequency of extended, nuclear, and single-parent families, class-bound and historically changing expectations about the appropriate level of educational attainment—all enter into this set of factors.

But the considerations affecting how workers respond to compensation go beyond this list. We can add other conditions that range from "economic" to "social."

1. The forms of the compensation package (cash, goods, fringe benefits, paid time off)
2. The degree to which the compensation is contingent on individual, group, or firm performance
3. The degree to which the compensation is linked to long-term job security and/or upward mobility
4. The desirability of nonpecuniary aspects of the job
5. Perceptions of the "fairness" of the compensation, typically defined with respect to reference groups of other workers

The last item, fairness, is clearly shaped by social relations and culture. The definition of the appropriate reference group, for example, is socially constructed. To whose wages does a woman textile worker compare her own? She must decide what restrictions of race, ethnicity, nationality, gender, age, occupation, industry, firm size, unionization status, location, and even historical period apply. In most cases, this decision is not an individual one; rather, it is shaped very strongly by the norms of groups in the workplace or cutting across workplaces. To white workers in the southern United States in the first half of the twentieth century, fairness meant that white employers accorded them privileges relative to black workers. Black workers strove for a nonracial definition of fairness.

But many of the other items on the list also respond to socially shaped values, not just individual tastes. Group values determine the importance that workers place on such nonpecuniary job characteristics as schedule flexibility or the ability to avoid getting one's hands dirty. Payment based on group performance is more acceptable to Japanese workers than U.S. ones. Annual, extended summer vacations are sacred among European workers, but not expected by many Americans.

Coercion rounds out the trio of incentives. From our standpoint of a capitalism staffed by free labor, work motivated primarily by coercion appears remote—a feature of precapitalist forms of labor and of certain exceptional organizations, such as armies and prisons. But as Jan Lucassen points out, "in world history, unfree, rather than free labor is the rule" (1993: 7). Large-scale coerced labor has consistently coexisted comfortably with capitalism. In seventeenth- and eighteenth-century England, most wage contracts took the form of indenture. The African slave trade exported an estimated 18 million slaves between 1500 and 1900, in addition to 8 million held in slavery on the continent itself (Manning 1990: 84). Poorer parts of the world (especially China and, even more so, India) exported about 2.1 million indentured servants between 1830 and 1920 (Northrup 1995: 156–158). Later in the twentieth century, forced labor prevailed in Hitler's concentration camps and Stalin's gulag alike. And forced labor continues. The International Labour Office (1993) documents outright chattel slavery in Mauritania and Sudan, debt bondage in Pakistan, India, and Peru (with workers in some cases bound by debts eight generations old), and other forms of forced labor in Brazil, Burundi, Cuba, the Dominican Republic, Haiti, Myanmar, Sri Lanka, Tanzania, and Thailand.

Coerced labor also persists closer to home. In 1995, U.S. Labor Department agents raided a sweatshop in El Monte, California, where Thai women worked in virtual slavery, sewing clothing 17 hours a day for less than $1 an hour, constrained from leaving by threats of violence against them and their families. U.S. officials estimated that Thai contractors smuggle 2,000 workers a month (from a variety of countries) into the United States, selling many at prices of up to $35,000 into slave-like conditions in sweatshops and brothels, where the workers must "earn" the purchase price (Sherer 1995).

Coercive elements crop up in other labor market work as well. Although we condemn the Thai labor contractor who misleads prospective workers about wages, hours, and working conditions, we have grown inured to compulsory overtime, unilateral management-imposed wage or piece-rate cuts, and speedups—refusal of which typically risks termination. Southern poultry plants maintain their 90-chickens-per-minute assembly line pace in part by restricting workers' bathroom breaks to two per day.

Outside of labor markets, coercion operates as well. Largely unnoticed by the general population, the United States of the 1980s and 1990s has invested heavily in reduction of unemployment by imprisoning a far higher proportion of its young men—especially young black men—than any other Western country. As of 1995, about 1.6 million Americans were in prison or jail; U.S. incarceration rates ran almost five times Canada's, seven or eight times those of most other Western countries, and fourteen times Japan's (Western & Beckett 1997: 11). If American rates of imprisonment fell to the levels of other comparable countries, unemployment would probably rise to significantly higher rates than now prevail in those countries—not only because many current prisoners would be unemployed but also because imprisonment reduces young men's future prospects for employment, and because the U.S. has made work as a correctional officer a major source of new employment. Coercion thus has powerful effects, both direct and indirect, on American working conditions. Along with commitment and compensation, coercion steers worker behavior in a wide range of employment—and unemployment—situations.

Bounding the Firm, Bounding the Worker

Employer behavior depends on the boundaries of the actor that we call the firm. In discussing boundaries, we necessarily simplify. Neither the formal boundaries defined by an organization chart nor the legal frontiers marked out by contract law adequately characterize the edges of the firm; it would be more precise to describe the firm, in Joseph Badaracco's words, as "a dense network at the center of a web of relationships" (1991: 314). Nonetheless, we can interpret the density and character of social and economic ties to draw a somewhat arbitrary boundary line.

Specifically, market work can be performed in a variety of contracting arrangements, which stretch or contract these boundaries. By contracting arrangements, we refer both to the balance between arms-length market relations and more intimate relations of command and commitment, and to the degree of permanence in the association of the person performing the work and the organization selling the goods or services created with the work. Capitalists can produce—and have produced—woven cloth for sale either via putting out that leaves production in the hands of individual contractors or in centralized factories under the control of corps of supervisors. Movies can be created either in studios employing large, long-term stables of employees or in temporary conglomerations that come together only long enough to complete a single project. Some houses are built in factories with a single chain of command; others are put together by several layers of contractors and subcontractors.

Differences in contracting arrangements across industries and over time reflect (1) the efficiency of different arrangements; (2) their contribution to organizational maintenance (including considerations of power); and (3) a historically grounded process of organizational innovation. Ronald Coase (1952 [1937]: 341) offered the classic efficiency-based formulation that the degree of *transaction costs* will determine what functions get centralized within firms: "a firm will tend to expand until the costs of organizing an extra transaction within the firm become equal to the cost on the open market or the costs of organizing in another firm." Oliver Williamson (1985) builds on this insight, adding that firms also internalize functions in order to reduce problems of bounded rationality and incentives. Economies of scale due to new types of machinery, new power sources, and a finer division of labor have also contributed to the growth of centralized factories (Landes 1969; North 1981, 1990).

Employers' organizational maintenance objectives also help determine firms' boundaries. This is clearest for the very largest employers—states and churches—whose scale is more a measure of power than efficiency. But capitalist firms as well incorporate this logic. British capitalists moved to centralize work in factories at least as much to impose discipline on a newly proletarianizing workforce as to reap efficiency gains (Marglin 1974). While in some industries U.S. industrialists created a closely controlled division of labor de novo, in others such as steel they had to break the power of craft-skilled foremen—essentially worker-subcontractors in control of their areas of work (Stone 1974). In a few sectors such as construction, union power as well as the relative absence of economies of scale and scope resulted in continued fragmentation among firms, extensive contracting, and craft control over the job.

In broad strokes, the evolution and subsequent partial devolution of large firms and quasi-permanent employment relationships can be described in terms of power shifts: Capitalists centralized production to increase their control; they established more permanent employment relationships partly to cement control and partly to respond to worker demands; they shed centralized and quasi-permanent employment—through increased subcontracting, temporary employment, and the like—to deflect and diffuse worker claims. Telling the tale in this way does not deny that economies of scale contributed to the formation of large firms or that flexibility-based advantages of networks of smaller firms helped to speed downsizing. However, it does assert that efficiency differences alone were not sufficient to drive this evolution. In fact, the economic contexts that determine the profitability of various scales (for example, mass product markets versus more fragmented, customized markets) have been constructed by firms' actions.

The drive for organizational maintenance not only powers historical change but also infuses the everyday life of firms. Every employer seeks loyalty as a central outcome of including actors within the boundaries of the firm. Firms have no monopoly on commitment since it thrives in informal networks as well, but constructing an organization with relatively explicit contractual relationships offers a straightforward way to elicit commitment where otherwise little would exist.

Capitalists and other firm-builders never draw from an open-ended menu of organizational forms. Rather, firms develop and diffuse organizational innovations in historically constrained ways. Organizational inertia exerts a powerful drag, so that innovation remains the exception rather than the rule. Alfred Chandler (1977, 1990, 1992) and William Lazonick (1991) demonstrate that enterprises' scale and scope consequently depend on their historically conditioned *organizational capabilities*. Innovations such as the multidivisional firm or the vertical integration of distribution functions have entered the capitalist repertoire in particular eras. "First movers"—the first firms in a particular industry to adopt organizational innovations—gain advantages that may last for decades. Path-dependent processes also render advantages to particular organizational forms: For instance, when an industry's dominant firms absorb the product distribution function, wholesalers and retailers adapt their systems in ways that advantage this particular arrangement.

The development of organizational capabilities depends on an array of historically given social institutions that cannot be conjured up by an individual firm, however large. For example, Lazonick (1991) argues that nineteenth- and early twentieth-century British manufacturers were trapped in a "proprietary capitalism" that centralized managerial power in the hands of proprietors, rather than establishing a powerful cadre of managers. Proprietary capitalism grew out of the ready availability of skilled craft labor and other resources (minimizing the need for managerial coordination), as well as British proprietors' emulation of the landed nobility. Consequently, the late–nineteenth-century managerial revolution took place in the United States—where labor shortages (and consequent mechanization) and broader suffrage steered capitalism in a different direction, while the creation of securities markets (which fragmented ownership) and the vast expansion of higher education (the training ground for managers) consolidated that direction.

The combination of efficiency, organizational maintenance, and organizational innovation threads through the history of firm boundaries in cotton, coal, and clinics. In British cotton textiles, economies of scale arising from the mechanization of the various phases of cloth production, capitalists' quest for greater control over the workforce, and a series of organizational experiments converged to move first spinning and then weaving into factories. Contractors gave way to employees. Healing in Britain and the United States shifted from dispersed private practices to concentrated hospitals, driven by the same three general influences, but in a manner quite distinct. The original transformation of hospitals from refuges of last resort to places of healing was spurred by economies of scale in therapeutic and diagnostic equipment and plant, as well as advances in contagion control that made group quarters compatible with healing. The chief organizational innovation was not the creation of hospitals, but their conversion to new uses and subordination to industry-wide standards. Managerial assertion of increasing control over the healing process propelled the subsequent incorporation of outpatient clinics and the transformation of physicians from contractors to employees.

Turning the telescope around, we can state that workers' boundaries also shift and vary. The object of interest is not workers' physiological boundaries, but the extent of employer control over workers' time and behavior. The present-day employment contract at a factory in Sri Lanka's Biyagama export processing zone illustrates the issue, especially in the following selected clauses:

You shall not damage the reputation and good name of the Management.

You shall not instigate your companion to be against the Management.
You shall not form and/or join any group in this establishment without
    prior written approval of the Management.
When you cause some moral/sexual misconduct with any of your com-
    panions which is normally unacceptable, you and he (she) shall agree
    to leave the services.
If you are [a] female employee, you shall agree to resign when and if
    you get married. (Fine 1995: 26)

Such requirements conjure up images of nineteenth-century industrial relations in Europe and the United States. In fact, in the West, the boundaries
of the worker have followed an arc. Substantial worker control over timing
of work and over behavior initially gave way to employer time-discipline over
most waking hours and, in many cases, extension of employer authority to a
wide range of worker behavior beyond the production process itself—widening the bounds of employers' claims. But workers' organizations and advocates gradually won restrictions on the working day, week, and year and limits on employers' long reach into nonproduction activities.

The initial proletarianization process had both economic and social drivers, corresponding to the rise of capitalist firms. Workers' ability to resist
this encroachment depended on both technologically grounded power and
organizational resources. Coal hewers, for instance, long resisted time-discipline both because their work was difficult for supervisors to observe and because they built powerful organizations. The subsequent narrowing of employers' claims resulted from hard bargaining and especially from
contentious labor union struggles culminating in state intervention.

In certain occupations, this cycle is more recent. In Arlie Hochschild's
1981 interviews with flight attendants, she found that airline rules from the
1960s and 1970s had extended to hair length, acceptable bust-waist-hips-
thigh measurements, eye shadow color (required to match the uniform at
American), and even underwear style (highlighted in Pan American's "girdle
check"). The "weigh-in" still prevailed at Delta Airlines, though age limits,
the exclusion of men from flight attendant jobs and the requirement that
women resign upon marriage had all crumbled under legal pressure
(Hochschild 1983: 101–103).

Workers and Firms in Networks

Boundaries matter, but so do the networks that intersect them. We have recurrently stressed that workers and employers do not act as isolated individuals. They act as participants in multiple, crisscrossing production and nonproduction networks. There are important networks of workers, of
managers, of subfirm units, and of firms themselves. Schematically, these

TABLE 6.2   Types of Networks

	Who Is Linked by the Networks		
Type of Network	*Workers*	*Sub-Firm Units*	*Firms*
Hierarchy	Craft guild	Levels of management	Parent + subsidiaries
Market	Temporary pool	Independent divisions	Subcontracting
Coalition	Industrial union	University departments	Keiretsu

networks group into hierarchies (characterized by asymmetrical coercion and commitment), markets (featuring symmetrical compensation), and coalitions (with symmetrical commitment), among others. Table 6.2 illustrates this typology with examples.

Networks form through repeated interaction, which may take the form of communication, association, or exchange. Production networks in particular coalesce out of the repetition of transactions and the proliferation of contracts. Therefore, whereas networks influence behavior, the reverse is also true: Worker and employer behavior builds, strengthens, and weakens networks, production and nonproduction alike. For example, Katherine Newman (1996), in her study of young inner-city workers starting jobs in the fast-food industry, found that as they persisted in their jobs, their social circle shifted to fellow workers, and they tended to choose mates who were also employed. They cut ties with former friends who remained unemployed, relied on welfare, or subsisted in the underground economy. A similar process of socialization alters the networks of those entering any job.

Informal, sometimes "invisible" networks often exist parallel to or even coextensive with formal networks. In the machine shop studied by Donald Roy (1954), for example, workers were linked by a formal division of labor and management hierarchy. At the same time, however, machinists collaborated with setup men, inspectors, tool-crib men, stockmen, and time-checkers in "making out," circumventing a series of piecework systems designed by management. Coalitions such as this one are particularly likely to be informal, though (black or gray) markets and hierarchies also sometimes take informal shapes.

Strong networks—those that form a basis for concerted action—tend to draw on multiple types of links. This is true in two senses. First, strong networks generally rely on some combination of compensation, coercion, and commitment. (This echoes our comment on Figure 4.1 that few work contracts rely on one incentive alone.) Thus, "pure" markets, hierarchies, and coalitions are of less interest as networks than hybrids. Stock markets and chain letters (to take two examples of networks based more or less entirely on compensation) offer little basis for joint action, much less for action extending beyond the arena spawning the network. Table 6.2 betrays this generalization, for in fact none of the examples partakes exclusively of compen-

sation, coercion, or commitment. For all the commitment holding an industrial union together, the exchange of dues for bargained pay raises also serves
as a central motor of unionism. And although independent divisions of a
corporation buy and sell services and goods-in-process, they are also linked
by subordination to the top levels of the corporate hierarchy.

Sturdy networks also build on multiple commonalities. Dennis Encarnation, reporting on India's powerful business houses (groups), noted that
within "each of these houses, strong social ties of family, caste, religion, language, ethnicity, and region reinforced financial and organizational linkages
among affiliated enterprises" (1989: 45, cited in Granovetter 1994: 464).
The correlation between strong networks and multiple solidarities flows
from several causal links. To start with, ties from the world of production
bind more strongly when they are aligned with ties from other social milieux. History plays a part in establishing such overlapping ties as well: When
actors set out to construct a network for concerted action (such as a union
or business association), they tend to use existing network connections as a
foundation. Seeking to organize first- and second-generation immigrant
workers, the CIO (Congress of Industrial Organizations) bypassed native-
dominated craft union nuclei and instead relied heavily on ethnically based
clubs and mutual assistance associations. Finally, history intervenes again
once a network exists since it then tends to strengthen itself by adding parallel connections: interlocking directorates, intermarriage, membership in
bowling leagues or country clubs. These additions result to some extent
from purposive attempts to reinforce the network, but to a much larger extent from nonpurposive actions shaped by the familiarity and ongoing contact networks bring.

Production networks vary widely in the relative importance of bonds of
compensation, coercion, and commitment, and thus of markets, hierarchies,
and coalitions. To simplify this field of variation, let us narrow our attention
to networks of employers (aided by an excellent review article by Mark Granovetter, 1994). We suggest that the mix of the three incentives in a given
national economy or a particular economic sector will follow several regularities. *Hierarchy* prevails where the state has privileged a small number of
businesses, where the product market tends toward monopoly, and where
preexisting authority relations form the basis for business networks. Marking
one extreme is state socialism, along with Saudi Arabia with its fusion of
state power, feudal authority, and business monopoly. South Korea and
Haiti, where for decades dictatorships accorded concessions (often with monopoly status) to small numbers of capitalists, also fit this mold. To this day,
South Korea's *chaebol* business groups maintain strict hierarchy.

Coalitions, on the other hand, are common where the state has fostered
collective business institutions, where businesses have worked out a division
of labor or carved out niches within the product market, and where business

networks build on preexisting relations of parity. Japan and the well-studied Third Italy region are examples. In Japan the national government has played an orchestrating role in research and new product development; in Emilia-Romagna and neighboring areas regional and local governments have led the construction of collective institutions for research and development, training, and marketing (Best 1990). Annalee Saxenian (1994) argues that California's Silicon Valley high technology region has evolved a similar form of cooperation with less conscious state intervention (though the U.S. Defense Department has played a central role in Silicon Valley's rise). Division of labor in the product market is an important element of this pattern: In general, it proves much easier to use commitment to maintain a production chain than to maintain a cartel. Cartels usually depend on coercion as well.

Finally, *markets* predominate where the state fosters decentralization and deconcentration, where product markets are relatively competitive (with easy entry), and where there are relatively few preexisting relations among businesses. The classic example, of course, is the United States. U.S. antitrust laws for decades discouraged business collaboration and, to a lesser extent, braked concentration. Locational mobility and the vertical integration of the largest companies also reduced ties of commitment and coercion among businesses. So despite limited cooperation in lobbying, U.S. businesses largely connect through markets—for example, deciding what other businesses to purchase from or sell to primarily based on price. Recently, however, employers influenced by the success of Japanese manufacturing have attempted to shift away from this model. For example, Ford, Chrysler, and General Motors (in addition to Japanese auto companies operating within the United States), have moved in their supply chain toward long-term relationships built on commitment and coercion.

Although this discussion has focused on employer networks in isolation, employer and worker networks influence each other greatly. This holds true at the micro-level of recruiting and supply networks, and it also applies at the level of national industrial relations systems. National employer associations and national union federations flourish together, especially where—as in Austria or Sweden—national governments facilitate or enforce national-level bargaining. On a more modest scale, the United Mine Workers of America and the Bituminous Coal Operators Association, bitter foes though they be, have each strengthened their unity and authority because of the other's existence.

What trends can we trace in the networks that intersect labor markets? Over a two hundred year span, growing urbanization, rising mobility (of labor, capital, and goods alike), and the increasing importance of global flows have all exerted an impact. The average worker or firm today holds membership in more networks, of greater geographic and cross-industry span, than in past generations. At the same time, extensive overlaps among networks have declined. There are still networks of businesses and workers that combine common region of origin, coethnicity, kinship ties, and a common industry, but such multiple links are considerably less common than in the past.

Commitment's role in gluing together networks has also expanded, as a number of analysts—perhaps most notably Michael Piore and Charles Sabel (1984; see also Best 1990)—have argued. Indeed, commitment's importance has perhaps followed something of a U-shaped trajectory. In preindustrial economies and early industrialization, various forms of commitment loomed large in binding together employers and workers. With the rise of mass production, capitalism's profile moved toward islands of hierarchy linked by markets. As "flexible specialization" has grown in importance, coalitions have become more common both within firms (as in the "matrix" firms studied by Rosabeth Kanter [1989]) and among firms (as in the industrial districts discussed by Piore and Sabel). We state these trends with a pinch of skepticism. Commitment-based networks often include a substantial element of hierarchy, as Bennett Harrison (1994, for example chapters 4 and 7) has pointed out. Furthermore, although coalitions may have waned and then waxed in the formal organization of production, informal networks have always drawn heavily on commitment. Arguably, much of the growth in the role of coalitions simply represents the formalization and strengthening of existing informal networks. Thus, the total profile of production networks has shifted toward commitment less than has the subset of formal production networks.

Other Actors: The Family

When workers step into the workplace, with its force fields of compensation, commitment, and coercion, they do not leave behind other sets of social relations. Families exercise particular influence over workers and constitute workers' key resource. In the United States and western Europe, nuclear families have been especially important since they have constituted the principal household unit since the seventeenth century (Hareven 1990: 233). Extended networks of kin also loom large in some contexts, but we will focus here on the nuclear family household.

Like other actors, families combined unified purpose with internal conflicts. Families' unified actions with respect to the economy constitute *family strategies* (Hareven 1990; Louise Tilly 1979). Family strategies include decisions about fertility, marriage, migration, education, entry of various members into the labor market, and tapping of other potential income sources (such as engaging in petty commerce, seeking transfer payments, or taking in boarders). In some cases, such strategies literally entail joint action. In the early years of the British coal and textile industries, family members took in work or went out to work together. Where a single industry dominated a community—as was often true in mining and textile industries—striking and strikebreaking pooled family efforts. Chain migration represents a family strategy par excellence. Antonia Bergeron told Tamara Hareven about her turn-of-the-century voyage from Quebec to Manchester, New Hampshire, to work in the textile mills:

> So when my neighbors went to the U.S., I decided to go with them. . . . I didn't know anyone when we arrived. . . . Then I met a woman who had taught me school in Canada when I was small. She worked in the mills here. She helped me, found me a job in the mills. . . . My mother came up later with my little brother and my little sister. . . . As time went on, we'd have another person come up, and another, and finally the whole family was here. (Hareven 1982: 86)

As this story makes clear, family ties are only one kind of network migrants draw on—but historically, it has been the most important one. Although joint action by families has become less common, as we will discuss later, family strategies persist.

Family strategies emerge from contestation and bargaining within the family. For instance, men sometimes use their power to limit their wives' participation in the paid workforce. In the same study by Hareven, the daughter of a male textile worker reported:

> My father didn't really want her [my mother, Marie Lacasse] to work. That was a big issue because she always wanted to go in and earn a little money. But the minute she said she wanted to work, there would be a big fight. He'd say, "No, you're not going to work. You're going to stay at home." And that's why she did other things. She'd make clothes for him, take in boarders, rent rooms. (Hareven 1982: 205)

On the other hand, Hareven found that women had substantial control over other areas, including birth control and decisions about when children should take paid jobs. And although family power relations and bargaining shape family members' participation in the paid labor force, that participation in turn reconfigures power within the family. Women who earn wages, on average, gain decisionmaking power within the family, and those who earn more wages gain more power (Coser 1990; England & Kilbourne 1990: 165).

Families also contribute to the gender roles and other cultural understandings that workers take into employment. This affects who seeks (and secures) particular jobs: Despite some recent mixing, physicians remain primarily male and nurses primarily female. Gender roles also modulate how male and female workers perform the same job: Arlie Hochschild (1983) found that male flight attendants were perceived as more authoritative and indeed exercised more authority, whereas female flight attendants were seen as more friendly and approachable and indeed spent more time responding to customer requests. Sallie Westwood (1982) discovered that women textile workers did their best to "domesticate" their workplaces, creating family-like relations with other workers to shield themselves from pressure by male overseers. In addition to gender, other elements of a worker's position within the family spill over into paid work. Age is an obvious example: Teenage workers often offer employers much the same mix of deference and rebellion that they accord their parents.

The family is the site of unpaid domestic labor. We have set aside consideration of such reproductive labor in this chapter's discussion. But the demands of housework leave fingerprints all over the world of paid work. The need for reproductive labor limits families' wage-labor strategies, sets the frame for contestation within families, and intertwines intimately with gender (and age) roles. On the other hand, the requirements of reproduction place a floor on compensation: Wages must be sufficient to sustain workers and their families. Sufficiency, of course, depends on a variety of historical and social factors: How capable are wives of making clothes, taking in boarders, and renting rooms, as Marie Lacasse did in the 1920s? What public or charitable supplements are available?

In the industrialized countries, families' strategies and activities have changed markedly over time. Families have moved (with the active population as a whole) from agriculture to industry, from rural areas to cities and suburbs, from acting as production units to acting as consumption units. Although the United States has seen a recent uptick in families working together, fueled by increased immigration from rural areas of Latin America and Asia, along with expansion of home-based work, the long-term trend sweeps the other way. With bans on child labor, the extension of schooling (and of childhood itself), and the establishment of universal pension programs, children have become less of an investment good created to share parents' work and support them in old age, more of a consumption good. Women have reduced and delayed fertility and are participating in paid labor at rising rates. Between 1948 and 1995, U.S. women's labor force participation climbed from 33 percent to 59 percent while men's declined from 87 percent to 75 percent; most other industrialized countries saw similar patterns.

All of these processes contribute to the individualization of family members' decisions about economically significant actions, weakening family strategies. Whereas coal strikes mobilized (and to some extent continue to mobilize) families and communities, hospital strikes usually do not. More importantly, the children of present-day coal miners and hospital workers are far more likely than their predecessors to make relatively independent decisions about whether and when to marry, where to seek employment, and how to use savings from their pay. One highly visible outcome of more individualized decisionmaking and action in the United States is elevated rates of single motherhood across all racial, class, and educational strata, with significant consequences for labor supplies of women and men alike.

Other Actors: The State

National, regional, and local states also join the by now crowded cast of actors on the stage of employment. Like families, states intervene in employment at a variety of points. Building on a useful discussion by Fred Block (1994), we can group such state actions into three areas of regulation: proletarianization, labor supply, and labor relations.

States regulate *proletarianization* by a variety of actions that expand or limit people's alternatives to working for wages. Most fundamentally, the state recognizes and defends certain property rights: When the British state upheld the gentry's enclosures of grazing land in the late eighteenth century, it privileged individual ownership over common claims on the land and pushed many of the landless into other activities, including the growing textile industry. Tax and transfer policies have also propelled or limited proletarianization. As Block notes (1994: 701), European colonists levied poll taxes on indigenous subsistence farmers to compel them to enter the cash economy—unlocking a new source of wage-labor. On the other hand, cash transfers (or public service employment programs) available to single mothers, the elderly, disabled people, and unemployed workers buffer them from the labor market's discipline. Government regulation of credit availability and price, finally, influences the availability of entrepreneurship as an alternative to employment.

State policies also expand and contract *labor supply* relative to demand. Actually, the most important policies in this regard act on the demand side: Fiscal and monetary policies to manage demand adjust the tightness of the labor market, as when the U.S. Federal Reserve's clampdown on credit precipitated the deep recessions of 1979–82, sending unemployment to its highest level since the Great Depression. But states wield a range of more delicate instruments on the supply side. States have long overseen skill creation, whether through guilds or schools. The engineering and business colleges at Chris Tilly's home institution, the University of Massachusetts at Lowell, trace their lineage back over 100 years to the Lowell Textile Institute, originally created by New England textile industrialists with government help to offset the advantage of low-wage southern manufacturers, later converted into a public institution. State certification of professional monopolies ratifies doctors' and nurses' strategies for limiting labor supply; state antidiscrimination policy, on the other hand, weakens ethnic groups' control over entry into the building trades. Child labor and compulsory schooling laws, protective legislation for women, and the like limit or cut off employers' access to categories of prospective workers.

Immigration laws also regulate labor supply. From the standpoint of the United States, we are most familiar with the immigration policies of a receiving country. But sending countries' states also do their best to manage emigration flows. In one peculiar example, the government of El Salvador, controlled by a right-wing party that orchestrated much of the repression during the 12-year civil war that ended in 1992, currently aids its nationals in filing for political asylum in the United States. Thus, paradoxically, the Salvadoran government is helping its citizens document that they face a continuing threat from the government or its allies. The paradox vanishes, however, once one realizes that the Salvadoran economy depends on the nearly $1 billion of remittances U.S.-resident Salvadorans send home each year and that anti-immigrant stirrings in the United States threaten to force many Salvadorans to return home (Carvajal 1995).

States weigh in on *labor relations,* first of all, by specifying rights and authority within the employment relationship. Consider, for example, the right to fire. It is much harder for West European businesses to fire employees than it is for U.S. businesses, due to government and union restrictions. Chinese state enterprises are attempting to make a wrenching transition from guaranteed employment (which has resulted in "overemployment" estimated at 20 percent or more in state enterprises) to an employment-at-will regime. Within the United States, laws do place a few restrictions on firing. Antidiscrimination laws forbid firing someone due to their race, gender, and so on (but not due to height, weight, disposition, or any number of other factors); the National Labor Relations Act bars sacking someone for attempting to organize a union (though this law has become something of a dead letter). However, virtually no other limitations apply. For instance, although the Occupational Safety and Health Act grants workers the right to a safe workplace, it offers no recourse to workers fired for refusing to work in (illegal) unsafe conditions. Pro-worker labor lawyers have attempted to get courts expand the few footholds into a concept of "wrongful discharge," projecting more comprehensive guidelines about when termination is justified—that is, they have tried to shift the state's stance on employers' authority to fire.

States also act on labor relations by regulating workers' collective action. As Samuel Bowles and Herbert Gintis (1986) have pointed out, over time workers have not only expanded their rights as citizens but have won from the state the extension of some of these rights to the workplace as well. The effects have been broad and deep. Consider one microcosm of this phenomenon: Hospital union organizing surged after 1974 when the federal government extended the National Labor Relations Act to the health care industry; it expanded again after 1990 when the National Labor Relations Board defined standard bargaining units for hospitals (reducing the lengthy and—for unions—debilitating arguments over the appropriate bargaining unit that typically delayed government-sanctioned union elections). State action was certainly not the only factor setting the pace of hospital union organizing; there was also an upsurge in the 1930s as part of the broader CIO ferment and one in the 1960s as an outgrowth of the Civil Rights movement. But even these counterexamples point to the potency of state action: The labor legislation of the 1930s and the Civil Rights Act of 1964, although silent on hospital unionization, gave encouragement to the movements and organizations that pursued this unionization.

Although states possess the authority to set out legitimate rules for the world of work, their authority is invariably leaky. Exhibit A in this regard is the collection of underground and informal economies that dodge state regulation and taxation in every country—in some cases growing as vast as the 74 percent of the labor force in metropolitan Lima, Peru, who are estimated to toil in the informal sector (Spalding 1992: 32). Even among formal, aboveground business and workers, compliance varies. In the United States, the 1992 Family and Medical Leave Act, which requires employers to grant up to 12 weeks of unpaid leave in cases of illness, illness of a family member, or the birth of a child, provides a case in point. During the debates leading up to the act's passage, an insurance company human resource official told Chris Tilly:

> The working parents issue is gaining much more national attention. There is a feeling in companies that if we don't respond, some state or federal regulations will be imposed. Companies like us don't tend to like to be regulated in this way. We prefer to be proactive. The parental leave act is coming up again—and there's a good chance it will pass. The problem with regulations is that they're generic—they don't necessarily fit our needs. (Chris Tilly 1996: 119–120)

Once the law was passed, compliance was spotty. According to a 1994 study, 40 percent of employers were failing either to offer 12 weeks of leave, to guarantee jobs after the leave, or to continue benefits during the leave. Almost two-thirds of surveyed workers who took leaves reported problems with their employers. Only "a very small minority of companies are really trying to implement the law," stated University of California professor Andrew Scharlach, coauthor of the study (Shellenbarger 1994, B1).

In addition, and not incidentally, states are far from monolithic. Legislative, executive, and judicial branches of government pursue overlapping but differing objectives, as do local, regional, and national governments (and international quasi-state bodies are growing in importance as regulators of international flows of credit, aid, and trade). Middle- and lower-level government bureaucrats and employees, not surprisingly, show the same limited autonomy from government policies that middle managers and workers show from employer policies.

Nonetheless, over time states have succeeded in writing themselves a large role in the script of employment processes. Wielding to a greater or lesser extent the three resources of legitimacy, coercive power, and a large budget, they have proven a powerful ally or a formidable foe to groups of workers and capitalists. Their reserves of commitment, coercion, and compensation

TABLE 6.3   Triads: Management Objectives, Worker Incentives,
Network Structures

		Network
Objective	*Incentive*	*Structure*
Quality	Commitment	Coalition
Efficiency	Compensation	Market
Power	Coercion	Hierarchy

expand from time to time (for example, during periods of popularly supported wars), allowing them to institutionalize new regulatory powers; un-
doing these powers is typically more difficult.

Curtain Call for the Actors

As we call the actors in labor markets out for another bow, let us recapitulate
the central points of our discussion. Employers, workers, families, and states,
in various ways, all pursue multiple objectives subject to bounded rationality.
The objectives that animate them and the constraints that bind them are
shaped and reshaped by historically formed social relations and by the shared
cultural understandings these social relations create and diffuse. Networks
built of established social relations link actors within firms, across firms, and
between firms and other elements of the society and economy. The boundaries of firms and workers do not mark sharply distinct, sealed packages of
social interaction but denote points at which the density and character of social relations change (for example, where relations of coercion and commitment within the firm give way to market relations between the firm and
other economic actors). Although the form and scope of organizations and
other networks does reflect efficiency advantages, efficiency only represents
one consideration, along with quality and power (often framed in terms of
organizational maintenance). Moreover, employers' choices of organizational structure (and other choices, such as those involving physical technology) take place in the context of relations and understandings handed down
from the past, which almost invariably exert an inertial drag.

We have referred repeatedly to employer objectives of quality, efficiency,
and power; to worker incentives of commitment, compensation, and coercion; and to the network forms of coalitions, markets, and hierarchies. The
isomorphism among these three triads is not accidental (Table 6.3). Employers seeking quality, efficiency, and power rely particularly on commitment,
compensation, and coercion, respectively, as motivators. Relations of commitment, compensation, and coercion, in turn, compound into coalitions,
markets, and hierarchies, respectively. Although the members of these triads
rarely, if ever, appear in pure form, these distinctions help map and explain

variation and changes in actors' behavior. Actors in labor markets build, break, adjust, and respond to ties founded on these three principles, and the resultant actions add up to the labor markets we see in the world.

This chapter and the two preceding ones have formulated an analytical framework and models of the behavior of the major actors in the world of waged work. Armed with these tools, we can now look more systematically at change and variation in work processes and labor markets. Chapter 7 launches this explication, considering change in terms of both the centuries-long evolution of labor markets and shorter-run changes in technology and the division of labor.

7
How Work Has Changed,
How Work Changes

Changing Work

Standard economic models of work pluck it out of culture and history to make it placeless and timeless. This simplification does not do justice to the tremendous changes work has undergone over the centuries. It also slights the daily, year-in and year-out process of change that attends any work process. What makes these long-term and short-term processes tick?

To understand change, we must start by acknowledging that work swims in culture and alters in response to a history far broader than that of work alone. By culture we mean shared understandings and their representations in symbols and objects. Culture permeates work in beliefs concerning which organizations of work are feasible, effective, and/or desirable; classifications of work as good or bad; grading of work's products; expectations about proper behavior of bosses and subordinates; standards of proper rewards for effort; and much more. Both these understandings and the organization of work change historically: They alter as a function of accumulated experience and constructed interpretations of that experience so that *when* something happens affects *how* it happens, and the order in which events occur affects their outcomes. Thus labor markets that emerge from disintegrating state socialism operate in distinctly different ways from those that grow out of mercantile capitalism not simply because they incorporate different principles of organization and different interpersonal networks but also because they operate in the context of different shared memories, understandings, and expectations. Again, labor unions crystallize at a certain time in relation to governments and employers only to retain their organization—at times to their own detriment—despite substantial alterations of capital, technology, and work. Struggle within well-established historical and cultural contexts dominates organizational change.

Our emphasis on bargaining and on interaction among a variety of technical and social forces contrasts sharply with conventional pictures of job change. Conventional accounts spotlight productivity-driven technological advance as if the invention and diffusion of new procedures for production at lower cost and/or higher return explained all job realignments. Even worker-friendly, antideterminist accounts of industrial organization commonly suppose that managers design organizations from scratch within constraints set by existing technologies. Business economist William G. Shepherd distinguishes between short-run management and long-run planning:

Current management is relatively routine. Setting future patterns is creative, difficult, and often risky—the term *entrepreneurship* glorifies it, but the task does require special talent. Investment levels and patterns must be selected. The firm's technology may need changing. Its organization chart may have to be redrawn. Personnel (including managers themselves) may have to be dropped or added. Even sticking with the old patterns often requires positive decisions to reject attractive new ways. (Shepherd 1979: 78)

The literature on job change itself—radical, conservative, and noncommittal alike—emits an astonishingly determinist tone, suggesting that technology pursues an inexorable logic which managers and workers can do no more than resist, subvert, mitigate, or adapt to. The introduction of the wheeled plow, the three-field rotation, the spinning jenny, the blast furnace, and the transistor made large differences in production through much of the West. However, job change linked to technological change is a special case. As we saw in Chapter 3, before the 1930s, large changes in the organization of British mining were driven primarily by labor-management bargaining, not by the invention of new technology. Moreover, the effects of technological change are invariably shaped, channeled, and at times blocked by the broader social, economic, and political context (Bijker, Hughes & Pinch 1987; Tushman & Rosenkopf 1992)—as we shall see in more detail later in this chapter.

Excessively technological and managerial narratives of organizational change result partly from managerial mythmaking, partly from the fact that major organizational recasting does often include shifts in productive techniques and partly from the fact that storytellers suppose a zero base—presume that beyond original development costs a new technology competes with existing technologies as if both were being newly installed. The last presumption violates important but often neglected principles of organizational change. Here are the most crucial principles, building on our discussion in Chapter 5:

1. In almost any organizational change, including those that seem entirely technological, what changes is not merely individual performances but relations among members of the organization. If transactions and contracts change, so then do jobs and the organization's overall structure.
2. In any organization, each change, deletion, or addition of a social relation costs something; costs include (a) creating the new form, (b) articulating it with existing and/or adjacent relations, (c) persuading the parties to adopt it, (d) teaching its use, (e) persuading powerful actors outside the organization—stockholders, trustees, courts, customers, fellow professionals—that the innovation is legitimate.
3. The more complex the organization and/or the more changes, the greater the cost of changing, deleting, or adding a relation.
4. Familiar forms of social structure, on the average, cost less to install than new forms.

5. To some degree, parties to all changes, deletions, and additions of relations bargain over the terms of the reorganization involved.
6. For these reasons, people rarely create wholly new organizations; instead, they typically piece together bits of existing social structure with novel social relations, understandings, and performances kept to a minimum.
7. Small, incremental changes occur incessantly and often invisibly as organization members renegotiate their relations through daily interaction. Changes in the members' external relations likewise cascade into incremental organizational changes.
8. Nevertheless, owners and managers usually take the visible, deliberate initiatives in these regards since they are more actively engaged than other organization members in responding to threats and opportunities outside the organization.
9. Owners and managers take such initiatives only to the degree that within some short run they estimate the returns (however measured) to exceed the transaction costs of innovation.
10. Building in familiar forms of social structure incorporates their external connections into the organization.

The final point is no doubt the most important and least familiar. To build existing gender distinctions into a firm, for example, incorporates symbolic codes, barriers, patterns of exploitation, family connections, and sometimes relations with sexual partners into the firm's social environment, thereby invoking whatever interests the parties may have in maintaining such distinctions outside the firm. Similarly, to recruit new employees by word of mouth through present employees (still standard practice in smaller American enterprises) gives present employees' interpersonal networks privileged access to the firm. These principles mean that productive organizations, once established, tend to retain their basic organizations far longer than static efficiency from a zero base would predict. Even dramatically cost-saving new technologies only enter production to the extent that their promoters overcome serious adoption costs. For these reasons, indeed, the original inventors of new techniques and machines rarely see them adopted until an entrepreneur arrives who intervenes directly in the affected organization and either adapts the invention to local conditions or beats down adoption costs.

Capitalism and the Rise of Labor Markets

Over the long sweep of human experience, major changes in the character of work have resulted from the interplay of technology, coercion, capital, existing social relations, and culture—changing productive procedures, changing uses of force, changing deployments of investment, changing connections to

surrounding communities, changing beliefs concerning the effects of different ways to organize work. The rise of capitalism in Europe and the United
States exemplifies this interplay. The near-monopolization of coercive means
by bourgeois-dominated states promoted the consolidation and protection
of bourgeois property, the elimination of multiple use rights in commons
and unseeded fields, and the extinction of claims on local communities for
subsistence of the poor and unemployed; these changes in property rights
advanced proletarianization of workers and investment of capitalists in the
fixed costs of factories, mills, and large shops. Changes in the organization of
capital such as the spread of joint-stock companies and the expansion of
credit likewise had fundamental, if indirect, effects on the character of work.

During the last century the largest alterations of work in western Europe
and North America have no doubt resulted from an interaction among the
mechanization of production and distribution, the expansion of communica-
tive and data-storage devices, the creation of large, heavily capitalized productive organizations, the imposition of centralized work-discipline, the
growth of public-sector employment, the shift from raw-material production
to manufacturing and services, and the extension of wage-labor—loosely
speaking, capitalist industrialization and proletarianization. These changes
constituted a huge increase in the proportion of all labor power offered for
sale compounded by a large decline in producer control of labor processes.

We stress that labor markets themselves represent an invention—and one
whose widespread adoption is comparatively recent. For centuries, capitalists
preferred not to promote labor markets, which require that employers invest
heavily in the means of production, organize and supervise the labor process,
create systems for hiring, firing, job assignment, and compensation, pay at
least a subsistence wage, and deal directly with interventions of public authorities, organized workers, or labor-supplying households in all of those
processes. Although European master craftsmen did organize both manufacture and sale of their products from medieval times onward, even they preferred to deal with formally autonomous outworkers during the early phases
of capitalist expansion; although outworkers typically produced goods of
lower and more uneven quality, those workers cost less and demanded much
less than established guild artisans (Kriedte 1983; Kriedte, Medick &
Schlumbohm 1981, 1992; Charles Tilly 1983). In general, larger merchants
arranged to buy the products of self-contained shops and households, whose
fates thereby depended heavily on the merchants but did not become the
merchants' moral or legal responsibility. Those shops and households created and supervised their own means of production.

Under European mercantile capitalism, a large share of all workers produced outside of labor markets; they strove within households and sold com-
pleted goods to merchants who resold them at a profit, as in the case of the
early textile industry. The chief exceptions were agricultural laborers, who

signed on with employers for a day, a season, or a year, received wages plus payments in kind, and moved frequently from job to job. Crafts such as stone-cutting and printing also created limited labor markets with stringent controls over entry into the trade and over commercial practice of its skills. Otherwise, few workers participated in labor markets of any significant extent.

Even waged workers, furthermore, enjoyed limited freedom. In England and America, the English Statute of Artificers (1562–63) and its variants codified the rules that (a) an apprentice, servant, or other worker signed for a term was subject to criminal penalties for leaving work before that term's end and (b) an unemployed worker in a given trade could be forced to work for a local master at the prevailing wage. As a result:

> In the seventeenth century, unfree labor represented the "normal" legal form that contractual labor took in the Anglo-American world. Free labor—labor undertaken under legal rules that did not give employers either the right to invoke criminal penalties for departure or the right to specific performance—represented, when it first appeared in the American colonies early in the eighteenth century, a special rather than universal form of contractual labor. For more than a century thereafter, free labor continued to be restricted to certain forms of the labor relationship. Not until the nineteenth century did it become the paradigm for normal employment. (Steinfeld 1991: 4)

In eighteenth-century England, miners, along with domestic servants, agricultural laborers, boatmen, salt makers, file makers and, of course, apprentices regularly worked on contracts binding them for a year or more; in Scotland, the system for miners came close to serfdom (Flinn 1984: 349–361). Indentured labor long remained the rule, not the exception (see Brass 1994; D. Montgomery 1993; Tomlins 1993).

With the accumulation and concentration of capital from the seventeenth to nineteenth centuries, nevertheless, a wide range of work proletarianized—reorganized so that workers received wages for labor they performed under capitalist supervision using employer-owned tools, materials, and premises. To be sure, church and state hierarchies had long specified tasks for limited groups of personnel (notably priests, monks, nuns, clerks, and soldiers), but universalization and regulation of labor markets made occupational affiliation the norm. With that proletarianization, not only employment but also unemployment became distinctive ideas, sets of practices, and legal conditions in ways that remained inconceivable before the nineteenth century (Keyssar 1986; Salais, Baverez & Reynaud 1986; Topalov 1994). Unemployment only constitutes a separate status where waged employment and labor markets dominate the world of work; a subsistence farmer may be idle, but only a would-be jobholder can be unemployed.

As capital concentrated, household economies came to depend heavily on wages rather than on self-produced goods and services or their sale. Labor markets proliferated. The law itself changed: Bourgeois law became dominant, with its hostility to multiple property rights in the same objects, its separation of use from ownership, its sharp distinction between the rights of capital and of labor, its similarly sharp distinction between criminal and civil offenses, and its requirement that civil plaintiffs prove material losses from others' illegal actions instead of merely demonstrating infringement of tradition, honor, or sacred prohibition. In different variants, workers came to articulate a labor theory of value and a class theory to match it: that the labor that went directly into an object's production constituted the object's true value; that through the fictions of ownership capitalists seized an unjust share of the value thus created; that a fundamental division of interest therefore separated workers from capitalists; that workers could only realize their true value by banding together to attack the system of property and power. As the self-styled Workingmen of Charlestown, Massachusetts, put it in their address of October 1840:

> We are men with the rights of men, with rights equal to those of the wealthiest and the proudest; but we are poor men; men obliged to labor for our daily bread; dependent on those who choose to employ us, and compelled by the invincible law of hunger to accept the wages they offer. They hold us then at their mercy, and make us work solely for their profit . . . The capitalist has no other interest in us, than to get as much labor out of us as possible. We are hired men, and hired men, like hired horses, have no souls . . . If we sicken and die, the loss is ours, not the employers. *There are enough more ready to take our places.* (Tomlins 1993: 10)

At the same time, British Chartists were building a great political movement around similar ideas.

As markets expanded and fixed capital increased in the forms of mines, mills, and machinery, capitalists turned to hiring labor for waged work under time-discipline on capitalist-owned premises; they created jobs. Although they frequently employed subcontractors and integrated previously existing relationships with workers in their new organizations, in the process capitalists also inadvertently formed labor markets. Sometimes they even deliberately promoted the formation of labor markets, as when they sought out scabs—new, cheaper, and more docile workers to replace those who were currently refusing to work on the capitalists' conditions. The abolition of slavery (in 1860, after all, slaves amounted to about 4 million of the 31 million U.S. residents) extended labor markets, even though in the short run many American ex-slaves became sharecroppers rather than wage-laborers. Eventually many capitalists began to exert direct control over hiring, routines of production, and systems of compensation for individual workers, coopting or eliminating the middlemen who so long made the immediate decisions in all three regards. They began to seek reliable, full-time, long-

FIGURE 7.1   The rise of labor markets

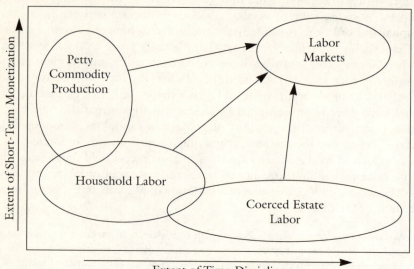

Extent of Short-Term Monetization

Petty
Commodity
Production

Labor
Markets

Household Labor

Coerced Estate
Labor

Extent of Time-Discipline

term workers who would cooperate with management's organization of production.

Figure 7.1 summarizes the momentous changes that occurred. Prior to
the rise of labor markets, petty commodity production, household labor, and
coerced estate labor represented three common ways of organizing work. In
petty commodity production, individuals, households, or small shops turned
out goods and services they marketed directly themselves. Such production
involved considerable short-run monetization—the limiting case being the
blacksmith or woodworker who produced on demand for cash—but not
much time-discipline in the sense of someone else's hour-by-hour specification and monitoring of work effort. (Remember, "short-term monetization"
means the extent to which workers invest effort, or fail to do so, contingent
on the prospect of monetary compensation in the immediate future—say
within a month or less. "Time-discipline" means the extent to which other
persons decide the disposition of a worker's effort within the working day.)

In the overlapping case of household labor, we find production within
households oriented chiefly to self-subsistence and organized around divisions of tasks that on the whole entailed little hour-by-hour supervision. In
the rather different circumstances of coerced estate labor—slaves' cane-cut-
ting on a sugar plantation provides an extreme example—we discover low
monetization but extensive time-discipline. In medieval Europe, two or
three of these organizations of work often coexisted, as households raised
much of their own food on small plots but sold poultry and fattened cattle

to pay rents, tithes, or taxes, while owing a certain number of days per year to the landlord for clearing, plowing, planting, and harvesting the landlord's fields. The movement toward labor markets reduced the roles of all these arrangements in favor of a great average increase in both monetization and time-discipline.

As Figure 7.1 suggests, actual trajectories toward labor markets differed markedly by point of origin. European households engaged in market-oriented petty commodity production (for example, spinning, weaving, and market gardening) for centuries before factory labor became common; households moving into labor markets from such milieux experienced relatively little monetization but drastic increases in externally imposed time-discipline. Slaves on Caribbean plantations, in contrast, knew plenty about time-discipline but at emancipation endured large increases in the monetization of their labor. The working conditions of former petty commodity producers and ex-slaves ended up resembling each other. Polemical Marxists called both wage-slaves.

American Proletarianization

Consider in more detail the U.S. experience. If we take "proletarian" to include anyone who works for wages at the command of someone else who owns the means of production, the United States is a very proletarian country and has been proletarianizing for a long time. By any standard, waged work—chiefly work within labor markets, the zone of jobs, employers, wages, and careers—has become enormously more prevalent in the United States over the two centuries since the country's founding. Figure 7.2 (drawn from Edwards, Reich & Weisskopf 1986: 124 and U.S. Dept. Of Commerce 1992: xiii) provides a crude indication of that change: A rise of wage and salary employees from 20 percent of the American labor force in 1780 to a peak of 83.5 percent in 1970, followed by a slight decline as salaried managers and administrators expanded to more than a tenth of the 1990 labor force.

The proportions in Figure 7.2 remain crude because the idea of "labor force" itself includes only those people census takers regard as gainfully employed or at least currently employable, which excludes many people who work in household enterprises or who live from nonmarket work of one kind or another. Before 1940, to be precise, U.S. census takers asked people their usual employment, if any; from household establishments they included in their tabulations only persons (usually male) they recognized as "heads" of households. Beginning with the 1940 census they asked whether respondents were currently working for pay or looking for paid employment. The share of all work done by people who fell into the official labor force, thus defined, greatly increased during the nineteenth century.

FIGURE 7.2   Wage and other work, U.S. labor force, 1780–1990

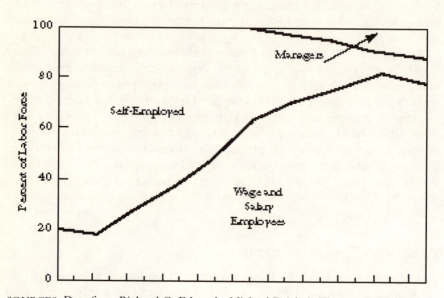

SOURCES: Data from Richard C. Edwards, Michael Reich & Thomas E. Weisskopf, eds., *The Capitalist System: A Radical Analysis of American Society* (Englewood Cliffs, N.J.: Prentice-Hall, 1986); U.S. Department of Commerce, *Statistical Abstract of the United States, 1995* (Washington, D.C.: U.S. Government Printing Office, 1995), xiii.

Proletarianization transformed the United States from a country in which the vast majority of people worked in household enterprises for little or no money to one in which the vast majority of adults worked in labor markets—held jobs for pay outside their own homes. To see the transition clearly, we must distinguish among four sets of changes, not all of which acted in the same direction:

1. Movement of people between work and nonwork
2. Movement of people between work outside the labor force (e.g., unpaid household work) and work inside the labor force (i.e., working for pay or looking for paid work but not necessarily in regular jobs)
3. Movement of people between (a) work within the labor force but outside labor markets and (b) work inside labor markets, with their firms, jobs, and monetary remuneration
4. Within labor markets, movement between wage-labor and other forms of work

FIGURE 7.3   Net movements among work statuses in United States, 1780–1990

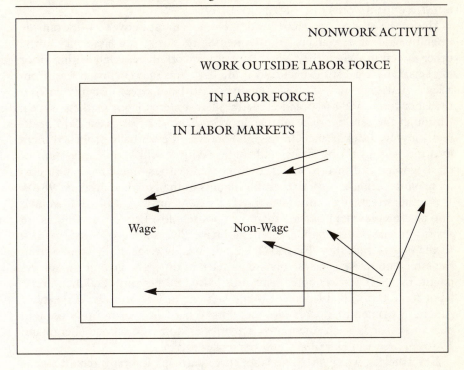

Figure 7.3 schematizes the relevant shifts, with their dominant directions. Under the first heading of change, Americans have actually seen a large net *reduction* of their work during the last two centuries; over an ordinary lifetime, the share of time spent outside of work—outside of activities that produce use value for other people—has greatly expanded. Among persons working for pay, average weekly hours have declined from almost 70 in 1830 to a little over 40 during the 1980s (Goldin 1994: Figure 5). The number of people outside the age range 18–64 who work in paid employment, furthermore, has sunk. Primary and secondary education have absorbed growing proportions of the population under 19, whereas retirement during one's sixties has become the rule. In 1860 about four-fifths of all free U.S. men older than 64 were working for money in firms or on farms; by 1980 that figure had fallen to about a quarter (Goldin 1994: Figure 6). Increases in life expectancy, finally, multiplied the effect of retirement patterns; higher and higher proportions of the total population fell into the very segment—65 and older—whose work time was decreasing so drastically. We have less evidence on nonmarket work, but U.S. time-budget studies for recent years indicate that housework time is declining, passive leisure such as television watching is rising, and volunteer ef-

forts are not increasing enough to make a difference to the overall downward trend in unpaid work (Juster & Stafford 1991).

Under the second and third headings—movement between work outside of and inside labor markets—the United States has seen a large shift in the other direction. When they work, Americans work increasingly within labor markets. One great surge occurred at the Civil War's end, when at least from a legal viewpoint almost all workers who had been slaves instantly entered the labor force, and as a practical matter many entered labor markets as well. Although the semibondage of sharecropping and debt peonage did not directly involve black farmers in wage-labor, even it eventually propelled them into the world of jobs, firms, and wages. With World War I, migration of black women and men to major metropolitan centers drained agriculture to fill manufacturing and service establishments in the North (Fligstein 1981).

Another great surge continues today: a steady movement of adult women into paid employment outside their own households. Labor force figures are sexist. Official statistics undercount, and have always undercounted, women to the degree that they live with men who qualify as gainfully employed in the same enterprise. The further we go back in time, the greater the undercount. In 1870, for example, the census placed 82 percent of all men in the labor force but only 14 percent of all women. In fact, the vast majority of American women then worked—and worked hard—on farms, in household enterprises, or in such uncounted activities as domestic service (Bergmann 1986: 21; see also Herr 1995 and references there).

Nevertheless, women's rising labor-force participation rates record a genuine change: a shift from work outside jobs and labor markets into that previously masculine world. In 1890, only about 15 percent of all American women 25–44 years of age qualified for inclusion in the labor force by virtue of running commercial enterprises, holding salaried jobs, or otherwise working visibly outside their homes; by 1990, the proportion had risen to 75 percent (Goldin 1994: Figure 7; for more detail, see Smith & Ward 1985, and for warnings about early undercounts of female domestic servants see Carter & Sutch 1996). Since 1940, moreover, the old tie between marriage and nonmarket work has started to dissolve; paid employment has risen more rapidly among younger married women than among all other women, married or unmarried.

The fourth component of change—movement within the labor market into waged work from other forms of employment—has likewise proceeded rapidly. As Figure 7.2 indicates, even if we exclude managers and administrators from employees the proportion of wage and salary employees in the American labor force has increased almost continuously since 1800. The great losers have been that strangely named category, the "self-employed": artisans, professionals, fisherfolk, and (overwhelmingly) farmers who instead of taking hourly or monthly pay from someone else earn their livelihood by

FIGURE 7.4   Changes in organization of cotton textiles, coal mining, and health care, 1800–1995

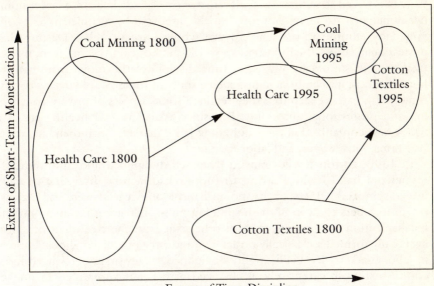

producing and selling goods or services. Although they survive in the form of shopkeepers, artists, and independent professionals, the self-employed have shrunk from a large majority to less than a tenth of the officially recognized American labor force. In the informal economy of street vendors, drug runners, and service providers, on the other hand, the "self-employed" surely loom much larger (Portes, Castells & Benton 1989).

These broad movements rippled through the cotton, coal, and health care industries of the United States. Figure 7.4 schematizes changes in the three sectors from 1800 to 1995 in terms of monetization and time-discipline. In 1800, all three industries were emerging from earlier origins in petty-commodity production, household work, and/or coerced labor, but none had arrived at anything like today's labor markets with their firms, jobs, wages, and labor mobility. All three followed the grand trend toward monetization and time-discipline, but in different manners and on quite distinct schedules.

Health care moved from a scattered set of crafts involving little time-discipline, depending heavily on unpaid home service, and varying enormously in payment patterns to a relatively monetized connected industry varying in time-discipline from supervising physicians (little) to kitchen workers (much). Throughout its history, it maintained a series of sharp gender divisions corresponding to real differences in power, prestige, and income: notably the division between physicians and surgeons (from predominantly to exclusively male in different eras) on one side and nurses (overwhelmingly female) on the other. As the industry consolidated, it moved from an essentially two-tiered structure—a small cadre of specialized healers, a larger number of helpers—to teams of professionals supported by technicians and contained by administrators who govern whole bureaucracies. Despite that professionalization, the industry as a whole shifted toward short-term monetization and significantly greater time-discipline; the move from private nomes to hospitals embodied just such a shift. In the U.S., physicians constituted the greatest exception; they retained some aspects of private contracting and professional autonomy. But since World War II health care as a whole has reorganized in thoroughgoing labor markets, with their characteristic firms, jobs, wages, and labor mobility.

In 1800, cotton textiles ranged from self-disciplined and intermittently monetized hand-loom weaving to the intense factory discipline of daily waged spinners' helpers; at that point, hand-loom weavers were still increasing in numbers to keep up with spinning mills' increasing production. The mechanization of weaving, then of other stages in the treatment of cloth, eventually formed a classically proletarian industry organized almost entirely in labor markets. By 1995, highly disciplined wageworkers produced most cotton textiles in extensively mechanized plants. Unlike garment manufacturing, which divided among elite couturiers' ateliers, large stitching mills, and thousands of low-wage sweatshops, cotton textiles continued as a classic example of factory production.

Coal mining always centered on the cash nexus, but over almost the entire period from 1800 to the present subcontracting played a larger part in coal than in health care or textiles, while hewers enjoyed greater autonomy and received payment by results rather than time-based wages. Mine owners managed to discipline the rest of their labor force during the nineteenth century, but only late in the twentieth century did coal mining mechanize and reorganize so extensively as to approach the short-term monetization and intense time-discipline of cotton textiles. Nevertheless, all three industries followed the general trend of capitalist industry toward short-term monetization and strong time-discipline.

At the time of the American Revolution, then, most Americans worked long weeks from childhood until near death but only intermittently, if ever, engaged in wage-labor; they rarely held jobs, as we understand them, and they almost never retired in anything like today's sense of the word. Now the world has turned. These days most Americans, male or female, have little to do with labor markets until their late teens, spend forty hours a week or so in jobs on other people's premises most of the time between ages 20 and 60, then start withdrawing massively from paid employment.

In some sense, everything that happened to the American economy from 1780 onward contributed to the transformation: monetization of daily life, growth of big cities, expansion of schooling, decline of fertility, aging of the population, increasing resort of unhappy couples to divorce, and much more. But the central changes occurred in the organization of work sites and their relations to the world outside them. In agriculture, capitalization, mechanization, and commercialization drove out the self-sustaining family farm in favor of two different sorts of entity: the small but capital- and labor-intensive operation producing fruits, vegetables, or poultry for delivery to merchants and processors; the land- and capital-intensive establishment shipping grain or livestock to national and world markets. (Although families often ran both sorts of enterprise, in recent decades they had little choice but to run them as competitive capitalist firms.)

In manufacturing, capitalization and mechanization widened the range of firms doing business, pushing small shops toward intensive specialization and production for larger industrial firms while creating huge organizations in the forms of factories, corporations, and conglomerate financial empires. In services, capitalization and mechanization took hold more slowly. Even there, technologies of recording, computation, and communication eventually assisted the growth of large, bureaucratized firms and multiunit organizations among the still-buzzing swarm of one-person and family enterprises. Extensive labor markets and time-disciplined waged work emerged as by-products and instruments of these vast changes.

Such changes in waged work cascaded into changes in work outside of capitalist premises: within households, in street trades, in schools, and elsewhere. The postwar increase in paid employment by American mothers, for example, generated new demands for child care. In 1965, about 3.8 million American children under age five had wage-earning mothers; by 1987, the figure had climbed to 9.1 million (see Table 7.1).

All of these arrangements involved work, but the portion of the necessary work supplied by nonrelatives outside the child's home was increasing rapidly; nonrelatives supplied 38 percent of the care in 1965 and 53 percent in 1987. The expanding involvement of married women in capitalist labor markets significantly affected their household allocations of work. Employers recognize their interest in reconciling household and work obligations: Although only about one employer in twenty provides on-site child care, over half of all U.S. employers offer some kind of help—information, financial aid, counseling, scheduling adjustments, or care itself (Reskin & Padavic 1994: 157–158).

Only recently have signs of reversal or redirection of these main trends shown up in the United States and the rest of the West, with possible moves toward fragmentation of productive organizations through computer technology, franchising, shifts of large-scale production (e.g., in ships, steel, and automobiles) away from the North and West, plus permanent unemployment, part-time and temporary employment, informal-sector employment,

TABLE 7.1   Distribution of Child-Care Arrangements, 1965 and 1987

	Percent of Children	
Source of Care	*1965*	*1987*
Child-care center	6.4	24.4
Relatives	46.7	37.0
Family day-care	15.8	22.3
In home day-care	15.3	6.2
Mother (at home or work)	15.0	8.9
Child cared for self	0.5	0.3
Other	0.3	1.0
Total	100.0	100.1

SOURCE: Touminen 1994: 232.

and underemployment of large portions of the potential labor force. "Self-service" in retail trade and health care has actually increased the amount of unpaid work that women do in both regards (Glazer 1993). After a century during which labor unions and government cooperated in restricting opportunities for women's homework on cigars, garments, and other industrial products, the U.S. government has recently turned to tolerating or even promoting white-collar homework as a reconciliation of household and market obligations (Boris 1994a). The U.S. temporary help industry, with its intermittent and often part-time employment, thin benefits, low pay, and overwhelmingly female labor force, rose from 184,000 workers in 1970 to 1.5 million in 1993 (Parker 1994: 29). These trends, too, deeply affect the general character of work in Western countries. Since welfare rights, pensions, and household well-being depend heavily on the employment of household members, such changes will affect the lives of Western populations for a long time to come.

Changes Large and Small

The grandeur of the story of labor markets' rise in Europe and the United States should not blind us to the fact that similar processes impel change in work on a smaller scale as well. In detail, work changes along two main dimensions: (1) direct alterations in the effort involved, and (2) shifts in relations to other persons entailed by that effort. Taylorist specification of work's timing and procedure certainly constituted changes in work, but so did the entry of foremen, shop stewards, government inspectors, and personnel specialists onto the shop floor. Housewives who welcomed the introduction of the electric iron, refrigerator, or washing machine (direct alterations in the effort of housework) soon discovered that other people's expectations concerning the products of iron, refrigerator, or washing machine had risen (shifts in relations to other persons) (see Vanek 1973; Cowan 1983).

Recognition that jobs consist of stipulated relations between workers and employers clears the way to a rough distinction among inventions and changes in work resulting from (a) deliberate initiatives of employers, (b) changes in workers' characteristics and social relations, (c) renegotiation of the relations between employers and workers. Olivier Zunz showed us all three in operation as corporations and white-collar work took shape in the United States. As the Du Pont company expanded, for example, the independent merchants who had served as its regional agents either lost their contracts or found themselves being absorbed into the company bureaucracy, with attendant loss of autonomy and shift from fees and commissions toward salary. A cohort of autonomous agents, typically hardware store owners, was replaced by a group of Du Pont corporate employees (Zunz 1990: 30–33).

As the Burlington and Missouri River Road sold land to encourage settlement along its rail lines, land department manager A. E. Touzalin

> began by reorganizing the department, defining tasks, and writing job descriptions. What should a cashier do? How do his responsibilities differ from those of an accountant? He also delegated specific tasks to his subordinates. One man wrote the contracts, another one responded to inquiries made by parties in person, while another tracked down delinquent accounts. Taxes also had to be attended to. So did land assessments and lawsuits. Each task was the responsibility of a specific person in his department. (Zunz 1990: 50)

Touzalin created jobs by identifying distinguishable tasks, a process that depended less on any internal logic than on relations of his organization with the rest of the world.

A related process imposed the increasingly bureaucratic organization of hospitals on the act of healing. But in this case the enormous power of the medical profession meant that doctors reorganized hospitals as much as hospitals organized doctors, along with other workers, into a specified division of labor. Other groups emulated—with varying degrees of success—physicians' sharp demarcation of professional boundaries and assertion of control over the education, training, and certification required for entry within those boundaries. Along the way, the professional, technical, and other job categories within health care acquired strong gender identities. Indeed, the typical result of the process of job definition is not only to create a set of jobs that stay in place with relatively little change but also to identify the job with a particular sort of person, marked not only by knowledge and experience but in many cases also by gender, race, ethnicity, age, citizenship, and/or class of origin.

Although the contours of jobs and the assignments of persons to them are initially arbitrary, once established they tend to endure. Ruth Milkman demonstrated the extreme sex-typing of work in electrical and automotive production before World War II. She then showed how Detroit's manufacturers, pressed by shortage of male workers during the war, reorganized some work into "women's jobs," even rationalizing the change by stressing women's superiority in work requiring dexterity and precision (Milkman 1987: 58–59). Yet at war's end employers, unions, and demobilized male workers collaborated in pushing women back into a limited number of sex-segregated jobs. In both the electrical and automotive industries, Milkman found, over the long run the gender assignment of a job, once made, tended to endure and to accumulate justifying mythology.

If the most dramatic changes in jobs result chiefly from deliberate initiatives of employers and/or changes in workers, renegotiation of relations between employers and workers occurs more continuously and with equally large effects. We have seen different versions of that renegotiation in the absorption of Du Pont agents into the company's central bureaucracy, the institutionalization of hospital-based health care, and the postwar reorganization of Detroit's industries. Renegotiation ranges from mass walkouts or wholesale firings to explicit bargaining to the minor adjustments that mold job to worker and vice versa. At one extreme, "when in 1885 the managers at the McCormick plant found themselves in a dispute with their unionized iron molders, they dismissed the entire force and installed molding machines and unskilled recruits in their places" (Rodgers 1974: 26). Likewise, at a U.S. textile mill in the late nineteenth century, one employer reported, "One Saturday afternoon after they [mule spinners] had gone home, we started right in and smashed a room full of mules with sledge hammers. On Monday morning [the spinners] were astonished to find that there was no work for them. That room is now full of ring frames run by girls" (Gordon, Edwards & Reich 1982: 115).

At the other extreme, we discover the daily stratagems of workers. All workers, ironically including those who work rigidly by the rules out of fear or spite, actually reshape their jobs to some degree. Political scientist Richard Pfeffer, who worked for seven months as a fork-lift driver in a Baltimore plant, found himself caught up in the job despite his radical analysis of capitalist work; on the one hand he began to resent the bosses, equipment, and fellow workers who made it hard for him to move his trash efficiently, while on the other he plotted innovations that made the job smoother, reduced the risk of accidents, and gave him larger blocks of personal time (Pfeffer 1979). Like radical sociologist Michael Burawoy in his Chicago area machine operator's job, Pfeffer worked harder and better than he had to, despite nagging awareness of playing management's game (Burawoy 1979). Yet by the same effort each of them wrested the job from management's prescriptions to stamp it as his own.

As these stories also illustrate, jobs actually change people. Not only the rewards—intrinsic and extrinsic—attached to particular jobs but also the routines and social relations built into jobs alter knowledge, skill, and personal style (Miller 1988: 340–349). Selection of certain types of persons for certain jobs accounts for some job-to-job variation in these regards, but long involvement in a job either accentuates or helps create job-specific style: the sociability of salesmen, the prolixity of professors, the profanity of sailors, and so on. In short, we are dealing with a powerful series of transactions in which jobs, or lack of them, shape people's lives while people reshape those jobs they have.

Technological Change

Two aspects of ongoing job change have attracted particular scholarly attention: technological change and alterations in the division of labor. Change in technology and in the division of labor have figured repeatedly in our narratives of change thus far. Closer examination of each case confirms the importance not just of the drive for efficiency, but also of social relations molded by history, rooted in culture, moved forward by bargaining and struggle.

That technology, coercion, capital, social relations, and culture interacted with variable results for work appears clearly in the history of particular inventions. "Form follows failure," announces Henry Petroski in his delightful book *The Evolution of Useful Things* (Petroski 1992: 22–33). Instead of looking resolutely toward the future, inventors typically stare at the defects of previous inventions. Patent applications, for example, stress how new inventions correct errors in existing solutions to problems. The vast majority of inventions emerge from criticism of previous devices meant for similar purposes. They therefore incorporate many existing features of those devices, not to mention accumulated understandings concerning how they work and what uses they serve. Invention, in Petroski's account, becomes an intensely path-dependent process, clinging to history like ivy to a wall. Petroski, himself a civil engineer, by no means denigrates mechanical inventions, but he rejects progressive applied-science accounts of their creation in favor of a story containing a great deal of uncertainty, trial and error, retrospective rationalization, and historical specificity (see also Bijker, Hughes & Pinch 1987).

Consider the history of metal-canned food, which began in Donkin and Hall's English "preservatory" toward the end of the Napoleonic Wars:

> Soldiers reportedly had to attack their canned rations with knives, bayonets, and even rifle fire, as American Civil War troops still would a half-century later. If Donkin and Hall wanted to sell their products to a broader clientele, they would certainly have to address the problem of how civilly to get what was inside a can out, but as late as 1824 a tin of roast veal carried on one of William Peary's Arctic expeditions bore the instructions "Cut round on the top near to the outer edge with a chisel and hammer." (Petroski 1992: 185–186)

The empty container weighed more than a pound. In certain regards it made an advance over dried beef and salted fish, but in others it was (both figuratively and literally) more burdensome. Most technical innovations have that mixed character, especially in their early phases. That is one reason why sheer efficiency explanations of technological change lack conviction. That is also why important technical innovations both emerge from and generate significant conflicts of interest.

As a first step toward a richer analysis of technological change, we must take employer interests and strategies into account. Employers have often taken advantage of new technologies to seek out different groups of workers, attractive for their lower wages, greater docility, or special skills. Women's historians have uncovered many instances like Philco's radical 1937–38 reorganization of radio production to replace higher-wage and seniority-accumulating men with cheaper, more docile, and more temporary women (Cooper 1991: 344–349). More generally, "over the long run, technological advances, proxied by a measure called total factor productivity, have been positively associated with the female intensity of a sector; that is, female-intensive sectors have had greater advances in technology" (Goldin 1987: 186). Notice, however, that increases in total factor productivity result from far more than technical inventions in any narrow sense of the term; they respond to recruitment of more qualified workers, more effective supervision, new incentive systems, better raw materials, and much more. We are dealing with an interaction between technical and organizational changes.

In fact, the character of entrepreneurship itself strongly affects the path of technological innovation. Invention and improvement of the sewing machine's successive versions, for instance, depended heavily on the interaction between such inventor-entrepreneurs as Isaac Singer and the various possible customers for different variants of the machine. Others had invented sewing machines well before Singer without being able to secure their widespread adoption. Singer was no technical genius, but he had a sharp eye for possible adaptations of his product to new uses; he spent much of his time seeking out potential users, creating appropriate variants of his machine, and selling their adoption; he facilitated the interplay between technology and market (Thomson 1984). By no means did the original invention's technical logic in itself determine the machine's subsequent integration into different labor processes.

Just as employers leave their imprint on technological change, so too do workers. In a classic case of technical changes in work, the introduction of the self-acting mule for the spinning of cotton in the United States led to the transformation of spinning into a foreman-supervised, time-driven occupation for an adult male who worked with one boy assisting him (see Chapter 3 for more details). Observing American workers alone, one might easily have thought the self-acting mule an inexorable instrument of deskilling. In England, however, the same device remained in the hands of subcontracting artisans who each hired their own two assistants, controlled entry into the trade, and successfully resisted speedups well into the twentieth century (Cohen 1985a; Freifeld 1986; Lazonick 1990). In terms of understandings, social relations, and power, mule spinning remained much more of a craft in England than in the United States, a fact that caused conflict and culture shock when English spinners emigrated to America (Cohen 1985b). Thus the same crucial invention integrated into distinctively different labor processes in the two countries.

As the English-American comparison illustrates, the character and organization of available workers shape employer-initiated technological innovations. Research on innovation has taken an excessively determinist form, tracing the "impact" of technical change on work and workers but rarely workers' impact on technical change. Employers do, as neoclassical accounts suggest, calculate the trade-offs among different mixes of labor, capital, and technology. But they do so not only to enhance productivity but also to maintain control over their organizations. Once again, criteria of power and quality intersect with criteria of efficiency. Workers, furthermore, care both about the character of their work and their control over it. P. K. Edwards points out the exceptional degree to which American strikes between the 1880s and the 1970s pivoted on struggles for job control rather than wages or benefits (Edwards 1981: 233–242). Although on balance American capitalists gained increasing power to reorganize labor processes, workers often won those strikes. Workers thereby affected the direction and pace of technical change.

The American printing industry exemplifies the mutual interaction of social relations and technology. The introduction of automatic typesetting machines from the Civil War onward could, in principle, have wiped out the compositors' trade. Instead, male compositors, organized in the powerful typographers' union, strengthened their monopoly over the trade's more esoteric skills, relegating women to less remunerative jobs up to the recent past. They absorbed a series of new technologies, including the advent of the word processor, into a resilient organization. New technologies have recently facilitated the entry of women into the higher reaches of printing but have by no means set the pace of change (Hartmann, Kraut & Tilly 1986: I, 29–32; see also Baron 1982).

The world of secretaries has witnessed a similar interaction. Since the largely female occupation of secretary began to displace the predominantly male world of clerks during the late nineteenth century, secretaries and their bosses have integrated a number of technical inventions—typewriters, recording machines, photocopiers, advanced telephones, computers, word processors—into their daily routines. In recent decades many large firms have reduced the ratio of word processing secretaries to executives dramatically. Yet in collaboration with the executives they work for, private secretaries have managed to exploit new machines in pursuit of their central responsibility: making life easier for their bosses. In the process they have gained considerable control over which machines their offices will buy, where the machines will stand, which computer software they will adopt, and what time schedule machine work will follow (Hartmann, Kraut & Tilly 1986: I, 32–47; Murphree 1987).

Furthermore, technologies in place reflect not just the current interaction of actors and forces, but also the residues of past decisions. The deliberate design of the slow but sure QWERTY typewriter keyboard to reduce key-stroke jams (and, some historians say, to help early typewriter salesmen tap out the word "typewriter" quickly from the top line alone) illustrates with greater clarity than usual the path-dependence of all technical innovations as a function of the ambient culture, social relations, economic organization, and adjacent technologies at each step of their development. In principle, it would now be more efficient to substitute any one of several alternative key-boards for QWERTY, but no one is likely to invest in the costs of organizing that substitution (David 1986; but for vigorous dissent see Liebowitz & Margolis 1990). Similarly, AC electrical power dominates some world regions, DC others, depending on which first gained a toehold. History has intervened.

Divisions of Labor

Adam Smith's pin factory casts a long shadow over discussions of the breadth of tasks incorporated into a single job. Describing the separation of pin making into drawing, straightening, cutting, pointing, and so on, Smith (1937) concluded that division of labor yields three cost advantages: in-creased dexterity due to specialization, reductions in set-up time, and greater opportunities for mechanization. In Smith's view, however, the extent of the market—and consequently the potential scale of production—places a limit on the division of labor.

Marxists have launched two pointed critiques of Smith's theory. Follow-ing Marx himself, Harry Braverman (1974) held that capitalists narrowed jobs in order to *deskill* them. Over the wide range of jobs, skill is not strictly correlated with job breadth: many of the least-skilled jobs (construction helper, nurse's aide) are extremely broad. But within the middle skill levels, skill tends to be tied to the diversity of tasks. Craft manufacturing workers and secretaries can perform more tasks than machine operators and file clerks. Employers can fill narrowed, deskilled jobs with less expensive grades of labor, cutting costs. In contrast with this cost-cutting explanation, Mar-glin (1974) posited that—as in the case of centralization—capitalists estab-lished a fine division of labor in order to wrest control of the labor process away from workers. Braverman stressed efficiency, Marglin power.

All of these theories call for a progressively finer and finer division of labor. But case studies demonstrate a far more complex pattern (Flynn 1985; Baran

& Parsons 1986; Hartmann, Kraut & Tilly 1986; Spenner 1988; Rumberger 1987; Kuhn 1990: 56–76). Narrowing and deskilling alternates or coincides with reskilling. Repetitive jobs are automated out of existence, while new, broad jobs are born. David Howell and Edward Wolff's (1991) careful study of changes in the skill composition of the U.S. workforce between 1960 and 1985 finds that overall, the mix of jobs shifted in the direction of *increasing* cognitive and interactive skills.

Indeed, deskilling often does not destroy skills so much as relocate them. Knowledge of production shifts from machinists to engineers or programmers (job categories that earlier did not exist in manufacturing settings). In turn, the work of engineering and programming deskills—or perhaps more accurately, stratifies into skilled and less-skilled categories (Kraft 1977). Work once performed by highly skilled physicians is now carried out by more moderately skilled registered nurses and nurse practitioners, resulting in narrowing of physician jobs but widening of nursing jobs (Chris Tilly 1984). When a health insurance company studied by Chris Tilly (1996) computerized the work of coding claims, it split the job into a far more routinized data entry job and a far more varied trouble-shooting job.

Even so, in broad terms we can identify a Taylorist trajectory toward narrower job definitions within most groups of jobs over the last century. The process moved relatively quickly in arenas such as the U.S. textile industry where managers firmly held the upper hand; it moved slowly in mining where skilled workers long controlled production via their grip on the local knowledge required for excavation. The narrowing of job definitions within many production jobs was accompanied by the emergence of new, broad jobs—engineer, maintenance person, middle manager—that consolidated functions once dispersed among other jobs. The cotton, coal, and health care industries all saw some version of these processes. The trio underwent major divisions of labor: cotton textiles early, coal mining relatively late, health care in several spurts of which one is still occurring. In the process, the average job narrowed considerably. Far from simplifying all work through finer subdivisions of tasks, however, those phases of differentiation typically divided production even more decisively between small numbers of technical tasks and larger numbers of standardized, easily learned routines. Whether tasks packaged into skilled and unskilled jobs depended not on the technologies alone but also on traditions, beliefs, and struggles within the industries. In none of the three industries can we make the case for a decisive deskilling of the average job, whereas in health care skill levels (as measured by required training time and replaceability) have surely risen significantly over the long run.

Recent innovations in management, particularly as pioneered by large Japanese corporations, have partially reversed the narrowing of production jobs. Continuous improvement, total quality management, and the like incorporate into the factory operative's job tasks that were once the domain of supervisors, quality control inspectors, maintenance mechanics, sweepers, and secretaries (Best 1990). The advantages of job splitting—whether due to heightened efficiency, cheapening of labor, or tighter control over labor—have apparently been offset by gains in worker commitment, adaptability to innovation, and increased throughput (some would say speedup) tied to broader job classifications.

What determines the spans of particular jobs? Employers combine considerations of cost minimization, flexibility, and control, within contexts shaped by a history of past practice, bargaining, and struggle. Workers and especially their unions, when present, weigh in: For example, American unions traditionally fought speedup by "job control unionism," defending the traditional bundling of tasks embodied in detailed job descriptions. Once widely established in jobs, bundles of tasks maintain a certain inertia, as employers and educational institutions organize training around certain accepted sets of tasks (secretary, chef).

Contention over the division of labor does not always pit managers against workers. Groups of workers may contend with each other over control of the content of neighboring jobs. As the nursing profession sought to expand its purview via the introduction of new, broader categories such as nurse practitioner, doctors counterattacked by promoting the creation of the physician's assistant to take on much the same tasks—but directly under the orders of a physician (Reverby 1976). Although this occupational turf battle may appear petty, much was at stake. After all, physicians had in part secured their privileged position within health care by building a symbiotic relationship with subordinate, largely female professional and technical workers. But as unionization and the women's movement stirred new ambitions among nurses, they came to threaten that cozy entente—and the combat began.

As the example of the physician's assistant illustrates, what's at stake in the division of labor is never simply who does what. Bundles of tasks and the sometimes-contested occupational labels associated with them link to status, compensation, position within a hierarchy of authority, and access to promotion. Employers and workers construct those links through collaboration and conflict, building on productivity considerations but also on a wide range of other beliefs, incorporating existing networks and axes of social segregation. In short, the complex, contentious, contingent processes that shape change in work also shape variation in work, and in particular variation among jobs. In the next few chapters, we explore how.

8
Varied Work, Segmented Work

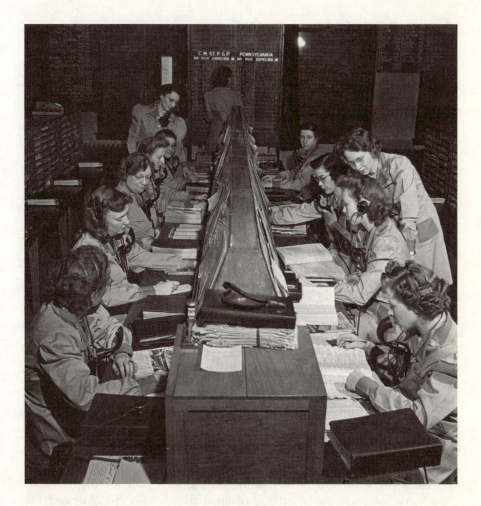

How and why does the quality of work and jobs vary? By now, it should be abundantly clear that we reject any simple functionalist logic linking a job's rewards solely to productivity. However, we do hold that job quality varies— and covaries—in systematic ways.

We start this chapter by discussing conceptual and measurement issues in job quality. Then we map covariation in key job characteristics and argue that segmentation theories offer useful leverage in understanding these patterns of covariation. In the two chapters that follow, we more closely examine variation in systems of matching, compensation, and mobility, before closing with a look to the future of labor market segmentation and internal labor markets.

A Good Job Is Hard to Define

We have defined a job as a cumulation of work contracts assigned durably and formally to a single person. Having specified what a job is, we still face conceptual difficulties on the way to defining a good job. This chapter's central conceptual issue is the extent to which various job characteristics cluster. According to a labor market segmentation perspective, particular sets of characteristics or governing rules travel in bunches: "It is not possible, as it were, to pick a rule from each category and establish a stable set of employment relationships," remarked Paul Osterman (1985: 58). Rather, only certain configurations of rules fit together. This points to multiple, qualitative distinctions between good and bad jobs. Labor market segmentation, in turn, is typically held to link production networks to other social networks of recruitment and supply—eroding the distinction between job and jobholder.

A neoclassical perspective, in contrast, adopts a hedonic view of job quality: Each job is a bundle of characteristics that may be varied at will (within certain limits) by employers; workers with varying valuations of these characteristics vote with their feet by choosing to apply for particular jobs, clearing the market. There is no reason to expect that a job that is bad in one way will also be bad in other ways; indeed, the theory of compensating differentials predicts that undesirable aspects of jobs will on average be offset by higher wages (Rosen 1986). This does not mean that all jobs are equally good, but it does imply that (1) the distinction between good and bad jobs is a finely graded continuum, rather than a qualitative break, and (2) there is no reason to expect that all (or even most) good jobs, nor all bad jobs, will have particular features in common.

Empirical research has not decisively resolved this choice between segmented and hedonic versions of job quality. Job characteristics do cluster— and, in particular, good jobs tend to be good along many dimensions—but the clustering is far from perfect or uniform. Compensating differentials are found in a few cases (particularly in compensating for the risk of death), but only a few. However, we will argue that a segmentation perspective offers more promise.

Other issues in defining job quality come in for less attention in this chapter but deserve to be recognized. For example, the term "good job" implies that certain jobs are good regardless of who holds them. In effect, we are assuming that the ranking of jobs is conceptually prior to the sorting of people among these jobs (Granovetter & Tilly 1988). But in fact, this is an oversimplification. A job's holder brings particular expectations to a job, and the employer's view of the job is colored by the worker holding it. Thus, jobholders shape jobs. In some cases they set out to mold their jobs in individualized and conscious ways (Miller 1988). In other cases, the talent, skills, or productivity of the incumbent are decisive: Established stars get paid more for acting in a movie than unknowns. But the largest impact of jobholder characteristics on jobs occurs when there is large-scale occupational or industrial segregation, such as job segregation by gender. Paula England and colleagues (1994) have demonstrated that in the United States, on average the higher the percent female in an occupation, the lower the pay offered to both women and men. Although gender segregation itself is a constant across societies, there is enormous variation in which jobs are defined as male and female (Reskin & Hartman 1986: 7). Despite this variation, women's jobs are in general valued less—indicating that jobholder characteristics, rather than the intrinsic characteristics of the job itself, contribute powerfully to the valuation process. Having noted this difficulty, we will frequently ignore it, treating jobs as independent of their holders to simplify the analysis.

Yet another two issues are familiar ones for many empirical investigators: the concealment of variation by measures of central tendency, and the choice between absolute and relative measures. Aggregation, and the use of measures of central tendency to summarize distributions, may obscure important variation. For example, based on mean characteristics, part-time jobs in the United States are bad jobs. They offer lower pay and fewer benefits and have higher turnover than other jobs. But although most part-time jobs do conform to this profile, a small subset are good jobs—in some ways better than the full-time jobs that surround them. These are part-time jobs, often at a professional level, created to meet the needs of valued employees. Such part-time jobs typically offer equal hourly wages and the standard benefit package (amounting to more benefits on a per-hour basis), long-term attachment to the business, and added schedule flexibility (Chris Tilly 1992, 1996). Similarly, tracking the mean or median wage over time as an indicator of job quality is inadequate if wage inequality is growing over time—as it has been in the United States and indeed in most of the wealthier countries.

Closely tied to issues of aggregation is the choice between absolute and relative measures of job quality. The absolute/relative distinction, of course, animates discussions over related concepts, such as poverty (Citro & Michael

1995; Ruggles 1990). Relative measures of job quality can be defined with reference to the distribution of jobs within a given country (for example, inquiring as to what proportion of jobs fall below half the median wage, or some other index of job quality), or with reference to international levels (for example, comparing one country's mean or median to those in some reference group of other countries). Absolute measures, in turn, can be defined with reference to some fixed standard (for example, the poverty line for a family of four) or with reference to the level in some base year.

A final conceptual/empirical issue is that the definition of a "good job" is itself a moving target. The meaning of a good job differs radically over time, place, culture, and class. In one very dramatic shift over time, succeeding generations of workers have placed decreasing emphasis on material rewards and more on enjoyment of the job and a feeling of making a meaningful contribution—what Daniel Yankelovich (1993) calls "expressive" values. Yankelovich documents that America has experienced a sea change in this direction. When a 1962 Gallup poll asked about the "formula for success in today's America," only 6 percent mentioned having a job that one enjoys doing; in a 1983 poll with similar wording the percentage rose to 49 percent. Among 30- to 40-year-old men and women surveyed in 1986, 60 percent stated that they placed much more emphasis on "pursuing satisfaction in a career" than their parents did; only 13 percent felt they placed less emphasis on such satisfaction.

Cross-national surveys show similar trends at work in most industrialized countries (Yankelovich et al. 1985). Particularly intriguing is the case of Sweden, whose economy's dominant sector has rapidly shifted from primary (agriculture, forestry, fisheries) to secondary (manufacturing) to tertiary (services). This shift is reflected in the attitudes toward work of successive age cohorts: The oldest cite survival and sustenance as the main reasons for work, Swedes in their middle years cite material success, and young Swedes are more likely than their elders to cite instead the realization of expressive values.

The move toward expressive values raises two important measurement issues. First, measurements of job characteristics along these dimensions are inevitably far more subjective than measures of—say—the purchasing power of a dollar of wages. Whether one can even imagine a job serving as a source of personal fulfillment is largely determined by social context—the shared values embedded in production networks and other social networks—as well as economic well-being. And second, a shift in values implies that the "weights" of different characteristics contributing to job quality are not themselves fixed. Both of these render assessment of changes in job quality over time more difficult, and indeed, no consistent time series of fulfillment on the job exists.

However, from the viewpoint of those of us struggling to measure job quality, it is comforting to note that the shift in values has not yet become a complete reversal. In no country has the emphasis on expressive values eclipsed material measures of success. In 1991, 40 percent of Americans still rated material success as most important, compared to only 22 percent putting intangibles at the top (Yankelovich 1993). Even among the Swedes, the nationality most likely to rate expressive values the most important aspect of work, fewer than one in four embraced this prioritization (Yankelovich et al. 1985). So while flagging this as a central problem for future research, we will pay little attention to jobs as a source of fulfillment in this chapter's discussion.

The State of the Art in Measuring Job Quality

The last significant advance in measuring job quality in the United States was accomplished by Christopher Jencks, Lauri Perman, and Lee Rainwater (1988). They conducted a Survey of Job Characteristics in 1980, asking each worker to rate his or her job on a (relative) ratio scale in which an average job scores 100 (so a job twice as good as the average job would be rated 200). Using the statistical technique of regression analysis, Jencks and colleagues analyzed how these scores were related to 48 job characteristics, including earnings, whether one gets dirty on the job, the degree of repetitiveness, and so on. They selected the 14 variables with the strongest relationships to workers' ratings and proposed the predicted job score based on this set of 14 variables as an Index of Job Desirability. Essentially, this empirically implements a hedonic model of job quality: Each characteristic is assumed to independently contribute to the overall quality of the job.

What makes this Index of Job Desirability (IJD) an advance? As Jencks and coauthors point out, in most work on job quality economists use a single measure—earnings; sociologists use another single measure—occupational status. Such single-measure choices are understandable since data are readily available to construct these measures. However, each of these measurement strategies has flaws. Earnings omits the impact of other job characteristics; Jencks et al. demonstrate that variation in nonmonetary elements of the IJD is more than twice as large as variation in earnings (see also Rosenthal 1989). Occupational categories combine vastly disparate jobs (consider the wide range of jobs falling within "salaried manager: business services"). Most variation in the 14 components of the IJD takes place within detailed (three-digit) occupational categories. The IJD does a better job of accounting for the impact of race, sex, education, and labor market experience on labor market success than do earnings or standard occupational status measures.

Examining the IJD immediately teaches us two lessons. First, despite their shortcomings, earnings and occupational status are not bad as quick-and-dirty measures of job quality. Both are strongly correlated with the IJD index itself. And both have the relationships with most of the components of the index that would be predicted by a segmentation perspective: a negative correlation with getting dirty on the job, a positive correlation with the number of vacation weeks, and so on. Second, both bread-and-butter job traits and issues of fulfillment at work contribute strongly to job satisfaction. The index includes earnings (+), weeks of vacation (+), and the risk of job loss (−) but also includes task repetitiveness (−), frequency of supervision (−), the average education of people in this job (+), and the ability to decide on one's own hours (+).

The problem with the IJD, of course, is that it was based on a one-time survey, rendering broader applications or tracking of change over time problematic. Furthermore, it finesses the issue of defining what a "job" is, taking workers' definitions of jobs for granted rather than distinguishing between jobs and less-formalized and durable work contracts.

Mapping Covariation in Work Contracts: Contracting and Autonomy

In spite of the spate of conceptual difficulties, we can begin to map differences among jobs. In fact, before zeroing in on labor markets and jobs, it is useful to take a step back to survey variation in work contracts more broadly conceived. What is of most interest is not simply variation in the characteristics of work, but covariation in these characteristics. Our specification of labor mechanisms provides a set of dimensions for arraying the quality of work. By examining a pair of labor mechanisms at a time, we can derive schematic maps of variation in work contracts. Figure 8.1 illustrates one approach, which ranges work contracts along dimensions of contracting (simplified to short-term monetization) and autonomy (simplified to time-discipline)—the same axes we used to trace the historical evolution of work in the previous chapter. The diagram also summarizes selected information on incentives and embeddedness.

In Figure 8.1, P stands for producer, R for recipient. "Time-discipline" refers to the immediate recipient's control over the producer's short-term disposition of work time, and "short-term monetization" refers to the prevalence of effort-by-effort, piece-by-piece, or hour-by-hour monetary compensation. Arrows portray balances of power expressed via incentives (summing the effects of compensation, coercion, and commitment), with a double-headed arrow indicating rough equality. Although a narrow "labor-management" mode of thinking suggests that producers generally dominate recipients, on a larger canvas this is obviously not true. For example, professionals often wield considerable power over their recipients—as many of us have found when consulting a doctor or lawyer.

In some cases, the diagram portrays multiple producers and recipients, with additional arrows schematizing the relationships among them, indicat-

FIGURE 8.1   Types of work contracts

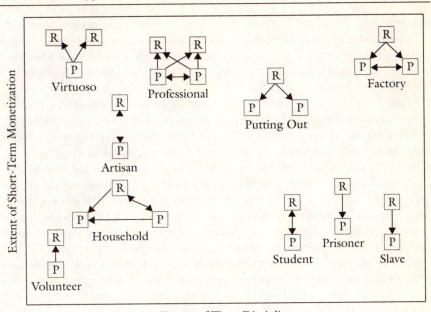

Extent of Time-Discipline

ing a single work contract's embeddedness in larger configurations of contracts. Asymmetries of connectedness generally give advantages to the connected side, as when journeymen in a well-organized craft divide and conquer the competing local entrepreneurs who employ them. Most work contracts connect with many other contracts, placing producers and recipients within larger hierarchies, coalitions, and markets. Even in terms of hierarchy within businesses, it is not only managers who manage. David Gordon (1996, Table 2.1) found that in a 1991 survey of the U.S. workforce, 80 percent of managers reported managerial or supervisory responsibilities, but so did 29 percent of professionals, 16 percent of clerical or sales workers, 12 percent of skilled workers, and even 2 percent of unskilled workers. In our diagram, we can only begin to capture this cat's cradle of power relations.

Starting at the upper left of Figure 8.1, a virtuoso works under little time-discipline from others, receives money performance by performance, and exerts considerable control over recipients who are little connected with each other; in these regards, a violin virtuoso differs little from the streetwise operator of a shell game. Industries centering on virtuosi, such as the performing arts, typically bring together organizers who are seeking to coordinate the work of virtuosi in the production of just enough innovation that paying audiences will recognize the novelty without finding it utterly bewildering.

Meanwhile, would-be virtuosi who seek to create their own individual styles and inventions compete for stardom. Interaction between organizers and virtuosi forms industries in which performers work by the project on short-term contracts, often hold multiple contracts simultaneously, frequently experience unemployment, and mostly fail to reach the individual opportunity for virtuosity that attracted them in the first place (Menger & Gurgand 1996).

Move right and downward in the diagram to see similarities and differences between virtuoso industries, on one side, and professional, artisanal, and putting-out systems, on the other. Strongly connected free professionals wield individual and collective influence over recipients of their services, who, like the virtuoso's clients, are little connected. In a putting-out system, a merchant contracts with a number of separate, relatively unconnected producers who nevertheless produce at rhythms the merchant's orders dominate, whereas in the drive system typical of assembly-line factories connected workers produce under close surveillance from their boss. Artisans sell individually produced objects to consumers on terms of relative equality.

Moving to the lower half of the diagram, households mix relations of equality and inequality in a fairly unmonetized world, with producers often exerting power over other producers but rarely under great time-discipline. Many unpaid volunteers work under little time-discipline, setting their own terms of service to recipients, whereas equally unremunerated slaves commonly work under great time-discipline imposed by the recipient of their products. A legal prisoner, in this illustration, resembles a slave but works under less time-discipline with greater short-term monetary return. Although students sometimes feel like slaves or prisoners, finally, they actually enjoy more control over their own time and exercise considerably greater influence over teachers by means of mutual commitment.

This diagram limits consideration of embeddedness to other producers and recipients located within a narrow perimeter of a given contract. But clearly other connections greatly determine the asymmetry of power and the ability of a given party to rely on coercion or commitment. The slaveholder, the teacher, and the straw boss all depend on a broader set of power relations to exercise their authority. The actual location of work contracts in this space depends on their relations to a larger web of networks and contracts, not all of them work-generated or even work-related.

As we saw in Chapter 3, work contracts in cotton, coal, and health care have crawled crabwise across this map over time, heading to the northeast in a process of proletarianization. Weavers of cotton shifted from household workers and artisans, to participants in a putting-out system, to factory workers. Coal hewers were able to stand their ground longer as craft workers (in close proximity, on Figure 8.1, to professionals and artisans) but eventually succumbed to mechanization and management control that made their work similar to factory work. In both Britain and the United States, health care of two centuries ago was shifting from households toward professional labor. Centralization of health care in hospitals and clinics continued to shrink the role of household care and added layers of less-professional workers subordinate to the physicians, subject to greater time-discipline and payment based on wages rather than fees. At the bottom of this hierarchy, workers in hospital laundries, kitchens, and instrument-processing departments have long labored in conditions little different from a factory. More recently, nationalized medicine in Britain and managed care in the United States have reshaped physicians' work contracts, shifting many of them away from their cherished status as independent professionals and toward salaried, time-disciplined activity (though U.S. physicians' median salary of $150,000 in 1994 still sets them apart from factory workers!).

We could fill in other types of work contracts, characterizing police, sailors, flight attendants, commission salespeople, prostitutes and their pimps, gangs of thieves, scientists within bureaucracies, and many more, each contract having its distinctive combination of time-discipline, monetization, incentives, and embeddedness. But this exercise already suggests a number of conclusions:

1. Work contracts vary systematically as a function of time-discipline and short-term monetization (more generally, of autonomy and contracting).
2. History and culture play significant parts in the character of such contracts (as illustrated by the disparate locations of factories, households, and slaves).
3. Relations to third parties deeply affect the character and enforcement of work contracts.
4. Full-fledged labor markets form especially in the zone combining high monetization with extensive time-discipline—the figure's upper-right corner.

Labor markets form in that zone rather than elsewhere because without monetization and time-discipline holders of capital have great difficulty detaching labor power from control of other claimants, who frequently strive at cross-purposes to them. Whatever long-run rationality might have prescribed, in the short run peasants, independent artisans, homeworkers, and other petty-commodity producers have generally resisted permanent incorporation into paid employment in jobs defined and disciplined by capitalists or bureaucrats. Through their advantages to capitalists, however, monetized, time-disciplined forms of production have drawn capital away from their otherwise-organized rivals and thereby reduced the viability of those rival forms.

Mapping Labor Markets and Their Relatives

Figure 8.2 closes in on the zone of high monetization and time-discipline, locating a number of different work contracts in or adjacent to labor markets. It summarizes the manner in which various sorts of contracts satisfy requirements for efficiency, quality, and power. Work lies within the labor market if its contracts integrate workers, employers, jobs, hiring, labor recruitment networks, and labor supply networks. Although labor markets in general give employers considerable choice among competing workers when it comes to hiring, job assignment, promotion, transfer, and separation, employers adopt very different incentive systems in response to worker power, available models of organization, and the requirements of production and sale. In the labor market, systems of loyalty characterize labor market jobs whose conditions of work encourage and rely heavily on commitment—which by no means precludes perquisites and high salaries as additional incentives. Loyalty systems shade off into prize arrangements offering premiums, bonuses, commissions, or enhanced status and privileges in reward for good performance. Tournament labor markets, such as internal labor markets for top management positions, combine characteristics of the two; as its prize, this sort of tournament offers the opportunity to be promoted.

Where employers see workers as more interchangeable and expendable, we find payment by results (PBR) and drive. PBR compensates employees for what they actually produce, either individually or collectively, in the form of piecework, taskwork, commissions, subcontracting, and similar arrangements. The system of drive, in contrast, gives employers extensive control over their workers' time and effort by means of monitoring, standardization of tasks, penalties, and threats of job loss. On the whole, incentive systems in the region of extensive time-discipline rely less heavily on the operation of previously existing interpersonal networks, whether work-generated or borrowed from outside of work. Of course, no sharp boundary exists between prize and payment by results, nor between loyalty systems and the fear-based system of drive. These labels simply mark out a few prominent clusters among the many conditions under which producers in labor markets actually work. However, within labor markets, short-term monetization and time-discipline correlate: The most common arrangements range more or less along the diagonal defined by roughly equivalent increases in both variables.

Labor Market Segmentation

Via Figures 8.1 and 8.2, we have asserted that work contracts—and in particular, jobs—cluster in certain areas of the planes of variation defined by various mechanisms of work and not in other areas. And indeed, there is plentiful evidence that many job characteristics covary systematically. For instance,

FIGURE 8.2   Labor markets and adjacent organizations of work

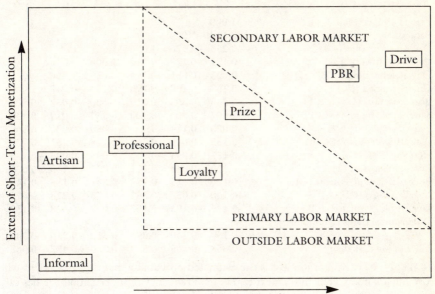

Jencks, Perman, and Rainwater (1988) demonstrate that virtually all of the characteristics that make a job "good" are pairwise positively correlated (Table 8.1). Higher earnings, access to on-the-job training, and ability to decide one's own hours are positively correlated with one another—and negatively correlated with frequent supervision, work repetitiveness, and the perceived risk of job loss.

Such empirical regularities have inspired the concept of segmented labor markets. The notion of labor market segmentation dates back at least as far as John Stuart Mill's *Principles of Political Economy;* Mill wrote of "noncompeting groups" in the labor market for whom hiring and wages were governed by custom and institutions (such as guilds and professions), rather than market competition. In the post–World War II United States, renewed interest in issues of industrial relations and poverty sparked attention to segmentation: Clark Kerr (1954) wrote of the "balkanization" of labor markets, and some years later Peter Doeringer and Michael Piore (1971) popularized the term "segmentation."

Indeed, segmentation implies not simply correlated mechanisms of work but also barriers to mobility among these clusters. Not uncommonly, workers spend most of their work lives within a single segment. Work in each segment operates under different rules, has different systems of qualification, and recruits from different networks. Employers and incumbent workers

TABLE 8.1   Correlations Among Selected Job Characteristics

	C1	C2	C3	C4	C5	C6
Frequent supervision (C1)	1.000					
Vacation weeks (C2)	0.149	1.000				
Decides own hours (C3)	−0.255	−0.170	1.000			
Gets dirty at work (C4)	0.121	−0.127	−0.117	1.000		
On-the-job training (C5)	−0.023	0.031	0.168	−0.059	1.000	
Union contract (C6)	0.167	0.198	−0.290	0.156	−0.147	1.000
Boss has a boss (C7)	0.343	0.362	−0.319	−0.100	−0.032	0.304
State/local employee (C8)	−0.002	0.206	−0.100	−0.053	−0.019	0.120
Federal employee (C9)	0.020	0.184	−0.107	−0.050	0.023	0.169
Proportion repetitive (C10)	0.132	−0.049	−0.264	0.148	−0.261	0.125
Hours > 35 (C11)	−0.137	−0.044	0.240	0.093	0.096	−0.175
Risk of job loss (C12)	0.120	−0.043	−0.111	0.077	−0.113	0.071
Educational requirements (C13)	−0.100	0.125	0.283	−0.381	0.183	−0.148
Log(Earnings) (C14)	−0.140	0.057	0.342	−0.058	0.228	0.025
Log(Earnings squared) (C15)	−0.129	−0.193	0.157	−0.039	−0.048	−0.112
Occupational status (Duncan score) (C16)	−0.159	0.140	0.294	−0.410	0.210	−0.209
Index of job desirability (F3)	−0.368	0.165	0.529	−0.370	0.427	−0.085

NOTE: N=621. Risk of job loss is the estimated probability that the respondent will lose the job completely in the next two years. Frequency of supervision scale has values for never (0), yearly or more but less than daily (0.5), daily (1). Other variables are self-explanatory.

SOURCE: Christopher Jencks, Lauri Perman & Lee Rainwater, "What Is a Good Job? A New Measure of Labor-Market Success," *American Journal of Sociology* 93 (1988):1322–1357 (Table A.1).

(*continues*)

alike defend the boundaries of various segments—especially those associated with relative privilege—from "inappropriate" interlopers. Appropriateness most assuredly entails skill (neither under- nor overqualified job seekers are appropriate) but also spills over to ascriptive characteristics and network ties. Labor market segmentation articulates with network segregation to produce categorical inequality.

What, then, are the segments? Let us limit our attention to the stratification of jobs—not of industries, firms, or demographic groups, although the stratifying principles of such alternative units of analysis certainly share much in common with job segmentation. Even within this limitation, labor market taxonomies for the United States have proliferated (Althauser & Kalleberg 1981; Caplow 1954; Edwards 1979; Gordon, Edwards & Reich 1982). Nonetheless, behind the welter of terminology there lurks a fairly strong consensus. First of all, we can usefully distinguish between primary and secondary labor markets. Primary labor market jobs have well-defined paths for advancement and the protection of rules of due process. Jobs in secondary

TABLE 8.1 *(continued)*

C7	C8	C9	C10	C11	C12	C13	C14	C15	C16	F3
1.000										
0.104	1.000									
0.150	−0.082	1.000								
0.091	−0.107	−0.030	1.000							
−0.279	0.041	−0.094	−0.176	1.000						
0.185	−0.051	−0.007	0.171	−0.092	1.000					
0.010	0.160	0.006	−0.378	0.115	−0.108	1.000				
−0.138	−0.022	−0.005	−0.304	0.349	−0.142	0.350	1.000			
−0.164	−0.093	−0.056	−0.037	−0.006	0.076	0.058	0.038	1.000		
−0.001	0.100	0.097	−0.361	−0.062	−0.152	0.588	0.321	0.029	1.000	
−0.259	−0.036	0.157	−0.536	0.438	−0.313	0.625	0.725	0.147	0.535	1.000

labor markets, in contrast, are unstable, high-turnover, unprotected, and typically low-skilled and low-paid. Turning back to Figure 8.2, the line between primary and secondary labor markets demarcates craft, professional, loyalty, and prize systems from payment by results and drive.

In turn, primary labor markets have during this century segmented into industrial, salaried, and craft jobs (Osterman 1987, 1988). The industrial labor market, which was, until recently, the standard model for manufacturing production workers, is defined by long tenure, job ladders, on-the-job skill acquisition, narrow job definitions, little decision-making power, and job security tempered by layoffs. The salaried labor market, on the other hand, corresponds to that of managers or company-based professional/technical workers, and again features long tenure, job ladders, and on-the-job training, but also has broad and flexible job definitions, substantial decision-making power and discretion, and an implicit lifetime employment guarantee.

Both industrial and salaried labor markets, then, entail internal labor markets—sets of jobs connected by rules of mobility and promotion and relatively sealed off from external access except at selected ports of entry. The craft labor market characterizes the situation of workers like the skilled carpenter or computer programmer: short tenure, loyalty to craft rather than to a particular firm, advancement by shifting from one firm to another or by accumulating skill rather than by climbing a ladder in a particular firm, and skills acquired off the job (through apprenticeship or education). Segmentation is a historical phenomenon. Sumner Slichter wrote in 1919 (p.436) that "employers so far have not fully appreciated as a means of combating unionism the tremendous possibilities of the plan of organizing the work in their plants into minutely subdivided jobs . . . [with]systematic lines of promotion." On the other hand, by 1971, Doeringer and Piore estimated (perhaps a bit generously) that 80 percent of the workforce toiled in internal labor markets with such characteristics.

History does not stand still. One obvious problem in applying these categories to United States labor markets is that the industrial and salaried segments, which had been relatively stable since the 1940s (and in the case of some larger companies, since the 1920s or even earlier), have been changing significantly since the early 1980s. Among the rank-and-file jobs typically grouped in industrial labor markets, "high performance work organization" management approaches have in many cases broadened job descriptions, amplified worker decision-making power, and expanded the role of off-job training and education. On the other hand, downsizing has shaken the implicit lifetime employment guarantee formerly accorded to large numbers of white-collar workers and, to a lesser extent, to blue-collar workers as well. Thus, elements of the craft and secondary labor markets have begun to grow in jobs formerly characterized by industrial or salaried structures. In management jargon, the model has shifted from one of open-ended employment to one of employability (in which workers gain new skills but have no assurance that their jobs will continue over the long term); internal labor markets are becoming increasingly externalized. At the end of Chapter 10, we will examine the extent of these changes—and will argue that our approach to labor market segmentation can help to explain them and forecast additional changes.

Logics of Segmentation

Theories of segmentation have typically adopted either functional or historical logics. Consider a few instances of each. Functional accounts, focusing on efficiency, include:

- Internal labor markets as incentive systems. The promise of advancement can help to deter shirking and to retain workers with valuable skills or proprietary knowledge. Marking an extreme in such systems were the company towns and family succession that characterized nineteenth-century coal mining.

- Division of demand into stable and fluctuating portions. Such segmentation of product demand may divide large firms with primary labor markets from small firms with secondary ones (Berger & Piore 1980) or may account for core and peripheral employees in a single company (Appelbaum 1987).
- Construction of system of matching, incentive, and mobility to meet varying patterns of availability of information about workers' performance. Thus, Arthur Stinchcombe (1990b, ch. 7) pointed out that workers with readily observed individual productivities—such as professional athletes—are recruited, compensated, and promoted based on those productivities; those holding jobs characterized by routine teamwork are rewarded based on supervisors' evaluations; and professionals (such as physicians) facing idiosyncratic, widely varying tasks are judged by peer review.

Clearly, the dimensions of efficiency which might underpin segmentation are quite various! But efficiency, multifaceted as it is, does not suffice to explain observed labor market segmentation. History once more intervenes. For instance, as Walter Licht (1991, p.71) has noted, the profusion of personnel policies in U.S. businesses is "notable for the persistence of old forms and old methods." And the deliberate, hard-fought creation of professional status by physicians and nurses illustrates the power of collective strategy. Historical accounts point to:

- The enormous power of inertia, enforced both by efficiency (based in the familiarity of current ways of doing things) and the defense of vested interests. The flexible Stinchcombe (1986, ch. 10), never one to pin himself down to a single explanation, observed that many jobs still reflect the organizational forms of their era of introduction: A case in point is the craft structures of the building trades.
- The tug-of-war of class struggle. Gordon, Edwards, and Reich (1982) attributed the initial homogenization and later segmentation of the U.S. proletariat to employer efforts to assert control over their workforces—first by deskilling the workers and later, in response to industrial unionism, by dividing them.

We repeat: Both functional and historical logics are necessary to explain segmentation. Incorporating history, and historically shaped culture, allows for far more satisfactory explanations of segmentation. Taking history into account, moreover, requires recognizing several principles. First, the historical unfolding of labor market segmentation is highly contingent. Although work has indeed systematically shifted to the "northeast" (toward greater time-discipline and short-term monetization) in Figure 8.1, the locations of particular jobs within that northeast corner have been set in large part by waves of bargaining. Teleological tales of the inevitable order imposed by industrialization offer little assistance in specifying these locations. Indeed, although the northeasterly trend is dominant, it is not without exceptions. As managed care has shortened hospital stays, it has shifted a portion of health care from the highly monetized, time-disciplined world of the hospital to home care—provided by less time-disciplined home health workers but also in large part by uncompensated family and friends (Glazer 1993).

Second, bargaining is a multiparty process. Employers do not set the matrix of labor market segmentation on their own. Workers, especially where unionized, push and pull on the boundaries, rules, and other features of labor market segments (Rubery 1978). For example, CIO industrial unions in U.S. industries such as longshore strenuously strove—often with success—to convert secondary labor markets into primary ones (Kahn 1976). The state has also stepped in repeatedly, often interceding when conflict between businesses and workers sharpened.

Third, patterns of historical transformation have differed markedly from one section of the labor market to another. Such variation renders broad generalizations risky. Gordon, Edwards, and Reich (1982) described the years from the 1870s to World War II as a period of homogenization of the U.S. working class and the subsequent decades as an era of segmentation. These broad strokes work tolerably well in depicting the labor markets faced by white men. But for white women and both women and men of color, a virtually opposite characterization proves more accurate (Albelda & Tilly 1994). The late nineteenth and early twentieth centuries were, on the whole, times of intense segmentation by race and gender, with African-Americans and Latinos concentrated in agriculture and domestic service (and Asians as well concentrated in a few sectors), middle-class women working primarily in the home, and women of all races and classes facing tremendous occupational segregation. In contrast, World War II and the postwar boom pulled, and the Civil Rights and women's movements pushed, such groups into a much wider array of workplaces, occupations, and industries—a (limited) integration into the mainstream of labor markets. For those exiting housework or sharecropping, the period was marked not so much by integration as by belated proletarianization (a process Gordon et al. [1982] associated with the 1820s to 1890s).

Segmentation groups and separates jobs. It does so by grouping and separating the seven mechanisms that mark a job or any other set of work contracts: incentive, embeddedness, contracting, autonomy, matching, mobility, and training. In the next two chapters we examine job variation and segmentation in more detail, by tracking variation in three particular mechanisms: matching, incentive, and mobility.

9
Inequality at Work: Hiring

*What determines a firm's decision to hire someone? The answer is
simple. A profit-maximizing firm hires someone if it thinks there's
money to be made by doing so. Unless there is, the firm won't hire the
person. So for a firm to decide whether to hire someone, it must compare the worker's* marginal revenue product *(the marginal revenue
it expects to earn from selling the additional worker's output) with
the wage that it expects to pay the additional worker.*

—David Colander, Economics
(1995: 666; emphasis in original)

*[Forty years ago in Los Angeles] the work force was Caucasian and
the lower end of the work force, the labor end, was black. . . . Through
civil rights and so forth, the black community elevated themselves
into positions that weren't there [previously]. . . . As that work force
disappeared and the great migration from the Latin countries [took
place], it became a Latino environment. We put an ad in the paper
we would have had very few Caucasian applicants. Even very few
black applicants.*

  *It seems that the black kids maybe just don't want to work. . . .
Why should they take an entry level job when they can make more on
some sort of welfare, unemployment, or dealing drugs? We have a lot
of poor people in the city, a lot of homeless, people asking for
money. . . . I was in the L.A. airport a while back and a black man
walks up to me and says, "Hey man, I need five bucks." It is a
"gimme" attitude. I can remember as a kid a man coming into my
father's store and saying, "I need money, can I sweep the floors for
fifty cents?" But that is not the way it is anymore, now it's "can you
spare a quarter" or "can you spare a dollar." Nobody wants to work
for it.*

*—White owner of a small manufacturing shop
in a Los Angeles suburb,
quoted in Moss & Tilly 1996: 265–266*

FOCUS GROUP MODERATOR: *What do you think employers
  are looking for when you walk through the door? What type of
  person are they looking for?*
RESPONDENT *(respondents are all young, inner-city black
  men): Hardworking. Neat, clean, hardworking.*
RESP: *Easy-tempered. Well, somebody who's going to keep their
  temper in check.*
RESP: *Qualifications. . . . Experience that would pertain to
  whatever.*
MOD: *What else do you think they're looking for?*
RESP: *White workers.*
MOD: *Why do you think white workers?*

> *RESP: Because they think we don't know what we're doing, that's how they see it.*
>
> *RESP: Because they know that their white government has all the stuff and the white students get school and everything. They already know what to expect from a white employee.*
>
> *RESP: Because there's so much negative about being black. So, that's in your mind. Everybody has that mind, they don't even think about that, so, if you're white and the guy's white, he's going to want someone of his own blood, because he's white.*
>
> *RESP: What a lot of young brothers don't understand is, the racism is not something—you can let the racism hold you back or you can overcome it. But, you also have to be realistic, a lot of people don't like to talk about race in this country—race is something that's not supposed to be talked about in government service and so forth, and you have to realize that, yes, you are [at] a disadvantage because of who you are, but I think young brothers need to be educated to the point of this can be something that I can overcome.*
>
> *Focus group of young, inner-city black men in the Boston area (Jobs for the Future 1995: 13–18)*

Ask an economist about who gets hired and how much they get paid, and typically you will get an answer that focuses on productivity. To be fair, economist David Colander, whom we quote above, does add, on a subsequent page, that "social interaction plays a role in determining wages. If you get along with the manager, his estimate of your marginal productivity is likely to be higher than if you don't" (1995: 670). But his main discussion addresses productivity, whereas the role of social interaction only merits a sidebar—an accurate reflection of the relative status of these two considerations in economic theory.

On the other hand, ask an employer or job seeker, and you will typically get an answer that emphasizes social interaction far more strongly—often packaged with moral lessons about enterprise, hard work, and opportunity or the lack thereof. Yes, productivity is part of the picture ("hard-working" and "qualifications" speak to productivity) but so are issues of power and organizational maintenance ("neat, clean" and "easy-tempered" have less to do with productivity per se than with the manager-worker relationship), and so are stereotypes and attitudes ("black kids maybe just don't want to work"; "they think we don't know what we're doing"). If you ask someone older, they will often cite historical change, as did the Los Angeles manufacturer quoted above.

We argue that *all* of these insights have value in explaining workforce inequality. It is necessary to combine functional explanations that highlight productivity and historical explanations that trace the emergence, consolidation, and evolution of social relations. The most visible (and most readily measurable) elements of workforce inequality are who gets hired, how much they get paid, and whether they get promoted. These three elements correspond to three of our seven mechanisms: matching, incentive (which includes compensation), and mobility. To illuminate inequality, we zero in on these three mechanisms—matching in this chapter, incentive and mobility in the next. For each, two overlapping questions stand out: What are the main systems of incentive, matching, and mobility, and what determines which system will prevail in each work contract? And cutting across the various systems, what generally determines who will be hired, how much they will be paid, and whether they will be promoted? For matching, incentive, and mobility alike, there are five main influences, all of which we have encountered before: productivity, preferences, networks, bargaining, and inertia.

Connections Among Matching, Incentive, and Mobility

Matching, incentive, and mobility are connected processes. Remember that work contracts specify, among other things, relations among workers and rewards accruing to the parties. In bundling certain work contracts together, employers and workers therefore simultaneously *link* jobs and *value* them relative to each other. Jobs link—one important form of embeddedness—to the extent that the same work contracts require interaction of their occupants. They differ in value to the extent that the compensation, coercion, and commitment attached to them differs. Valuation does not always produce a single continuous hierarchy: One job offers higher pay, another more pleasant working conditions, a third more power, and so on. But in segmented labor markets these varied rewards tend to be correlated—allowing us to learn much from focusing on the contours of compensation alone or from promotion opportunities alone. In bureaucratized firms, moreover, both the linking and the valuation acquire visible official expression in the hierarchical forms of organization charts, perquisites, pay scales, and standard job progressions. Even in the absence of such devices, however, links and values form in the very process of bundling.

We should take care, however, to distinguish linking and valuation from **matching** of persons with jobs—which will be addressed in more detail in the rest of this chapter. Linking and valuation relate jobs to each other, whereas matching links persons to jobs. Figure 9.1 summarizes the distinction. In firms, gross person-to-job matching occurs chiefly through hiring, contracting, promotion, separation, and transfers, whereas fine matching takes the form of day-to-day modification in a jobholder's work contracts. In the course of gross matching, the parties sometimes also renegotiate a job's

FIGURE 9.1   Linking, valuing, and matching

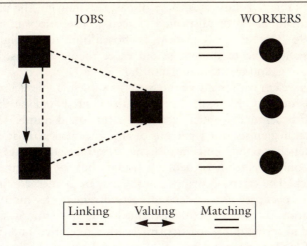

contents, links, and value, as when a star athlete gets major concessions for signing with a failing team. Employers typically shape particular jobs, furthermore, in the light of ideas about who will be available to fill them; in announcements of job qualifications, they adapt content, links, and values to anticipated matches. We separate definition, linking, valuation, and matching of jobs for analytical purposes, but in practice they interact incessantly.

In a nineteenth-century cotton mill, for example, "mule spinner" designated a job with well-defined, crucial responsibilities: work contracts tying the position to other workers, to helpers, and to foremen. Although the job centered on tending a machine, its actual execution depended heavily on its *links* to other jobs. In terms of pay, prestige, and autonomy, it clearly ranked between helper and foreman; it occupied an intermediate *value*. A man acquired the job either by moving up from helper or by the foreman's hiring him from outside; two forms of *matching* filled the job. But an experienced mule spinner recruited his own helper, negotiated his own working conditions within customary limits, imposed his own style on daily work routines, and struck up his own ties of cooperation and command with fellow workers. Thus linking, valuing, and matching intertwined. Nonetheless, we can to some degree unthread matching and view the forces shaping the matching process for a given job.

Matching Workers and Jobs

As we scan the landscape of work, we do not find various ascriptive categories of people spread uniformly across it. Divisions and disproportions by gender, race, ethnicity, and nationality, among other categories, sculpt the topography. Table 9.1 illustrates these disparities, showing the proportions who were female, black, or Hispanic in selected occupations in the United States in 1994. The set of occupations is chosen both to highlight occupational segregation and to illuminate our three thematic industries: health care, coal mining, and textile manufacturing.

Familiar as we are with many of the patterns shown, Table 9.1 still has the capacity to astound. Can it really be that in the United States at the verge of the twenty-first century, women account for (in round numbers) 100 percent of dental hygienists and 1 percent of auto mechanics? That 38 percent of farmworkers but only 2 percent of farm operators and managers are Hispanic? That only 3 percent of dental assistants but 29 percent of nursing aides are black? The variation swings most widely by gender, confirming that at the level of occupations, gender segregation remains far more profound than segregation by race and ethnicity. But blacks and Latinos, as well, are concentrated in certain jobs—particularly service, operative, and (in the case of Latinos) farm labor occupations.

Because of the occupational breakdown that the data are drawn from (which is not, after all, an industry breakdown), we learn more about health care than about mining or textiles from Table 9.1. Health care is a predominantly female industry: For example, managers and technical workers in health care fields are almost twice as likely to be women as in the economy as a whole. But even within this largely feminine domain, gender variations by occupation are striking. Dental hygienists and assistants are overwhelmingly women; dentists are overwhelmingly men. Men only rarely fill jobs as nurses or aides but fill almost four out of five physician jobs. Blacks concentrate at the bottom of the health care hierarchy. Compare the black shares among physicians, registered nurses, dietitians, licensed practical nurses, and aides: As status and pay decline in this chain of caregivers, the proportion black consistently increases. There is little pattern among Hispanics, who have made relatively limited inroads into health care occupations.

The table does give us a glimpse at mining and textiles as well. Women have a near lock on jobs as textile machine operators—a presence quite distinct from women's underrepresentation in most machine operator jobs. Women engineers are even rarer than women machine operators. And mining—represented here by extractive occupations—equals auto repair in terms of women's nearly absolute invisibility. Blacks and Latinos crowd operative jobs, and particularly textile machine operator jobs, but are generally underrepresented among miners and engineers.

What's going on here? Labor market organization and social segregation are logically separate processes, but the maneuvers of employers and workers often make them coincide. A closer look at matching helps to understand why and how. Matching actually comprises three flows: hiring, promotion,

TABLE 9.1   Percent of Workers in Selected Occupations Who Are Female, Black, or Hispanic, United States, 1994

	Percent Who Are:		
	Female	*Black*	*Hispanic*
Total	46%	10%	9%
Executive, administrative, managerial	43	7	5
Managers, medicine and health	80	5	4
Administrators, education and related fields	62	12	5
Professional	53	7	4
Industrial engineers	15	6	4
Physicians	22	4	5
Dentists	13	4	5
Registered nurses	94	9	3
Dietitians	92	14	2
Technical	52	10	5
Dental hygienists	100	0	3
Licensed practical nurses	95	19	4
Radiologic technicians	74	8	8
Engineering technologists and technicians	20	7	6
Sales	49	7	7
Supervisors and proprietors	28	4	3
Cashiers	84	10	5
Administrative support, including clerical	79	12	8
Supervisors	60	14	7
Secretaries	99	8	6
Postal clerks, except mail carriers	44	28	8
Service	60	17	13
Private household cleaners, servants	96	20	31
Firefighting occupations	2	9	5
Dental assistants	97	3	10
Nursing aides, orderlies, attendants	89	29	9
Precision production, craft, repair	9	8	10
Automobile mechanics	1	7	11
Extractive occupations	1	6	9
Precision production	24	9	12
Operators, fabricators, laborers	24	15	14
Machine operators, assemblers, inspectors	38	15	15
Textile, apparel, and furnishings machine operators	74	22	20
Textile sewing machine operators	86	19	24
Motor vehicle operators	11	15	10
Farming, forestry, and fishing	19	5	17
Farm operators and managers	25	0	2
Farm workers	17	7	38

SOURCE: U.S. Department of Commerce, *Statistical Abstract of the United States, 1995* (Washington, D.C.: U.S. Government Printing Office, 1995), Table 649.

and separation (whether through quits or discharges). Although promotion and especially hiring generally receive the most attention, differing rates of exit may also greatly affect the employment mix. For example, a personnel official at a large local government agency told Moss and Tilly (1996: 261), "My own personal feeling is that a lot of these young black men who are being tough, scare some of their supervisors. And so rather than address their behavior problems and deal with the issues, [the supervisors] will back away until they can find a way to get rid of them." Nonetheless, similar factors shape hiring, promotion, and separation. We will address promotion in more detail in the next chapter; here we simplify by primarily confining our attention to hiring.

In the simplest neoclassical models, the matching of people with jobs occurs through a mutual search process in which employers search for the cheapest worker they can find who possesses the human capital required for entry into a given job (or the most highly skilled worker available at a specified wage), whereas workers search for the most highly rewarded job they can get with the human capital they possess. Both sides of the search are driven by the quest for productivity: on the one hand productivity in production, on the other hand productivity toward the worker's goal of maximizing satisfaction. In gross, this standard theory has some merit. Within limits, employers do prefer cheaper and/or better-qualified labor, the emphasis on qualifications generally rising with the amount of capital at risk per worker.

In detail, however, the standard theory is obviously false. Employers do not make effective searches for the cheapest potential workers of a given quality, who in the United States typically consist of women, older workers, and members of racial minorities; only by including gender, age, and race in the "quality" of labor power required can we make standard theory explain such anomalies. As Reskin and Roos (1990) put it, job queues describe the relative desirability of jobs from the perspective of workers, but "quality" queues (in the Reskin-Roos analysis, gender queues) order the desirability of workers from the perspective of employers; workers who stand higher in quality queues move up farther in job queues. All parties bring with them larger agendas than matching price, quality, and quantity. A more complete model must incorporate the social relations that construct these larger agendas.

We can broaden the formulation of matching, then, by adding to productivity four other important factors: preferences, networks, bargaining, and inertia. These factors are not fully distinct: They are overlapping and mutually reinforcing. How does each structure the matching process?

Productivity in Matching

Productivity, in the form of *worker qualifications,* constitutes the beginning and end of human capital theory's account of matching but only the beginning of our discussion. The relevant qualifications depend crucially on the product or service in question and on the objectives pursued by the work recipient. Aleksandr Solzhenitzyn (1975: 265–266) described the disjunction between the reward system in a concentration camp and that in the outside world: "In camp it was advantageous to be a medical assistant, a barber, an accordion player, I daren't go any higher. You would get along all right if you were a tinsmith, a glass blower, or an automobile mechanic. But woe on you if you were a geneticist, or, God help you, a philosopher, an art historian, then you had had it. You would kick the bucket on general work in two weeks."

On the other hand, apparently disparate work situations may call for very similar qualifications. Peter Reuter, Robert MacCoun, and Patrick Murphy (1990) discovered that among young men in the Washington, D.C., area who reported selling drugs, three-quarters also had earnings from a legitimate job, with the large majority working five days a week or more at paid employment. In fact, men who earned more per hour from drug dealing, also tended to earn a higher wage in legitimate jobs! This correlation would not surprise petty-criminal-turned-author Nathan McCall:

> I quickly discovered that dealing wasn't as easy as it seemed. Selling reefer was a round-the-clock hustle that required more time and energy than I wanted to invest. . . . I eventually built up a decent clientele but discovered that that, too, had its drawbacks. . . . Dudes always wanted me to meet them in out-of-the-way places to deliver the goods. . . . I had to . . . work the streets and stay there most of the time. . . . Among the dealers the competition was stiff. I tried to gain an edge by offering more weight than the next man, which cut down on my profits unless I padded the reefer with a little oregano. I'd also try to lure buys by putting out the word that I had some exotic brand of reefer known for its potency. . . . I also found out that I damned near had to be an accountant to stay in business. I had to save the money I made and invest and manage it properly so that I could reinvest. . . . Eventually, I realized it was too much work for me to try to hawk herb alone [so I hired a friend]. . . . With him dealing for me, I had to keep track of how much dope I gave him to sell and how much money I was due. . . . I finally had to admit that I lacked the discipline to be a good dealer. Dealing drugs is harder than any job I've had, then or since. To this day, I laugh when I hear folks say drug dealers are lazy people who don't want to work. (McCall 1994: 124–127)

In short, successful drug dealing requires hard work, discipline, and skills including marketing, finance, accounting, and management—very similar to the skills required of other kinds of entrepreneurs and managers.

Employers screen workers on a variety of educational credentials, experience criteria, and demonstrations or certifications of skill. Screening plays a particularly critical role in what the M.I.T. Commission on Industrial Productivity (Dertouzos et al. 1989, ch. 6) calls "pattern A" countries such as the United States, Sweden, and Britain, where most specialized skills are acquired via formal education, as opposed to "pattern B" countries (Japan, West Germany) where employer training confers most general as well as specialized work skills. In Canada, educational requirements for entry-level jobs have been rising with the rated cognitive complexity of those jobs for more than half a century (Hunter 1988). In other words, the matching mechanism interacts intimately with the training mechanism.

Since access to education is stratified by class, race, and gender (Bowles and Gintis 1976), screening on educational credentials filters according to these categories. Education, however, has little impact on employment prospects for large realms of the world of work. Based on interviews with young men in three predominantly white working-class neighborhoods of Boston, Howard Wial (1991: 406) reports that "higher education . . . is dismissed as relatively unimportant [for the transition from secondary to primary jobs], even by workers who had attended college."

Screening on experience or work-acquired skills can also reproduce categorical inequality. The personnel director of a machine shop in the Detroit area told Moss and Tilly (1992) she doesn't get black applicants because "I don't know of anybody [black] who has ever worked in a machine shop, that's done the work." Workers applying for jobs in this middle-sized shop are expected to have experience and training from a smaller shop. However, entrepreneurs and skilled workers in the trade are overwhelmingly white. Thus both the hiring networks of small shops and the preferences of the shops' owners and workers—who provide the training—tend to exclude blacks. Similarly, Roger Waldinger (1986–87: 389) observed that in New York, "groups may enter the labor market with skills that influence their initial placement: Greeks from the province of Kastoria, where a traditional apprenticeship in furmaking is common, tend to enter the fur industry; Israelis move into diamonds, a traditional Jewish business centered in New York, Tel Aviv, and Antwerp; Indians from Gujarat, previously traders, become small storeowners." Skills, then, are often passed on through networks.

Each decision to screen is also, implicitly or explicitly, a decision *not* to train. This point came up in the focus group of young African-American men that provided one of the opening quotes for this chapter (Jobs for the Future 1995: 7):

MODERATOR: Why are there some jobs you just don't go after?
RESPONDENT 1: You don't qualify.
RESPONDENT 2: Excuse me, I ain't dumb. If you teach me something, I'm going to get it right. I may take a little longer on some things, but I may do it a little faster on something else. But if they keep you, I'm going to get it. But, a lot of them want you to come in with experience off the top, mostly, too.

As the second respondent points out, on-the-job training or a prerequisite of experience are substitutes for each other. To demand a prerequisite, an employer must have confidence that surrounding training systems or migration streams can supply sufficient workers who meet that prerequisite. When labor shortages squeeze, employers will often relax hiring requirements more than they will increase wages.

Both the assessment of qualifications needed for a given job and assessment of the qualifications possessed by a given worker, moreover, invariably include subjective elements. A majority of the Detroit and Los Angeles area employers interviewed by Philip Moss and Chris Tilly (1996) cited "soft skills"—motivation and the ability to interact comfortably with supervisors, customers, and coworkers—as among the most important qualifications for jobs requiring no more than a high school education. A smaller majority stated that black men are deficient in such skills. But Moss and Tilly conclude that this view mixes in substantial amounts of stereotypes and cultural gaps—and that furthermore, comfort of interaction depends on supervisors, customers, and coworkers themselves, not just the prospective worker. Large majorities of the employers rated the pre-employment interview as their most important screening device. But many agreed that, as a public sector human resource official in the Los Angeles area put it, "woven into that [the interview assessment] is all of the individual interviewer prejudices, how they see the job, how they evaluate the candidate, and how they present it. You cannot get away from that" (Moss & Tilly 1996: 270). So employer preferences and beliefs—and choices based on them—infiltrate the weighing of qualifications.

Preferences in Matching

Employer and worker **preferences** and perceptions thus also contribute to matching workers and jobs. This parallels productivity in the sense that employers and workers can be viewed as each seeking to maximize their satisfaction (and not just to maximize the business's profits or the wages received). For a given employer that may mean hiring someone who is less qualified but is a co-ethnic; for a worker that may mean choosing a job that pays less but offers interaction with friends. Theoretically, this is a small step away from the standard, neoclassical model of matching. Practically, however, the step may be larger.

How large? At first glance, one might suppose that preferences and beliefs would not greatly divert matching from strict production efficiency. After all, in the previously quoted words of economist David Colander, "a profit-maximizing firm hires someone if it thinks there's money to be made by doing so." As for workers, Jencks, Perman, and Rainwater (1988) report that the view of what represents a good job does not vary significantly by race, gen-

der, age, or years of education. Even the streetwise African-American youths
of the focus group we heard from earlier sound—at least at times—much
like *homo economicus,* shrewdly trading off leisure and wages:

> MODERATOR: What kind of jobs do you generally look for, when you
> do look for a job?
> RESPONDENT 1: You're looking for the highest paying job you can
> get. That's what I look for, anyway.
> RESPONDENT 2: I look for the easiest job that you can get, because,
> usually, you know what I'm saying, without an education, they don't
> hire you. You've got to take what you can get, you know. (Jobs for
> the Future 1995: 7)

But as we saw in Chapters 5 and 6, employers and workers pursue multiple
objectives subject to bounded rationality. The result is not just random noise
but systematic patterns of variation: Capitalist labor markets and professions
ordinarily organize in ways that sustain categorical inequality. Employers contribute to that result, however unintentionally, by allocating work according
to categorical distinctions that correspond to religion, class, race, ethnicity,
nationality, gender, age, or sexual orientation. In short, employers discriminate—preferentially hiring one categorical group over another based on their
own preferences and beliefs or those of customers, incumbent workers, or
suppliers who will come into contact with workers. Before World War II,
Pittsburgh's steel mills segregated their divisions exquisitely by national origin. A foreman there developed "an elaborate three-color chart that catego-
rized 36 ethnic groups in Pittsburgh according to the type of work to which
they were most adaptable. East Europeans, he concluded, were most adaptable to 'carrying' jobs, as boiler firemen, and in work in which the tempera-
tures and atmospheric conditions varied considerably. They also were considered 'good' at dirty work" (Weber & Morawska 1985: 292–293).

Occupational labeling facilitates ethnic, racial, class, citizenship, and gender discrimination in employment since it encourages officials and employers
to draw sharp distinctions between categories of work that are actually similar in performance and entry requirements but (for whatever reason) recruit
different kinds of workers. An unusually vivid example emerges from the
complaint of a female machinist in a large industrial plant:

> I do the same work on the bench lathes as the men who do work on the big lathes
> . . . We do the *same thing* to the pieces . . . We have the *same equipment* and the
> same training. All the women welders went to welding school [run by the com-
> pany] the same as the men. We passed the same tests to be certified as welders . . .
> The only difference is that when we got through training, they sent all the women
> to be welders at a rate 14, while all the men went to a rate of 18. The women
> work on smaller pieces than the men, but we have to have the same skill and do

the same welding work . . . In fact, our work used to be part of the men's welding job, but the men didn't like it . . . So [management] broke that part of the job off and put women on it, at a lower rate. (Reskin & Hartmann 1986: 49)

In all sorts of work, individual differences in compensation do not issue chiefly from differential pay within the same jobs but from compensation differentials *among* jobs. The great bulk of male-female wage differences has long resulted from the fact that most men and women work in differentially rewarded sex-segregated jobs. That is precisely the argument for "comparable worth," the enforcement of equal wages for predominantly male and predominantly female jobs that have different labels but essentially the same requirements in human capital and current performance (England 1992).

The creation of clerical work as a distinct occupational category, and the concomitant feminization of these jobs, illustrates the historical processes involved in demographic typing of jobs (Miller 1988). With the expansion of administrative work in the late nineteenth and early twentieth centuries, businesses began to separate clerical from managerial work. Their initial objective was to reduce wages and increase control over what became clerical jobs. Women entering the workforce provided a workforce willing to tolerate lower wages, truncated career ladders, and subordinate status; men gravitated to now-separate managerial and professional job classes within administration. The feminization of clerical jobs, in turn, consolidated the jobs' status as a separate occupational group, as well as the lower wages offered. The process resulted in a new occupation. Robust occupational barriers now limited mobility to and from other occupations from which clerical work was once indistinguishable (and with which it still shared tasks: coordination remains a central activity of both secretaries and managers). The process also yielded powerful sex-typing of the occupation (compare the percentage female among secretaries and among managers in Table 9.1!).

Workers produce a complementary effect to that achieved by employers, by organizing their searches for employment and their control of occupational niches within the categories established by the same distinctions. Although workers across race, ethnic, and gender lines may agree on what a good job is, they also prefer to work with people who are demographically similar (Shellenbarger 1993b; Tajfel & Turner 1986). This helps account for the power that preexisting networks wield in matching. Even if an excluded categorical group succeeds in getting hired, barriers remain. Coworkers can welcome or block new workers, as Susan Eisenberg (1992a) demonstrates with accounts of women trying to break into the building trades in the United States. To bar women, male construction workers took actions including refusal to train, shunning, verbal harassment, sabotage, and physical violence. Groups not welcomed by their coworkers tend to exit rapidly and enter the trade in decreasing numbers.

Prospective workers also make choices based on life circumstances and culture. Immigrants and students who expect their time at a job to be short avoid jobs with lengthy training periods and are often willing to take jobs that would be undesirable over the long term. Teenagers, women with young children, and older workers disproportionately choose part-time work. Women sometimes limit their job options based on an internalized view of what jobs are "appropriate" for a woman. Cultural conventions about appropriate work, indeed, matter to a wide variety of groups. The Chinese-Filipino personnel officer of a Los Angeles-area local government agency employing primarily blue-collar workers told Moss and Tilly (1992) that few Asians apply because such manual work is "not looked at as one of the 'acceptable' professions."

Networks in Matching

Employer and worker preferences and beliefs affect matching most powerfully when they are linked to interpersonal networks (Powell & Smith-Doerr 1994). Matching results from the connection of **recruitment networks** through which employers seek workers with **supply networks** through which potential workers seek jobs. Both kinds of networks are always smaller and more selective than standard labor-market theories assume. One extension of such theories posits that internal labor markets modify the bargain by restricting the employer's choice to workers who already hold jobs within the relevant firm(s); they arise, according to standard theory, because accumulated experience within a firm transfers from job to job and because the performance of a worker in one job gives high-quality information about the worker's capacity to do other jobs; workers recruited from outside lack firm-specific knowledge and are harder to judge. But again, recruitment networks, whether internal or external, actually do more for employers than such theories of internal labor markets suggest; they facilitate the creation of patron-client chains including employers, forward selectivity (hence discrimination) in hiring, and guarantee some accountability of suppliers for the quality of workers supplied.

Although in any concrete instance recruitment and supply networks merge, the distinction between the two matters analytically. Both kinds of networks differ dramatically by gender, ethnicity, race, age, citizenship, and residence; their articulation therefore has a strong impact on what sorts of workers actually get into given firms. As a result, very different sorts of people enter similar jobs in different firms. Once in place, furthermore, the connection between them tends to sustain itself; people in the networks recruit new workers like themselves. "The tendency toward occupational closure is strong," Waldinger (1986–87: 390) points out, "because networks of information and support are often ethnically bounded." Indeed, the effects work in both directions: As the differential histories of immigrant populations indicate, mutual aid and information identified with common origin reinforce or even help create ethnicity (Portes & Rumbaut 1990; Yans-McLaughlin 1990). Osterman (1980) notes that different networks for young black and white men in Boston launch them on differing job trajectories. Networks may also follow gender lines: Eisenberg (1992a) found that whereas the sons of construction workers knew when and how to apply for apprenticeship programs, women had to make extraordinary efforts to submit applications.

Personal contacts and informal local institutions generate most job matches (Granovetter 1981, 1986, 1995; Corcoran, Datcher & Duncan 1980; Holzer 1987). Networks play a critical role in hiring for the smallest businesses—for example, the 4.5 million firms of less than 50 employees that employ over 40 percent of the workforce in the United States (U.S. Department of Commerce 1988). But even in larger, more bureaucratized organizations, ethnic groups may "capture" particular departments or entire establishments, combining the selective effects of networks plus a work environment shaped by a critical mass of a given ethnic group. When asked why blacks didn't apply to a large auto parts manufacturer in the Los Angeles area, a Latina company spokesperson responded, "Maybe because they only see Spanish around" (Moss & Tilly 1995: 26). Furthermore, as noted in the machine shop example cited above, large employers may require skills and experience only available from smaller firms that themselves rely on networks.

Among workers, tales of such connections circulate widely; as a Polish immigrant reported in the 1970s (referring to a job held decades earlier):

> The only way you got a job (was) through somebody at work who got you in. I mean this application, that's a big joke. They just threw them away. No matter how many . . . to get a job with the railroad, my brother-in-law got it for me. My job at the hospital, my dad got it for me. I got the job at this meat place . . . the boy I used to play ball with, he got it for me. So, in other words, so far as your application goes, that was a big joke. (Bodnar, Simon & Weber 1982: 56–57)

From the viewpoint of workers, the process looks like pure favoritism. Employers interested in wresting control over hiring from subordinates or in complying with outside pressure for fairer hiring have often installed personnel departments and bureaucratized hiring procedures. Yet they, too, frequently save effort and avoid uncertainty by drawing more workers from networks that have already yielded reliable employees.

Most hiring involves some prior personal contact between current and prospective employees, often as a result of a boss simply asking a worker, Do you know anyone who . . . ? As the head of a large fish-processing firm in Aberdeen, Scotland, speaking of his female workers, told Margaret Grieco:

> I couldn't tell you exactly what the connections between them all are but there's a lot of family there. And it's a good bet, if one of them asks you to start somebody she'll stay—and what's more she'll be a good worker too. We don't train

anybody, but we turn a blind eye if somebody brings in a youngster and trains them up, provided the work doesn't suffer that is. Yes, it's a pretty good bet that if they know people here before they arrive they'll stay. (Grieco 1987: 13)

Such procedures greatly lower the cost of labor market information. They also reinforce existing patterns of selectivity and discrimination. And they are common. A 1993 survey of mostly small and midsized U.S. businesses found that 88 percent employed people who were related to each other. At one 6,700-employee print shop, half of the employees are relatives of other employees (Shellenbarger 1993a)!

The most dramatic cases of network domination of matching appear when long-distance migration networks organize around a supply of jobs and exert a near-monopoly over those jobs. Chain migration (the arrangement in which a stream of migrants from a single origin to a single destination maintain multiple connections, providing information and aid that facilitates movement back and forth in response to opportunities at either end) has an ancient and important history among major flows of labor. Within migration chains migrant individuals and households (1) frequently send substantial remittances to relatives at the origin, (2) retain major claims on property and enterprises at the origin, (3) return for ritual occasions, dead seasons at the destination, or retirement, (4) create collective identities and ethnic enterprises at the destination, and (5) operate long-distance systems of marriage as well.

Once established as a supply network for a particular set of jobs, a stream of chain migration provides advantages to both its members and its employers. For the workers, *paesani* send word home about the chances of employment and offer a variety of supports—information, lodging, companionship, a collective identity as well as help in finding jobs—at the destination. For employers, the migrants provide a flexible, even disposable, flow of workers having certain proven characteristics, ensuring some solidarity on the job, and offering a collective guarantee of reasonable performance if only because of possible collective retaliation for misbehavior.

Exactly parallel processes appear in the formation of ethnic enterprises, except that there the availability of pooled capital and credit becomes crucial (Light & Karageorgis 1994). In Los Angeles of the late 1970s, after all, start-up costs for the first three months of a 3000-square-foot table-service restaurant ran in the vicinity of $250,000, the minimum for a leased gas station close to $50,000 (Light & Bonacich 1988: 243). To start such enterprises, Korean immigrants relied heavily on rotating credit associations (*kye*) operated by their countrymen. Kye drew on existing solidarities among immigrants but also created new solidarities, as many of them dined together, financed ritual occasions, and got involved willy-nilly in each other's careers. Small enterprises started with rotating credit ordinarily involved a single household and its unpaid labor, whereas larger ones typically employed kinsmen among their fellow immigrants. Thus migration, credit, enterprise, and employment locked together in a closed system virtually excluding non-Koreans.

With varying degrees of tightness, such systems flourish throughout the worlds of enterprise and employment not only in the United States but in all parts of the world. As Mark Granovetter (1995: 140–141) reported, recent surveys have found that 30 to 40 percent of British workers found jobs through friends and relatives (Harris et al. 1987: 94; Fevre 1989: 92), 35 percent of Japanese workers (and 55 percent of male workers surveyed in the Tokyo area) found jobs through personal contacts (Watanabe 1987), and 61 percent of top Dutch managers found their jobs through contacts (Boxman, DeGraaf & Flap 1991).

Beyond a certain geographic scale, network connections are typically swamped by simple spatial proximity or distance. For a neighborhood employer—say, a small shop paying close to the minimum wage—the particular set of neighborhood residents who obtain jobs is greatly shaped by networks. But the shop's location itself is the main factor determining who will work there. After all, most potential workers cannot afford to travel far for a minimum wage job!

In the United States, racial residential segregation thus decisively shapes job access (Jencks & Mayer 1990; Kirschenman, Moss & Tilly 1996). Employers offering jobs requiring only moderate skills (particularly manufacturers) have shifted to suburban areas more distant from concentrated neighborhoods of color. Business locations have shifted in part due to "neutral" business-related reasons, such as land costs or access to highways. But employers' location choices also often turn on factors related to the race and class composition of the areas chosen: They avoid areas in which they perceive high crime, question workforce quality, or simply feel uncomfortable. The resulting "spatial mismatch" between jobs and minority population affects access to jobs in at least three ways. First, transportation costs impose a barrier for distant job seekers. Physical distance drives up the cost of commuting from minority areas. Second, information about job openings diminishes with distance, holding all else equal. The networks that form a key information source are in part spatially determined. However, all else is not always equal. As long distance chain migration shows, physical distance is not invariably a bar. Third, most minority job applicants bear the stigma associated with their area of residence.

Business location choices are shaped by recruitment networks (access to workers is a key locational consideration). Such choices also shape recruitment networks (geographic access to jobs nurtures some existing networks and creates new ones). Despite a number of dramatic stories about plant relocations, these spatial effects primarily work through the location of new start-ups and branches, not relocation of existing facilities. And the relevant geographic scale depends on the jobs in question: Whereas a small shop re-

cruits workers from walking distance, a transnational corporation may recruit a CEO from another continent.

Bargaining and Inertia in Matching

Bargaining by the parties molds matching outcomes. **Bargaining** consists of
interactions in which two or more parties exchange rewards, punishments,
threats, and promises contingent on agreements with respect to future performance. Bargaining escalates to contention to the extent that it entails mutual, collective making of claims. Disputes are not always resolved through
bargaining. In many cases, workers and employers use exit rather than voice
(in Albert Hirschman's terminology) to register dissatisfaction with an employment situation: Individual workers quit or forgo seeking employment at
a particular business, and employers fire workers or fail to hire them in the
first place. However, bargaining does emerge in both external labor and internal labor markets. Bargaining occurs in external labor markets particularly
when significant barriers restrict labor supply, as in the case of long-distance
migration: In the history of the United States, the African slave trade, the
immigration of Chinese men to work on the railroads, and the bracero program resulted from bargaining (as well as coercion) among governments,
employers, and other principals. A smaller-scale example is Henry Ford's decision, during the labor shortage of World War I, to encourage black religious leaders to recruit southern blacks to work in previously segregated divisions of Ford's Detroit works (Granovetter & Tilly 1988).

Bargaining is more common in internal labor markets, where workers
hold firm-specific knowledge, have some control over the pace and quality of
production and training, and have the opportunity to organize collectively.
Workers may use bargaining to exclude particular groups, as when cigar-
making unions barred Chinese workers from the industry. Given the propensity of U.S. employers in the late nineteenth and early twentieth century to
use previously excluded ethnic groups in breaking strikes, the success or failure of a strike often had major consequences for the ethnic mix in a given
workplace or industry. Similarly, as the United Farm Workers organized California ranches in the 1960s and 1970s, they struggled to stabilize a U.S.-
based Chicano, Filipino, and Arab-American workforce, whereas antiunion
growers often sought to displace this workforce with Mexican migrants. And
as public and private workforces shrank during the economic and fiscal con-
tractions of the 1970s and 1980s, many U.S. unions sought to uphold a seniority rule for layoffs, while some governments and employers pushed for
affirmative action layoff rules that preserved jobs for less senior women and
people of color. In all these cases, bargaining extended to the point of contention: Collectivities such as unions confronted employers, often drawing
the state into the conflict.

Subordinate groups of workers—with or without unions—often use bargaining to press their claims. One common routine is for a group of workers to press for the appointment of a supervisor from their group; that supervisor then often recruits preferentially from the group. Chris Tilly (1989a) found that bargaining by professional women resulted in the creation of a new category of professional part-time jobs at a number of insurance companies during the 1970s and 1980s. The women, upon having children at mid-career, demanded part-time hours with the same pay and benefits; since the companies could not easily replace the women's professional expertise, they complied. Women who in an earlier era would have left the company now remained within the professional ranks.

The parties involved in bargaining each bring particular resources—coercive power, legitimate claims, special knowledge, and so on—to the bargaining process. Such parties often extend beyond the employer and prospective worker to include incumbent workers, unions, labor contractors, government, and other organizations. The most important resource for a party is often an alliance with a powerful other party. In particular, members of categories that suffer exclusion as a result of matching processes gain redress primarily by appealing to third parties, especially the state. For example, when women began entering the U.S. building trades in the late 1970s, they were able to penetrate apprenticeship programs because the federal government placed pressure on unions and contractors. Although unions complied with federal requirements for apprenticeship placements, they were far less consistent in defending women against hostile male coworkers. With a change in government in 1981, federal pressure relaxed, and the number of women in the building trades dwindled (Eisenberg 1990, 1992a, 1992b).

Finally, **inertia** lays a heavy hand on the matching of workers and jobs. It does so in two ways. First, inertia greatly influences *who*—both individually and categorically—holds particular jobs. As Arthur Stinchcombe (1990b: 253) pointed out, "Overall, the central institutional feature of employers is that, by and large, they will employ the same workers in the same jobs this year as they did last year." The spot markets of contingent or day labor remain the exception, not the rule. And when a worker is replaced, homogeneous recruitment and supply networks, along with bargaining based in vested interests, tend to reproduce the race, ethnicity, and gender of the former incumbent. The manager of subcontracted housekeeping workers at a Los Angeles area hospital told Philip Moss and Chris Tilly:

> If you have a high population employed in an area like, say, here [at this hospital] a high Hispanic population, blacks through word of mouth are going to tend to not apply here. If there are primarily blacks in an area, Hispanics are going to tend not to apply there. An example that comes to mind is our contract at [another company] with mostly blacks—it was very difficult to get Hispanics to come in even though we had a Hispanic manager at the account. . . .

When you are talking black-Hispanic differences, the black on the job will tend to feel very isolated because the Hispanic individuals cluster together, they speak their native language and you or I or a black person would feel outside of that group automatically. (Moss & Tilly 1992)

Second, inertia also stabilizes matching procedures themselves. Unionized hiring halls, day-labor shape-ups, recruitment networks, and want-ad placement procedures, once in place, all gain the same advantages as other established mechanisms. Incumbents know how to use them and see them as appropriate. Vested interests grow up, both on the side of employers and on the side of job seekers, with a stake in the preservation of current approaches to matching. Thus, for example, it took substantial technological change, child labor laws, and increased working-class mobility to shake coal mining in Britain and the United States out of reliance on family succession to staff the mines.

Job requirements also acquire inertia, as struggles over deskilling and upskilling document. For example, hospitals have sought to staff some nursing duties—such as bathing, feeding, and bed making—with lower-paid nurses' aides, displacing nurses. But predictably, nurses have protested, in some cases slowing down or stopping such changes. A managing partner of health care consulting company APM Inc., which makes a business out of teaching hospitals how to make the switch, concedes, "This is a tough issue. We are taking out layers, and we get noise from people about it. But if you don't have noise, you aren't doing the job" (Anders 1995: B1). On the other hand, employers (or workers) may seek to *change* the job structure precisely to *preserve* other social relations. Paul Osterman (1979) found that after a sex discrimination case was filed against a major publisher, the company promoted several female employees to be staff editors, but simultaneously created a new position of "senior staff editor," and promoted several men into this job—"suggesting that the job structure was manipulated to maintain status differences between men and women"(p.463).

Mixing and Matching

The interplay of productivity, networks, bargaining, and inertia tends to reproduce categorical inequality—but not always in the same way. This interplay has generated strikingly different matches of groups of workers to groups of jobs over space and time. For example:

There is a great deal of variability across societies as to which gender is expected to do what job, even in the West. For example, dentists are primarily female in Denmark, Poland, and the Soviet Union, in contrast with the United States, where dentistry is 93 percent male . . . In the Soviet Union, both physicians and street cleaners are usually female . . . Beyond industrial society, there is yet more

TABLE 9.2   Relationships Between Ethnicity and Occupation, 1990

Ethnic Origin	Males		Females	
Jewish	medical, health	10.2	sales supervisors	4.3
Portuguese	construction labor	9.2	cleaners	10.3
Chinese	chefs, waiters	5.2	sewing	3.5
West Indian	medical, health	3.9	nursing aides	7.1

SOURCE: Breton, Isajiw, Kalbach & Reitz 1990:166.

variability. Household servants, predominantly female in the West, are typically male in India . . . , and construction labor is shared by the sexes . . . West African women engage in highly organized long-distance trading that is elsewhere an exclusively male occupation. (Reskin & Hartman 1986: 7)

Chris Tilly encountered this variability in two consecutive medical records clerk jobs he held, one at a hospital in Boston, the other in San Francisco. Although the jobs were essentially identical, the predominantly female workforce in the Boston record room viewed the job as women's work, whereas the largely Filipino, majority male workforce in the San Francisco record room saw it as heavy work unsuitable for a woman. Inequality and job segregation are the constants, not the specific matches of jobs to particular networks or groups.

As a result of network-mediated differential recruitment, most local and regional labor forces end up highly segregated by race, national origin, and gender. Because cross-region variation cancels out when aggregating to the national level, local occupations show far more intense segregation than the national-level data we examined earlier in the chapter. For example, in Toronto, as of 1971, Italians were 16.8 times more likely than other male workers to be employed as masons or tile setters, Italian females 11.5 times more likely than non-Italian females to be employed in textiles. Italian males also concentrated disproportionately among barbers (14.4), construction laborers (12.6), plasterers (11.4), and excavation or paving (6.0). Other high concentrations can be seen in Table 9.2.

That stereotypes such as the Chinese restaurateur and the Jewish doctor immediately catch the eye is no coincidence; although the stereotypes often endure past the time when they had some validity, they originate in the sharp categorical differentiation of jobs and enterprises.

Differentiation entails inclusion for some, exclusion for others; it therefore produces discrimination (see Granovetter & Tilly 1988 for a much more extensive discussion). If our analysis is correct, alas, the identification, explanation, and elimination of categorical discrimination in employment become much more complex than neoclassical reasoning ordinarily implies. Neoclassical analysis neatly limits the explanation of job assignments to two factors: (1) marginal productivities (which in turn are supposed to depend on human capital), plus (2) exogenous preferences of employers, workers, or consumers (as played out in discrimination [Becker 1957] or compensating differentials [Rosen 1986]). Our much more ragged alternative suggests that job assignment results from incessant bargaining among multiple actors, that employers and job seekers alike heavily exploit segregated networks in the matching process, that employers and advantaged workers have concrete interests in far more than the sheer skills of any potential worker, and that all parties spend much of their effort creating and maintaining solidarities, thereby protecting their powers, privileges, prestige, and autonomies within the firm. Such added baggage carries over, as well, to wages and promotion.

10

Inequality at Work:
Wages and Promotion

Beyond Human Capital Theory

What determines wage levels? Without doubt, the theory of wage determination that has enjoyed the greatest acceptance is human capital theory: More productive workers get paid more, human capital (abilities and skills) largely determines productivity, and there is much variation in the extent to which people are endowed with and invest in human capital. But human capital theory leaves much unexplained. Standard human capital research uses regression analysis to discover how much of the variation in wages among individuals can be explained by differences in human capital. Table 10.1, adapted from Erica Groshen (1991), shows typical results from such research.

Without getting into technical details, note that a person's education and age are the human capital variables. Age imperfectly represents workforce experience, as well as captures any wisdom accumulated through aging itself. The square of age is included because mathematically this allows the positive impact of age on earnings to level off and even become negative with increasing age (which indeed it does). Table 10.1 reveals that the standard human capital variables only account for about one-quarter of the variation in wage levels among individuals. Taking account of each individual's occupation, industry, race, sex, and whether they are unionized doubles this but still leaves 49 percent of the variation unaccounted for.

More detailed studies highlight that pesky 49 percent, finding large wage differences even among similar jobs in similar workplaces within local areas. Langton and Pfeffer (1994) cited a number of such studies:

- John Dunlop (1957) found that in Boston, truck drivers hauling scrap metal earned $1.27 an hour, whereas truck drivers who carried magazines received $2.49 an hour, almost 100 percent more—despite belonging to the same union.
- Donald Treiman and Heidi Hartmann (1981, Table 12) pointed out that the U.S. Bureau of Labor Statistics's Area Wage Surveys (now renamed Occupational Compensation Surveys) typically turn up wide variations in the wages paid to narrowly defined jobs within specific metropolitan areas. Table 10.2 illustrates this variation, showing the ratio of highest to lowest wages found in six jobs in the Atlanta, Detroit, and Los Angeles metropolitan areas in the early 1990s. If we consider the full range of wages for a given job in a given city, the highest-paying businesses pay up to four times much as the lowest—and only rarely pay less than twice as much. Even when we throw out the highest one-quarter and lowest one-quarter of wages, focusing on the "middle range," the highest wage in this range is typically 30 percent or more above the lowest, and in some

TABLE 10.1   The Percentage of Wage Variation Among Individuals Accounted for by Human Capital and Other Variables, United States, 1986

Explanatory Variables	Percent of Wage Variation Explained
Years of education, Age, Age²	26%
Years of education, Age, Age², Occupation	42%
Years of education, Age, Age², Occupation, Race, Sex, Union status	48%
Years of education, Age, Age², Occupation, Race, Sex, Union status, Industry	51%

NOTES: Sample includes all people aged 18–54 employed for wages and salaries in nonagricultural industries in the United States. Dependent variable is log(hourly earnings). Occupation and Industry denote dummy variables at the two-digit level.

SOURCE: Data from Erica Groshen, "Five Reasons Why Wages Vary Among Employers," *Industrial Relations* 30 (1991):350–381, Table 1.

cases is twice as great. Not surprisingly, registered nurses, with their readily transferable, certified skills, show the least variation. Janitors show the most variation: Given the limited skill required for this job, their pay will depend far more on the specific institutional setting in which they are employed. Variation in other forms of compensation is even greater (U.S. Bureau of Labor Statistics 1991b): In the Atlanta area, the number of paid holidays for production workers spanned from zero to sixteen; office workers' hours of vacation after five years of service extended from zero weeks to eight!

- Jonathan Leonard (1989) found that ratios like the ones in Table 10.2 are present even within the electronics industry in two California counties. The highest-paying firm paid twice as much, or more, as the lowest-paying firm for secretaries, janitors, stock clerks, and production supervisors.

All of this unexplained variation does not in itself sink a human capital model of earnings (Baker, Jensen & Murphy 1988). Unexplained differences in wages can always be attributed to unobserved differences in ability, and hence productivity. But a more satisfactory response is to seek to build richer models of compensation and other rewards. In our framework, this quest starts by considering compensation as only one form of incentive among several.

Incentive Systems

Incentive systems combine compensation with coercion and commitment. Systematic variation in incentives can be traced on the maps of work in Fig-

TABLE 10.2   Ratio of Highest to Lowest Wage Rate, for Full Range and "Middle Range" of Pay Rates in Specific Jobs in Selected U.S. Metropolitan Areas, 1990–1991

| | *Ratio of Highest to Lowest Wage in Full Wage Range* | | |
	Atlanta	*Detroit*	*Los Angeles*
Hourly wage (straight time)			
Truck drivers	2.3	2.9	4.3
Forklift operators	2.9	3.5	3.0
Janitors	3.8	3.8	3.8
Weekly wage (straight time)			
Receptionists	2.0	2.7	2.3
Registered nurses[1]	1.7	1.5	1.8
Computer programmers,			
trainee level	2.1	1.9	2.2
	Ratio of Highest to Lowest Wage in Middle Range		
	Atlanta	*Detroit*	*Los Angeles*
Hourly wage (straight time)			
Truck drivers	1.8	–	1.4
Forklift operators	2.0	1.3	1.3
Janitors	1.2	1.8	1.5
Weekly wage (straight time)			
Receptionists	1.4	1.3	1.2
Registered nurses[1]	1.1	1.2	1.3
Computer programmers,			
trainee level	1.5	1.3	1.2

[1]Registered nurses include only registered industrial nurses in Atlanta and Los Angeles, only level 1 registered nurses in Detroit.

NOTE: The "middle range" is defined by two rates of pay: one-fourth of the workers earn the same as or less than the lower of these rates and one-fourth earn the same as or more than the higher rate.

SOURCES: Data from U.S. Bureau of Labor Statistics, *Area Wage Survey: Los Angeles–Long Beach, California, Metropolitan Area, December 1990.* Bulletin 3055-55 (1991); U.S. Bureau of Labor Statistics, *Area Wage Survey: Atlanta, Georgia, Metropolitan Area, May 1991.* Bulletin 3060-14 (1991); U.S. Bureau of Labor Statistics, *Occupational Compensation Survey: Pay and Benefits—Detroit, Michigan, Metropolitan Area, December 1991.* Bulletin 3060-60 (1992).

ures 8.1 and 8.2; for convenience we reproduce Figure 8.1 here as Figure 10.1. Where do coercion, compensation, and commitment fall on these maps? Examine Figure 10.1: Coercion-intensive contracts cluster in the area of low monetization and high time-discipline, where disparities of power greatly favor recipients. The purer forms of compensation (here exemplified by virtuosi but joined in principle by drug dealers, street peddlers, confi-

FIGURE 10.1   Types of work contracts

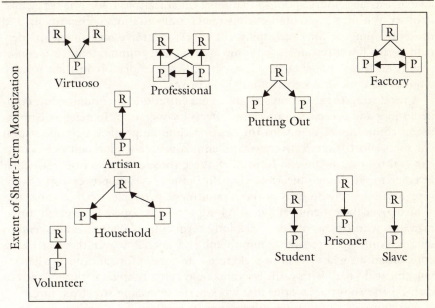

Extent of Short-Term Monetization

Extent of Time-Discipline

dence men, and arbitrageurs), cluster in the area of high monetization and low time-discipline, with power differentials tending to favor producers. Mixed coercion and compensation correlates with high monetization and extensive discipline, in cases where the relative power of producers and recipients is more nearly equal and/or contested.

Finally, systems giving greater stress to commitment (represented by professionals, artisans, households, and volunteers in Figure 10.1, extending to loyalty and prize systems in Figure 8.2) appear in an intermediate zone where the work that available compensation unaided by commitment can buy is of insufficient quality to sustain the enterprise; in that zone, organizations relying exclusively on coercion and/or compensation fail and disappear. Although employers of nurses have varied greatly in their emphasis on coercion and compensation, for example, since Florence Nightingale they have almost always stressed commitment.

Underlying these patterns is the fact that resources deployed in compensation, coercion, and commitment overlap, albeit incompletely. Think about organized respect as a resource: rewarding performance with respect (compensation), threatening to withdraw respect (coercion), and acquiring respect through symbolically charged external connections (commitment) overlap with each other. Although resource-rich organizations such as elite military units pour on all three kinds of incentives, such investments draw on an exhaustible resource pool so that most organizations trade one off against another. Within a given budget constraint, compensation, commitment, and coercion compete for overlapping resources; extensive investment in coercion means fewer resources for compensation and commitment. As a consequence, actual producing organizations differ considerably in their relative emphasis on one or another of these incentives.

A producing organization's relative concentration on commitment, compensation, and coercion significantly affects its operation. In general, emphasis on commitment maintains the organization, emphasis on compensation enhances short-run effectiveness, and emphasis on coercion enhances short-run control over members. In parallel, these three emphases offer particular leverage for attaining objectives of quality, efficiency, and power respectively. Organizations relying heavily on commitment generally sacrifice short-run control over their members but gain long-term allegiance. Conversely, organizations whose powerholders seek long-term control over members tend to choose contracts stressing commitment and coercion over those stressing compensation, whereas those seeking a one-time effort and no further involvement do it all with cash. No one could run a hospital with the kinds of cash-on-the-spot transactions that work perfectly well in street vending.

A combination of history, culture, productive logic, and embeddedness in other social structures accounts for the location of different activities with respect to commitment, compensation, and coercion, which in turn affects the position of those activities on the scales of monetization and time-discipline. Thus far in this mapping exercise, we have emphasized productive logic. But the enormous importance of history, culture, and embeddedness becomes clear in making international comparisons and in tracking change over time.

Compared to the United States, Japanese work contracts tend to rely more on commitment, whereas volatile labor relations in South Korea reflect attempted coercion by both employers and workers. One reflection of such variation is the span of control—the number of workers per manager. Coercion correlates with more intense supervision, hence fewer workers per manager. Figure 10.2, calculated from the work of David Gordon, tabulates the span of control for sixteen industrialized nations. Among these nations, the United States imposes the heaviest management control, with about one manager per six workers. The hand of management is far lighter in Japan, with a manager for every sixteen workers. But the most laid-back countries of all are Italy, Sweden, and Switzerland, all with 25 workers or more per manager. Surely the requirements for producing Fords, Toyotas, Fiats, and Volvos do not differ this greatly! Nor does the mix of productive activities across the sixteen countries vary so widely. Instead, these patterns reflect the historical paths labor relations have taken in the sixteen countries and the

FIGURE 10.2 Variation in span of control across industrialized countries, 1980

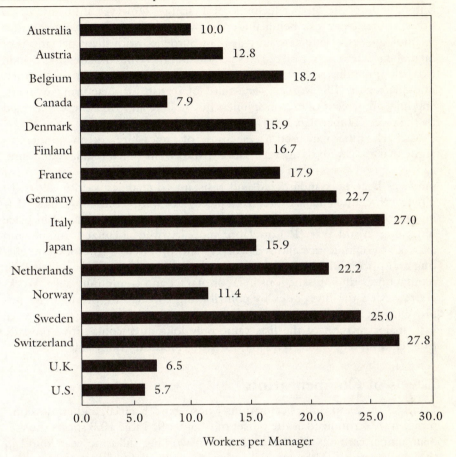

NOTE: National-level span of control computed as the ratio of clerical, service, and production workers to administrative and managerial workers.

SOURCE: Computed from David Gordon, "Bosses of Different Stripes: A Cross-National Perspective on Monitoring and Supervision," *American Economic Review* 84(2) (1994):375–379 (Figure 1).

norms and other shared understandings the march along these historical paths has trod out. Gordon (1994) found that the span of control is highly correlated with worker bargaining power and a strong welfare state.

Explaining change—or lack of change—over time in incentive systems also requires going beyond functional, production-based logic. Consider piece rates in the cotton textile industry. When technology changes rapidly in a competitive industry, piece rates pose a dilemma for firms. If proprietors cut rates based on rising productivity, they risk provoking workers to restrict output and oppose further technological change. However, if businesses do not cut rates, they risk being undercut by other firms employing the new technology—especially new start-ups not burdened with the expectations of incumbent workers. Yet piece rates persisted in the United States and Britain from the preindustrial era well into the twentieth century: At midcentury, one-quarter of U.S. workers, one-third of British manufacturing workers, and fully 85 percent of cotton spinners in Cheshire and Lancashire were paid by the piece (Huberman 1996).

Michael Huberman used a case study of Lancashire cotton spinners to argue that "a feature of 'mature' labor markets—in which regular communications exist between the parties—is that multiple wage-and-employment practices become standardized and resistant to change" (1996: 396). In nineteenth-century Lancashire, fixed piece rates were set in "wage lists" dating in some cases back to the 1820s which, remarkably, remained in place until after World War II. Low labor mobility, well-organized unions, and close-knit communities allowed workers and proprietors to block rate cutting and price undercutting. Firms that attempted to cut rates sullied their reputations, bringing sanctions in labor market and community alike. Workers rewarded the high rates by contributing to ongoing productivity improvements. Given workers' and owners' massive investment in the wage lists, major revision of the lists came only long after competitive pressure from cheap foreign labor rendered the British industry nonviable.

Levels of Compensation

Consider once more the occupations whose gender, racial, and ethnic composition we scrutinized at the outset of Chapter 9. Table 10.3 shows the median annual earnings of men and women working full-time year-round in these occupations. Although the occupational breakdown is not as detailed as the one we examined earlier, mineworkers are still visible as "extractive occupations," and their pay is quite handsome for manual work. Textile operatives (who are predominantly women) are approximated in Table 10.3 by female machine operators, who earn on average less than half as much as the overwhelmingly male miners. Health care workers' pay straddles that of the two industrial groups: Doctors earn far more than miners, nurses about as much as miners, whereas women health service workers receive about the same yearly pay as their machine operator counterparts.

Looking beyond these particular groups of workers, certain regularities emerge. Within occupations, supervisors earn more than other workers. Women earn less than men in *every* occupation, without exception, for which reliable estimates for both sexes were available. The differences often yawn wide. Moreover, within each broad occupational category, the higher

TABLE 10.3 Who's Getting Paid: Total Annual Earnings of Men and Women Who Worked Full-Time, Year-Round, and Percent Female, by Selected Occupations, United States, 1992

	Median Annual Earnings of:		
	Men	Women	Percent Female
Total	30,538	21,440	41%
Executive, administrative, managerial	42,509	27,945	41
Professional	44,015	31,261	48
Engineers	47,765	41,955	6
Physicians and other health diagnosing	87,224	52,233	18
Registered nurses and other health assessment and treating	41,418	36,006	85
Technical	33,092	24,681	46
Health technologists and technicians, except licensed practical nurses	34,413	22,949	70
Licensed practical nurses	–	22,936	94
Other technical workers	33,328	27,030	30
Sales	31,346	17,924	38
Supervisors and proprietors, salaried	33,888	19,872	33
Cashiers	14,230	11,928	73
Administrative support, including clerical	27,186	20,321	77
Supervisors	38,099	26,599	61
Secretaries, stenographers, typists	–	20,614	98
Service	20,606	12,931	51
Private household	–	9,668	89
Police and firefighters	36,136	–	8
Health service	17,291	15,243	88
Precision production, craft, repair	28,923	19,045	8
Automobile mechanics	20,933	–	1
Extractive occupations	37,977	–	2
Precision production	30,817	17,481	19
Operators, fabricators, laborers	23,005	16,609	23
Machine operators and tenders	23,315	15,019	36
Motor vehicle operators	25,566	17,436	7
Farming, forestry, and fishing	14,897	10,079	11
Farm operators and managers	15,294	12,801	11
Other farm occupations	12,213	–	15

NOTES: More recent editions of this publication do not include this information. Percent female is for full-time, year-round workers. Median earnings for technical workers as a whole imputed by authors.

SOURCE: U.S. Department of Commerce, *Money Income of Households, Families, and Persons in the United States, 1992* (Washington, D.C.: U.S. Printing Office, 1993).

the percentage of women in the job, the lower tends to be the pay that both men *and* women receive in that job.

As with matching, a combination of productivity, preferences, networks, bargaining, and inertia sets these pay scales. In particular, compensation of workers in labor markets varies as a function of nine main variables:

1. market power of the firm
2. amount of capital per worker in the firm
3. extent of the worker's discretionary control over the firm's capital
4. impact of the worker's performance on the firm's aggregate performance
5. substitutability of that impact
6. worker's membership in favored ascriptive categories
7. worker's network proximity to others scoring high on items 3, 4, 5, and 6
8. the nature of institutions regulating compensation in the firm, industry, or occupation
9. inertial effect of earlier configurations with respect to 1–8

Thus we find very high compensation (wages, benefits, and nonmonetary perquisites) for a worker belonging to a privileged demographic group (men, for example) in an oligopolistic, heavily capitalized firm; who disposes of expensive machinery or other assets; whose expertise in using that machinery or those assets is both hard to reproduce and crucial to the firm's profitability; who is closely connected with other workers (including managers) having nonsubstitutable expertise and extensive discretionary control of capital; who benefits from the intercession of a union, professional organization, or government bureaucracy; and whose job has historically been blessed by these advantages. Conversely, we find low compensation for a member of a less-favored demographic group working in a weakly capitalized firm exposed to competition, who is easily replaced, has little access to the firm's capital, remains distant from its crucial handlers of capital, enjoys no institutional protections, and has a job long marked by this set of curses.

Specific examples illustrate the theory. Textile machine operators, who are predominantly women, easily replaced, working in a moderately capitalized industry facing sharp competition, earn far less than overwhelmingly male miners, with harder-to-replace skills, working with more capital in a more concentrated industry—and represented by a powerful, though shrinking, union. Looking beyond cotton and coal, note that managers, who exercise considerable discretion over the use of capital and contribute substantially to a firm's performance, are the highest-paid workers, although certain professionals with valuable, specialized knowledge and the protection of a professional association also gain high earnings. The substitutability concern means that physicians or lawyers must be well paid even when their contributions to firm performance are limited since the earnings must be sufficient to win them away from other jobs available to them. Secretaries of important decisionmakers earn more than other secretaries with equal skills both because of their heightened impact on the firm's functioning and because of their network position. Market power, capital per capita, and regulatory institutions offer a partial explanation of the fact that high-paying and low-paying firms and industries exist, even for jobs and workers who appear identical in all observable characteristics.

As with matching, the standard economic theory stresses *productivity*-based determinants of pay: capital per worker, discretionary control over capital, and the worker's impact on firm performance. But preferences, networks, bargaining, and inertia insistently place their thumbs on the scale. *Preferences* account for part of the pay differences among ascriptive categories. Not all: We know, for example, that most of the difference between women's and men's wages results from the fact that women and men work in different jobs. But in fact, as Table 10.3 documents, women do earn less than men even within the same occupation (and—though this cannot be determined from the table—even after controlling for differences in human capital). Furthermore, as advocates of comparable worth are wont to point out, the fact that "women's" jobs pay less than "men's" jobs surely reflects the preferences and perceptions of employers, embodying judgments deeply ingrained in culture. Similar invidious distinctions trail other ascriptive traits. In nineteenth-century California, rural construction, which was carried out by a Chinese workforce, was viewed as unskilled, whereas urban construction, which employed white men, was considered skilled (Johnson 1989).

Ascriptive characteristics do not matter equally in all settings. Jeffrey Pfeffer (1977), for example, discovered that the impact of socioeconomic origins on salary was greater in staff rather than line positions, in smaller organizations, and in financial businesses relative to manufacturing ones. "The results," he concluded, "are consistent with the hypothesis that the use of ascriptive characteristics will increase to the extent performance is difficult to evaluate or to the extent linkage in a high socioeconomic status network is itself an important determinant of performance" (p.553).

Moreover, the effects of ascriptive characteristics spill over to both productivity and networks. When they find themselves an unwelcome minority, women construction workers may be less productive—not because they are less able, but because resentful male coworkers may refuse to train and cooperate with them and may even sabotage their work. The connection with *networks* is even more decisive. Social networks segregate, to some extent, by ascriptive characteristics. Networks, in turn, determine who is likely to get what jobs (as we saw in Chapter 9), as well as what other workers will be network-linked to a given employee. Thus, much difference in wages by demographic group reflects the working of networks in matching and promotion rather than worker productivity or employer wage discrimination.

Indeed, networks affect the job one is able to find, the pay level for a given job, and in some cases the entire system of compensation. It is tempting to suppose that finding a job through a contact brings a wage advantage. But the wage effect, of course, depends on to whom the network connects a job searcher. Luis Falcón and Edwin Melendez (1996), studying workers in Boston, discovered that although non-Latino whites who found their jobs through contacts received higher wages than those who did not, blacks and to a lesser extent Latinos actually paid a penalty—in wages, hours, and/or benefits—for finding a job via networks. Networks bend compensation most when they are powerful enough to alter the system of compensation. The New England fishing industry, for instance, bifurcates into "kinship" fishing vessels, whose Italian and Portuguese immigrant crews are linked by strong family and kinship ties, and "capitalist" boats, whose Yankee, Norwegian, and other non-Mediterranean owners hire from the labor market at large. Kinship vessels pay crew members according to an income-sharing system, whereas capitalist fishing boats pay market wages (Doeringer, Moss & Terkla 1986).

Compensation differences among New England fishing vessels point as well to the fundamental role of *bargaining* in setting pay. A wide variety of institutions condition and structure bargaining. Although family ties may be the most important such institutions aboard fishing vessels, unions and civil service systems play the same role in other industries. Wage tribunals in Australia or France's sectoral bargaining—in which agreements between unions and employer associations are binding on all employers in a given sector, whether or not they were a party to the agreement—exert highly visible influence on compensation. But even in the notoriously flexible, unregulated labor market of the United States, tens of millions of workers have wages set by unions, minimum wage laws (federal, state, and local), or prevailing wage laws. Bargaining generates wage patterns that diverge markedly from those predicted by a "pure" market model. Within the unionized sector of the United States, steady patterns of wage growth, little affected by shifts in labor demand, have long alternated with sharp, dramatic adjustments. Such adjustments took place in the early 1920s, early 1960s, and early 1980s; in each case employers seem to have suddenly realized that their bargaining power had increased (Mitchell 1986).

Bargaining mediates the effect of the firm's market power on wages. Although greater market power denotes greater ability to pay, only the bargaining process can determine whether that ability will actually translate into higher wages. Among businesses in concentrated industries, unionization correlates with lower profits: Evidently unions compel oligopolies to share their windfalls (Freeman & Medoff 1984).

And even in work contracts untouched by unions or government regulations, norms of fairness inevitably emerge. Alfred Marshall (1925: 213, cited in Solow 1990) declared about a century ago that "the basis of the notion that there should be given 'a fair day's wage for a fair day's work' is that every man who is up to the usual standard of efficiency of his trade in his own neighborhood, and exerts himself honestly, ought to be paid for his work at the usual rate for his trade and neighborhood; so that he may be able to live in that way to which he and his neighbors in rank of life have been accustomed."

Notions of fairness blossom particularly within internal labor markets, and Paul Pigors and Charles Myers (1981: 362, cited in Solow 1990) described the consequences: "Wage and salary differentials are a mark of social status in almost every organization. If they do not correspond to the relative significance of jobs, as employees view them, the employee's sense of justice is outraged." But although conceptions of fairness are universal, their content varies across regions and countries and changes over time.

Finally, *inertia* slows change in compensation, prolonging wage patterns well beyond the factors that initially gave rise to them. Just as the best predictor of who will hold a job today is who held it yesterday, the best predictor of today's wage is yesterday's wage. Longitudinal studies of wages paid to individuals over their tenure with particular employers find strong serial correlation: The wage in each period is tightly correlated with the wage in the previous period (Baker & Holmstrom 1995). Nominal wage cuts, common in the United States during the 1910s and 1920s, have become extremely rare, although arguably the increasing use of bonuses and profit sharing creates ways for compensation to fluctuate downward as well as upward. When firms seek to cut wages, they typically lower wages for new hires—not incumbent workers. Norms of fairness surely play an important part in the downward rigidity of wages: Opinion surveys in the United States demonstrate a powerful public antipathy for nominal wage cuts (Jacoby & Mitchell 1990; Kahneman, Knetch & Thaler 1986). Nothing new there: Marshall, quoted previously, continued his statement by adding, "And further, the popular notion of fairness demands that [the worker] should be paid this rate ungrudgingly; that his time should not be taken up in fighting for it; and that he should not be worried by constant attempts to screw his pay down by indirect means" (1925: 213, cited by Solow 1990).

Inducing Work Effort

Efficiency wage theories mark an important effort to broaden and rehabilitate a model of wage determination based on productive logic. Such theories start from the observation that for employers, compensation serves two main functions: attracting workers, and getting workers to exert effort and stay at the job. Until recently, standard economic models largely overlooked the latter function. The problem of inducing work effort—which neoclassicals label the principal/agent problem, Marxists the extraction of labor from labor power—immediately raises broader issues of power.

Efficiency wage models (Akerlof & Yellen 1986), which have proliferated since the early 1980s, incorporate the incentive problem. In the basic effort-regulation efficiency wage model (Shapiro & Stiglitz 1984), employers seek to deter workers from shirking with the threat of discharge. To make job loss costly for workers, they raise their wage above the market-clearing level. When many employers raise their wages, the result is equilibrium unemployment, giving employers the upper hand.

This sort of model expands the neoclassical conception of employer power. Standard economic theory generally limits its attention to Walrasian power—the power to do business with somebody else, for example by discharging an employee, quitting a job, or switching to another contractor. Efficiency wage models additionally incorporate what Samuel Bowles and Herbert Gintis (1993) call "short-side" power—the power enjoyed by sellers in a shortage or buyers in a surplus, in this particular case the power that employers gain due to persistent unemployment. But efficiency wage models still flatten the complex and contested nature of power. Such models take production technology (including the ease of monitoring worker effort level) as exogenous. But capitalists redesign technology to enhance their control over labor. Indeed, Richard Edwards (1979) pointed out that capitalists adopt a variety of different approaches to controlling labor, including direct supervision (simple control), machine pacing (technical control), and inducing workers to internalize the rules and goals of the firm (bureaucratic control). In turn, workers, individually and collectively, struggle to expand their control over their work. Codified rules are invariably ambiguous and subject to negotiation or subversion.

As Edwards's category of bureaucratic control illustrates, employers rely on loyalty and other ideologies, not simply naked power, to extract effort. George Akerlof (1982) developed a "partial gift exchange" model as an alternative to the neoclassical approach. According to Akerlof, workers in a particular unit set norms for a "fair day's work," based on sentiment for each other and the firm generated by daily interaction. Firms pay above-market wages as a "gift" to workers, who in return offer a gift of above-minimum effort. The gift exchange is not the only explanation of how ideology affects effort: For example, Michael Burawoy (1979) described worker effort as the outcome of a "game" orchestrated by the employer.

The history of employer-employee interaction determines operative norms and bargains. Workers' degree of compliance also depends on their perceptions of alternatives to the job in question—perceptions molded by individual and group history. For example, employers often draw on migrant streams to fill less attractive jobs since migrants compare these jobs with even less attractive alternatives in their region of origin. But once immigrants or their offspring see themselves as permanent members of the economy they have migrated to, their view of alternative jobs shifts, and not uncommonly, they rebel (Piore 1979b; Sabel 1982).

A Case Example:
Growing Wage Inequality in the United States

In principle, our approach can help to explain changes in the distribution in compensation in the aggregate, as well as variation and change at the level of firms and industries. Consider movements in earnings inequality. Between the 1940s and the 1970s, most industrialized countries saw at least moderate equalization of earnings and well-being. But since the early to mid-1970s, the tide has flowed toward widening inequality. Among highly industrialized countries, this trend has been most pronounced by far in the United States. Since the 1970s, earnings inequality in the United States has surged dramatically. Between 1979 and 1993, the hourly earnings of a full-time worker at the 90th percentile (earning more than 90 percent of other workers) relative to a worker at the 10th percentile, increased by 31 percent for men and by 42 percent for women (Table 10.4, calculated from Houseman 1995, Table 6).

In fact, American earnings inequality widened along most dimensions: by race, by level of education, by industry (though the gender wage gap actually narrowed). The ratio of the median hourly wage of men with college education or more to that of male high school dropouts expanded by nearly 50 percent between 1979 and 1993 (Houseman 1995, Table 7). But earnings inequality also grew *within* each education category. Even among college graduates, many struggled. In 1991, one in six working male college graduates aged 25–34 with no postbaccalaureate degree, and one in four of their female counterparts, earned *less than the poverty level for a family of four* (about $16,000 in today's dollars) (Danziger & Gottschalk 1995). Widening point-in-time wage inequality does not necessarily imply growing disparities in mobility over time, but in fact the United States has simultaneously seen decreased upward mobility (and increased downward mobility), as we discuss in more detail at the end of the chapter when we evaluate the future of internal labor markets.

In earlier sections of this chapter we have mainly considered compensation in terms of the ordinal ranking of jobs. However, falling earnings inequality during the 1940s to 1970s and rising inequality thereafter have altered not the ranking order but rather the distances among ranks. In the earlier decades, economic growth, expanding welfare states, and union power dur-

TABLE 10.4   The Distribution of U.S. Hourly Wages, 1979–1993 (wages in 1993 dollars)

	1979	*1989*	*1993*
MEN			
Levels			
10th percentile	$ 6.79	$ 5.80	$ 5.21
50th percentile	$13.46	$12.08	$11.39
90th percentile	$23.81	$23.92	$23.93
Ratio of 90th to 10th	3.51	4.12	4.59
As % of 1979 level			
10th percentile	100%	85%	77%
50th percentile	100	90	85
90th percentile	100	100	101
Ratio of 90th to 10th	100	118	131
WOMEN			
Levels			
10th percentile	$ 5.69	$ 4.69	$ 4.78
50th percentile	$ 8.31	$ 8.72	$ 8.72
90th percentile	$15.25	$17.40	$18.19
Ratio of 90th to 10th	2.68	3.71	3.81
As % of 1979 level			
10th percentile	100%	82%	84%
50th percentile	100	105	105
90th percentile	100	114	119
Ratio of 90th to 10th	100	138	142

NOTE: All figures exclude agricultural and self-employed workers.

SOURCE: Data from Susan N. Houseman, "Job Growth and the Quality of Jobs in the U.S. Economy," *Labour,* special issue (1995): S93–S124 (Table 6).

ing and after World War II combined to lift the bottom of the wage distribution relative to the top. Since the 1970s, all three have reversed. Thus, our thumbnail account of the forces driving inequality down and up highlights bargaining and particularly the roles of unions, employers, and the state.

To illustrate, let us examine in more detail the surge of inequality the United States has experienced over the past twenty-odd years. Three main areas of economic change help to explain the trends in inequality. The first is increased sharpness and fluidity of competition. Globalization represents one aspect of this heightened competitiveness but not the only aspect—after all, the total of imports and exports still equaled only one-fifth of U.S. output in 1994. Deregulation, accelerated technological change, and the increased impact of shareholder impatience through actual or threatened buyouts all contributed to this rise in competitiveness as well, dislodging formerly comfortable oligopolies and opening new industries to competition. The second major change is sped-up technological change itself. In addition to creating new openings for competition, technological change has spurred worker displacement and job redefinition.

For each of these two factors, the story is not just one of inexorable market-based productivity shifts, but also of alterations in institutions and social relations. Deregulation, changed rules of trade, and even the emergence and evolution of the transnational corporation represent institutional shifts wrought by the strategic interaction of states, businesses, and to a lesser extent workers and their organizations. The computer, the premier engine of recent technological change, was created and developed not to further profit seeking, but census taking and war making. In any case, technological change does not translate unproblematically, via productivity, into new wage configurations. True, statistical analysis finds an association between using a computer on the job and higher wages (Krueger 1993). But a study of German earnings (DiNardo & Pischke 1996; U.S. data do not include the relevant information) discovered that approximately the same wage premium accrues to workers who use handheld calculators, pens, pencils, or work sitting down! Clearly status, and not just skill, enters the wage-setting process.

Indeed, history and culture have not simply influenced wage inequality by shaping the institutional settings for product markets and technological change. Our central claim is that the labor market itself is decisively shaped by social relations. Like the United States, the rest of the industrialized world has experienced increased global competitiveness (and to a lesser extent other escalations in competitive pressure) and speedier technological change. But despite significant stress on their industrial relations systems, no other country has experienced the kind of burst in inequality that the United States has undergone. Explaining this difference is the third factor: U.S. businesses have for the most part responded to new competitive pressures by cutting costs and speeding up production rather than enhancing quality. This entails a concerted effort to keep wages low for the production workforce but increasing rewards for the managers and professionals implementing the strategy.

Employers have mounted a concerted assault on unions: Between the mid-1970s and the mid-1990s, the rate of union membership fell by about one-half. They have prevailed on the state to slow growth in the minimum wage: After adjusting for inflation, the federal minimum wage lost about one-third of its value between 1979 and 1989; recent increases have only recouped a fraction of the loss. They have stretched and battered at the norms of fairness that earlier limited managerial pay. "U.S. companies now dominate the labor market to an unprecedented degree," declared *Business Week* in 1995 (Bernstein 1995: 56). Rising inequality in the United States is the outcome of bargaining in which one party's power has grown disproportionately.

Of course, wage inequality is only one element of economic inequality; there are many other sources of income, wealth, and consumption besides wages. But wage inequality contributes more powerfully and directly to income inequality in the United States than it does in most other industrialized countries, for a number of reasons related to the thinness of the U.S. welfare state. Various levels of government in the United States provide far more limited cash assistance than counterpart governments in other wealthy countries. In addition, health insurance and pension benefits are to a much larger extent provided by private employers, rather than the government—and such benefits correlate positively with wage levels. Moreover, the great bulk of cash transfers provided by the U.S. government depend on or differentiate by present or past work experience: social security, Medicare, unemployment compensation, workers' compensation, and now increasingly welfare. Instead of compensating for low wages or no wages, the U.S. government tends to reinforce the inequalities generated by the country's wage structure.

Promotion and Mobility

In addition to compensation, the other major reward offered by firms is **promotion**. Promotion marks one particular form of **job mobility**. Mobility matters to employers, who depend on job-to-job movement to provide training and motivate workers. It matters also to workers, who use mobility to gain advancement. Most people find promotion rewarding not only because it brings increased perquisites and pay, but also because recognition, deference, power, and greater proximity to capital are gratifying in themselves. In the United States, many hold long-term jobs. The median tenure of a 45–54-year-old man with his current employer was over 12 years in 1991. At the same time, however, U.S. workers experience surprisingly vigorous occupational churning. Ten percent of the workforce (including eight percent of those aged over 25) change occupations each year (U.S. Bureau of Labor Statistics 1992b). This combination of statistics points to multiple models of job mobility.

Three main patterns of mobility predominate. Craft workers, such as plumbers or computer programmers, move, at times rapidly, from job to job but consistently ply a particular skilled trade and may rise formally or informally within the ranks of that trade. Secondary workers bounce from employer to employer, and often occupation to occupation, without accumulating significant skills. Employers utilizing secondary labor markets often experience annual turnover rates of 200 to 300 percent among "permanent" workers (Chris Tilly 1996). Finally, within salaried and industrial internal labor markets, workers advance with a particular employer through promotion. The rules for internal advancement typically turn on seniority (for blue-collar and some lower level white-collar jobs) or merit (for managerial and professional jobs).

Mapping Mobility

Arraying work contracts by time-discipline and short-term monetization, as in Figure 10.1, told us much about incentives. A grid of mobility and training sheds considerable light on variation in other dimensions of work and labor markets (Figure 10.3). We classify work contracts by the degree to which training takes place within a given work contract and by a mobility spectrum from turnover, through stagnation, to promotion. (The latter axis oversimplifies since certain "up or out" work contracts combine promotion and turnover but foreclose stagnation.)

A number of regularities emerge. First, mobility and training correlate: Most work contracts—and particularly most contracts within labor markets—fall on the diagonal running from turnover and extra-contractual training to promotion and internal training. Craft, unskilled, and temporary workers huddle in the turnover/outside-contract corner. Managers, military officers, and clergy hobnob in the opposite corner, where promotion and in-house training predominate. Criminals and semiskilled workers loiter closer to a stagnant mobility pattern, where slaves and small family business employees—both trained primarily within their contracts—stand shackled by bonds of coercion and commitment. Housewives and professionals fall between the two poles.

The groupings at the two ends of the diagonal differ in other ways as well. They correspond to external and internal labor markets. In the one case, the key social relations that embed the work contract tend to fall outside the firm or other productive organization; in the other case, many of these social relations fall within. Although the proverbial CEO-who-started-as-a-file-clerk travels the length of the diagonal, more commonly careers stay within a relatively small section of the training-mobility plane. Today's fast-food chains, for example, commonly concentrate the great bulk of their workers in the diagram's lower left corner—outside recruitment and high turnover—but keep an eye out for the occasional worker who has the personal style and social characteristics to enter a promotion ladder as a potential manager.

The split workforce adopted by fast-food chains, in fact, is widespread in labor markets. Although the mix of high-turnover and promotion-ladder jobs varies widely across businesses, most large firms create at least two distinct internal labor markets. One consists of low-ceiling or dead-end jobs whose entrants work under close supervision with little hope of advancement within the firm, the other of hierarchically arranged jobs whose occupants, much more closely screened for compatibility with the firm's high officers, enter directly into the firm's system of command, patronage, information, promotion, and solidarity. We might call the first a **turnover pool**, the second a **command pool**. Even where the entry-level jobs differ little in direct compensation or intrinsic difficulty, the two pools commonly

FIGURE 10.3   Work contracts by training and mobility

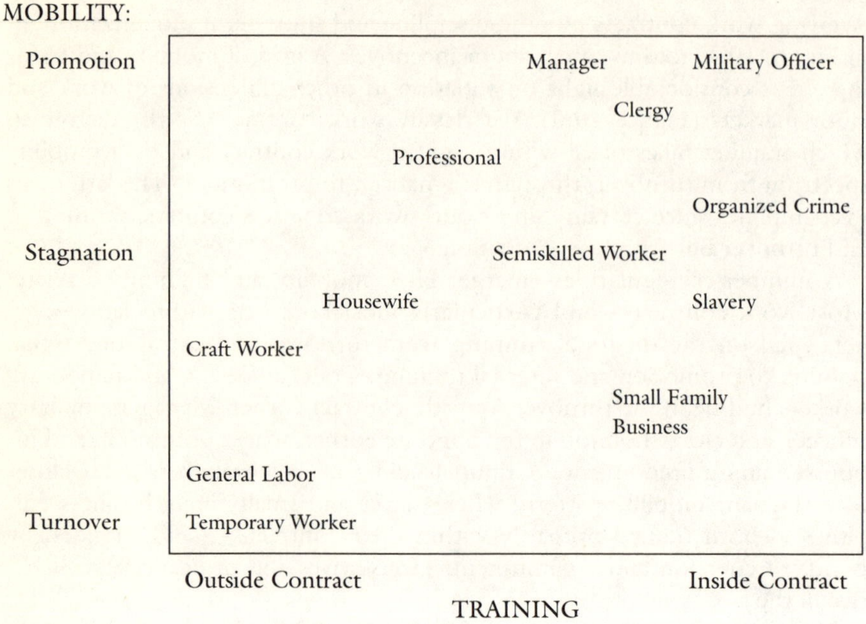

MOBILITY:

Promotion		Manager Military Officer
		Clergy
	Professional	
		Organized Crime
Stagnation		Semiskilled Worker
	Housewife	Slavery
	Craft Worker	
		Small Family Business
	General Labor	
Turnover	Temporary Worker	

        Outside Contract   Inside Contract
                            TRAINING

contrast dramatically in dress, demeanor, perquisites, class origin, race, ethnicity, gender, and citizenship. Such arrangements create a bifurcated power structure within the firm.

Businesses do their best to mobilize compensation and coercion to direct the turnover pool, and commitment to motivate the command pool. The mobility-training plane diagrammed in Figure 10.3 grounds less directly in issues of control than does the monetization/time-discipline plane we saw in Figure 10.1. Nonetheless, incentives once more vary systematically across this plane. Commitment grows in importance as one moves from turnover to promotion and from external to internal training. (Craft workers and professionals, who substitute commitment to craft or profession for commitment to firm, constitute the major exception.) Compensation looms larger as one moves in the opposite direction; in the absence of long-term attachments craft and temporary workers are motivated primarily by short-term pecuniary rewards. Coercion is used most extensively in stagnant or high-turnover work contracts, then held in reserve for the policing of unruly craft and professional workers.

Describing only two classes of pools oversimplifies: More generally, the segmentation of internal labor markets forms a continuum from pools containing nothing but command jobs to other pools containing nothing but dead-end jobs. Incentives vary accordingly, spanning a spectrum from loyalty to direct surveillance. Compensation likewise varies accordingly, with long-term salary, nonmonetary perquisites, and pensions more common at the loyalty end of the continuum, hourly wages with minimum benefits and perquisites more common at the surveillance end. The differential assignment of workers to segments of internal labor markets by race, ethnicity, citizenship, class origin, and gender therefore produces systematic differences in compensation across those categories as well.

The same logic that distinguishes command from promotion pools within firms also accounts for variation among firms and industries. Firms and industries differ greatly in the extent to which employers and workers (in combination, sometimes with state officials or labor unions) bargain out different combinations of incentive systems, routines of labor recruitment, compensation, and allocation of jobs among command and turnover pools. Broadly speaking, the same conditions that produce high compensation—capital intensivity, workers' discretionary control over capital, high and unsubstitutable impact of worker performance on aggregate performance, worker membership in favored ascriptive groups, network proximity of workers to other high-impact workers, firm market power, and strong institutional protections for compensation—also favor loyalty systems, worker control of recruitment, and extensive command pools.

But the character of the pools themselves also varies across firms and industries. Even in turnover pools, on the whole heavily capitalized firms and industries offer higher wages, more extensive benefits, and greater job security to their workers than do those having low ratios of capital per worker. Since workers in such industries, on the average, enjoy greater capacity to organize and greater leverage in bargaining (Conell 1980, 1989; Hanagan 1989b), employers are more inclined to preempt their unionization and collective action by providing company unions and paternalistic welfare programs. These tendencies have given rise to the distinction between "core" and "peripheral" industries.

Explaining Promotion Patterns

Differences among firms and industries in patterns of internal promotion raise three questions about internal labor markets. First, what determines the extent to which a given organization fills higher-status jobs via promotion, and *which* jobs do they fill by promotion? Data gathered by George Baker, Michael Gibbs, and Bengt Holmstrom (1994, Table II) illustrate the question. The medium-sized U.S. service firm they studied had eight levels of employment. The percentage of jobs filled from inside at each level, ranked from lowest to highest, was:

Level 1:	1%
Level 2:	73%
Level 3:	70%
Level 4:	75%
Levels 5–8:	90%

Why fill three-quarters of level 2–4 jobs internally, rather than 1 percent or 90 percent? Why fill a higher proportion of jobs by promotion at the upper levels of the organization?

Productive logic provides a starting point. Firms use promotion more where firm-specific knowledge requirements are greater and where screening and evaluation of outside candidates are difficult. Imbuing workers with firm-specific knowledge is costly, and businesses seek to husband that investment once it is made. Promotion ladders also give employers an opportunity to assess worker abilities and separate the wheat from the chaff.

Firms are also more likely to promote when they rely more on commitment rather than other incentive systems (though the choice of incentive system and job-filling mechanism are—conceptually—simultaneous). Hiroshi Ishida and colleagues (1995), studying large Japanese and American financial sector firms, found that among college graduates entering the companies, initial promotions were essentially automatic. In the Japanese company, nearly every employee was promoted to deputy section chief, and about 90 percent attained the rank of section chief. However, promotion to deputy section chief required at least ten years of seniority (most were promoted after thirteen years) or reaching the age of 33. Neither the universality of the promotions nor the uniformity of their timing can be readily explained by learning or screening processes. Instead, they constitute encouragements for loyalty.

For Japanese corporations, which offer lifetime employment for some classes of employees, loyalty may trump skill. At many companies, job applicants with previous experience and job-related skills are actually *disadvantaged*, since "Japanese companies prefer to hire motivated but inexperienced students and provide on-the-job training" (Ishida et al. 1995: 7). Loyalty considerations, along with firm-specific knowledge and screening, help explain why promotion from within is more common at higher levels of a firm's hierarchy.

The history and current configuration of bargaining also alters the degree of reliance on promotion. Workers and their organizations press for opportunities for upward mobility. In the U.S. hospital industry, in which the boundaries among job strata have been virtually impermeable, unions have bargained to establish education and training programs. Managers' response to proposals such as these depends in part on productivity costs and benefits but also on their assessment of the extent to which promotion can serve to coopt workers (as opposed to giving workers the opportunity to infiltrate management!). More generally, businesses take worker expectations and desires into account when designing or redesigning mobility systems. They may design promotion systems to satisfy those expectations—or to forestall them. Illustrating the latter case, increasing numbers of U.S. businesses, including manufacturers, are conducting initial hires through temporary help agencies, then screening the temporary employees for possible promotion to permanent employment. This device heads off new hires' claims on benefits or even on continued employment during the screening period.

Widespread conceptions of what is fair or just also underlie another finding by Baker et al. that is remarkable precisely because it is so unremarkable: *Demotions* are virtually nonexistent. Why should this be? As with pay cuts, incumbent workers would not tolerate demotion. Companies kick nonperformers upstairs, duplicate their jobs, fire and replace them—anything but demote them.

Established channels of promotion do not necessarily imply that workers exercise substantial control over their upward mobility; quite the opposite may be true. About one-third of Japanese companies use career development programs (CDP), which offer employees consultations on career orientation in order to facilitate individual career choices. But in a survey of Japanese firms "reputedly using CDP effectively," a large majority of employees responded to "What will your next position be?" with either "It's not up to me but up to the firm to consider such matters," or "I am considering these matters, but being short of information I have only a vague image of my career" (Amaya 1990: 46–50).

A second query about promotion: Given that jobs are filled through promotion, what forms the paths leading into these jobs? Typically we find clusters of jobs linked by promotion ladders. Baker, Gibbs, and Holmstrom discovered that at the medium-sized service business for which they obtained personnel records, all jobs fed primarily into one or two other jobs, aggregating into seven major career paths. The clusters are often bounded both vertically and horizontally. For example, insurance companies studied by Chris Tilly (1996) had separate ladders for service, clerical, and professional/managerial jobs; within the professional/managerial stratum, ladders were distinguished by functional area. Within each cluster, there are typically both turnover pools and command pools, although the ratio of command to turnover positions declines as one climbs the hierarchy.

Once more, productive logic specifies one factor in this clustering: Companies create paths or ladders based on overlap in firm-specific knowledge (hence separate ladders by functional area). Other factors include networks (so that coethnicity may pave promotion paths), preferences and perceptions (based on views of what groups will be most loyal, what groups will command the most loyalty, and what promotion paths are appropriate or legitimate), and bargaining.

Discrimination based on preferences and perceptions can radically reshape promotion ladders, particularly when the beneficiaries of the discrimination are disposed to defend their claims. Railroads in the southern United States at the beginning of the twentieth century hired African-Americans for the midlevel jobs of brakeman and fireman but barred their advancement to conductor or engineer. This peculiarity prevented southern railroads from creating seniority-based promotion ladders, which had become standard on other North American railroads. White-dominated unions not only defended the promotion bar, but fought to drive blacks from the midlevel jobs as well (Sundstrom 1990).

Detailed patterns of discrimination in promotion can be quite varied, depending on institutional history and needs. In one Pittsburgh insurance company, part-timers are forbidden to bid for full-time jobs; managers explained to Chris Tilly (1996) that this provision was designed to attract only people who wanted long-term part-time work. On the other hand, in numerous grocery stores—and in the U.S. Postal Service—virtually every worker must enter through a part-time position.

Once promotion ladders have been established, precedent freezes them in place. Since changing the rules for promotion can spark confusion and resentment in an incumbent workforce, firms generally alter ladders only when major shifts in the environment require it. A Boston insurance company official told Chris Tilly,

> Typically, [the company's] culture was that we hired at the entry level, and moved people up at a steady rate—not extremely rapid . . . But that's beginning to change . . . particularly in a couple of areas—financial, data processing. We're really having to fight for a highly skilled labor supply. It would take too much time to promote from within—our needs are growing and changing too rapidly. So we . . . are bringing in more MBAs at midstream. This does cause problems in employee relations . . . MBAs hired in at grade 14 or 15 have the same attitude as people at the *bottom*—"I've been here a couple of years, where's my promotion?" The old-style managers say, "We've already given you a break, we've given you an opportunity that we and your co-workers never had." We have no plan yet for how to handle this problem—it's sink or swim. The good ones [MBAs] move up to 16 or 17. That creates some resentment below. Or, they get frustrated and leave. (Chris Tilly 1989b)

A third and final question is who—in categorical terms—follows promotion paths. Who moves up depends on worker knowledge—but in this case, less on firm-specific skills than on groups' differential access to credentials and general job-related skills. Networks and discrimination (which may be at work both in the promotion process itself and in the mentoring and training that sets the stage for promotion) also loom large. For example, the "glass ceiling" confronting women in U.S. corporations is well-known. In the large corporation studied by Rosabeth Kanter, "male" and "female" jobs differed systematically in the mobility chances they offered. For women, therefore, mobility was so rare and the chance for social contact so great in office jobs that strong peer networks easily developed. It was also easier for the women to support a culture devaluing hierarchical success because of tradition and because they had few women upward in the hierarchy with whom to identify. Then, the distribution of men and women throughout the organization also shaped the psychological filter through which these women viewed promotion. As a woman rose in Indsco, she was likely to find fewer and fewer female peers, whereas men found a male peer group at every level of the system. So concern about "leaving friends" and the social discomforts of a promotion were often expressed by women in the clerical ranks; men in management had no such problem. (Kanter 1977: 151; see also Epstein 1981)

Similar mobility problems beset members of racial and ethnic minorities within large firms.

Networks bulk particularly large in the determination of upward mobility within internal labor markets. The importance of networks for promotion varies inversely with the formality of promotion procedures. Pyramid selling marks one extreme—networks alone create the opportunity to rise within the organization—but the same pattern holds across other types of business as well. Shirley Mark (1990) reported that engineers in high technology firms move upward by participating in the formation of project groups—an informal process structured by networks of acquaintance that disproportionately exclude Asian-American engineers. A similar process marginalized women in the advertising firm studied by Herminia Ibarra (1992). Jomills Braddock and James McPartland (1987) found that jobs filled by promotion from within are more likely to have white employees if the employer approaches employees directly to offer the job or to solicit applications for the job; they are less likely to have white employees if a written job description is posted or circulated. A portion of the exclusion commonly attributed to discriminatory attitudes thus results instead from network segregation. In addition to networks and discrimination, access to promotion also turns crucially on explicit or implicit bargains among powerful actors, often embodied in policies such as seniority and affirmative action.

The End of Internal Labor Markets?

Ironically, as researchers developed taxonomies of U.S. labor market segments over the last two decades, the labor market began to change in ways that render these taxonomies obsolete. The portion of the workforce fitting an industrial profile—long-term, rule-bound subordinate employment—has shrunk, for reasons including a shift of employment from manufacturing to services and employers' responses to heightened global competition (Harrison & Bluestone 1988; Albelda & Tilly 1994). More generally, U.S. employers have widely shifted away from internal labor markets in both their industrial and salaried varieties, toward a system relying far more on external educational institutions for training, combined with greatly increased mobility among firms. This widespread externalization results in part from the rapid growth of institutions for adult and continuing education, in part from firms' attempts to "get lean" and stay "poised for contraction" (Appelbaum 1987; Noyelle 1987; Carré, duRivage & Tilly 1995). Workers' heightened mobility takes the voluntary form of job-hopping but also the involuntary form of downsizing. Although some growing job groups fit the pattern of secondary or craft segments, others combine features of various segments in new ways.

As AT&T geared up to lay off an estimated 40,000 workers in early 1996, Vice President for Human Resources James Meadows told the *New York Times,* "People need to look at themselves as self-employed, as vendors who come to this company to sell their skills." He added, "In AT&T, we have to promote the whole concept of the workforce being contingent, though most of the contingent workers are inside of our walls." Instead of jobs, people increasingly have "projects" or "fields of work," he remarked, leading to a society that is increasingly "jobless but not workless" (Andrews 1996: D10). Meadows's statement holds that employment has devolved from jobs toward contracts—and in the limit, is tending toward individual transactions. Large-scale surveys reveal a similar shift in attitudes and expectations: Workers and managers alike rate employees' commitment to their current employer, and employers' commitment to their current workers, far lower than in earlier decades (Cappelli 1995). Even that most long-term of employers, the United States Postal Service, has expanded noncareer part-time jobs and created a "transitional" workforce as they automated and outsourced mail-sorting systems.

Are jobs in the United States really becoming less permanent? Yes and no. Jobs are becoming less permanent for men, particularly older and less-educated men, and more permanent for women (Farber 1995; Rose 1995, 1996). When these changes are combined, the net effect is no detectable trend (Farber 1995, though some measures do show an overall decrease in tenure; see Swinnerton & Wial 1995). However, this netting out does not necessarily imply that the changes are neutral. Arguably, women's growing tenure reflects a shift in labor supply—women are more likely to choose to stay at jobs rather than quitting. But men's declining tenure presumably primarily reflects a shift in labor demand—meaning that employers are more likely to lay off or fire workers or shut down. For the purposes of assessing the opportunities available to workers, the shift in labor demand is the decisive element.

Evidence from the Census Bureau's Displaced Worker Survey (DWS) also suggests reduced opportunity for long-duration jobs (Farber 1996). The DWS focuses on an extreme set of events: permanent layoffs. Displacement rates in 1991–93, nominally years of recovery from a mild recession, were higher than during the deep recession years of 1981–83. In turn, displacement rates for the 1980–92 period as a whole exceeded job loss rates during 1968–79, according to research based on the Panel Study of Income Dynamics (Boisjoly, Duncan & Smeeding 1994). Between these two periods, the percentage of people laid off increased by one-third, and the percentage fired doubled.

Do shortening job durations harm workers' interests? Some in the business press have argued that frequent job changes facilitate ongoing learning and advancement or have argued that rather than viewing shorter tenure as a setback, it should simply be seen as a change in the patterns and rules of job-holding. Journalists have introduced us to beneficiaries of mobility from one short-term job to another, such as 25-year-old temporary worker Jayson Elliot, who comments, "I don't want a job. I would never take one" (Flynn 1996). Providing some scholarly support for a benign view is the flexible specialization literature launched by Piore and Sabel (1984). Flexible specialization theorists argue that smaller firms and more volatile employment herald a return to craft forms of organization, marked by attachment to a trade, rather than a firm, with possibilities of advancement within that trade.

However, an instructive counterpoint to high-tech temp Elliot is provided by the words of temporary manual labor pool workers in the Carolinas. The Carolina Alliance for Fair Employment held a workshop with such temporary workers in 1994 and asked each participant to supply four words to describe how he/she felt about his/her work life (Gardner & McAllister 1995). Although the list yielded a few positive terms (qualified, hopeful, capable, competent), the bulk were negative: discouraged (five times), unimportant (twice), sad, bad, unpredictable, abused, rough, angry, disappointed, disgusted, tired of looking, expendable, on the outside, insecure, used, underpaid, aggravated, no future, pressured, threatened, unhappy, out of place, depressed, could be better, sucks, demanding, hate, stinks, poor, unfair, tired, and overworked!

Although temporary work marks one extreme in impermanence, Jencks, Perman, and Rainwater (1988) found that in general, a 10 percent increase in the expected risk of job loss in the next two years reduces the job's rating as much as a 10 percent pay cut. And although the earnings penalty associated with job changes was lower in the 1980s than in the 1970s, it remained a penalty. Even among job-changes who stayed within the same occupation, men who changed employers at most once during the 1980s earned 11 percent more per year than those who changed two or three times; the corresponding earnings premium among women was 32 percent (Rose 1995). The preponderance of the evidence indicates that most workers experience shorter-term employment as a contraction of employment opportunity.

Closely related to the issue of permanence is the question of mobility over time. Overall wage mobility decreased between the 1970s and early 1990s

(Buchinsky & Hunt 1996). What's more, *downward* mobility has become markedly more common in the United States. Tracing the trajectories of individual prime-age adults, Stephen Rose (1994) found that about one-fifth experienced declines of five percent or more in real earnings over the decade of the 1970s; that proportion rose to one-third during the 1980s. As in some of the other indicators, men and women crisscrossed: Men's likelihood of losing annual earnings increased, whereas women became less likely to lose. However, in terms of *hourly wages* (factoring out the effect of changes in weeks and hours worked, which enter into annual earnings), both groups became more likely to experience declines in the later decade.

What heightened the probability of downward mobility? Rose accounts for half of men's greater probability of an earnings drop by the increased frequency of job changes. But data about other firm-level changes suggest a more complex picture. Although the frequency of job *changes* increased, the benefits of job *stability* decreased at the same time. The payoff to accumulating seniority with a single employer, long a standard feature of compensation, diminished sharply during the 1980s (Chauvin 1994; Marcotte 1994). Employers also significantly decreased the amount of formal training they provided in order to qualify employees for jobs (Constantine & Neumark 1994). And new forms of work organization have removed layers of management and folded unskilled blue-collar jobs into multifunctional teams, taking out rungs in traditional job ladders (Cappelli 1993; Cappelli & O'Shaughnessy 1995). In short, the possibilities of upward mobility with a particular employer contracted, but the opportunities for ascent via movement from job to job have not offset this contraction.

The new "casualization" of labor attachment marks not only the United States, but also France, Italy, Japan, and other countries. The apparent convergence of these countries may be deceptive, however. In France and Italy, employers have shifted to less formal employment and subcontracting in large part to fend off the worker militancy of the late 1960s and early 1970s as well as to evade strict government and union regulations restricting discharge. U.S. employers, pressed by growing global and domestic competition, have acted more to blunt worker *expectations* of long-term employment than to dodge specific rules. Japanese expansion of nonregular employment initially represented employers' attempts to cope with a labor shortage by absorbing more women, students, and hundreds of thousands of illegal workers and later responded to a sharp recession induced by currency fluctuation. Although some have argued that the economies of Japan and Germany are now gravitating toward U.S.-style low-commitment labor markets (*Economist* 1996), such predictions seem premature.

Is this the end of internal labor markets in the United States? Clearly, the old internal labor market model is dissolving, especially for men. The U.S. business press has embraced the notion that there is a new career model founded on interemployer movement. In this "employability" model, much like a craft labor market, employers' commitment to workers is not continued employment, but provision of skills that render the worker more employable. But at present, although job-hopping surely offers new opportunities to some, on the average sustained attachment to a single employer still offers the greatest payoff to men and women alike. U.S. workers will strive to find ways to shield themselves from labor market insecurity, as workers everywhere have always done. Although workers have lost bargaining power due to decreased unionization and intensified product market competition, their power—and particularly their ability to rally the state as a sometime ally—is still to be reckoned with.

Given all of this, the labor market situation in the United States in the late 1990s looks like a transitional phase, not a stable new system. It is difficult to predict the final outcome. The reconstruction of some sort of within-firm internal labor markets is one possibility, though not the strongest one. Alternatively, worker security can be rebuilt based on a state-provided or required "safety net" of benefits portable from job to job, or new forms of unionization or other worker organization that impose standards for worker mobility across firms in an industry or geographic area—or some combination of these elements. What is certain is that in any new system, mechanisms of incentive and mobility will, as always, be shaped by productivity, preferences, networks, bargaining, and inertia. What is also certain is that the new system will be hammered out through contention among workers, employers, and the state.

11
Contention at Work

After the long Fascist containment of workers and the chaos of World War II, Italian management, labor, and state resumed the boom-and-bust of industrial conflict Italy had known before Mussolini seized power in the 1920s. From 1944 onward a vigorous, violent, and often victorious labor movement began to coalesce. In 1948 a nationwide general strike dramatized the determination of Italy's workers, but the late 1940s' strike wave soon subsided. Strikes then remained relatively small and infrequent until during the early 1960s a slow, irregular buildup of industrial conflict occurred. The dam soon broke: a great burst of struggle between 1968 and the mid-1970s, including the intense conflict of what Italians call the *autunno caldo*—hot autumn—of 1969.

In those heady times students, Catholic activists, and a great variety of workers all mobilized to make sweeping demands, sometimes together, often at cross-purposes, now and then with novel forms of claim-making. The strike waves of that period brought remarkable innovation to the forms of industrial conflict:

> A whole new vocabulary of strike forms developed, from the *sciopero bianco* (go-slow) to the *sciopero a singhiozzo* (literally, hiccup strikes), the *sciopero a scacchiera* (chessboard strikes), the *corteo interno* (marches around the factory grounds to carry along undecided workers), and the *presidio al cancello* (blocking factory gates to prevent goods from entering or leaving the plant). These innovations were not "wild"; their logic was to create the maximum amount of disruption with the minimum expenditure of resources. (Tarrow 1989: 188)

At the same time, forms of working-class action other than strikes multiplied: demonstrations, mass meetings, antistate violence. Then, after 1975, came a large decline in strike activity; although the pattern of large, brief, demonstrative strikes that had emerged during the early 1970s persisted, their sheer number declined radically.

Italy's postwar industrial conflict and its powerful left parties attracted worldwide political attention at the time and considerable scholarly interest in retrospect. Since the huge workers' mobilization that followed World War I had given way to Fascist seizure of power, lovers of democracy worried whether Italy was again becoming vulnerable to a right-wing movement. Both radicals and conservatives also asked (in hope or fear) whether postwar Italy, with its momentous class struggles and hulking Communist party, harbored the potential for revolution. Subsequent political experience has reduced the retrospective plausibility of a revolutionary scenario as well as of Fascism's full return but has only increased the fascination with those Italian conflicts.

For example, from close examination of Italian strikes during the years from 1950 through 1978, sociologist Roberto Franzosi drew important conclusions concerning causes and effects of industrial conflict in general

(Franzosi 1995). By expertly probing and flexing a wide variety of evidence, Franzosi showed the following:

1. Although they never disappeared entirely, Italian postwar strikes concentrated in waves covering multiple industries.
2. During each postwave downturn, scholars and political commentators began to speak of a general collapse or extinction of organized labor, only to be surprised by the next wave's timing, intensity, form, and locus; each round of strikes set new conditions for the next round.
3. Each wave left behind significant changes in industrial relations; the *autunno caldo,* for example, established plant-level organizing structures for workers and debilitated the old national employers' associations.
4. Employers typically responded to major surges in strike activity by trying to substitute other labor for organized workers and other factors of production for labor in general; how well they succeeded in either regard depended in part on available technologies. But it also depended on the current power positions of management and organized labor with respect to each other and the state.
5. Far from driving the entire system, employers' investments in new technologies and capital-intensive production followed the rhythms of labor militancy with a lag for search and imposition of the new forms.
6. Conventional periods for labor-management contracts (for this period, legally sanctioned but out-of-phase three-year cycles at national and plant levels) introduced regular rhythms into strike activity.
7. Other effects held constant, both antilabor governments and unemployment depressed strike activity, whereas union organizational strength and economic expansion promoted it.

Some of these findings (for example, the depressing effect of unemployment on strike activity) confirmed well-known phenomena, whereas others (for instance, transformation of bargaining structures and technologies by strike waves) challenged widely held assumptions about industrial conflict. Although Franzosi himself took a modified Marxist-institutionalist position resembling our own, his findings offered something for everyone: Marxist, institutionalist, and neoclassical analysts alike.

By the same token, Franzosi's conclusions challenge the standard versions of each view in some respects. The conclusions shake Marxists in their frequent supposition that to merely withdraw labor power collectively in support of workplace demands (the defining features of strikes) instead of joining revolutionary movements actually reinforces the existing system of production. The conclusions dare institutionalists to explain the widespread mobilization of allegedly opportunist yet custom-bound workers for risky confrontations. They deny the neoclassical presumption that neither strikes nor political intervention can prevail against the market's supreme adjudicative force. Franzosi's discoveries point to a view of strikes not as straightforward expressions of workers' discontent or of their interests alone but as episodes in continuing struggles over serious stakes among workers, employers, and the state.

No one will understand the findings without taking seriously the history of relations among Italy's major economic actors, of institutions their struggles laid down, of connections between strikes and other forms of struggle, and of production's continuously changing organization. Although observers have the habit of explaining the major actors' behavior in such struggles as if they acted exclusively from inner motives—the frustration of workers, the rapacity of employers, and similar attributions—Franzosi places strategic interaction at the center of his analysis. "It takes two to tango," he declares (Franzosi 1995: 15). Strikes and their preparation involve heavy dancing.

Industrial conflict is, as Franzosi says, a prominent form of **contention:** mutual, collective making of claims which, if realized, affect other people's interests. Contention is thus a particular, collective form of bargaining. Contention joins three elements: (1) claim-making and (2) strategic interaction involving (3) the deployment of commitment, coercion, and compensation as incentives for supporters, allies, rivals, and objects of claims. The minimum set of actors in contention consists of a *claimant* and an *object* of claims, but claims commonly run in both directions and often engage more than two parties. Contentious claims parallel, and frequently overlap, work contracts. Workers who contest the firing of a union activist, for example, sometimes invoke work contracts contentiously by arguing that the activist fulfilled all her job obligations and that the discharge violated established rules for expulsion from the firm.

Far from being an epiphenomenon of more basic economic changes, furthermore, contention over work makes a difference to the organization of production. Franzosi demonstrates how, for example, conflicts of the 1960s ended the centrality to both production and industrial conflict of the "mass worker"—the large-plant, continuous-process producer operating under intense time-discipline—in favor of work teams in big plants and extensive subcontracting to more flexible, less strike-prone smaller firms. Industrial conflict deeply influenced the very organization of work, a transformation which in turn affected further prospects for industrial conflict.

Franzosi's analysis also shows how Italian strike patterns resulted from strategic interaction among multiple actors. Relevant actors included foreign powers: From the late 1940s onward, American politicians, businessmen, and union leaders feared Soviet influence in Italy. Beginning in 1950, well-laundered American money subsidized formation of Italy's non-Communist labor unions as counterweights to the Communist-allied Italian General Confederation of Labor (CGIL) which had emerged from wartime Resistance coalitions and had spearheaded the great strikes of 1948 to 1950 (Franzosi 1995: 114–115). Many Italian employers then played the ancient game of divide and conquer, not only negotiating agreements with non-Communist unions while refusing to bargain with the CGIL but also offering bonuses to workers who quit the CGIL or allowing the CGIL's rival unions to control production-line hiring and firing within their plants. During the struggles of the 1960s, however, the CGIL began to form effective alliances with other unions, a strategy that paid off in great gains for workers. Simultaneously the previously solid front between large and small employers was splitting, a fissure that augmented the strategic advantages of unified workers.

How and Why Workers Contend

Italian postwar experience of industrial conflict articulates neatly with the transactional analyses we have urged in previous chapters. It brings out the centrality of continuously renegotiated work contracts to collective action by all major actors: not only workers but also labor-supplying households, unions, firms, employers' associations, political parties, and members of various state agencies. For each of them, incentives, opportunities, and capacities for concerted action depended on currently shared understandings with other actors and on the history of their relations with other actors. Innovations in forms of collective action followed the pattern of institutional changes elsewhere: sometimes concentrating in remarkable waves of invention and adoption, but always building on previous forms, and often consisting of modifications at the edge of well-established routines. Even in the heat of struggle, transaction costs sorted possible ways of making claims, favoring those that drew on existing social relations and culture. Waves of action and change, furthermore, did not occur on the side of workers alone; all parties responded to new opportunities and threats by means of reorganization, technical innovation, and strategic maneuvering. On the side of management, waves of lockouts and of changes in production resulted from the same processes that propagated strike waves among workers.

Within the systematic study of collective contention, the shift from individualistic to relational analyses we are urging on analyses of work has already been proceeding for a decade. Earlier, individualistic explanations—both rationalist and irrationalist—of participation prevailed, as analysts sought to show either that individual interests sometimes stacked up neatly into collective action or, contrariwise, that social movements, strikes, and other forms of contention attracted individuals driven by passions, illusions, and/or mistaken conceptions of their interests. Careful students of such phenomena came to realize that they were dealing with continuous social interactions, not with solo performances that individualistic models (whether rationalist or antirational) could adequately represent.

In studies of revolutions and social movements, specialists began to create models of strategic interaction among multiple parties in which participants responded to changing political opportunities, mobilized and demobilized, formed coalitions, tried tactical innovations, pursued collective ends, and scrutinized the outcomes of their interactions with care (for reviews, see Goodwin 1994; Marwell & Oliver 1993; Tarrow 1994). They also recognized increasingly the deep grounding of collective contention in existing social organization, for example the crucial part played by predisposing network ties in recruitment to social-movement activism (McAdam & Paulsen 1993). Students of contention outside of work, in short, were uncovering the same socially embedded interactive processes that Franzosi stressed in his analysis of Italian strikes and that we have identified in routines of work and labor markets.

Unlike large-scale collective contention, much bargaining over work contracts occurs almost invisibly, on a person-to-person scale, as bosses reinterpret the rules, employees evade the directions supervisors give them, and workers collaborate with each other to reshape daily routines. Since work organizes around contracts and since contracts always leave some uncertainty with respect to obligations, incentives, monitoring, and enforcement, all work entails continuous small-scale negotiation. Existing work mechanisms—mixes and levels of incentives, embedding, contracting, autonomy, matching, mobility, and training—offer constant occasions for renegotiation. In that sense almost all work involves the making of claims that, if realized, affect other people's interests. As earlier chapters have documented, such claim-making often takes collective forms. To that degree our earlier analyses of work relations have concerned contention. Capitalist firms also engage in frequent contention on a larger scale: takeover battles, stockholder-management fights, struggles with regulators and citizens over such matters as environmental pollution, splits within management over succession and competing directions for the firm. But sustained, overt, collective contention fully involving ordinary workers occurs more rarely and entails social processes that do not happen every day.

Given great asymmetries of power and organization between capitalists and workers, indeed, large-scale worker-initiated contention poses difficult explanatory problems. Like good Walrasian street vendors refusing to sell for too low a price, why don't workers individually walk away from unsatisfactory contracts to look elsewhere for better bargains? A proper answer contains three points:

First, dissatisfied workers do often quit, shirk, sabotage, or maneuver at an individual scale to modify their contracts.

Second, for workers as well as for managers the costs of finding alternatives to an operating set of contracts typically run from substantial to overwhelming.

Third, under some circumstances workers combine the interest, the capacity, and the opportunity to act in concert for improvements in their position or for defense against its degradation.

The first two points we have encountered repeatedly in earlier analyses of work routines. The third—how, when, and why workers contend effectively and collectively—engages us here.

Workers who act together on behalf of shared interests face something like the situation schematized in Figure 11.1. (We call the figure an "accounting scheme" rather than something more pretentious because it does not embody a precise causal logic—it makes, for example, no allowance for feedback from contention to shared understandings—but it does group the main elements any explanation must take into account.) Workers find themselves in *precipitating conditions* including established work mechanisms; preferred configurations of power, quality, and efficiency; existing social networks; a range of threats and opportunities affecting their interests and possibilities of action; and established means of coordination for their action. They activate *shared definitions* of actions they might undertake and likely outcomes of those various actions.

Such shared definitions depend heavily on interaction between the surrounding culture and the previous history of contention. They limit *collective contention,* which includes collective claims on others; deployment of incentives (commitment, coercion, and compensation) with respect to other participants and objects of claims; and strategic interaction with those others. Our scheme simplifies enormously by representing the position of just one actor at a time, which hides second-guessing and strategic interaction. At least it conveys the complexity and contingency of the process. Our causal accounting system, then, contains ten elements:

1. Variable *work mechanisms,* and challenges to them, typically supply both immediate precipitants and substantive claims of collective contention over work.
2. Workers and capitalists alike commonly embed their *preferred configurations* in stories connecting the history of their relations with rights, justice, and moral obligations.
3. Relevant *networks* center on those built into production itself—but significant networks also often include unions, gender divisions, racial solidarities, and old boys' connections that figure on no official organization chart.
4. The *threats* in question often spring from management initiatives: wage cuts, speedups, plant closings. *Opportunities* frequently result

FIGURE 11.1   Accounting scheme for work-based contention

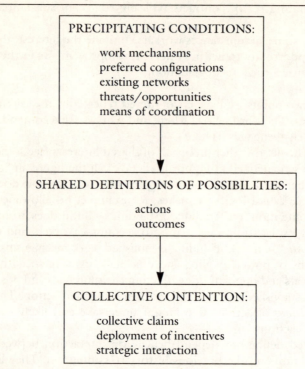

from increased availability of external allies in the form of other
workers, supportive communities, unions, or public officials.

5. Known *means of coordination* typically include informal communication on the job, union meetings, slowdowns, sabotage, grievances,
   and strikes. At times they also extend to external lobbying, demonstrations, boycotts, mutual-aid programs, political campaigns, adver-
   tisements, and other social-movement activities.

6. Envisaged *actions* include this whole repertoire of known means and
   possible variants on them—for example the new strike-demonstra-
   tions invented by Italian workers during the *autunno caldo*.

7. Shared conceptions of probable *outcomes* blend preferred configurations with memories of what happened the last time someone tried a
   certain action.

8. *Collective claims* focus on defense or alteration of existing work contracts.

9. *Incentives* at work consist of commitment, compensation, and coercion in varying combinations applied to both (a) fellow claimants

and (b) objects of claims; in a common scenario, workers deploy coercion and appeals to commitment in demands for compensation.

10. *Strategic interaction* with employers, allies, state officials, and other
parties pervades the process.

Any such formulation, to be sure, has an air of circularity; how can we identify relevant threats, opportunities, work mechanisms, and the remaining elements other than by observing the contention we are trying to explain? The
answer falls into two parts. First, the three clumps of factors—precipitating
conditions, shared definitions, and contention—specify what we have to explain, thereby narrowing the search for explanations and breaking it into
manageable bits. Second, the formulation tells us where to look for explanations and their confirmation: not in the abstractly conceived interest or motivation of an average individual worker, but in the social relations and culture laid down by previous interactions of work and contention.

We are asking, then, (1) how work generates collective contention, (2)
what accounts for variation and change in the issues, forms, and intensities
of contention about work, and (3) how work-based contention is changing
today. Our glance at Italian industrial conflict has already suggested answers
to the first two questions: Work generates contention through its impact on
opportunity structure, interaction networks, means of coordination, work
incentives (among other work mechanisms), and preferred configurations of
power, quality, and efficiency, as filtered through shared definitions of possible actions and their outcomes. Variation in these regards (whether produced by work as such or factors external to work) induces differences and
changes in the character of contention.

Those two answers also offer perspective on the third question—contemporary shifts in work-based contention. We should expect today's contention (its collective claims, strategic interaction, and deployment of incentives) likewise to alter in response to transformations of work mechanisms,
shared preferences, opportunity structure, interaction networks, means of
coordination, and work incentives, again as filtered through shared definitions of possible actions and their outcomes. For today's changes, we must
of course scrutinize the actual record of work-based contention, but we already have the injunction to focus on mutations in these elements while
keeping an eye on the way in which history and culture are reshaping managers' and workers' shared definitions of possibilities.

History, Culture, and Repertoires of Contention

We represent the strategic choices of a single actor in the matrix of Figure
11.2. Within the matrix lurk causal theories connecting possible ways of
making claims (e.g., occupying a factory) each attached to an array of likely

FIGURE 11.2   Shared definitions of claim-making and its outcomes

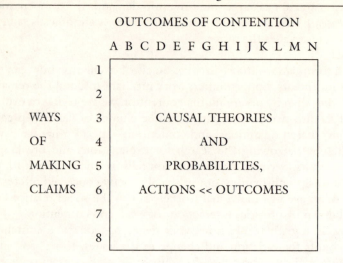

outcomes to those claim-making actions (e.g., wage gains, management concession to worker power, or ignominious defeat, and each assigned some rough probability). Actors rarely state probabilities and causal theories explicitly, but that does not reduce their force. Each cell connects one conceivable action with one conceivable outcome of that action, linking them by means of an estimated probability and a causal theory; thus cell D4 might connect Italy's go-slow (*sciopero bianco*) to replacement of a hated foreman with a probability of .10—one chance in ten that a go-slow will induce management to fire the foreman—on the simple theory that managers would rather sacrifice the foreman than take a cut in production. In the same matrix, C4 might say that a go-slow would lead to firing of workers with a probability of .30, an estimate making the tactic unattractive.

Such a matrix permits forward reasoning from actions to likely outcomes (If we occupy the factory, what are the chances the police will drag us out?) as well as backward reasoning from desired or feared outcomes to actions that will promote them (If we want to avoid arrest, what actions will help us?). Experience of interaction modifies each element: knowledge of possible actions, awareness of possible outcomes, estimated probabilities that one will produce the other, causal theories positing links between actions and outcomes. During a go-slow, for example, workers may well learn that replacement workers are waiting outside the plant gates, a bit of intelligence that reduces their estimates of success by changing the causal scenario.

By comparison with the forms of claim-making that are technically feasible in a given situation, any set of contending parties (the minimum set consist-

ing of a single claimant and a single object of claims) has at its disposal a radically limited array of actions. At one time or another, workers confronting
ruthless employers have beaten them, killed them, sued them, run them out
of town, broken their plant windows, smashed their machines, thrown
garbage at their houses, attacked their families, occupied their offices, torn
up their papers, appealed to their competitors, seized control over their enterprises, performed humiliating ceremonies, sung demeaning songs, presented petitions, posted anonymous handbills, sabotaged production, so-
licited intervention from priests, quit jobs en masse, formed competing
cooperatives, held material or equipment hostage, and otherwise harassed
owners. Most of these forms have disappeared; all have lost their standing as
recognized forms of contention.

The word "strike" itself probably derives from disgruntled British merchant sailors' striking of their ships' sails in defiance of orders from masters
to weigh anchor and set off from shore. Similarly, the French word for strike,
grève, comes from the tendency of seventeenth-century Parisian day workers
to mill on the Place de Grève, a major site of daily hiring, plotting action
against ungenerous masters. Both terms denoted actions that had long disappeared by the time British and French states legalized firm-by-firm strikes
during the nineteenth century. Historically, these various means of claim-
making have repeatedly figured as central actions rather than mere by-products of strikes or political movements. Today's aggrieved American workers,
however, generally restrict themselves to filing complaints with unions or
public officials, threatening to strike, quitting individually, and engaging in
covert resistance. For making claims on employers, they use a limited number of well-defined means.

To capture this restriction of means, a theatrical metaphor serves us well. A
continuous sequence of actions by which an actor makes a claim is a *performance*. All performances that characterize claim-making among a specified set
of collective actors constitute that set's *repertoire of contention*. Most repertoires resemble the tunes known to a jazz ensemble rather than the strict
scores of a military band: They encourage improvisation and combination
within well-established patterns rather than precise repetition. Performances
veer away from rote recitation because they form part of strategic interaction
in which situations change continuously, because surprise often gives advantages, and because workers are more likely to join an action if something
marks off the situation as a crisis requiring more than ritual participation. Yet
a number of factors push them toward selectivity and standardization in the
same way that work contracts repeat themselves: Familiarity greatly lowers
the cost of mobilizing people and guiding them safely through the interaction; familiar routines convey their messages to significant audiences with less
ambiguity than unfamiliar ones; performances build on existing interpersonal
networks and contracts; established rights and obligations, including those

installed in legal codes, always favor a limited range of interactions and subject many other possible interactions to penalties.

Western governments, to take the most obvious example, generally recognized the legal right of workers to strike during the latter half of the nineteenth century. But that recognition (a) narrowly defined which persons counted as workers eligible to strike against a given employer, not to mention which individuals and organizations could speak for the workers and what qualified as justifiable strike demands, (b) outlawed a number of performances, such as physical attacks on strikebreakers, that had frequently accompanied earlier work stoppages, (c) established stringent rules for such matters as picketing, entering workplaces, blocking entry, seeking arbitration, and even calling a strike, (d) pushed the entire process toward an orderly, nonviolent withdrawal of one firm's wageworkers (or some recognized subset of them) from the employer's premises, designation of representatives to conduct negotiations with similarly designated representatives of management, ratification of a settlement through systematic consultation of the workers in question, followed by an orderly return to work.

At the same time, governments set up agencies to monitor, contain, and sometimes arbitrate strikes when they occurred. Legally constituted trade unions formed to represent workers throughout these proceedings and acquired grudging governmental recognition as interested parties. None of this regularization precluded rage, vituperation, sabotage, trickery, lying, or covert maneuvering. But it did establish the strike as a highly recognizable, increasingly standardized set of routines engaging workers and employers with each other repeatedly through much of the Western world. In the United States, "wildcat" came to designate a strike that did not conform to well-recognized rituals, especially due announcement by the locally certified labor union.

The firm-by-firm strike and its concomitants displaced an equally well-established earlier repertoire of worker-worker and worker-employer performances—for example donkeying, in which workers seized a fellow worker who had been accepting a lower than standard wage or otherwise violating local rules, placed him on a donkey (or a substitute such as a fence rail), paraded him through town, cursed him roundly, and pelted him with garbage or stones as he proceeded. Sailors and port workers used tarring and feathering to similar effect. The expression "ride someone out of town on a rail" refers to a closely related practice. These forms of claim-making have practically disappeared from worker-worker repertoires.

Most directly, strikes replaced turnouts: occasions on which a small group of dissatisfied workers from a local trade marched from shop to shop in that trade, called out the workers in each shop to join their march, and if successful, held a meeting in a nearby field, deliberated a set of demands on all the local masters in their trade, sent delegates to meet with the assembled masters or their representatives, and tried to keep anyone from returning to work until the masters had offered a satisfactory settlement. Clearly the turnout and the firm-by-firm strike corresponded to different organizations of production: The turnout fit most easily with small-shop trades divided sharply between relatively equal masters on one side and relatively equal journeymen on the other. The strike, properly speaking, belonged to larger firms with more differentiated workforces. Yet the firm-by-firm strike did not simply displace the turnout smoothly as the organization of production altered. Jurisprudence, local practices, worker organization, and collective memory kept variants of the turnout—increasingly labeled as illegal conspiracies—well into the age of factories and heavily capitalized firms. To some extent, marches around factory grounds during Italy's *autunno caldo* reinvented the turnout, substituting a capital-intensive plant for the industrial village.

History and culture intertwine in the transformation and use of contentious repertoires. We can think of history as the dynamic aspect of culture, the process by which shared understandings and their representations change as a consequence of collective experience. Or we can think of culture as a residue laid down by history, the current accumulation of shared memories, explanations, justifications, condemnations, and representations of the possible. In either view, previous experience severely constrains the forms of contention that are now available for use. Struggle generates its own means.

Repertoires both limit and facilitate contentious action because the actors involved have learned their parts in established performances, because in general participants mobilize more easily for performances whose routines and outcomes they can predict, because meanings those performances convey have acquired some stability, because performances attach to existing networks and contracts, because they therefore intersect with important rights and obligations backed by known sanctions, procedures, and likelihoods of third-party intervention. Rights are publicly enforceable claims that command assent from significant third parties. Workers have a right to strike that involves far more parties than workers and employers alone: police, judges, legislators, consumers, workers' families. Although with legal sanction guilds once set and enforced rates of payment for all their members, these days most workers enjoy no such right to attack the person, property, or tools of fellow workers who toil for less than the prevailing wage. When Teamster truckers beat nonunion drivers who are working at less than Teamster rates, they risk arrest and conviction for assault. The chief exceptions nowadays are professionals, who can still use legal procedures to drive ratecutters out of business. History and culture have intervened.

As our stories suggest, states figure importantly in work-based contention even when state officials do not intervene directly. They enact and enforce laws making some forms of claim-making permissible and others liable to punishment. They codify, regulate, and adjudicate rights of workers and owners. They define opportunity structures ranging from strict repression of workers' organization to direct participation in government by workers' representatives and allies. Franzosi's findings for Italy, with antilabor governments depressing strike activity, conform to patterns widely observed elsewhere. Examining Brazilian strikes from 1945 to 1989, for example, Salvador Sandoval identifies an important feature of the pattern: Under repressive military regimes, strikes certainly declined, but they also became more pointedly political in claims and consequences; with democratization, strikes responded more directly and exclusively to shifts in the Brazilian economy (Sandoval 1993: 57–75). National politics set important limits within which changing conditions of work generated contention.

The Organization of Work
as Basis and Object of Contention

How, then, does work generate contention? Let us break the question into two segments: (1) How does the organization of work generate potentially contentious issues? (2) Under what conditions do parties to work contracts acquire the capacity and propensity to struggle over those issues?

First, where do contentious issues come from? When the performance of one party, the uncertainty of obligations, incentives, monitoring, and enforcement, or the manifest balance of advantages changes notably, incitements to small-scale contention appear. Where many workers and managers are parties to the same contracts and such changes occur, the situation becomes ripe for collective contention on a large scale. Our enumeration of work mechanisms—incentives, embedding, contracting, autonomy, matching, mobility, and training—provides a rough checklist of work's features that are likely to become contentious issues:

Incentives (commitment, compensation, coercion): wages, hours, perquisites, discipline

Embeddedness (multiple producers, multiple recipients, nonproduction networks): categorical hiring, union recognition and rights

Contracting (incorporation, sustained contracting, job contracting, purchase): outsourcing, subcontracting of jobs

Autonomy (producer or recipient control over specification of the work process): intensity of monitoring, quality control, hours and work schedules

Matching (merit, network, categorical, walk-in): categorical hiring, firing, and promotion

Mobility (promotion, turnover, stagnation): job security

Training (formal education, on-the-job training, apprenticeship): qualifications for hiring, retention, and promotion

Because every work contract necessarily occupies a position in each of these
regards, the give and take of routine work put all of them at issue on the
small scale. They become more salient issues when managers try to shift existing contracts along any of the dimensions—cut pay, attempt to decertify a
union, terminate subcontracts, alter quality control, institute a new hiring
system, lay people off, impose new training requirements for promotion, and
so on. They also gain salience when economic expansion gives workers opportunities to act on long-nurtured grievances.

Small-scale struggles over such issues occur all the time. Few of them,
however, become objects of sustained collective contention. Workers initiate
such contention chiefly when they can see that collective action has a chance
of gaining them more in these regards, or at least of losing them less, than
collective inaction. Workers' "seeing" operates, of course, within the limits
set by existing work mechanisms, preferred configurations, current
threats/opportunities, available connecting networks, known means of coordination, plans for strategic interaction, disposable incentives, and shared
definitions of possible action-outcome combinations. As with technological
invention, innovation in contention follows strongly path-dependent trajectories, referring repeatedly to accumulated, reinterpreted experiences in past
and present.

In very broad terms, nevertheless, the same conditions that favor high
compensation for workers also give them more leverage in contention: location in firms with substantial market power, high capital-labor ratios, extensive worker discretionary control over firm capital, high impact of worker
performance on firm's aggregate performance, worker membership in privileged groups, and institutions confirming worker rights. Workers who can
easily disrupt production, impose large replacement costs by quitting, and
put substantial capital at risk have great collective-action advantages over
their fellows. So do those whose work, training, or nonwork connections
give them more extensive internal communication.

Underground coal miners provide an excellent example of workers who
once enjoyed great advantages in these regards: well-connected within mine
and community, easily capable of bringing the whole expensive mine apparatus quickly to a standstill, accumulating unshared local knowledge of the
seams they were working. These factors vary in potency over time, with a
firm that faces an urgent delivery deadline or perishable stocks obviously
more vulnerable to worker performance than one operating overstaffed in
slack season. Once American coal production moved from the cyclical market of heavy industry and home heating to power generation for large utilities, miners' advantages in these regards diminished enormously, as did their

TABLE 11.1   Strike Issues and Striker Rates, United States, 1980

Issue	*Percent Distribution of Strike Issues*			
	All Industries	*Textiles*	*Mining*	*Services*
General wage change	62.4	87.3	18.5	41.6
Wage adjustment	3.1	0.0	1.9	39.7
Job security	14.7	0.0	8.3	11.3
Plant administration	10.4	1.8	49.7	1.3
Union organization	1.7	0.0	13.6	0.4
Other	7.7	10.9	8.0	5.7
Total	100.0	100.0	100.0	100.0
Number of strikes*	3,885	33	297	262
Number of strikers*	1,366,300	5,500	116,600	85,600
Strikers*/1,000 workers employed in industry	15	6	113	3

*Strictly speaking, "work stoppages" and "workers involved."

SOURCE: Data from U.S. Bureau of Labor Statistics, *Analysis of Work Stoppages, 1980.* Bulletin 2120 (Washington, D.C.: U.S. Government Printing Office, 1982).

propensity for seasonal strikes. The well-known tendency of strikes (especially strikes for new benefits) to concentrate in periods of economic expansion reflects working-class awareness of this variable leverage.

As a result of organizational differences, industries vary greatly in both their levels and kinds of strikes. A crude indication appears in Table 11.1, which shows the distribution of major issues in American strikes during 1980. (We lack comparable information for later periods because the Reagan administration saved money by radically reducing reports of strikes from 1981 onward.) We return to textiles and mining, substituting services as a whole for health services, whose strike issues are not available separately. As it happens, none of 1980's major strikes occurred in textiles, mining, or health care; industrial conflict for the year centered on Gulf Oil and other petroleum refining companies, copper manufacturing, motion picture production, New York City public transit, construction in California and New York, California retail groceries, and public schools of Chicago and Philadelphia (U.S. Bureau of Labor Statistics 1982: 13–15). Still, 117,000 workers went on strike in mining, and another 86,000 in services.

Strike patterns differed sharply from industry to industry. Although the workforce as a whole produced 15 strikers for every thousand workers during the year, services and textiles produced only 3 and 6 per thousand respectively. Miners, however, struck at 7.5 times the national rate: 113 strikers per thousand workers. Major strike issues likewise differed dramatically among industries. While general wage changes (common at the expiration of contracts) and wage adjustments (more often involving abrupt wage cuts)

TABLE 11.2 Percent Distribution of Strikers by Occupational Category and Industry, United States, 1980

Category	All Industries	Textiles	Mining	Services
Professional/technical	12.1	0.0	0.0	55.5
Clerical	0.3	0.0	0.0	0.7
Sales	1.4	0.0	0.0	0.6
Production/maintenance	72.8	100.0	100.0	11.3
Protection	1.0	0.0	0.0	0.2
Service	1.6	0.0	0.0	19.0
Combinations	10.9	0.0	0.1	12.5
Total	100.1	100.0	100.1	99.8
Total Strikers	1,366,300	5,500	116,600	85,600

SOURCE: Data from U.S. Bureau of Labor Statistics, *Analysis of Work Stoppages, 1980.* Bulletin 2120 (Washington, D.C.: U.S. Government Printing Office, 1982), 40–42.

together accounted for about two-thirds of U.S. strikes in 1980, wages motivated 81 percent of service strikes and a full 87 percent of textile strikes. Again miners differed, with almost half their strikes concerning plant administration—job control and related issues—and another 13.6 percent attributable to struggles over union representation.

Understandably, the occupational categories involved in strikes varied as well. Table 11.2 shows the distributions. This time, services stand out from the other industries. Professionals such as the teachers who struck in Chicago and Philadelphia loomed large in service strikes while remaining practically nonexistent in all the rest. They occupied positions similar to nurses who began to organize and strike seriously during the 1960s and 1970s. If production workers predominated nationally, they amounted to only 11.3 percent of strikers in service industries, while combinations of different occupational categories allied more frequently in service strikes than elsewhere. That underpaid, overworked professionals with organizational leverage concentrate in service industries helps explain, of course, those industries' distinctive profile of strike participation. The organization of production obviously shapes patterns of contention.

Conditions that promote worker collective-action advantages do not necessarily promote strikes in a linear fashion—the more of X, the more of Y. From workers' perspectives, strikes are often costly alternatives to established grievance procedures, informal persuasion, invocation of governmental authorities, and other available measures; under conventions that crystallized during the nineteenth century, striking workers forsake their wages for whatever support union strike funds, local credit, and family resources can supply them. (If that arrangement seems natural and inevitable, consider how nineteenth- and twentieth-century conventions also establish that many workers do collect wages while [1] temporarily disabled, [2] on scheduled vacations, [3] benefiting from parental leave, [4] idled by involuntary plant shutdowns or [5] approaching retirement—not to mention that discharged workers commonly collect government-supervised unemployment benefits. Wage payments in cases [3] and [4] are far more common in Europe than in the United States. All of these arrangements issued from hard-won bargaining that could in principle have included continuation of wages during strikes.) Because of wage loss during strikes, long strikes—more likely when workers and owners have relatively equal power—have many disadvantages for both very weak and very strong categories of workers.

Workers who enjoy great leverage vis-à-vis employers can often get their way without striking at all. Workers who have few of these organizational advantages (little capacity to disrupt production, low capital-labor ratios, thin internal connections, and so on) are neither inclined to strike nor likely to win if they do strike. They usually recognize how hopeless a strike would be. Hence strikes work best, and have the greatest appeal, for intermediate workers, workers who neither run the place nor lack all stake in it. To the extent that unions specialize in striking, threatening to strike, negotiating strike settlements, and monitoring compliance with resulting contracts, they appeal chiefly to those intermediate workers. Neither house surgeons nor sweepers strike or join unions very often.

Workers who persist in given firms and industries accumulate imperfect but substantial knowledge of their strategic positions from daily experience and from collective memory of contentious episodes. Strikes and their outcomes themselves, when they occur, provide all parties with new information about their relative strengths and weaknesses. Samuel Cohn has used careful econometric studies to identify conditions for miners' success in strikes in the French mining industry from 1890 through 1935. Success was measured not by whether the workers immediately gained satisfaction of their explicit demands, but by wage changes over the years (Cohn 1993). Whereas Franzosi's study of Italian strikes concentrated on *causes*, Cohn's study of French strikes stressed *effects*. Here are some of Cohn's more remarkable findings:

1. Frequent strikes produced wage gains even when strikes themselves failed; over the long run, employers made larger wage settlements to militant workers than to those who struck infrequently.
2. Strikes over working conditions and political issues produced larger long-run gains than strikes over salary.
3. Short strikes produced larger gains than long strikes.
4. Bureaucratized, centralized unions gained fewer advantages for their members than decentralized unions.
5. Ideologically divided dual unions tended to reduce worker advantages by encouraging employers' steering of benefits to less militant workers.

6. All these advantages depended, however, on the existence of a credible strike threat including (a) ability to mobilize workers and (b) employer costs imposed by work stoppage.

Some of these results follow directly from the principles we have already laid out. Few readers, for example, will find the relative weakness of dual unions astonishing.

Other findings are more puzzling; why should losing strikes, for example, produce wage gains? Militant workers struck more often, even to their short-run disadvantage, and more often struck over nonwage issues. Workers who acquired a reputation for militancy—read "trouble"—more often attracted both preventive wage rises and government intervention to reduce conflict. (Once French socialists and trade union supporters entered the national legislature late in the nineteenth century, the French government became much more likely than the American to enter labor disputes on the side of workers or at least in favor of a compromise settlement [Friedman 1988].) Bureaucratized, centralized unions installed leaders who developed closer ties to managers, who had more to lose in all-out conflict, and who therefore became more reluctant to risk open confrontations than their confreres in decentralized unions. At least in France, an effective threat of disruption, hence greater likelihood of gain from strikes, included not only direct blockage of work routines but also workers' public political action and the attraction of government intervention into local disputes and the lives of firms.

French strikes between 1890 and 1935 underscore the importance of conditions outside any particular firm for levels and forms of industrial conflict. Over that period, strikes bunched significantly in waves, with the waves of 1893, 1899–1900, 1904, 1906, and 1919–20 (15 percent of the years) accounting for 35 percent of all strikers during the period in question (computed from Shorter & Tilly 1974: 361–362; "strike waves" include all years in which both number of strikes and number of strikers exceeded the mean of the previous five years by at least 50 percent). Every strike wave brought together multiple firms, regions, and industries. Just as Franzosi's analysis of later Italian strikes teaches us to expect, each of them also intersected with national politics, responding to opportunities or threats established by the current governmental situation, becoming a political issue in itself, and causing changes in existing political alignments.

The great French strike wave of 1906, for example, included 1,354 strikes and 437,800 strikers. It benefited from a great organizational consolidation of French labor in 1904–1905. Those years brought the formation of a Unified Socialist Party that became the French Section of the Workers' International, organizational ancestor of both the French Socialist and Communist parties of postwar years. The central labor federation, Confédération Générale du Travail (CGT), decided to launch a decisive campaign for the eight-hour day with a general strike on May Day 1906. (The French campaign focused more sporadic agitation that had been going on in France since 1890; it followed by two decades the American Federation of Organized Trades' initiation of a similar campaign on May 1, 1886, by 16 years the Second International's first effort at a multinational general strike on behalf of the eight-hour day, May 1, 1890.) During the spring of 1906, a violent struggle over disestablishment of Catholic schools and monasteries continued into the opening of a turbulent national electoral campaign. Together, they provided an immediate political context for the strike wave, as did Georges Sorel's publication in 1906 of his *Reflections on Violence,* which advocated the General Strike as the means of revolution.

In this political setting, a literally explosive event started the strike wave. On March 10, a gas explosion at Courrières, near Lens, killed 1,200 miners. The disaster precipitated protests led by anarchist unions (no oxymoron in those days), soon joined by their syndicalist and socialist rivals. Before long almost a third of all France's miners were on strike. Then the balance shifted from mining; Paris-based union leaders began to coordinate a national movement in which Parisian workers themselves participated enthusiastically. Mass meetings, marches, demonstrations, and manifestos accompanied the firm-by-firm organization of walkouts. France's interior minister, Georges Clemenceau, and the prefect of the Seine (whose district included Paris) set their spies and detectives to following labor activists and having those who violated the law arrested.

On April 20, the prefect's staff typed out predictions of May Day's activities and strike turnout. They expected much greater response to the May Day call in Paris than elsewhere. One report for the Seine concluded:

> Leaving aside the typographers and the goldsmiths, who are already striking, we can count on 185,000 strikers in Paris. But since the voluntary idleness of some leads to the forced idleness of others (for example, ruglayers can't work if painters go on strike), the total number of strikers can be estimated at 200,000. The most troublesome will be construction laborers, bakers, grocers, and hairdressers; having little hope of getting benefits by means of peaceful strikes, they will try to intimidate their employers through sabotage. (Archives Nationales, Paris, F⁷ 13267)

The staff's predictions came close to the mark. Over the year as a whole, the Seine's workers supplied 29 percent of the entire country's strikers. The strike wave spread greatly with May Day. Eventually typographers and smelters brought large numbers into the fray; automobile workers (who concentrated in the Paris suburbs) came out in force for the first time ever. Almost every industrial category, in fact, contributed far more strikers than its usual number (Shorter & Tilly 1974: 118–122). The government reacted energetically, arresting national union leaders, ransacking the CGT's Paris headquarters, looking far and wide for evidence of a revolutionary conspiracy.

France as a whole then teemed with small-scale revolutionary conspiracies, but they did not cause the wave of workers' contention during 1906. The wave roared in from a conjunction of the factors we have been stressing: favorable shifts in existing networks, means of coordination, and opportunities for labor at a national scale; expanding shared definitions of possible actions and their outcomes; ready examples of claims, deployment of incentives, and strategic interaction from miners' reactions to the Courrières disaster. Although it took French industrial workers another thirty years to reach their eight-hour day—the momentous strike wave of the 1936 Popular Front and its accompanying political struggles made that particular gain—by the early twentieth century worker-initiated contention was making a substantial difference to both the organization of production and national politics.

Work and Contention in the United States

Throughout the capitalist world, relations among workers, managers, and the state have played a significant part in national politics for at least a century. As our glances at Italy and France have already indicated, work-based contention has brought other Western countries much closer to revolutionary crisis than the United States (Cronin 1984; Haimson & Tilly 1989; Haimson & Sapelli 1992; Korpi & Shalev 1979, 1980). Not that American workers have always behaved more moderately than their Canadian, Latin American, and European counterparts; with massive railroad struggles and the growth of the Knights of Labor, for example, the 1870s and 1880s brought U.S. labor militancy to epic levels. The differences arose thereafter, as the American state sided with capital more decisively than any other Western state, state-led or state-tolerated repression drove militant workers underground, and politically moderate craft unions came to dominate organized labor (Friedman 1988; Sexton 1991; Voss 1993). Toleration and expansion of industrial unions under the New Deal gave a boost to American union membership. Even then, U.S. management allowed unions very little say about production decisions. Major unions accepted that exclusion. As longtime labor reporter John Hoerr puts it,

> when organized labor became an insider, so to speak, in the economic system, it lost interest in what was happening in the work process. The union presence remained strong on the factory floor in the person of the steward or grievance committeeman. But he or she fulfilled a narrow quasi-legal function of filing grievances when members complained about management decisions such as disciplinary actions or job assignments. The union took virtually no part or responsibility in making the workplace more productive, or in gaining a direct voice for its members in operations. (Hoerr 1988: 34)

In 1948, for example, Walter Reuther essentially abandoned his earlier calls for worker participation in production management when his United Auto

Workers signed a long-term wage agreement with General Motors featuring automatic cost-of-living increases but restricting the union largely to matters of wages and hours (Hoerr 1988: 612).

Cold War repression of left-wing unions, furthermore, soon checked labor militancy and reestablished the political advantages of American capital. As American manufacturing began to face acute international competition, union leaders took increasingly cautious positions, concentrating on wage issues, their members' job security, and saving their own organizations. Government deregulation of trucking and other transportation industries promoted hiring of lower-cost nonunion workers, undercutting even such aggressive unions as the Teamsters (Belzer 1995). Union members lost confidence in their leadership, and unions failed to organize new groups of workers. Union membership, which had reached 35.5 percent of U.S. nonagricultural employees in 1945 and remained close to that level until 1954, declined massively after then (Goldfield 1987: 8–22). Union members' occupational composition shifted dramatically; while the labor force as a whole was moving from 17 percent professional and technical in 1935 to 30 percent in 1990, professional and technical workers comprised essentially 0 percent of union members in 1935, 9 percent in 1970, a full 25 percent in 1990 (Form 1995: 41).

Capitalist countries vary greatly in union density: the proportion of all legally organizable wageworkers who belong to unions. Around 1980, union density broke down as follows (Rothstein 1992: 42):

80 percent or more: Sweden, Denmark, Finland
50–79 percent: Iceland, Belgium, Ireland, Norway, Austria, Australia
20–49 percent: United Kingdom, Canada, Italy, Switzerland, West Germany, Netherlands, Japan
under 20 percent: United States, France

Although France (where workers can and do easily drop their union memberships between strike waves, only to join up again as conflict rises) bottomed the list at 15 percent, the United States came close at 18 (and has subsequently fallen even farther).

In these huge differences we see long-term effects of capital's hegemony as mediated by the character of the state. With roughly equal weights, three factors—presence of leftist politicians in government, union involvement in the administration of unemployment benefits, and the size of the labor force in unionizable industries—explain almost all the country-to-country variation in union density (Rothstein 1992; see also Western 1993; Zolberg 1986). Differences in unionization then reciprocally affect the ability of workers to get their way with management and the state. Here is one ironic consequence: Countries high on union density tend to have few strikes, whereas workers in the low-ranking countries, lacking other means, strike frequently.

In the United States, nevertheless, the collapse of organized labor in manufacturing since the 1950s has depressed strike activity as well. For a century, American workers engaged their employers in longer, less successful strikes than their confreres in other capitalist countries (Edwards 1981: 41–46). But they certainly struck often. Figure 11.3 reports strikers per 1,000 workers from 1881 through 1995 (Edwards 1981; Statistical Abstract of the United States, 1996; U.S. Bureau of Labor Statistics 1982; the Edwards series, grouped for blocks of years, uses nonagricultural employment as its base, whereas the Bureau of Labor Statistics includes all employees except private household, forestry, and fisheries; nevertheless the two series coincide closely). In the United States, as elsewhere, strikes have concentrated in great waves, and those waves have reached their greatest heights in years immediately following major wars. Despite a surge in the later 1960s, the trend of American strike activity since World War II has run massively downward. By 1980 striker rates were touching the lowest levels they had reached for a century. Those low levels of strike activity reflected American labor's disintegration.

Not all American workers have fallen into a postwar collective-action slump. David Wellman drew on three years of close observations on San Francisco's docks to conclude that the longshoremen's union remains activist and radical

> not because it permitted communists to join in the 1950s, or because its founding leaders were sympathetic to socialist causes, or because it supported unpopular foreign policy issues. Nor is it radical in conventional terms that equate radical with ultra-left politics. It is radical because it promotes trade union values, because it is based on the principles of solidarity, equality, and democracy. It is radical because, in addition to the collectivist impulses contained in the values of solidarity and equality, the union practices and promotes insubordination and individualism. (Wellman 1995: 306)

Although containerized cargo-handling has drastically changed work routines and productivity on the waterfront, with a consequent decline in the total number of workers, it has actually sustained or even enhanced some of the conditions that favor workers' collective action: location in firms with substantial market power, high capital-labor ratios, extensive worker discretionary control over firm capital, high impact of worker performance on firm's aggregate performance, and institutions confirming worker rights. The carryover of reputations and relations from the days of conventional handwork has given longshoremen additional advantages in asserting their rights.

Looking at detailed evidence from California, Paul Johnston (1994) pointed out that public-sector workers grew increasingly organized, militant, and strike prone from the mid-1960s to 1980 before shifting to political ac-

FIGURE 11.3   Strikers per 1,000 workers, United States, 1881–1995

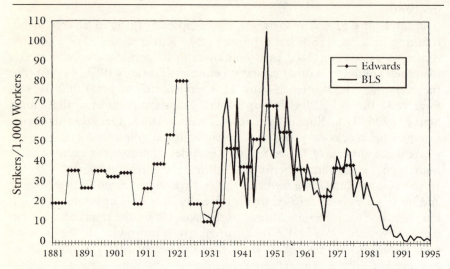

SOURCES: Data from U.S. Bureau of Labor Statistics, *Analysis of Work Stoppages,
1980.* Bulletin 2120 (Washington, D.C.: U.S. Government Printing Office, 1982)
Statistical Abstract of the United States, 1996 (Washington, D.C.: U.S. Government
Printing Office, 1996), and P. K. Edwards, *Strikes in the United States 1881–1974*
(Oxford: Blackwell, 1981).

tion in defense of threatened public services—and their own jobs. Johnston, a
union organizer for United Farm Workers, Service Employees International
Union, and other organizations in northern California until his "involuntary
retirement" into professional sociology in 1982, emphasizes the relative success of California's public employees. His case studies include female administrative workers in San Jose and San Francisco as well as city nurses in San Francisco, all of whom effectively deployed demands for comparable worth during
the 1970s. He extended his analysis to private-sector registered nurses (who
organized regionally but excluded other nursing personnel from their campaigns) and to a Justice for Janitors campaign that bridged public and private
sectors, seeing both as catching some of their fire from public-sector examples.

Whereas private-sector workers contend chiefly within the firms that employ them, strive strenuously to control labor markets, and turn to public
appeals as a last resort, the opposite is true of governmental employees:
From the start their contention brings them into the political arena. Since
government employees and their families can account for up to 30 percent
or so of a U.S. locality's registered voters, they can wield direct threats to the
tenure of elected officials; correspondingly, 43 percent of government employees belonged to unions in 1990 (Form 1995: 77). For those unions, or-

ganizational leverage depends less on the ability to stop production—although shutdowns of schools and garbage collection have dramatic impacts on large number of citizens—than on political alliances and popular support.

In terms of our accounting scheme, precipitating conditions based on work still interact with shared definitions of possibilities, but in the case of public-sector workers both clusters of causes involve elected public officials, political factions, and mobilized citizens much more immediately than in private-sector contention. Almost by definition, their workplaces cannot contain them. The struggles of public employees resemble those of miners in company towns. Public-sector "towns," however, extend from incorporated villages to big cities to states to the federal government.

Collective contention at work emerges from essentially the same processes that produce work in general. History, culture, past social relations, work objectives, and labor mechanisms all govern the loci, forms, and intensities of contention. Four major features, however, distinguish work-based collective contention from everyday production:

First, people involved face problems of collective action and interaction for which everyday routines will not suffice; they must ensure commitment, limit defections, organize consensus in the face of risk, and distribute costs and benefits effectively.

Second, strategic interaction entails anticipation, surprise, second-guessing, and disruption of opponents' valued procedures, assets, or identities; everyday work limits the scope of all these threats to orderly production.

Third, relations to persons, networks, and institutions outside the immediate setting of work figure more directly and visibly in collective contention concerning questions of work: Families, friends, neighbors, political actors, state officials, police, and others who rarely intervene in everyday production frequently get involved in sustaining, containing, mediating, or repressing work-based contention.

Finally, collective contention often results in deliberate, abrupt reorganizations of work and its personnel instead of the incremental, piecemeal, trial-and-error alterations that characterize most transformations: mass firings, new work rules, changes in wage schedules, introduction of novel labor processes, and more.

By no means all contention produces advantages for workers. Sometimes workers who contend would have been better off leaving work contracts as they were. Nevertheless each struggle leaves a residue in memories, shared understandings, interpersonal networks, work contracts, and jobs. A circle runs from the everyday organization of work through collective contention back to altered organizations of work.

12
Conclusions

So what? Why should workers, managers, officials, citizens, or students of work care about what the eleven dense chapters that precede this one have said? Mostly because our analysis clarifies how and why the social organization of work varies so much from setting to setting and time to time. If we understand how and why work is changing today, how it differs from work in the past, then we can map possibilities for work in the future–under some circumstances even help create more desirable forms of work. Since the kinds of work people do, and what they get for their effort, strongly affect their well-being in and out of work, the stakes are serious. If we want to vivify work, we must first explain its forms.

Our book has looked for better explanations of work under capitalism. It has concentrated on features of work that are widely recognized but badly explained by existing economic theories. Most available theories of work assume that one central, normal organization of work exists, most often in the image of well-defined jobs in orderly labor markets; other sorts of work then become variants on the theme or deviations from it. In contrast, we begin with the idea of work as multifarious by its very nature and search for principles of variation. As we closed our first sketches of cotton textile, coal mining, and health care, we laid out the questions that have guided our inquiry:

- Why do workers devote variable degrees of their available effort, knowledge, and care to work?
- In a given work setting, what determines the relative predominance of
  - A. use of labor markets, as opposed to household production, other petty commodity production, and the informal economy?
  - B. hiring via internal versus external labor markets?
  - C. different systems of supervision and reward?
  - D. purchase, subcontracting, and supervised production?
- What factors shape the scope, definition, and remuneration of particular jobs?
- What produces categorically selective hiring, promotion, and separation? What produces boundaries in segmented labor markets? Does the same process account for both?
- What sets the wages and other rewards of different workers? Why do whole categories of workers (especially categories of age, sex, race, and ethnicity) differ substantially in rewards from work?
- What explains people's varied individual voyages in work careers?
- How and why have these relationships and patterns changed over time?

We have offered partial answers, some of them familiar and some of them novel, to all these questions. On the whole, we have rejected prevailing stories about work, in which five main things happen: (1) available technologies and their changes shape the possibilities of production, with more efficient technologies rapidly driving out their predecessors; (2) adopting the most efficient technologies available, owners and managers of capital design systems of production, including jobs for workers within those systems; (3) the same owners and managers offer jobs, one by one, to the least expensive available workers who can meet the job requirements; (4) individual workers offer their services to the employer who will pay the highest price for someone with their qualifications; (5) firms that do not meet these conditions fail in competition with other lower-cost firms.

Within strong limits set by technology and market conditions, according to this sort of account, a single decision-making worker bargains with a single decision-making employer; compounded, bargains of this kind generate variable organizations of work. Such stories, in our view, give far too much weight to individual performances and far too much credit to market efficiency. They greatly underestimate the significance of networks, organizational structure, culture, history, and collective action.

What alternative have we provided? Drawing on institutionalist, Marxist, and organizational analyses, we have built an interactional model of work. We start with transactions among individuals rather than the individuals themselves, observe the bundling of transactions into different sorts of work contracts, and follow the elaboration of contracts into highly variable systems of production and distribution. We watch the unequal distribution of power affect the content and execution of work contracts. We also examine how the embedding of transactions in culture—in historically accumulated shared understandings and their representations—affects their operation. People who work and make others work do so on the basis of strong understandings about what forms of interaction are possible, desirable, and effective for what likely outcomes. Our recurrent comparisons of cotton textiles, coal mining, and health care have illustrated the historical building of culture into the very organizations of different industries and firms.

Most economic theorizing about work assumes that it occurs in efficiently organized labor markets. Our account differs in emphasizing that labor markets embody an unusual, historically specific organization of work. Labor markets presume formally free labor. They package work for hired producers in jobs within firms. Their elements include not only jobs and firms but also workers, employers, hiring, recruitment networks, supply networks, and contracts among the parties to work.

Such labor markets have indeed become much more central to work during the last century or so, but they have not obliterated other organizations of work. Even in capitalist countries, the bulk of work goes on outside of tightly organized labor markets. It takes place in households, schools, prisons, the informal economy, family farms, petty commodity production, and other settings that lack the apparatus of firms and jobs.

All real labor markets, furthermore, incorporate extensive segmentation—barriers to mobility from one kind of job to another; selective recruitment to jobs and firms as a function of race, ethnicity, gender, citizenship, schooling, and friendship; and large variations in perquisites, working conditions, and forms of compensation among firms, industries, and categories of work. Within the world of labor markets, workers and employers often create or incorporate major organizational barriers to the free movement of qualified labor: professional monopolies, organized crafts, labor recruitment networks based on particular migration streams, segregated job ladders within firms, citizenship requirements for hiring, and many more.

Detecting such barriers, we typically discover both (a) that employers and workers are continuously bargaining over organizational arrangements and (b) that all concerned are pursuing multiple objectives—for example, survival of their firm, standing in their community, order on the shop floor—in addition to monetary return. Pursuing multiple objectives from their side, employers offer a mix of coercion, commitment, and compensation as incentives for workers' performance rather than relying on compensation alone. But workers also pursue multiple objectives. We have repeatedly seen groups of workers preferring job security and autonomy to the maximum possible wage.

While criticizing conventional stories about the organization of work, we have disciplined the inquiry into work processes by means of our own stylized story. It runs as follows:

- Work centers on the production of use value.
- The elementary relationship links a *producer* to a *recipient* of use value.
- Producers and, especially, recipients of work-created value pursue objectives of *quality, efficiency, and power,* whose relative salience depends on both the task at hand and the culture—shared understandings and their representations—emerging from the previous history of the social relations involved.
- In pursuit of particular mixtures of those objectives, producers and recipients bargain out *work contracts;* all the work contracts connecting a given worker to other positions constitute a *job,* whereas all the social relations established by a set of connected work contracts concatenate into a *production network.* Thus jobs acquire links to each other (e.g., surgeon-anesthetist) and value relative to each other (e.g., master mechanic versus janitor), while entailing matching processes that identify particular persons with particular jobs.
- Producers and recipients of use value often incorporate existing interpersonal networks (for example, connections among the graduates of an elite technical school or among migrants from the same village) into the social relations of work; those networks then significantly affect the quality and outcomes of work.

- Networks that are salient in work include *hierarchies, markets, and coalitions,* each having somewhat different qualities.
- Segments of hierarchies, markets, and coalitions compound into *organizations:* clearly bounded network segments in which at least one position holds authority to commit social relations binding other positions. Organizations of work include firms, but they also include households, governments, and associations of various kinds.
- Work contracts and production networks embody various *mechanisms* (incentive, embeddedness, contracting, autonomy, matching, mobility, and training) to meet requirements of quality, power, and efficiency in ways that satisfy recipients' objectives.
- Among those mechanisms, the provision of *incentives*—commitment, compensation, and/or coercion—plays a central part in motivating work.
- Demands of recipients for quality, efficiency, and power constrain the availability of alternative mechanisms, thus shaping contracts and organizations.
- The configuration of any contract at any point in time, however, is not a determinate outcome of short-run demands for quality, efficiency, and power but rather depends on a *historically contingent bargaining process set within a cultural framework.*

Using different versions of this story, our book has done three main things: (1) described current change and variation in work within capitalist economies; (2) placed current work processes in historical perspective; (3) provided partial explanations of change and variation—past and present—in the character of work. Although our descriptions may be helpful in understanding current economic circumstances, the value of our analysis depends ultimately on the validity and fruitfulness of the explanations we offer. Let us review, then, the kinds of answers we have given to our guiding explanatory questions.

Why do workers devote variable degrees of their available effort, knowledge, and care to work?

We have generally replied that this is because workers and their employers have bargained varying mixes of coercion, commitment, and compensation into work contracts. Although a good deal of the relevant bargaining consists of everyday give-and-take, some of it occurs in the form of outright contention: collective and mutual making of interest-affecting claims.

In a given work setting, what determines the relative predominance of (a) use of labor markets, as opposed to household production, other petty commodity production, and the informal economy? (b) hiring via internal versus external labor markets? (c) different systems of supervision and reward? (d) purchase, subcontracting, and supervised production?

On the whole, our answers to these questions have invoked the reduction of transaction costs in pursuit of varying combinations of quality, efficiency, and power within important limits set by intertwining culture and interpersonal networks. While granting that under favorable institutional conditions full-fledged labor markets promote short-run efficiency and that in some intensely competitive industries efficiency-emphasizing conditions sometimes obtain, we have denied that competitive labor markets constitute the normal case from which all others must be counted as undesirable deviations.

What factors shape the scope, definition, and remuneration of particular jobs?

We see the bundle of work contracts attached to a particular one-person position—the job—as an outcome of incessant bargaining among producers and recipients under variable conditions of relative power. But bargaining does not start from zero with each new hiring. Because all work contracts connect a new jobholder to previously established workers, because managers copy organizational forms from existing firms or other segments of the same firm, and because which forms of contract are even conceivable depends on the institutional setting—visible American employers cannot get away with slavery, even if their ancestors did—the structure of jobs changes only slowly and incrementally.

As concomitants and consequences of proletarianization and capital concentration, on the average long-term trends have moved jobs under capitalism toward a combination of short-term monetization and extensive time-discipline. Within capitalist work, nevertheless, working conditions and compensation vary enormously as a function of workers' relations to capital; the crude division among drive, payment-by-result, prize, loyalty, professional, and artisanal forms of control captures some of that variability. So does our characterization of compensation levels (as well as hiring and promoting practices) as the result of interaction among productivity goals, employer and worker preferences, networks, bargaining, and inertia that favors existing ways of doing business. More specifically, we summarize wage determination in full-fledged labor markets as a function of

1. market power of the firm;
2. amount of capital per worker in the firm;
3. extent of the worker's discretionary control over the firm's capital;
4. impact of the worker's performance on the firm's aggregate performance;
5. substitutability of that impact;
6. worker's membership in favored ascriptive categories;

7. worker's network proximity to others scoring high on items 3, 4, 5, and 6;
8. the nature of institutions regulating compensation in the firm, industry, or occupation;
9. inertial effect of earlier configurations with respect to 1–8.

The list's miscellaneous character identifies it as more like a research agenda than a testable theory. Yet it enumerates the sorts of organizational processes that affect not only wages but differentiation among conditions of work in general.

What produces categorically selective hiring, promotion, and separation?

Two sets of causes intersect: First, managers and workers within firms create segmented clusters of jobs, each of them characterized by a distinctive pattern of remuneration, supervision, security, job-to-job mobility, and relation to organizational power; the most general divisions of this kind segregate command-and-promotion pools from turnover pools. Having established such divisions, managers and workers often recruit newcomers to them categorically, for example by assigning jobs on one side of the boundary to men and jobs on the other side to women.

Second, members of networks that cross firm boundaries—for example, friendship networks, migration streams, and graduates of certain schools—organize their own preferential access to certain job clusters. Professions and licensed trades take preferential access to the extreme by enlisting government support in the exclusion of workers who have not met their standards. Once internal segmentation and external access intersect, the sheer economy and reliability of recruitment through existing workers tilts the whole process of matching workers with jobs toward the reproduction of existing divisions.

What produces boundaries in segmented labor markets? Does the same process account for both categorical selectivity in matching of persons with jobs and boundaries in segmented labor markets?

Labor market segmentation results from functional, efficiency-driven processes (though typically ones that economize on information and transaction costs rather than production costs per se), as well as from historical processes of bargaining and inertia. In general, intersection of within-firm segmentation with segregated boundary-crossing networks causes both categorical divisions within firms and larger-scale boundaries in labor markets. At the larger scale, however, sheer costs of information and transportation start mattering more. Within large metropolitan areas, for example, residential segregation by race limits the access of segregated minorities to desirable jobs they could actually fill. Similarly, the passing of much information about available jobs by word of mouth and localized media means that categorical segmentation of information networks—for instance, the difference between English-language and Spanish-language worlds in the United States—promotes labor-market segmentation over and above the effects of organized preferential access to jobs.

What sets the wages and other rewards of different workers? Why do whole categories of workers (especially categories of age, sex, race, and ethnicity) differ substantially in rewards from work?

Here again intersection between within-firm segmentation of job clusters and categorically differentiated networks of recruitment and job seeking plays the central part. Within job clusters, individual performance certainly induces employers to offer differential rewards. Workers' categorical memberships often influence their job performances, if only because cooperation with other workers affects job performance and depends on categorical membership. Yet large categorical differences within firms and labor markets do not result from differential performance and discrimination within the same jobs; they result from categorical differences in the processes that match workers with jobs.

What explains people's varied individual voyages in work careers?

Once more, productivity, preferences, networks, bargaining, and inertia all shape worker mobility. Networks play a particularly large role. For the reasons we have just summarized, workers' network memberships strongly affect not only their access to successive jobs but also their work histories, whether in well-defined jobs or otherwise. Whether, when, how, and in what sequence workers are employed, unemployed, retired, engaged in entrepreneurship, involved in the informal economy, working in their own households, or performing work elsewhere depends crucially on the networks—including the categorically segregated networks—to which they belong. To be sure, schooling and job experience themselves create network memberships, thus producing significant correlations between individual capacities for different kinds of work and actual engagement in that work; training and mobility reinforce each other and therefore correlate. But in contrast to the common idea that efficient markets match individual workers with the best jobs for which they are qualified, close examination of work under capitalism reveals the enormous mediating influence of network membership.

How and why have these relationships and patterns changed over time?

Over the long run of capitalism, proletarianization and concentration of capital produced a decisive movement of work into labor markets, waged jobs, and hierarchical workplaces. Over the last century or so, such changes within major capitalist countries have altered the structure of inequality from one with the majority of the population living near bare subsistence to a majority living in relatively comfortable material circumstances between a small number of very rich people and a larger number of very poor. Relation to labor markets—in or out, but also where within them—has come to matter crucially for well-being.

Between 1940 and 1975, some equalization of income, wealth, and well-being occurred in capitalist countries as well-paid jobs in manufacturing expanded, labor unions exerted pressure for improvement in their members' conditions, and welfare states provided income and services for poor people. In expanding economies, labor shortages gave bargaining advantages to workers and their representatives. Since 1975 or so, those trends have all reversed in the capitalist world; inequality continues to rise as managers and owners of capital take larger shares of added value and ever more potential workers find themselves relegated to marginal jobs or none at all. As managers receive more of the rewards—although not necessarily the job security—of loyalty-based incentive systems, ordinary workers get squeezed out of loyalty systems into drive and payment-by-result systems of supervision and remuneration. At least in the United States, employers are also weakening internal labor markets as they turn both to external hiring for specialized skills and to part-time or temporary employment. The causal processes relating work to well-being continue to operate as before, but with very different consequences for the actual distribution of well-being.

And the future? We cannot read it well, for by our own account the future of work depends not just on shifts in technology and markets but on complex network-mediated organizational processes, many entailing contingent bargaining. Yet our analysis points both to futures that are *not* likely to materialize and to some that have some likelihood of happening.

Speculations about the future of work often move heedlessly from what technologies might make possible to what is actually going to occur—computers organizing and executing all work, new communications technologies mediating all transactions, and so on. More cautious predictions depend on interactions between technologies and markets, with cost-reducing technologies displacing their more expensive predecessors only within limits of market demand. While agreeing that technical innovation and market reorganization will continue to impinge on work in the future as they have in the past, our own analysis indicates that organizational requirements channel the adoption of new technologies and the transformation of work routines to accommodate them. Most technically possible futures will not materialize.

What will? Most people will continue to work for most of their lives, simply because the production of added value will remain for most people the only feasible way to acquire the means of bargaining for desired goods; few will live from theft, inheritance, nature's bounty, or authoritative redistribution of other people's wealth. Existing culture and social relations, both derived from accumulated historical experience, will continue to limit innovations in organizational forms of production. Interventions of outside actors, notably governments and households, will keep on influencing the organization of work settings. Beyond such obvious continuities, we should look for changes in the character of work where

- the relative bargaining power of different groups of producers and recipients shifts significantly;
- new actors intervene in the production of use value;
- whole new organizational models become available through diffusion and authoritative intervention; and
- the relative attractiveness of quality, efficiency, and power to those who control producing organizations alters notably.

Genuinely massive changes in the quality of work such as those we associate with the Industrial Revolution occur when most or all of these organizational transformations arrive together.

Conclusion: Work is unlikely to change character massively during the next few decades because low-wage workers in poorer countries compete their capitalist cousins out of business, because capitalist workers' preferences shift from wages to leisure, or because someone invents the ultimate labor-saving device. It is likely to change because international circuits of capital are gaining power, because governments are losing their capacity or propensity to enforce workers' established rights, and because long-distance migration is bringing new groups of workers into previously closed labor markets. Changing power relations will have larger impacts than new technologies or alterations in market efficiency. The character of work under capitalism has always depended on hard bargaining within stringent institutional limits established by the previous histories of shared understandings and social relations. Future work will continue to depend on struggle–muted, routinized, or openly contentious.

References

Abbott, Andrew (1988): *The System of Professions. An Essay on the Division of Expert Labor*. Chicago: University of Chicago Press. (1993): "The Sociology of Work and Occupations," *Annual Review of Sociology* 19: 187–209.

Abrahamson, Eric & Lori Rosenkopf (1995): "Social Network Effects on the Extent of Innovation Diffusion: A Computer Simulation," unpublished paper, Department of Management of Organizations, Graduate School of Business, Columbia University.

Adams, Walter, ed. (1977): *The Structure of American Industry,* 5th ed. New York: Macmillan.

Adelson, Andrea (1997): "Physician, Unionize Thyself: Doctors Adapt to Life as H.M.O. Employees," *New York Times,* April 5, 35–36.

Aglietta, Michel (1976): *Régulation et Crise du Capitalisme*. Paris: Calmann-Lévy.

Akerlof, George A. (1982): "Labor Contracts as Partial Gift Exchange," *Quarterly Journal of Economics* 97: 543–569. (1984): "Gift Exchange and Efficiency Wage Theory: Four Views," *American Economic Review Proceedings* 74: 79–83.

Akerlof, George A. & William Dickens (1982): "The Economic Consequences of Cognitive Dissonance," *American Economic Review* 72: 307–319.

Akerlof, George A. & Janet L. Yellen, eds. (1986): *Efficiency Wage Models of the Labor Market*. Cambridge: Cambridge University Press.

Albelda, Randy & Chris Tilly (1994): "Towards a Broader Vision: Race, Gender, and Labor Market Segmentation in the Social Structure of Accumulation Framework," in David M. Kotz, Terrence McDonough & Michael Reich, eds., *Social Structures of Accumulation*. Cambridge: Cambridge University Press, 212–230.

Aldrich, Howard, Trevor P. Jones & David McEvoy (1984): "Ethnic Advantage and Minority Business Development," in Robin Ward & Richard Jenkins, eds., *Ethnic Communities in Business: Strategies for Economic Survival*. Cambridge: Cambridge University Press.

Allen, Robert C. (1982): "The Efficiency and Distributional Consequences of Eighteenth-Century Enclosures," *Economic Journal* 92: 937–953.

Alonso, William & Paul Starr, eds. (1987): *The Politics of Numbers*. New York: Russell Sage Foundation.

Althauser, Robert P. & Arne L. Kalleberg (1981): "Firms, Occupations, and the Structure of Labor Markets: A Conceptual Analysis," in Ivar Berg, ed., *Sociological Perspectives on Labor Markets*. New York: Academic Press, 119–149.

Amaya, Tadashi (1990): "Recent Trends in Human Resource Development," Japanese Industrial Relations Series No.17, Japan Institute of Labor, Tokyo.

Amin, Shahid & Marcel van der Linden, eds. (1997): "'Peripheral' Labor? Studies in the History of Partial Proletarianization," *International Review of Social History,* supplement 4, entire issue.

Amott, Teresa L. & Julie A. Matthaei (1991): *Race, Gender, and Work: A Multicultural Economic History of Women in the United States*. Boston: South End Press.

Amsden, Alice (1990): "South Korea's Record Wage Rates: Labor in Late Industrialization," *Industrial Relations* 29 (1): 77–93. (1994): "Convergence, Technological Competition, and Transmission of Long-Run Unemployment," forthcoming in John Eatwell, ed., *Unemployment at Century's End*. White Plains, N.Y.: M. E. Sharpe.

Anders, George (1995): "Nurses Decry Cost-Cutting Plan That Uses Aides to Do More Jobs," *Wall Street Journal*, January 20, B1, B6.

Anderson, Grace M. (1974): *Networks of Contact: The Portuguese and Toronto*. Waterloo, Ontario: Wilfrid Laurier University Publications.

Andrews, Edmund L. (1996): "Don't Go Away Mad, Just Go Away: Can AT&T Be the Nice Guy As It Cuts 40,000 Jobs?" *New York Times*, February 13, D1, D10.

Appelbaum, Eileen (1987): "Restructuring Work: Temporary, Part-Time, and At-Home Employment," in Heidi I. Hartmann, ed., *Computer Chips and Paper Clips: Technology and Women's Employment*. Vol. II: Case Studies and Policy Perspectives (Washington, D.C.: National Academy Press).

Apple, Rima D., ed. (1990): *Women, Health, and Medicine in America: A Historical Handbook*. New York: Garland.

Aronson, Robert L. (1991): *Self-Employment: A Labor Market Perspective*. Ithaca: ILR Press.

Arrow, Kenneth (1950): "A Difficulty in the Concept of Social Welfare," *Journal of Political Economy* 58: 328–346. (1994): "Methodological Individualism and Social Knowledge," *American Economic Review, Papers and Proceedings* 84: 1–9.

Arthur, W. Brian (1989): "Competing Technologies, Increasing Returns, and Lock-In by Historical Events," *Economic Journal* 99: 116–131.

Ashenfelter, Orley C. & Albert Rees, eds. (1973): *Discrimination in Labor Markets*. Princeton: Princeton University Press.

Ashenfelter, Orley C. & Richard Layard, eds. (1986): *Handbook of Labor Economics*. Amsterdam: North-Holland.

Ashworth, William (1986): *The History of the British Coal Industry*. Volume 5, *1946–1982: The Nationalized Industry*. Oxford: Clarendon Press.

Attewell, Paul (1987): "The Deskilling Controversy," *Work and Occupations* 14: 323–346.

Averitt, Robert T. (1968): *The Dual Economy*. New York: McGraw-Hill.

Badaracco, Joseph (1991): "The Boundaries of the Firm," in Amitai Etzioni & Paul R. Lawrence, eds., *Socio-Economics: Toward a New Synthesis*. Armonk, N.Y.: M. E. Sharpe, 293–328.

Bae, Kyu Han & William Form (1986): "Payment Strategy in South Korea's Advanced Economic Sector," *American Sociological Review* 51: 120–131.

Baer, Ellen D. (1990): "Nurses" in Rima D. Apple, ed., *Women, Health, and Medicine in America: A Historical Handbook*. New York: Garland.

Bahl, Vinay (1989): "Women in the Third World: Problems in Proletarianization and Class Consciousness," *Sage Race Relations Abstracts* 14: 3–27. (1995): *The Making of the Indian Working Class: A Case of the Tata Iron and Steel Company, 1880–1946*. New Delhi: Sage.

Bain, G. S. & Robert Price (1980): *Profiles of Union Growth: A Comparative Statistical Portrait of Eight Countries*. Oxford: Blackwell.

Baker, George & Bengt Holmstrom (1995): "Internal Labor Markets: Too Many Theories, Too Few Facts," *American Economic Review, Papers and Proceedings* 85: 255–259.

Baker, George, Michael Gibbs & Bengt Holmstrom (1994a): "The Internal Economics of the Firm: Evidence from Personnel Data," *Quarterly Journal of Economics* 109: 881–919. (1994b): "The Wage Policy of a Firm," *Quarterly Journal of Economics* 109: 921–955.

Baker, George P., Michael C. Jensen & Kevin J. Murphy (1988): "Compensation and Incentives: Practice vs. Theory," *Journal of Finance* 43: 593–616.

Baker, Thomas H. (1994): "First Movers and the Growth of Small Industry in Northeastern Italy," *Comparative Studies in Society and History* 36: 621–648.

Baran, Barbara & Carol Parsons (1986): "Technology and Skill: A Literature Review." Berkeley: Berkeley Roundtable on the International Economy, University of California, January.

Barnes, Samuel H. & Max Kaase (1979): *Political Action. Mass Participation in Five Western Democracies.* Beverly Hills: Sage.

Baron, Ava (1982): "Women and the Making of the American Working Class: A Study of the Proletarianization of Printers," *Review of Radical Political Economics* 14: 23–42. (1991): eds., *Work Engendered: Toward a New History of American Labor.* Ithaca: Cornell University Press.

Baron, Harold (1971): "The Demand for Black Labor: Historical Notes on the Political Economy of Racism," *Radical America* 5: 1–46.

Baron, James N. (1984): "Organizational Perspectives on Stratification," *Annual Review of Sociology* 10: 37–69.

Baron, James N. & Michael T. Hannan (1994): "The Impact of Economics on Contemporary Sociology," *Journal of Economic Literature* 32: 1111–1146.

Baron, James N. & William T. Bielby (1980): "Bringing the Firm Back In: Stratification, Segmentation, and the Organization of Work," *American Sociological Review* 45: 737–755. (1984): "The Organization of Work in a Segmented Economy," *American Sociological Review* 49: 454–473.

Barrett, Michele & Mary McIntosh (n.d.): "The Family Wage: Some Problems for Socialists and Feminists," *Capital and Class* 11: 51–72.

Bean, Charles R. (1994): "European Unemployment: A Survey," *Journal of Economic Literature* 32: 573–619.

Becker, Gary S. (1957): *The Economics of Discrimination.* Chicago: University of Chicago Press. (1964): *Human Capital: A Theoretical Analysis with Special Reference to Education.* New York: Columbia University Press for National Bureau of Economic Research. (1976): *The Economic Approach to Human Behavior.* Chicago and London: University of Chicago Press.

Begg, David K. H. (1982): *The Rational Expectations Revolution in Macroeconomics: Theories and Evidence.* Baltimore: Johns Hopkins University Press.

Belchem, John (1990): *Industrialization and the Working Class: The English Experience, 1750–1900.* Aldershot, England: Scolar Press.

Belzer, Mike (1995): "Truckers' Travails: Deciphering a Decade of Decline," *Dollars & Sense* 201 (September/October), 20–23.

Berg, Ivar, ed. (1981): *Sociological Perspectives on Labor Markets.* New York: Academic Press.

Berg, Ivar & Janice Shack-Marquez (1985): "Current Conceptions of Structural Un-employment: Some Logical and Empirical Difficulties," *Research in the Sociology of Work* 3: 99–117.

Berg, Maxine (1985): *The Age of Manufactures: Industry, Innovation and Work in Britain, 1700–1820.* Oxford: Blackwell.

Berg, Maxine, Pat Hudson & Michael Sonenscher (1983): *Manufacture in Town and Country Before the Factory.* Cambridge: Cambridge University Press.

Berger, Suzanne & Michael J. Piore (1980): *Dualism and Discontinuity in Industrial Society.* Cambridge: Cambridge University Press.

Bergmann, Barbara R. (1986): *The Economic Emergence of Women.* New York: Basic Books.

Berk, Sarah Fenstermaker (1985): *The Gender Factory: The Apportionment of Work in American Households.* New York: Plenum.

Bernstein, Aaron (1995): "The Wage Squeeze," *Business Week*, July 17.

Berridge, Virginia (1990): "Health and Medicine," in F.M.L. Thompson, ed., *The Cambridge Social History of Britain 1750–1950.* Volume 3, *Social Agencies and Institutions.* Cambridge: Cambridge University Press.

Best, Michael H. (1990): *The New Competition: Institutions of Industrial Restructuring.* Cambridge: Harvard University Press.

Best, Norman (1990): *In Celebration of Work.* Lincoln: University of Nebraska Press.

Bielby, Denise D. & William T. Bielby (1988): "She Works Hard for the Money: Household Responsibilities and the Allocation of Work Effort," *American Journal of Sociology* 93: 1031–1059.

Bielby, William T. & James N. Baron (1986): "Men and Women at Work: Sex Segregation and Statistical Discrimination," *American Journal of Sociology* 91: 759–799.

Biernacki, Richard (1995): *The Fabrication of Labor: Germany and Britain, 1640–1914.* Berkeley: University of California Press.

Biggart, Nicole Woolsey (1989): *Charismatic Capitalism. Direct Selling Organizations in America.* Chicago: University of Chicago Press.

Bijker, Wiebe E., Thomas P. Hughes & Trevor J. Pinch (1987): *The Social Construction of Technological Systems: New Directions in the Sociology and History of Technology.* Cambridge, Mass.: MIT Press.

Blanchard, Olivier & Lawrence Summers (1986): "Hysteresis and the European Unemployment Problem," in Stanley Fischer, ed., *NBER Macroeconomics Annual.* Cambridge, Mass: MIT Press, 15–78.

Blau, Francine D. & Lawrence M. Kahn (1992): "The Gender Earnings Gap: Some International Evidence." Cambridge, Massachusetts: National Bureau of Economic Research Working Paper 4224. (1994): "Rising Wage Inequality and the U.S. Gender Gap," *American Economic Review, Papers and Proceedings* 84: 23–28.

Blau, Francine D. & Marianne A. Ferber (1985): "Women in the Labor Market: The Last Twenty Years," in *Women and Work: An Annual Review* 1: 19–49. (1986): *The Economics of Women, Men, and Work.* Englewood Cliffs, N.J.: Prentice-Hall.

Blau, Judith R. (1984): *Architects and Firms. A Sociological Perspective on Architectural Practice.* Cambridge, Mass.: MIT Press.

Blewett, Mary H. (1991): "Manhood and the Market: The Politics of Gender and Class among the Textile Workers of Fall River, Massachusetts," in Ava Baron, ed.,

Work Engendered: Toward a New History of American Labor. Ithaca: Cornell University Press.

Bloch, Marc (1970): *Feudal Society*. Volume 1, *The Growth of Ties of Dependence*. Translated by L. A. Manyon. Chicago: University of Chicago Press.

Block, Fred (1985): "Postindustrial Development and the Obsolescence of Economic Categories," *Politics and Society* 14: 70–103. (1990): *Postindustrial Possibilities: A Critique of Economic Discourse*. Berkeley: University of California Press. (1994): "The Roles of the State in the Economy," in Neil Smelser & Richard Swedberg, eds., *Handbook of Economic Sociology*. Princeton and New York: Princeton University Press and Russell Sage Foundation, 691–710.

Bluestone, Barry & Irving Bluestone (1992): *Negotiating the Future: A Labor Perspective on American Business*. New York: Basic Books.

Bluestone, Barry, Mary Huff Stevenson & Chris Tilly (1994): "Public Policy Alternatives for Dealing with the Labor Market Problems of Central City Young Adults: Implications from Current Labor Market Research." Occasional Paper, John W. McCormack Institute of Public Affairs, University of Massachusetts, Boston.

Bodnar, John (1982): *Workers' World: Kinship, Community, and Protest in an Industrial Society, 1900–1940*. Baltimore: Johns Hopkins University Press. (1985): *The Transplanted: A History of Immigrants in Urban America*. Bloomington: Indiana University Press.

Bodnar, John, Roger Simon & Michael P. Weber (1982): *Lives of Their Own: Blacks, Italians, and Poles in Pittsburgh, 1900–1960*. Urbana: University of Illinois Press.

Boisjoly, Johanne, Greg J. Duncan & Timothy Smeeding (1994): "Have Highly Skilled Workers Fallen from Grace? The Shifting Burdens of Involuntary Job Losses from 1968 to 1992." Mimeo, University of Quebec, Rimouski.

Bolin-Hort, Per (1989): *Work, Family and the State: Child Labour and the Organization of Production in the British Cotton Industry, 1780–1920*. Lund, Sweden: Lund University Press.

Boris, Eileen (1994a): *Home to Work: Motherhood and the Politics of Industrial Homework in the United States*. Cambridge: Cambridge University Press. (1994b): "The Home as a Workplace: Deconstructing Dichotomies," *International Review of Social History* 39: 415–428.

Borjas, George J. (1988): *International Differences in the Labor Market Performance of Immigrants*. Kalamazoo, Mich.: W. E. Upjohn Institute for Employment Research. (1995): "Ethnicity, Neighborhoods, and Human Capital Externalities," *American Economic Review* 85: 365–390

Botwinick, Howard (1993): *Persistent Inequalities: Wage Disparity Under Capitalist Competition*. Princeton: Princeton University Press.

Bound, John & Richard B. Freeman (1992): "What Went Wrong? The Erosion of the Relative Earnings and Employment of Young Black Men in the 1980s," *Quarterly Journal of Economics* 107: 201–232.

Bourke, Joanna (1994): "Housewifery in Working-Class England 1860–1914," *Past & Present* 143: 167–197.

Bowles, Samuel (1985): "The Production Process in a Competitive Economy: Walrasian, Neo-Hobbesian, and Marxian Models," *American Economic Review* 75: 16–36.

Bowles, Samuel & Herbert Gintis (1976): *Schooling in Capitalist America: Educational Reform and the Contradictions of Economic Life.* New York: Basic Books. (1986): *Democracy and Capitalism: Property, Community, and the Contradictions of Modern Thought.* New York: Basic Books. (1993): "The Revenge of Homo Economicus: Contested Exchange and the Revival of Political Economy," *Journal of Economic Perspectives* 7: 83–114 (with comments by Oliver Williamson and Joseph Stiglitz).

Boxman, Ed, Paul De Graaf & Henrik Flap (1991): "The Impact of Social and Human Capital on the Income Attainment of Dutch Managers," *Social Networks* 13: 51–73.

Boyer, Robert & Jacques Mistral (1978): *Accumulation, Inflation, Crises.* Paris: Presses Universitaires de France.

Bradbury, Katharine L. (1990): "The Changing Fortunes of American Families in the 1980s," *New England Economic Review* July/August: 25–40.

Braddock, Jomills Henry II & James M. McPartland (1987): "How Minorities Continue to Be Excluded from Equal Employment Opportunities: Research on Labor Market and Institutional Barriers," *Journal of Social Issues* 43: 5–39.

Brass, Tom (1994): "Some Observations on Unfree Labour, Capitalist Restructuring, and Deproletarianization," *International Review of Social History* 39, part 2: 255–276.

Brass, Tom, Marcel van der Linden & Jan Lucassen (1993): *Free and Unfree Labour.* Amsterdam: International Institute for Social History.

Braverman, Harry (1974): *Labor and Monopoly Capital: The Degradation of Work in the Twentieth Century.* New York: Monthly Review Press.

Breman, Jan (1994): *Wage Hunters & Gatherers: Search for Work in the Urban and Rural Economy of South Gujarat.* Delhi: Oxford University Press.

Breton, Raymond, Wsevolod W. Isajiw, Warren E. Kalbach & Jeffrey G. Reitz (1990): *Ethnic Identity and Equality: Varieties of Experience in a Canadian City.* Toronto: University of Toronto Press.

Bridges, William P. (1982): "The Sexual Segregation of Occupations: Theories of Labor Stratification in Industry," *American Journal of Sociology* 88: 270–295.

Brines, Julie (1994): "Economic Dependency, Gender, and the Division of Labor at Home," *American Journal of Sociology* 100: 652–688.

Brinton, Mary C., Yean-Ju Lee & William L. Parish (1995): "Married Women's Employment in Rapidly Industrializing Societies: Examples from East Asia," *American Journal of Sociology* 100: 1099–1130.

Brody, David (1990): "Labour Relations in American Coal Mining: An Industry Perspective," in Gerald D. Feldman & Klaus Tenfelde, eds., *Workers, Owners, and Politics in Coal Mining: An International Comparison of Industrial Relations.* New York: Berg.

Broman, Thomas (1995): "Rethinking Professionalization: Theory, Practice, and Professional Ideology in Eighteenth-Century German Medicine," *Journal of Modern History* 67: 835–872.

Brooks, Clem (1994): "Class Consciousness and Politics in Comparative Perspective," *Social Science Research* 23: 167–195.

Brown, Charles (1980): "Equalizing Differences in the Labor Market," *Quarterly Journal of Economics* 94: 114–134.

Brown, James N. & Orley Ashenfelter (1986): "Testing the Efficiency of Employment Contracts," *Journal of Political Economy* 94 (June): 55–78.

Brunsson, Nils (1985): *The Irrational Organization: Irrationality as a Basis for Organizational Action and Change*. Chichester: Wiley. (1989): *The Organization of Hypocrisy: Talk, Decisions, and Actions in Organizations*. Chichester: Wiley.

Buchinsky, Moshe & Jennifer Hunt (1996): "Wage Mobility in the United States." Working Paper 5455, National Bureau of Economic Research, Cambridge, Massachusetts.

Bulow, Jeremy I. & Lawrence H. Summers (1986): "A Theory of Dual Labor Markets with Application to Industrial Policy, Discrimination, and Keynesian Unemployment, *Journal of Labor Economics* 4: 376–414.

Burawoy, Michael (1979): *Manufacturing Consent: Changes in the Labor Process Under Monopoly Capitalism*. Chicago: University of Chicago Press. (1985): *The Politics of Production*. London: Verso. (1990): "Marxism as Science: Historical Challenges and Theoretical Growth," *American Sociological Review* 55: 775–793.

Burawoy, Michael & János Lukács (1992): *The Radiant Past: Ideology and Reality in Hungary's Road to Capitalism*. Chicago: University of Chicago Press.

Burbridge, Lynn C. (1994): "The Reliance of African-American Women on Government and Third-Sector Employment," *American Economic Review, Papers and Proceedings* 84: 103–107.

Burgess, Keith (1980): *The Challenge of Labour: Shaping British Society 1850–1930*. New York: St. Martin's.

Burrow, James G. (1977): *Organized Medicine in the Progressive Era: The Move Toward Monopoly*. Baltimore: Johns Hopkins University Press.

Burt, Ronald S. & Marc Knez (1995): "Kinds of Third-Party Effects on Trust," *Rationality and Society* 7: 255–292.

Butler, Richard J. & James B. McDonald (1986): "Income Inequality in the United States, 1948–1980," *Research in Labor Economics* 8: 85–140.

Buttrick, John (1952): "The Inside Contract System," *Journal of Economic History* 12: 205–221.

Byron, Reginald (1994): "The Maritime Household in Northern Europe," *Comparative Studies in Society and History* 36: 271–292.

Bythell, Duncan (1969): *The Handloom Weavers: A Study in the English Cotton Industry During the Industrial Revolution*. Cambridge: Cambridge University Press.

Caferro, William (1994): "Mercenaries and Military Expenditure: The Costs of Undeclared Warfare in XIVth Century Siena," *Journal of European Economic History* 23: 219–248.

Campbell, Angus, Philip E. Converse & Willard L. Rodgers (1976): *The Quality of American Life: Perceptions, Evaluations, and Satisfactions*. New York: Russell Sage Foundation.

Campbell, Karen E., Peter V. Marsden & Jeanne S. Hurlbert (1986): "Social Resources and Socioeconomic Status," *Social Networks* 8: 97–117.

Campbell, Karen E. & Rachel Rosenfeld (1986): "Job Search and Job Mobility: Sex and Race Differences," *Research in the Sociology of Work* 3: entire issue.

Cannings, Kathleen & William Lazonick (1978): "The Development of the Nursing Labor Force in the United States: A Basic Analysis" in Samuel Wolfe, ed., *Organization of Health Workers and Labor Conflict*. Farmingdale, N. Y.: Baywood.

Caplow, Theodore (1954): *The Sociology of Work*. Minneapolis: University of Minnesota Press.

Cappelli, Peter (1993): "Are Skill Requirements Rising? Evidence for Production and Clerical Workers," *Industrial and Labor Relations Review* 46: 515–530. (1995): "Rethinking Employment," *British Journal of Industrial Relations* 33: 563–602.

Cappelli, Peter & K. C. O'Shaughnessy (1995): "Skill and Wage Change in Corporate Headquarters, 1986–1992." National Center on the Educational Quality of the Workforce, University of Pennsylvania, Philadelphia.

Card, David (1990): "Strikes and Bargaining: A Survey of the Recent Empirical Literature," *American Economic Review, Papers and Proceedings* 80: 410–415.

Carney, Judith (1996): "Rice Milling, Gender, and Slave Labour in Colonial South Carolina," *Past & Present* 153: 108–134.

Carré, Françoise, Virginia L. duRivage & Chris Tilly (1995): "Piecing Together the Fragmented Workplace: Unions and Public Policy on Flexible Employment," in Lawrence G. Flood, ed., *Unions and Public Policy*. Westport, Conn.: Greenwood Press, 13–37.

Carroll, Glenn R. & J. Richard Harrison (1994): "On the Historical Efficiency of Competition Between Organizational Populations," *American Journal of Sociology* 100: 720–749.

Carter, Susan B. & Richard Sutch (1996): "Fixing the Facts: Editing of the 1880 U.S. Census of Occupations with Implications for Long-Term Labor Force Trends and the Sociology of Official Statistics," *Historical Methods* 29: 5–24.

Carvajal, Doreen (1995): "Salvador Helps Refugees Filing for Asylum in U.S.," *New York Times*, October 27, A1, B4.

Case, Anne C. & Lawrence F. Katz (1991): "The Company You Keep: The Effect of Family and Neighborhood on Disadvantaged Youths." Working Paper 3705, National Bureau of Economic Research, Cambridge, Massachusetts, May 1991.

Casparis, John (1982): "The Swiss Mercenary System: Labor Emigration from the Semi-Periphery," *Review* 5: 593–642.

Castles, Stephen & Mark J. Miller (1993): *The Age of Migration: International Population Movements in the Modern World*. New York: Guilford Press.

Chandler, Alfred (1977): *The Visible Hand: The Managerial Revolution in American Business*. Cambridge: Harvard University Press. (1990): *Scale and Scope: The Dynamics of Industrial Capitalism*. Cambridge: Belknap/Harvard University Press. (1992): "Organizational Capabilities and the Economic History of the Industrial Enterprise," *Journal of Economic Perspectives* 6: 79–100.

Chapkis, Wendy (1997): *Live Sex Acts: Women Performing Erotic Labor*. New York: Routledge.

Charles, Maria (1992): "Cross-National Variation in Occupational Sex Segregation," *American Sociological Review* 57: 483–502.

Charlot, Bernard & Madeleine Figeat (1985): *Histoire de la formation des ouvriers, 1789–1984*. Paris: Minerve.

Chauvin, Keith (1994): "Firm-Specific Wage Growth and Changes in the Labor Market for Managers," *Managerial and Decision Economics* 15: 21–37.

Cheng, Lucie & Edna Bonacich, eds. (1984): *Labor Immigration Under Capitalism: Asian Workers in the United States Before World War II*. Berkeley: University of California Press.

Chiswick, Barry R., Carmel U. Chiswick & Paul W. Miller (1985): "Are Immigrants and Natives Perfect Substitutes in Production?" *International Migration Review* 19: 674–685.

Christopherson, Susan (1988): "Production Organization and Work Time: The Emergence of a Contingent Labor Market," in Kathleen Christensen & Mary Murphree, eds., *Flexible Work Styles: A Look at Contingent Labor,* Conference Summary. Washington, D.C.: U.S. Department of Labor Women's Bureau.

Church, Roy (1986): *The History of the British Coal Industry.* Volume 3, *1830–1913: Victorian Pre-eminence.* Oxford: Clarendon Press. (1990): "Employers, Trade Unions, and the State, 1889–1987: The Origins and Decline of Tripartism in the British Coal Industry," in Gerald D. Feldman & Klaus Tenfelde, eds., *Workers, Owners, and Politics in Coal Mining: An International Comparison of Industrial Relations.* New York: Berg.

Citro, Constance F. & Robert T. Michael, eds. (1995): *Measuring Poverty: A New Approach.* Washington, D.C.: National Academy Press.

Clark, Anna (1995): *The Struggle for the Breeches: Gender and the Making of the British Working Class.* Berkeley: University of California Press.

Clarkson, L. A. (1971): *The Pre-Industrial Economy in England, 1500–1750.* London: Batsford.

Clawson, Dan (1980): *Bureaucracy and the Labor Process.* New York: Monthly Review Press.

Clines, Francis X. (1994): "Self-esteem and Friendship in a Factory on Death Row," *New York Times,* January 12, A1, A8.

Coase, Ronald (1952): "The Nature of the Firm," *Economica* 4: 386–405 (1937), reprinted in George Stigler & Kenneth Boulding, eds. *Readings in Price Theory.* Chicago: Irwin. (1992): "The Institutional Structure of Production," *American Economic Review* 82: 713–719.

Cockburn, Cynthia (1983): *Brothers: Male Dominance and Technological Change.* London: Pluto Press.

Cohen, Isaac (1985a): "Workers' Control in the Cotton Industry: A Comparative Study of British and American Mule Spinning," *Labor History* 26: 53–85. (1985b): "American Management and British Labor: Lancashire Immigrant Spinners in Industrial New England," *Comparative Studies in Society and History* 27: 608–650.

Cohen, Joshua & Joel Rogers (1983): *On Democracy: Towards a Transformation of American Society.* New York: Penguin.

Cohen, Lizabeth (1990): *Making a New Deal: Industrial Workers in Chicago, 1919–1939.* Cambridge: Cambridge University Press.

Cohen, Robert, P.C.W. Gutkind & P. Brazier, eds. (1979): *Peasants and Proletarians: The Struggles of Third World Workers.* London: Hutchinson.

Cohn, Samuel (1985): *The Process of Occupational Sex-Typing: The Feminization of Clerical Labor in Great Britain.* Philadelphia: Temple University Press. (1993): *When Strikes Make Sense—And Why.* New York: Plenum.

Cohn, Samuel & Mark Fossett (1994): "Why Racial Employment Inequality Is Greater in Northern Labor Markets: An Investigation of Regional Differences in White-Black Employment Differentials," unpublished paper, Texas A&M University. (1995): "What Spatial Mismatch? The Proximity of Blacks to Employment in Boston and Houston," unpublished paper, Texas A&M University.

Cohn, Steve (1990): "The Political Economy of Nuclear Power (1945–1990): The Rise and Fall of an Official Technology," *Journal of Economic Issues* 24: 781–811. (1994): "The Future of Nuclear Power in the United States." Paper presented at the Annual Meeting of the Allied Social Science Associations, Boston, Mass., January 3–5, 1994.

Colander, David C. (1995): *Economics*, 2nd ed. Chicago: Richard D. Irwin.

Cole, Jonathan R. & Harriet Zuckerman (1984): "The Productivity Puzzle: Persistence and Change in Patterns of Publication of Men and Women Scientists," *Advances in Motivation and Achievement* 2: 217–258.

Cole, Robert (1979): *Work, Mobility, and Participation: A Comparative Study of American and Japanese Industry*. Berkeley: University of California Press.

Coleman, James S. (1990): *Foundations of Social Theory*. Cambridge: Harvard University Press. (1991): "Matching Processes in the Labor Market," *Acta Sociologica* 34: 3–12.

Collins, Randall (1975): *Conflict Sociology: Toward an Explanatory Science*. New York: Academic Press. (1979): *The Credential Society: An Historical Sociology of Education and Stratification*. New York: Academic Press.

Commons, John R. (1934): *Institutional Economics: Its Place in Political Economy*. New York: Macmillan.

Conell, Carol (1980): "The Impact of Union Sponsorship on Strikes in Nineteenth-Century Massachusetts." Doctoral dissertation in sociology, University of Michigan. (1989): "The Local Roots of Solidarity: Organization and Action in Late Nineteenth-Century Massachusetts," *Theory and Society* 17: 365–402.

Constantine, Jill M. & David Neumark (1994): "Training and the Growth of Wage Inequality." Working Paper, National Center on the Educational Quality of the Workforce, University of Pennsylvania, Philadelphia.

Cooper, Frederick (1981): "Peasants, Capitalists, and Historians: A Review Article," *Journal of Southern African Studies* 7: 284–314. (1983): ed., *Struggle for the City: Migrant Labor, Capital, and the State in Urban Africa*. Beverly Hills: Sage.

Cooper, Patricia (1991): "The Faces of Gender: Sex Segregation and Work Relations at Philco, 1928–1938," in Ava Baron, ed., *Work Engendered: Toward a New History of American Labor*. Ithaca: Cornell University Press.

Corcoran, Mary, Linda Datcher & Greg J. Duncan (1980): "Most Workers Find Jobs Through Word of Mouth," *Monthly Labor Review* (August): 33–35.

Corcoran, Mary & Sharon Parrott (1992): "Black Women's Economic Progress." Paper presented at Social Science Research Council conference on "The Urban Underclass: Perspectives from the Social Sciences," Ann Arbor, Mich., June 8–10.

Coser, Lewis A., Charles Kadushin & Walter W. Powell (1985): *Books: The Culture and Commerce of Publishing*. Chicago: University of Chicago Press. First published in 1982.

Coser, Rose Laub (1990): "Power Lost and Status Gained: A Step in the Direction of Sex Inequality," in Kai Erikson & Steven Peter Vallas, eds., *The Nature of Work: Sociological Perspectives*. New Haven: Yale University Press and American Sociological Association, 71–87.

Costa, Dora L. (1993): "Explaining the Changing Dynamics of Unemployment: Evidence from Civil War Pension Records." National Bureau of Economic Research,

Working Paper Series on Historical Factors in Long-Run Growth, Historical Paper 51, Cambridge, Massachusetts.

Coverman, Shelley (1983): "Gender, Domestic Labor Time, and Wage Inequality," *American Sociological Review* 48: 623–636.

Cowan, Ruth Schwartz (1983): *More Work for Mother: The Ironies of Household Technology from the Open Hearth to the Microwave*. New York: Basic Books.

Crafts, N.F.R. (1985): *British Economic Growth During the Industrial Revolution*. Oxford: Clarendon Press. (1989): "Real Wages, Inequality, and Economic Growth in Britain, 1750–1850: A Review of Recent Research," in Peter Scholliers, ed., *Real Wages in 19th and 20th Century Europe: Historical and Comparative Perspectives*. New York: Berg.

Cronin, James E. (1979): *Industrial Conflict in Modern Britain*. London: Croom Helm. (1984): *Labour and Society in Britain 1918–1979*. London: Batsford.

Daniel, Josh (1995): "Nurses vs. Catholic Hospital: Sisters, Can You Spare a Dime?" *Nation*, July 10: 54–57.

Danziger, Sheldon & Peter Gottschalk, eds. (1992): *Uneven Tides: Rising Inequality in the 1980's*. New York: Russell Sage Foundation. (1995): *America Unequal*. New York: Russell Sage Foundation; Cambridge: Harvard University Press.

Darity, William, Jr., ed. (1984): *Labor Economics: Modern Views*. Boston: Kluwer-Nijhoff. (1992): "Dressing for Success? Economic History and the Economic Performance of Racial and Ethnic Minorities in the USA," forthcoming in *Cambridge Economic History of the United States*. Cambridge: Cambridge University Press.

David, Paul A. (1986): "Understanding the Economics of QWERTY: The Necessity of History," in William N. Parker, ed., *Economic History and the Modern Economist*. Oxford: Blackwell.

Davies, Margery W. (1975): "Woman's Place Is at the Typewriter: The Feminization of the Clerical Labor Force," in Richard Edwards, Michael Reich & David Gordon, eds., *Labor Market Segmentation*. Lexington, Mass.: D.C. Heath. (1982): *Woman's Place Is at the Typewriter: Office Work and Office Workers, 1870–1930*. Philadelphia: Temple University Press.

Davis, John (1992): *Exchange*. Minneapolis: University of Minnesota Press.

Dawley, Alan (1976): *Class and Community: The Industrial Revolution in Lynn*. Cambridge: Harvard University Press.

Dembe, Allard E. (1996): *Occupation and Disease: How Social Factors Affect the Conception of Work-Related Disorders*. New Haven: Yale University Press.

Dente, Leonard A. (1977): *Veblen's Theory of Social Change*. New York: Arno Press.

Dertouzos, Michael, Richard Lester, Robert Solow & the M.I.T. Commission on Industrial Productivity (1989): *Made in America: Regaining the Competitive Edge*. Cambridge, Mass.: M.I.T. Press.

De Schweinitz, Dorothea (1932): *How Workers Find Jobs: A Study of Four Thousand Hosiery Workers in Philadelphia*. Philadelphia: University of Pennsylvania Press.

De Soto, Hernando (1989): *The Other Path: The Invisible Revolution in the Third World*. New York: Harper & Row.

DeVault, Marjorie (1991): *Feeding the Family: The Social Organization of Caring as Gendered Work*. Chicago: University of Chicago Press.

Dewerpe, Alain (1985): *L'Industrie aux champs. Essai sur la proto-industrialisation en Italie du Nord (1800–1880)*. Rome: Ecole Française de Rome. (1992): "Taylorismo e filantropia in un dossier fotografico della Citroën (1917)," *Ventesimo Se-colo* 2: 121–154.

Dicken, Peter (1992): *Global Shift: The Internationalization of Economic Activity,* 2nd ed. New York: Guilford Press. First published in 1986.

Dickens, William T. & Kevin Lang (1985): "A Test of Dual Labor Market Theory," *American Economic Review* 75: 792–805.

Digby, Anne (1975): "The Labour Market and the Continuity of Social Policy After 1834: The Case of the Eastern Counties," *Economic History Review,* 2d series, 28: 69–83. (1978): *Pauper Palaces.* London: Routledge & Kegan Paul.

di Leonardo, Micaela (1987): "The Female World of Cards and Holidays: Women, Families, and the Work of Kinship," *Signs* 12: 440–453.

DiMaggio, Paul & Walter Powell (1991): Introduction to Walter Powell & Paul DiMaggio, eds., *The New Institutionalism in Organizational Analysis.* Chicago: University of Chicago Press, 1–38.

DiNardo, John E. & Jorn-Steffen Pischke (1996): "The Returns to Computer Use Revisited: Have Pencils Changed the Wage Structure Too?" Working Paper 5606, National Bureau of Economic Research, Cambridge, Massachusetts.

Dix, Keith (1977): *Work Relations in the Coal Industry: The Hand-Loading Era, 1880–1930.* Morgantown: Institute for Labor Studies, West Virginia University.

Dobbin, Frank, John R. Sutton, John W. Meyer & W. Richard Scott (1993): "Equal Opportunity Law and the Construction of Internal Labor Markets," *American Journal of Sociology* 99: 396–427.

Dobson, C. R. (1980): *Masters and Journeymen: A Prehistory of Industrial Relations 1717–1800.* London: Croom Helm.

Doeringer, Peter B., Kathleen Christensen, Patricia M. Flynn, Douglas T. Hall, Harry C. Katz, Jeffrey H. Keefe, Christopher J. Ruhm, Andrew W. Sum & Michael Useem (1991): *Turbulence in the American Workplace.* New York & Oxford: Oxford University Press.

Doeringer, Peter B. & Michael J. Piore (1971): *Internal Labor Markets and Manpower Analysis.* Lexington, Mass.: D.C. Heath.

Doeringer, Peter B., Philip I. Moss & David G. Terkla (1986): "Capitalism and Kinship: Do Institutions Matter in the Labor Market?" *Industrial and Labor Relations Review* 40: 48–60.

Dosi, Giovanni (1988): "Sources, Procedures, and Microeconomic Effects of Innovation," *Journal of Economic Literature* 26: 1120–1171.

Dosi, Giovanni, Renato Giannetti & Pier Angelo Toninelli, eds. (1992): *Technology and Enterprise in a Historical Perspective.* Oxford: Clarendon Press.

Dow, Gregory K. (1993): "Why Capital Hires Labor: A Bargaining Perspective," *American Economic Review* 83: 118–134.

Doyal, Lesley (1981): *The Political Economy of Health.* Boston: South End Press. First published in 1979.

Dublin, Thomas (1979): *Women at Work: The Transformation of Work and Community in Lowell, Massachusetts, 1826–1860.* New York: Columbia University Press. (1994): *Transforming Women's Work: New England Lives in the Industrial Revolution.* Ithaca: Cornell University Press.

Duin, Pieter van (1992): "White Building Workers and Coloured Competition in the South African Labour Market, c. 1890–1940," *International Review of Social History* 37: 59–90.

Dunk, Thomas W. (1992): *It's a Working Man's Town: Male Working-Class Culture in Northwestern Ontario*. Montreal: McGill-Queen's University Press.

Dunlop, John (1957): "The Task of Contemporary Wage Theory," in John Dunlop, ed., *The Theory of Wage Determination*. London & New York: Macmillan & St. Martin's Press, 3–27.

Earle, Carville (1993): "Divisions of Labor: The Splintered Geography of Labor Markets and Movements in Industrializing America, 1790–1930," *International Review of Social History* 38, supplement 1: 5–38.

Easterlin, Richard (1973): "Does Money Buy Happiness?" *Public Interest* 30: 3–10.

Ebbinghaus, Bernhard (1993): "Labour Unity in Union Diversity: Trade Unions and Social Cleavages in Western Europe, 1890–1989," unpublished doctoral dissertation, European University Institute, Florence.

Eccles, Robert G., Nitin Nohria & James D. Berkley (1992): *Beyond the Hype*. Boston: Harvard Business School Press.

Economist (1996): "Stakeholder Capitalism: Unhappy Families," February 10: 23–25.

Edwards, Ness (1926): *The History of the South Wales Miners*. London: Labour Publishing Company.

Edwards, P. K. (1981): *Strikes in the United States, 1881–1974*. Oxford: Blackwell. (1986): *Conflict at Work: A Materialist Analysis of Workplace Relations*. Oxford: Blackwell.

Edwards, Richard C. (1979): *Contested Terrain: The Transformation of the Workplace in the 20th Century*. New York: Basic Books. (1986): *Trade Unions in Crisis: A Six Country Comparison*. Boston: Auburn House.

Edwards, Richard C., Michael Reich & Thomas E. Weisskopf, eds. (1986): *The Capitalist System: A Radical Analysis of American Society*. Englewood Cliffs, N.J.: Prentice-Hall.

Ehrenreich, Barbara & Deirdre English (1973): *Witches, Midwives, and Nurses: A History of Women Healers*. Old Westbury, N.Y.: Feminist Press.

Eichengreen, Barry & Henry A. Gemery (1986): "The Earnings of Skilled and Unskilled Immigrants at the End of the Nineteenth Century," *Journal of Economic History* 46: 441–454.

Eisenberg, Susan (1990): "Shaping a New Decade: Women in the Building Trades," *Radical America* 23(2–3): 29–38. (1992a): "Welcoming Sisters into the Brotherhood," *Sojourner: The Women's Forum* 18: 20–21. (1992b): "Tradeswomen: Pioneers—or What?" *Sojourner: The Women's Forum* 17: 17–18.

Elster, Jon (1983): *Explaining Technical Change: A Case Study in the Philosophy of Science*. Cambridge: Cambridge University Press. (1985): *Making Sense of Marx*. Cambridge: Cambridge University Press.

Encarnation, Dennis (1989): *Dislodging Multinationals: India's Comparative Perspective*. Ithaca: Cornell University Press.

Engels, Frederick (1969): *The Condition of the Working Class in England*. London: Granada. First published (in German) in 1845. (1978): "Socialism: Utopian and Scientific," in Robert Tucker, ed., *The Marx-Engels Reader*, 2nd ed. New York: Norton, 683–717. First published in 1880.

Engelsing, Rolf (1973): *Zur Sozialgeschichte deutscher Mittel- und Unterschichten*. Göttingen: Vandenhoeck & Ruprecht.

England, Paula (1992): *Comparable Worth: Theories and Evidence*. New York: Aldine de Gruyter.

England, Paula & Barbara Stanek Kilbourne (1990): "Marriages, Markets, and Other Mates: The Problem of Power," in Roger Friedland and A. F. Robertson, eds., *Beyond the Marketplace: Rethinking Economy and Society*. New York: Aldine de Gruyter, 163–188.

England, Paula & George Farkas (1986): *Households, Employment, and Gender: A Social, Economic, and Demographic View*. Chicago: Aldine de Gruyter.

England, Paula, George Farkas, Barbara Stanek Kilbourne & Thomas Dou (1988): "Explaining Occupational Sex Segregation and Wages: Findings from a Model with Fixed Effects," *American Sociological Review* 53: 544–558.

England, Paula, Melissa S. Herbert, Barbara S. Kilbourne, Lori L. Reid & Lori M. Megdal (1994): "The Gendered Valuation of Occupations and Skills: Earnings in 1980 Census Occupations," *Social Forces*, 73: 65–99.

Epstein, Cynthia Fuchs (1981): *Women in Law*. New York: Basic Books.

Erikson, Kai & Steven Peter Vallas, eds. (1990): *The Nature of Work: Sociological Perspectives*. New Haven: Yale University Press.

Esping-Anderson, Gøsta, ed. (1993): *Changing Classes: Stratification and Mobility in Post-Industrial Societies*. Newbury Park, Calif.: Sage.

Espinosa, Juan G. & Andrew S. Zimbalist (1978): *Economic Democracy: Workers' Participation in Chilean Industry, 1970–1973*. New York: Academic Press.

Falcón, Luis & Edwin Melendez (1996): "The Role of Social Networks in the Labor Market Outcomes of Latinos, Blacks, and Non-Hispanic Whites." Paper presented at Multi-City Study of Urban Inequality Conference on "Residential Segregation, Social Capital, and Labor Markets," Russell Sage Foundation, New York City, February 8–9.

Farber, Henry S. (1986): "The Analysis of Union Behavior," in Orley Ashenfelter & Richard Layard, eds., *Handbook of Labor Economics* II. Amsterdam: North-Holland, 1039–1090. (1995): "Are Lifetime Jobs Disappearing? Job Duration in the United States: 1973–1993." Working Paper 341, Industrial Relations Section, Princeton University, Princeton, N.J. (1996): "The Changing Face of Job Loss in the United States, 1981–1993." Working Paper 360, Industrial Relations Section, Princeton University, Princeton, N.J..

Farkas, George & Paula England, eds. (1988): *Industries, Firms, and Jobs: Sociological and Economic Approaches*. New York: Plenum.

Feldman, Gerald D. & Klaus Tenfelde, eds. (1990): *Workers, Owners, and Politics in Coal Mining: An International Comparison of Industrial Relations*. New York: Berg.

Felmlee, Diane H. (1993): "The Dynamic Interdependence of Women's Employment and Fertility," *Social Science Research* 22: 333–360.

Feltes, N. N. (1992): "Misery or the Production of Misery: Defining Sweated Labour in 1890," *Social History* 17: 441–452.

Fernández-Kelly, M. Patricia (1994): "Broadening the Scope: Gender and the Study of International Development," in A. Douglas Kincaid & Alejandro Portes, eds., *Comparative National Development: Society and Economy in the New Global Order*. Chapel Hill: University of North Carolina Press.

Fevre, Ralph (1989): "Informal Practices, Flexible Firms, and Private Labour Markets," *Sociology* 23: 91–109.

Fine, Janice, with Matthew Howard (1995): "Women in the Free Trade Zones of Sri Lanka," *Dollars & Sense* (November/December): 26–27, 39–40.

Fink, Leon & Brian Greenberg (1979): "Organizing Montefiore: Labor Militancy Meets a Progressive Health Care Empire," in Susan Reverby & David Rosner, eds., *Health Care in America: Essays in Social History*. Philadelphia: Temple University Press.

Fligstein, Neil (1981): *Going North: Migration of Blacks and Whites from the South, 1900–1950*. New York: Academic Press. (1997): "Social Skill and Institutional Theory," *American Behavioral Scientist* 40: 397–405.

Flinn, Michael W. (1984): *The History of the British Coal Industry. Volume 2: 1700–1830: The Industrial Revolution*. Oxford: Clarendon Press.

Floud, Roderick & Kenneth W. Wachter (1982): "Poverty and Physical Stature: Evidence on the Standard of Living of London Boys, 1770–1870," *Social Science History* 6: 422–452.

Flynn, Laurie J. (1996): "For Some, Steady Job Isn't the End of the Road," *New York Times*, May 20, D8.

Flynn, Patricia M. (1992): "The Impact of Technological Change on Jobs and Workers," in Patricia M. Flynn, ed., *Technology Life Cycles & Human Resources*. Lanham, Md.: University Press of America.

Fogel, Robert W. (1993): "New Sources and New Techniques for the Study of Secular Trends in Nutritional Status, Health, Mortality, and the Process of Aging," *Historical Methods* 26: 5–43. (1994): "Economic Growth, Population Theory, and Physiology: The Bearing of Long-Term Processes on the Making of Economic Policy," *American Economic Review* 84: 369–395.

Folbre, Nancy (1993): "Women's Informal Market Work in Massachusetts, 1875–1920," *Social Science History* 17: 135–160.

Form, William (1987): "On the Degradation of Skills," *Annual Review of Sociology* 13: 29–47. (1995): *Segmented Labor, Fractured Politics: Labor Politics in American Life*. New York: Plenum.

Fox, N. E. (1978): "The Spread of the Threshing Machine in Central Southern England," *Agricultural History Review* 26: 26–28.

France, Bureau de la Statistique Générale (1910): *Répertoire technologique des noms d'industries et de professions*. Paris: Berger-Levrault.

Franzosi, Roberto (1981): "La conflittualità in Italia tra ciclo economico e contrattazione collettiva," *Rassegna Italiana di Sociologia* 22: 533–575. (1989): "One Hundred Years of Strike Statistics: Methodological and Theoretical Issues in Quantitative Strike Research," *Industrial and Labor Relations Review* 42: 348–362. (1995): *The Puzzle of Strikes: Class and State Strategies in Postwar Italy*. Cambridge: Cambridge University Press.

Freeman, Richard B. & James L. Medoff (1984): *What Do Unions Do?*. New York: Basic Books.

Freeman, Richard B. & Joel Rogers (1994): "Worker Representation and Participation Survey: First Report of Findings," London School of Economics and University of Wisconsin Law School, December.

Freidson, Eliot (1984): "The Changing Nature of Professional Control," *Annual Review of Sociology* 10: 1–20. (1990): "Labors of Love in Theory and Practice: A Prospectus," in Kai Erikson & Steven Peter Vallas, eds., *The Nature of Work: Sociological Perspectives*. New Haven: Yale University Press and American Sociological Association, 149–161.

Freifeld, Mary (1986): "Technological Change and the 'Self-Acting' Mule: A Study of Skill and the Sexual Division of Labor," *Social History* 11: 319–344.

Frenk, Julio & Luis Durán-Arenas (1993): "The Medical Profession and the State," in Frederic W. Hafferty & John B. McKinlay, eds., *The Changing Medical Profession: An International Perspective*. New York: Oxford University Press.

Friedland, Roger & A. F. Robertson, eds. (1990): *Beyond the Marketplace: Rethinking Economy and Society*. New York: Aldine de Gruyter.

Friedlander, Dov (1973): "Demographic Patterns and Socioeconomic Characteristics of the Coal-Mining Population in England and Wales in the Nineteenth Century," *Economic Development and Cultural Change* 22: 39–51.

Friedman, Gerald (1988): "Strike Success and Union Ideology: The United States and France, 1880–1914," *Journal of Economic History* 48: 1–25.

Friedman, Milton (1962): *Capitalism and Freedom*. Chicago & London: University of Chicago Press.

Friedmann, Harriet (1978a): "Simple Commodity Production and Wage Labour in the American Plains," *Journal of Peasant Studies* 6: 71–100. (1978b): "World Market, State, and Family Farm: Social Bases of Household Production in the Era of Wage Labor," *Comparative Studies in Society and History* 20: 545–586.

Frisch, Michael H. & Daniel J. Walkowitz, eds. (1983): *Working-Class America: Essays on Labor, Community, and American Society*. Urbana: University of Illinois Press.

Gabaccia, Donna R. (1988): *Militants and Migrants: Rural Sicilians Become American Workers*. New Brunswick, N.J.: Rutgers University Press.

Galbraith, John Kenneth (1952): *American Capitalism: The Concept of Countervailing Power*. Boston: Houghton Mifflin.

Gallie, Duncan (1978): *In Search of the New Working Class: Automation and Social Integration Within the Capitalist Enterprise*. New York: Cambridge University Press.

Gardner, Florence & Jean McAllister (1995): "Temporary Workers: Flexible or Disposable?" *Poverty & Race* (newsletter of the Poverty & Race Research Action Council) (November/December): 9–14.

Geary, Roger (1985): *Policing Industrial Disputes: 1893 to 1985*. Cambridge: Cambridge University Press.

Gilder, George (1981): *Wealth and Poverty*. New York: Basic Books.

Gittleman, Maury B. & David R. Howell (1995): "Changes in the Structure and Quality of Jobs in the United States: Effects by Race & Gender, 1973–1990," *Industrial and Labor Relations Review* 48: 420–40.

Glass, Jennifer & Valerie Camarigg (1992): "Gender, Parenthood, and Job-Family Compatibility," *American Journal of Sociology* 98: 131–151.

Glazer, Nona Y. (1991): "'Between a Rock and a Hard Place': Women's Professional Organizations in Nursing and Class, Racial, and Ethnic Inequalities," *Gender & Society* 5: 351–372. (1993): *Women's Paid and Unpaid Labor: The Work Transfer in Health Care and Retailing*. Philadelphia: Temple University Press.

Godard, Jean-Luc & Anne-Marie Miéville (1976): *Six Fois Deux*, video for French television.

Goebel, Thomas (1994): "Professionalization and State Building: The State and the Professions in Illinois, 1870–1920," *Social Science History* 18: 309–337.

Goffman, Erving (1967): *Interaction Ritual.* New York: Doubleday Anchor.

Goldfield, Michael (1987): *The Decline of Organized Labor in the United States.* Chicago: University of Chicago Press.

Goldin, Claudia (1987): "Women's Employment and Technological Change: A Historical Perspective," in Heidi Hartmann, ed., *Computer Chips and Papers Clips: Technology and Women's Employment,* Volume 2. Washington, D.C.: National Academy Press. (1990): *Understanding the Gender Gap: An Economic History of American Women.* New York: Oxford University Press. (1994): "Labor Markets in the Twentieth Century." National Bureau of Economic Research, Working Paper Series on Historical Factors in Long-Run Growth, Historical Paper 58, Cambridge, Massachusetts.

Goodman, David & Michael Redclift (1981): *From Peasant to Proletarian and Agrarian Transitions.* Oxford: Blackwell.

Goodnow, Jacqueline & Jennifer M. Bowes (1994): *Men, Women and Household Work.* Oxford: Oxford University Press.

Goodrich, Carter (1925): *The Miner's Freedom: A Study of the Working Life in a Changing Industry.* Boston: Marshall Jones.

Goodwin, Jeff (1994): "Toward a New Sociology of Revolutions," *Theory and Society* 23: 731–766.

Gordon, David (1972): *Theories of Poverty and Underemployment.* Lexington, Mass.: D.C. Heath. (1988): "The Global Economy: New Edifice or Crumbling Foundations?" *New Left Review* 168: 24–65. (1990): "Who Bosses Whom? The Intensity of Supervision and the Discipline of Labor," *American Economic Review, Papers and Proceedings* 80: 28–32. (1994): "Bosses of Different Stripes: A Cross-National Perspective on Monitoring and Supervision." *American Economic Review* 84(2): 375–379. (1996): *Fat and Mean: The Corporate Squeeze of Working Americans and the Myth of Managerial "Downsizing."* New York: Free Press.

Gordon, David M., Richard Edwards & Michael Reich (1982): *Segmented Work, Divided Workers: The Historical Transformations of Labor in the United States.* New York: Cambridge University Press.

Gottfried, Heidi (1991): "Mechanisms of Control in the Temporary Help Service Industry," *Sociological Forum* 6: 699–714.

Gottfried, Heidi & David Fasenfest (1984): "Gender and Class Formation: Female Clerical Workers," *Review of Radical Political Economics* 16: 89–103.

Grafteaux, Serge (1985 [1975]): *Mémé Santerre: A French Woman of the People.* Translated by Louise A. Tilly & Kathryn L. Tilly. New York: Schocken.

Graham, Laurie (1995): *On the Line at Subaru-Isuzu: The Japanese Model and the American Worker.* Ithaca: ILR Press.

Graham, Lawrence Otis (1992): "Invisible Man," *New York* 25(32): 26–34.

Granovetter, Mark (1981): "Toward a Sociological Theory of Income Differences," in Ivar Berg, ed., *Sociological Perspectives on Labor Markets.* New York: Academic Press. (1985): "Economic Action and Social Structure: The Problem of Embeddedness," *American Journal of Sociology* 91: 481–510. (1986): "Labor Mobility, Internal Markets, and Job-Matching: A Comparison of the Sociological and the Economic Approaches," *Research in Social Stratification and Mobility* 5: 3–39. (1988): "The Sociological and Economic Approaches to Labor Markets," in George Farkas & Paula England, eds., *Industries, Firms, and Jobs: Sociological and*

Economic Approaches. New York: Plenum. (1994): "Business Groups," in Neil Smelser & Richard Swedberg, eds., *Handbook of Economic Sociology.* Princeton and New York: Princeton University Press and Russell Sage Foundation, 453–475. (1995): *Getting a Job: A Study of Contacts and Careers,* 2nd ed. Chicago: University of Chicago Press. First published in 1974.

Granovetter, Mark & Charles Tilly (1988): "Inequality and Labor Processes," in Neil J. Smelser and Richard Swedberg, eds., *Handbook of Sociology.* Newbury Park, Calif.: Sage.

Green, James & Chris Tilly (1987): "Service Unionism: Directions for Organizing," *Labor Law Journal* 38: 486–495.

Grieco, Margaret (1987): *Keeping It in the Family: Social Networks and Employment Chance.* London: Tavistock.

Grob, Gerald N. (1995): "The Paradox of Deinstitutionalization," *Society* 32: 51–59.

de Groot, Gerjan & Marlou Schrover (1995): "Between Men and Machines: Women Workers in New Industries, 1870–1940," *Social History* 20: 279–296.

Groshen, Erica (1991): "Five Reasons Why Wages Vary Among Employers," *Industrial Relations* 30: 350–381.

Gueron, Judith M. (1987): "Reforming Welfare with Work," Occasional paper no. 2, Ford Foundation Project on Social Welfare and the American Future. New York: Ford Foundation.

Guillemard, Anne-Marie & Martin Rein (1993): "Comparative Patterns of Retirement: Recent Trends in Developed Societies," *Annual Review of Sociology* 19: 469–503.

Gullickson, Gay L. (1986): *Spinners and Weavers of Auffay: Rural Industry and the Sexual Division of Labor in a French Village, 1750–1850.* Cambridge: Cambridge University Press.

Gunderson, Morley (1989): "Male-Female Wage Differentials and Policy Responses," *Journal of Economic Literature* 27: 46–72.

Gutmann, Myron P. (1988): *Toward the Modern Economy: Early Industry in Europe, 1500–1800.* Philadelphia: Temple University Press.

Hagen, William W. (1988): "Capitalism and the Countryside in Early Modern Europe: Interpretations, Models, Debates," *Agricultural History* 62: 13–47.

Haimson, Leopold & Charles Tilly, eds. (1989): *Strikes, Wars, and Revolutions in an International Perspective: Strike Waves in the Late Nineteenth and Early Twentieth Centuries.* Cambridge: Cambridge University Press.

Haimson, Leopold & Giulio Sapelli, eds. (1992): *Strikes, Social Conflict and the First World War: An International Perspective.* Milan: Feltrinelli. Fondazione Giangiacomo Feltrinelli, *Annali* 1990/1991.

Haines, Michael R. (1975): "Fertility and Occupation: Coal Mining Populations in the Nineteenth and Early Twentieth Centuries in Europe and America," Western Societies Occasional Paper 3, Cornell University, Ithaca, New York.

Hakim, Catherine (1992): "Explaining Trends in Occupational Segregation: The Measurement, Causes, and Consequences of the Sexual Division of Labor," *European Sociological Review* 8: 127–152.

Halaby, Charles N. & Davied L. Weakliem (1993): "Ownership and Authority in the Earnings Function: Nonnested Tests of Alternative Specifications," *American Sociological Review* 58: 16–30.

Halle, David (1984): *America's Working Man: Work, Home, and Politics Among Blue-Collar Property Owners.* Chicago: University of Chicago Press.

Halpern, Rick (1992): "Race, Ethnicity, and Union in the Chicago Stockyards, 1917–1922," *International Review of Social History* 37: 25–58.

Hanagan, Michael P. (1980): *The Logic of Solidarity: Artisans and Industrial Workers in Three French Towns, 1871–1914.* Urbana: University of Illinois Press. (1989a): *Nascent Proletarians: Class Formation in Post-Revolutionary France.* Oxford: Basil Blackwell. (1989b): "Solidary Logics: Introduction," *Theory and Society* 17: 309–328.

Hareven, Tamara (1982): *Family Time and Industrial Time: The Relationship Between the Family and Work in a New England Industrial Community.* Cambridge: Cambridge University Press. (1990): "A Complex Relationship: Family Strategies and the Processes of Economic and Social Change," in Roger Friedland & A. F. Robertson, eds., *Beyond the Marketplace: Rethinking Economy and Society.* New York: Aldine de Gruyter, 215–244.

Harris, Chris C., P. Brown, R. Fevre, G. G. Leaver, R. M. Lee, and L. D. Morris (1987): *Redundancy and Recession in South Wales.* Oxford: Basil Blackwell.

Harrison, Bennett (1994): *Lean and Mean: The Changing Landscape of Corporate Power in the Age of Flexibility.* New York: Basic Books.

Harrison, Bennett & Barry Bluestone (1988): *The Great U-Turn: Corporate Restructuring and the Polarizing of America.* New York: Basic Books.

Hartmann, Heidi, Robert E. Kraut & Louise A. Tilly, eds. (1986/1987): *Computer Chips and Papers Clips. Technology and Women's Employment.* Washington, D.C.: National Academy Press. 2 vols.; vol. 2 edited by Heidi Hartmann.

Hartmann, Heidi & Ann Markusen (1980): "Contemporary Marxist Theory and Practice: A Feminist Critique," *Review of Radical Political Economics* 12: 87–94.

Hatcher, John (1993): *The History of the British Coal Industry.* Volume 1, *Before 1700: Towards the Age of Coal.* Oxford: Clarendon Press.

Hatton, Timothy J. & Jeffrey G. Williamson (1992): "International Migration and World Development: A Historical Perspective," National Bureau of Economic Research, Historical Paper 41, Cambridge, Massachusetts.

Haydu, Jeffrey (1988): *Between Craft and Class: Skilled Workers and Factory Politics in the United States and Britain, 1890–1922.* Berkeley: University of California Press.

Henderson, Rebecca M. & Kim B. Clark (1990): "Architectural Innovation: The Reconfiguration of Existing Product Technologies and the Failure of Established Firms," *Administrative Science Quarterly* 35: 9–30.

Herr, Elizabeth (1995): "The Census, Estimation Biases, and Female Labor-Force Participation Rates in 1880 Colorado," *Historical Methods* 28: 167–181.

Hersch, Joni & Leslie S. Stratton (1994): "Housework, Wages, and the Division of Housework Time for Employed Spouses," *American Economic Review, Papers and Proceedings* 84: 120–125.

Hershberg, Theodore, ed. (1981): *Philadelphia: Work, Space, Family, and Group Experience in the 19th Century.* New York: Oxford University Press.

Hessing, Melody (1994): "More than Clockwork: Women's Time Management in their Combined Workloads," *Sociological Perspectives* 37: 611–634.

Heyzer, Noeleen (1986): *Working Women in South-East Asia: Development, Subordination, and Emancipation.* Milton Keynes, England: Open University Press.

Hicks, J. R. (1963): *The Theory of Wages*. London: Macmillan.

Higby, Gregory J. & Teresa C. Gallagher (1990): "Pharmacists" in Rima D. Apple, ed., *Women, Health, and Medicine in America: A Historical Handbook*. New York: Garland.

Hine, Darlene Clark (1985): "Co-Laborers in the Work of the Lord. Nineteenth-Century Black Women Physicians," in Ruth J. Abram, ed., *"Send Us a Lady Physician": Women Doctors in America, 1835–1920*. New York: W. W. Norton.

Hirsch, Paul M. & Michael Lounsbury, "Toward a Reconciliation of 'Old' and 'New' Institutionalisms," *American Behavioral Scientist* 40: 406–418.

Hirsch, Susan (1986): "Rethinking the Sexual Division of Labor: Pullman Repair Shops, 1900–1969," *Radical History* 35: 26–48.

Hirschman, Albert O. (1970): *Exit, Voice, and Loyalty: Responses to Decline in Firms, Organizations, and States*. Cambridge: Harvard University Press.

Hirschman, Charles (1982): "Immigrants and Minorities: Old Questions for New Directions in Research," *International Migration Review* 16: 474–490.

Hobsbawm, Eric (1964): *Laboring Men: Studies in the History of Labor*. New York: Basic Books.

Hochschild, Arlie Russell (1983): *The Managed Heart: Commercialization of Human Feeling*. Berkeley: University of California Press.

Hodgson, Geoffrey M. (1988): *Economics and Institutions: A Manifesto for a Modern Institutional Economics*. Philadelphia: University of Pennsylvania Press.

Hodson, Randy (1995): "Worker Resistance: An Underdeveloped Concept in the Sociology of Work," *Economic and Industrial Democracy* 16: 79–110.

Hoerder, Dirk, ed. (1983): *American Labor and Immigration History, 1877–1920s: Recent European Research*. Urbana: University of Illinois Press.

Hoerr, John P. (1988): *And the Wolf Finally Came. The Decline of the American Steel Industry*. Pittsburgh: University of Pittsburgh Press.

Hoffman, Emily P., ed. (1991): *Essays on the Economics of Discrimination*. Kalamazoo, Mich.: W. E. Upjohn Institute for Employment Research.

Hoffnar, Emily (1995a): "One Bad Apple: Discrimination and Strategic Complementarities in the Labor Market," unpublished paper, Department of Economics, University of North Texas. (1995b): "Applications of the Strategic Complementarities Model of Job Segregation," paper presented at the annual meeting of the International Association for Feminist Economics.

Holden, Constance (1997): "Population Control for Docs," *Science* 275: 1571.

Holloway, S.W.F. (1964): "Medical Education in England, 1830–1858," *History* 49: 299–324.

Holmstrom, Bengt & Paul Milgrom (1991): "Multitask Principal-Agent Analysis: Incentive Contracts, Asset Ownership, and Job Design," *Journal of Law, Economics, and Organization* 7: 24–52. (1994): "The Firm as an Incentive System," *American Economic Review* 84: 972–991.

Holzer, Harry J. (1987): "Informal Job Search and Black Youth Unemployment," *American Economic Review* 77: 446–452.

Horan, Patrick M. & Thomas A. Lyson (1986): "Occupational Concentration in Work Establishments," *Sociological Forum* 1: 428–449.

Houseman, Susan N. (1995): "Job Growth and the Quality of Jobs in the U.S. Economy," *Labor,* special issue: S93–S124.

Howell, David R. & Edward N. Wolff (1991): "Trends in the Growth and Distribution of Skills in the U.S. Workplace, 1960–1985," *Industrial and Labor Relations Review* 44: 486–502.

Huber, Joan (1986): "Trends in Gender Stratification, 1970–1985," *Sociological Forum* 1: 476–495.

Huberman, Michael (1996): "Piece Rates Reconsidered: The Case of Cotton," *Journal of Interdisciplinary History* 26: 393–418.

Hudson, Pat (1986): *The Genesis of Industrial Capital: A Study of the West Riding Wool Textile Industry c. 1750–1850*. Cambridge: Cambridge University Press. (1990): ed., *Regions and Industries: A Perspective on the Industrial Revolution in Britain*. Cambridge: Cambridge University Press.

Huffman, Matt L. (1995): "Organizations, Internal Labor Market Policies, and Gender Inequality in Workplace Supervisory Authority," *Sociological Perspectives* 38: 381–398.

Huggins, Martha Knisely (1985): *From Slavery to Vagrancy in Brazil*. New Brunswick, N.J.: Rutgers University Press.

Humphries, Jane (1977): "Class Struggle and the Persistence of the Working Class Family," *Cambridge Journal of Economics* 1: 241–258. (1990): "Enclosures, Common Rights, and Women: The Proletarianization of Families in the Late Eighteenth and Early Nineteenth Centuries," *Journal of Economic History* 50: 17–42.

Hunt, E. H. (1981): *British Labor History, 1815–1914*. London: Weidenfeld & Nicolson.

Hunter, Alfred A. (1988): "Formal Education and Initial Employment: Unravelling the Relationships Between Schooling and Skills Over Time," *American Sociological Review* 53: 753–765.

Ibarra, Herminia (1992): "Homophyly and Differential Returns: Sex Differences in Network Structure and Access in an Advertising Firm." *Administrative Science Quarterly* 37: 442–47.

Independent Sector (1986): *The Charitable Behavior of Americans: A National Survey*. Washington, D.C.: Independent Sector.

Ingrao, Charles W. (1987): *The Hessian Mercenary State: Ideas, Institutions, and Reform Under Frederick II, 1760–1785*. Cambridge: Cambridge University Press.

International Labour Office (1968): *International Standard Classification of Occupations,* revised edition. Geneva: International Labour Office. First published in 1958. (1992): *World Labour Report, 1992*. Geneva: ILO. (1993): *World Labour Report 1993*. Geneva: ILO. (1995): *World Employment 1995*. Geneva: ILO.

Ishida, Hiroshi, Seymour Spilerman & Kuo-Hsien Su (1995): "Educational Credentials and Promotion Prospects in a Japanese and an American Organization." Working Paper 92, Center on Japanese Economy and Business, Columbia University, New York, N.Y.

Jackson, Robert Max (1984): *The Formation of Craft Labor Markets*. Orlando: Academic Press.

Jacobs, Jerry A. (1989): *Revolving Doors: Sex Segregation and Women's Careers*. Stanford: Stanford University Press. (1992): "Women's Entry into Management: Trends in Earnings, Authority, and Values Among Salaried Managers," *Administrative Science Quarterly* 37: 282–301. (1995): ed., *Gender Inequality at Work*. Thousand Oaks, Calif.: Sage.

Jacobs, Jerry A. & Ronnie J. Steinberg (1990): "Compensating Differentials and the Male-Female Wage Gap: Evidence from the New York State Comparable Worth Study," *Social Forces* 69: 439–468.

Jacobs, Jerry A. & Suet T. Lim (1992): "Trends in Occupational and Industrial Sex Segregation in 56 Countries, 1960–1980," *Work and Occupations* 19: 450–486.

Jacoby, Sanford M. (1985): *Employing Bureaucracy: Managers, Unions, and the Transformation of Work in American Industry, 1900–1945.* New York: Columbia University Press. (1990): "The New Institutionalism: What Can It Learn from the Old?" *Industrial Relations* 29: 316–340. (1991): ed., *Masters to Managers. Historical and Comparative Perspectives on American Employers.* New York: Columbia University Press.

Jacoby, Sanford M. & Daniel J. B. Mitchell (1990): "Sticky Stories: Economic Explanations of Employment and Wage Rigidity," *American Economic Review, Papers and Proceedings* 80: 33–37.

Janoski, Thomas (1990): *The Political Economy of Unemployment: Active Labor Market Policy in West Germany and the United States.* Berkeley: University of California Press.

Jasso, Guillermina & Mark R. Rosenzweig (1995): "Do Immigrants Screened for Skills Do Better than Family Reunification Migrants?" *International Migration Review* 29: 85–111.

Jencks, Christopher & Susan E. Mayer (1989): "The Social Consequences of Growing Up in a Poor Neighborhood: A Review," Center for Urban Affairs and Policy Research Report, Northwestern University, Evanston, Illinois. (1990): "Residential Segregation, Job Proximity, and Black Job Opportunities," in Laurence E. Lind & Michael McGeary, eds., *Inner City Poverty in the United States.* Washington, D.C.: National Academy Press, 111–196.

Jencks, Christopher, Lauri Perman & Lee Rainwater (1988): "What Is a Good Job? A New Measure of Labor-Market Success," *American Journal of Sociology* 93: 1322–1357.

Jessop, Bob (1972): *Social Order, Reform, and Revolution: A Power Exchange and Institutionalization Perspective.* London: Macmillan.

Jobs for the Future (1995): "The Club Focus Group," April 18. Unpublished focus group transcript, Jobs for the Future, Boston, Mass.

Johnson, Mark (1989): "Capital Accumulation and Wage Rates: The Development of the California Labor Market in the Nineteenth Century," *Review of Radical Political Economics* 21(3): 76–81.

Johnston, Paul (1994): *Success While Others Fail.* Ithaca: ILR Press.

Joyce, Patrick, ed. (1987): *The Historical Meanings of Work.* Cambridge: Cambridge University Press.

Juravich, Tom (1985): *Chaos on the Shop Floor: A Worker's View of Quality, Productivity, and Management.* Philadelphia: Temple University Press.

Juster, F. Thomas & Frank P. Stafford (1991): "The Allocation of Time: Empirical Findings, Behavioral Models, and Problems of Measurement," *Journal of Economic Literature* 29: 471–522.

Kahn, Lawrence M. (1976): "Internal Labor Markets: San Francisco Longshoremen," *Industrial Relations* 15: 333–337.

Kahne, Hilda & Janet Z. Giele (1992): eds., *Women's Work and Women's Lives. The Continuing Struggle Worldwide*. Boulder: Westview Press.

Kahneman, Daniel, Jack L. Knetch & Richard Thaler (1986): "Fairness as a Constraint on Profit-Seeking: Entitlements in the Market," *American Economic Review* 76: 728–741.

Kalb, Don (1994a): "Expanding Class: Power and Everyday Politics in Industrial Communities, North Brabant Illustrations, ca. 1850–1950," unpublished doctoral dissertation in General Social Sciences, University of Utrecht. (1994b): "On Class, the Logic of Solidarity, and the Civilizing Process: Workers, Priests, and Alcohol in Dutch Shoemaking Communities, 1900–1920," *Social Science History* 18: 127–152.

Kalleberg, Arne L. & Aage B. Sørensen (1979): "The Sociology of Labor Markets," *Annual Review of Sociology* 5: 351–379.

Kanter, Rosabeth Moss (1977): *Men and Women of the Corporation*. New York: Basic Books. (1989a): "The Changing Basis for Pay," *Society* 26: 54–65. (1989b): *When Giants Learn to Dance*. New York: Simon and Schuster.

Kaplan, Hillard (1994): "Evolutionary and Wealth Flows Theories of Fertility: Empirical Tests and New Models," *Population and Development Review* 20: 753–792.

Kato, Shuichi (1981): "The Japan Myth Reconsidered," *Democracy* 1: 98–108.

Katz, Lawrence (1986): "Efficiency Wage Theories: A Partial Evaluation," in Stanley Fischer, ed., *NBER Macroeconomics Annual*. Cambridge, Mass.: MIT Press.

Katz, Lawrence & Anna Revenga (1989): "Changes in the Structure of Wages: The U.S. vs. Japan," unpublished paper, Harvard University and the National Bureau of Economic Research, Cambridge, Mass., July.

Katznelson, Ira & Aristide Zolberg (1986): *Working-Class Formation: Nineteenth-Century Patterns in Western Europe and the United States*. Princeton: Princeton University Press.

Kazal, Russell A. (1995): "Revisiting Assimilation: The Rise, Fall, and Reappraisal of a Concept in American Ethnic History," *American Historical Review* 100: 437–471.

Kellenbenz, Hermann (1976): *The Rise of the European Economy: An Economic History of Continental Europe from the Fifteenth Century*. London: Weidenfeld & Nicolson.

Kern, William S., ed. (1992): *From Socialism to Market Economy: The Transition Problem*. Kalamazoo, Mich.: W. E. Upjohn Institute for Employment Research.

Kerr, Clark (1954): "The Balkanization of Labor Markets," in E. Wright Bakke, P. M. Hauser, G. L. Palmer, C. A. Myers, D. Yoder & Clark Kerr, eds., *Labor Mobility and Economic Opportunity*. Cambridge, Mass.: MIT Press, 92–110.

Kessler-Harris, Alice (1982): *Out to Work: A History of Wage-Earning Women in the United States*. Oxford: Oxford University Press. (1985): "The Debate Over Equality for Women in the Work Place: Recognizing Differences," *Women and Work: An Annual Review* 1: 141–161. (1989): "Gender Ideology in Historical Reconstruction: A Case Study from the 1930s," *Gender & History* 1: 31–49. (1990): *A Woman's Wage: Historical Meanings and Social Consequences*. Lexington: University Press of Kentucky.

Keynes, John Maynard (1964): *The General Theory of Employment, Interest, and Money*. New York & London: Harcourt, Brace, Jovanovich. First published in 1936.

Keyssar, Alexander (1986): *Out of Work: The First Century of Unemployment in Massachusetts.* Cambridge: Cambridge University Press.

Kilbourne, Barbara Stanek et al. (1994): "Returns to Skill, Compensating Differentials, and Gender Bias: Effects of Occupational Characteristics on the Wages of White Women and Men," *American Journal of Sociology* 100: 689–719.

Killingsworth, Mark (1986): "Female Labor Supply: A Survey," in Orley Ashenfelter & Richard Layard, eds., *Handbook of Labor Economics.* Amsterdam: North-Holland, 103–204.

Killingsworth, Mark R. & James J. Heckman (1986): "Female Labor Supply: A Survey," in Orley C. Ashenfelter & Richard Layard, eds., *Handbook of Labor Economics.* Amsterdam: North-Holland.

Kirschenman, Joleen, Philip Moss & Chris Tilly (1996): "Space as a Signal, Space as a Barrier: How Employers Map and Use Space in Four Metropolitan Labor Markets." Paper presented at the meetings of the Social Science History Association. New Orleans, October.

Kjellberg, Anders (1992): "Sweden: Can the Model Survive?" in Anthony Ferner & Richard Hyman, eds., *Industrial Relations in the New Europe.* Oxford: Blackwell.

Klein, Herbert S. (1983): "The Integration of Italian Immigrants into the United States and Argentina: A Comparative Analysis," *American Historical Review* 88: 306–329.

Klepper, Steven & Elizabeth Graddy (1990): "The Evolution of New Industries and the Determinants of Market Structure," *Rand Journal of Economics* 21: 27–44.

Knoke, David (1994): "Cui Bono? Employee Benefit Packages," *American Behavioral Scientist* 37: 963–978.

Knoke, David & Arne L. Kalleberg (1994): "Job Training in U.S. Organizations," *American Sociological Review* 59: 537–546.

Kobrin, Frances E. (1985): "The American Midwife Controversy: A Crisis of Professionalization," in Judith Walzer Leavitt & Ronald L. Numbers, eds., *Sickness and Health in America: Readings in the History of Medicine and Public Health.* Madison: University of Wisconsin Press, 197–205.

Kochan, Thomas, Harry C. Katz & Robert B. McKersie (1986): *The Transformation of American Industrial Relations.* New York: Basic Books.

Kochar, Anjini (1995): "Explaining Household Vulnerability to Idiosyncratic Income Shocks," *American Economic Review, Papers and Proceedings* 85: 159–164.

Kocka, Jürgen (1983): *Lohnarbeit und Klassenbildung. Arbeiter und Arbeiterbewegung in Deutschland 1800–1875.* Berlin: Dietz.

Kornai, Janos (1992): *The Socialist System: The Political Economy of Communism.* Princeton: Princeton University Press.

Korpi, Walter (1991): "Political and Economic Explanations for Unemployment: A Cross-National and Long-Term Analysis," *British Journal of Political Science* 21: 315–348.

Korpi, Walter & Michael Shalev (1979): "Strikes, Industrial Relations, and Class Conflict in Capitalist Societies," *British Journal of Sociology* 30: 164–187. (1980): "Strikes, Power, and Politics in the Western Nations, 1900–1976," in Maurice Zeitlin, ed., *Political Power and Social Theory.* Greenwich, Conn.: JAI Press.

Kotz, David M., Terrence McDonough & Michael Reich (1994): eds., *Social Structures of Accumulation: The Political Economy of Growth and Crisis.* Cambridge: Cambridge University Press.

Kraft, Philip (1977): *Programmers and Managers: The Routinization of Computer Programming in the United States*. New York: Heidelberg Science Library; Springer-Verlag.

Kriedte, Peter (1983): *Peasants, Landlords, and Merchant Capitalists: Europe and the World Economy, 1500–1800*. Cambridge: Cambridge University Press.

Kriedte, Peter, Hans Medick & Jürgen Schlumbohm (1981): *Industrialization Before Industrialization*. Paris: Maison des Sciences de l'Homme. Cambridge: Cambridge University Press. (1992): "Sozialgeschichte in der Erweiterung—Proto-industrialisierung in der Verengung? Demographie, Sozialstruktur, moderne Hausindustrie: ein Zwischenbilanz der Proto-Industrialisierungs-Forschung," *Geschichte und Gesellschaft* 18: 70–87, 231–255.

Krueger, Alan (1993): "How Computers Have Changed the Wage Structure: Evidence from Microdata, 1984–1989," *Quarterly Journal of Economics* 108: 33–60.

Kuhn, Sarah (1990): "Working Conditions in the United States Service Sector: A Review of the Literature," unpublished paper, Department of Policy and Planning, University of Massachusetts-Lowell, January.

Kussmaul, Ann (1981): *Servants in Husbandry in Early Modern England*. Cambridge: Cambridge University Press.

Ladd-Taylor, Molly (1994): *Mother-Work: Women, Child Welfare, and the State, 1890–1930*. Urbana: University of Illinois Press.

Lamphere, Louise (1987): *From Working Daughters to Working Mothers: Immigrant Women in a New England Industrial Community*. Ithaca: Cornell University Press.

Landes, David S. (1969): *The Unbound Prometheus*. Cambridge: Cambridge University Press. (1986): "What Do Bosses Really Do?" *Journal of Economic History* 46: 585–623.

Lane, Robert E. (1991): *The Market Experience*. Cambridge: Cambridge University Press.

Langton, Nancy & Jeffrey Pfeffer (1994): "Paying the Professor: Sources of Salary Variation in Academic Labor Markets," *American Sociological Review* 59: 236–256.

Larson, Magali Sarfatti (1977): *The Rise of Professionalism: A Sociological Analysis*. Berkeley: University of California Press.

Laurie, Bruce (1980): *Working People of Philadelphia, 1800–1850*. Philadelphia: Temple University Press.

Lazear, Edward P. (1979): "Why Is There Mandatory Retirement?" *Journal of Political Economy* 87: 1261–1264. (1981): "Agency Earnings Profiles, Productivity, and Hours Restrictions," *American Economic Review* 71: 606–620. (1989): "Symposium on Women in the Labor Market," *Journal of Economic Perspectives* 3: 3–8. (1990): "Pensions and Deferred Benefits as Strategic Compensation," *Industrial Relations* 29: 263–280. (1991): "Labor Economics and the Psychology of Organizations," *Journal of Economic Perspectives* 5: 89–110. (1992): "The Job as a Concept," in William Bruns, ed., *Performance, Measurement, Evaluation, and Incentives*. Boston: Harvard Business School Press. (1995): "A Jobs-Based Analysis of Labor Markets," *American Economic Review, Papers and Proceedings* 85: 260–265.

Lazear, Edward P. & Sherwin Rosen (1981): "Rank-Order Tournaments as Optimal Labor Contracts," *Journal of Political Economy* 89: 841–864.

Lazonick, William (1990): *Competitive Advantage on the Shop Floor*. Cambridge: Harvard University Press. (1991): *Business Organization and the Myth of the Market Economy*. Cambridge: Cambridge University Press.

Leavitt, Judith Walzer (1986): *Brought to Bed: Childbearing in America 1750 to 1950*. New York: Oxford University Press.

Lee, Ching Kwan (1993): "Familial Hegemony: Gender and Production Politics on Hong Kong's Electronics Shopfloor," *Gender & Society* 7: 529–547. (1995): "Engendering the Worlds of Labor: Women Workers, Labor Markets, and Production Politics in the South China Economic Miracle," *American Sociological Review* 60: 378–397.

Lee, Ok-Jie (1993): "Gender-Differentiated Employment Practices in the South Korean Textile Industry," *Gender & Society* 7: 507–528.

le Grand, Carl (1991): "Explaining the Male-Female Wage Gap: Job Segregation and Solidarity Wage Bargaining in Sweden," *Acta Sociologica* 34: 261–278.

Leidner, Robin (1993): *Fast Food, Fast Talk: Service Work and the Routinization of Everyday Life*. Berkeley: University of California Press.

Leigh, J. Paul (1991): "No Evidence of Compensating Differentials for Occupational Fatalities," *Industrial Relations* 30: 382–395.

Leonard, Jonathan (1989): "Wage Structure and Dynamics in the Electronics Industry," *Industrial Relations* 28: 251–275.

Leonard, Robert J. (1995): "From Parlor Games to Social Science: von Neumann, Morgenstern, and the Creation of Game Theory, 1928–1944," *Journal of Economic Literature* 33: 730–761.

Leontief, Wassily (1951): *The Structure of the American Economy*. New York: Oxford University Press.

Lesieur, Henry R. & Joseph F. Shelley (1987): "Illegal Appended Enterprises: Selling the Lines," *Social Problems* 34: 249–260.

Levine, David, ed. (1984): *Proletarianization and Family History*. Orlando, Fla.: Academic Press.

Levine, David & Keith Wrightson (1991): *The Making of an Industrial Society: Whickham 1560–1765*. Oxford: Clarendon Press.

Levine, David I. (1993): "Demand Variability and Work Organization," in Samuel Bowles, Herbert Gintis & B. Gustafsson, eds., *Democracy and Markets: Participation, Accountability, and Efficiency*. Cambridge: Cambridge University Press.

Levine, David I. & Laura D'Andrea Tyson (1990): "Participation, Productivity, and the Firm's Environment," in Alan S. Blinder, ed., *Paying for Productivity*. Washington, D.C.: Brookings Institution, 183–243.

Levine, Philippa (1994): "Consistent Contradictions: Prostitution and Protective Labour Legislation in Nineteenth-Century England," *Social History* 19: 17–36.

Levy, Frank & Richard J. Murnane (1992): "U.S. Earnings Levels and Earnings Inequality: A Review of Recent Trends and Proposed Explanations," *Journal of Economic Literature* 30: 1333–1381.

Lewin-Epstein, Noah & Moshe Semyonov (1994): "Sheltered Labor Markets, Public Sector Employment, and Socioeconomic Returns to Education of Arabs in Israel," *American Journal of Sociology* 100: 622–651.

Lewis, Ronald L. (1987): *Black Coal Miners in America: Race, Class, and Community Conflict, 1780–1980*. Lexington: University Press of Kentucky.

Licht, Walter (1983): *Working for the Railroad: The Organization of Work in the Nineteenth Century.* Princeton: Princeton University Press. (1991): "Studying Work: Personnel Policies in Philadelphia Firms, 1850–1950," in Sanford Jacoby, ed., *Masters to Managers: Historical and Comparative Perspectives on American Employers.* New York: Columbia University Press. (1992): *Getting Work: Philadelphia, 1840–1950.* Cambridge: Harvard University Press.

Lie, John (1992): "The Concept of Mode of Exchange," *American Sociological Review* 57: 508–523.

Lieberson, Stanley (1980): *A Piece of the Pie: Blacks and White Immigrants Since 1880.* Berkeley: University of California Press.

Liebowitz, S. J. & Stephen E. Margolis (1990): "The Fable of the Keys," *Journal of Law and Economics* 33: 1–27.

Light, Donald W. (1993): "Countervailing Power: The Changing Character of the Medical Profession in the United States," in Frederic W. Hafferty & John B. McKinlay, eds., *The Changing Medical Profession: An International Perspective.* New York: Oxford University Press.

Light, Ivan (1984): "Immigrant and Ethnic Enterprise in North America," *Ethnic and Racial Studies* 7: 195–216.

Light, Ivan & Edna Bonacich (1988): *Immigrant Entrepreneurs: Koreans in Los Angeles, 1965–1982.* Berkeley: University of California Press.

Light, Ivan & Stavros Karageorgis (1994): "The Ethnic Economy," in Neil T. Smelser & Richard Swedberg, eds., *The Handbook of Economic Sociology.* Princeton: Princeton University Press, 647–671.

Lin, Nan (1982): "Social Resources and Instrumental Action," in Peter V. Marsden & Nan Lin, eds., *Social Structure and Network Analysis.* Beverly Hills: Sage.

Lin, Nan & Mary Dumin (1986): "Access to Occupations Through Social Ties," *Social Networks* 8: 365–385.

Link, Bruce G., Mary Clare Lennon & Bruce P. Dohrenwend (1993): "Socioeconomic Status and Depression: The Role of Occupations Involving Direction, Control, and Planning," *American Journal of Sociology* 98: 1351–1387.

Lipartito, Kenneth (1994): "When Women Were Switches: Technology, Work, and Gender in the Telephone Industry, 1890–1920," *American Historical Review* 99: 1074–1111.

Lipkind, Karen L. (1995): "National Hospital Ambulatory Medical Care Survey 1993: Outpatient Department Summary," *Advance Data.* National Center for Health Statistics, no. 268.

Lipset, Seymour Martin (1990): "The Work Ethic—Then and Now," *Public Policy* 98 (Winter): 61–69.

Lis, Catharina (1986): *Social Change and the Labouring Poor. Antwerp, 1770–1860.* New Haven: Yale University Press.

Lis, Catharina, Jan Lucassen & Hugo Soly (1994): "Before the Unions: Wage Earners and Collective Action in Europe, 1300–1850," *International Review of Social History*, 39, Supplement 2, entire issue.

Litoff, Judy Barrett (1978): *American Midwives 1860 to the Present.* Westport, Conn.: Greenwood.

Littler, Craig (1982): *The Development of the Labour Process in Capitalist Societies: A Comparative Study of the Transformation of Work Organization in Britain, Japan, and the USA.* London: Heinemann.

Littler, Craig & Graeme Salaman (1984): *Class at Work: The Design, Allocation, and Control of Jobs.* London: Batsford.

Lloyd, Cynthia B., ed. (1975): *Sex, Discrimination, and the Division of Labor.* New York: Columbia University Press.

Lloyd, Peter (1982): *A Third World Proletariat?* London: George Allen & Unwin.

Lloyd-Jones, Roger & M. J. Lewis (1988): *Manchester and the Age of the Factory: The Business Structure of Cottonopolis in the Industrial Revolution.* London: Croom Helm.

Long, Diana Elizabeth & Janet Golden, eds. (1989): *The American General Hospital: Communities and Social Contexts.* Ithaca: Cornell University Press.

Long, Priscilla (1989): *Where the Sun Never Shines: A History of America's Bloody Coal Industry.* New York: Paragon House.

Lorenz, Edward H. (1992): "Trust and the Flexible Firm: International Comparisons," *Industrial Relations* 31(3): 455–472.

Lucassen, Jan (1987): *Migrant Labour in Europe, 1600–1900: The Drift to the North Sea.* London: Croom Helm. (1993): "Free and Unfree Labour Before the Twentieth Century: A Brief Overview," in Tom Brass, Marcel van der Linden & Jan Lucassen, *Free and Unfree Labour.* Amsterdam: International Institute for Social History, 7–18.

Lüdtke, Alf (1993): "Polymorphous Synchrony: German Industrial Workers and the Politics of Everyday Life," *International Review of Social History* 38, Supplement 1: 39–84.

Luxton, Meg (1980): *More than a Labour of Love: Three Generations of Women's Work in the Home.* Toronto: Women's Press.

MacKay, Lynn (1995): "A Culture of Poverty? The St. Martin in the Fields Workhouse, 1817," *Journal of Interdisciplinary History* 26: 209–231.

MacLeod, Jay (1987): *Ain't No Makin' It: Leveled Aspirations in a Low-Income Neighborhood.* Boulder: Westview Press.

Madden, Janice Fanning (1985): "The Persistence of Pay Differentials: The Economics of Sex Discrimination," *Women and Work: An Annual Review,* 1: 76–114.

Mahini, Amir (1990): "A New Look at Trade," *McKinsey Quarterly* (Winter): 42.

Maller, Judy, ed. (1992): *Conflict and Co-operation: Case Studies in Worker Participation.* Johannesburg: Ravan Press.

Mallett, M. E. (1974): *Mercenaries and Their Masters: Warfare in Renaissance Italy.* Totowa, N.J.: Rowman and Littlefield.

Maloney, Thomas N. (1995): "Degrees of Inequality: The Advance of Black Male Workers in the Northern Meat Packing and Steel Industries Before World War II," *Social Science History* 19: 31–62.

Mandemakers, Kees & Jos van Meewen (1983): "Industrial Modernization and Social Developments in the Centre of Dutch Shoe Industry, Central Noord-Brabant, 1890–1930," *Centrum voor Maatschappijgeschiedenis* 10 (entire issue)

Manning, Patrick (1990): *Slavery and African Life: Occidental, Oriental, and African Slave Trades.* Cambridge: Cambridge University Press.

March, James G. (1972): "Model Bias in Social Action," *Review of Educational Research* 42: 413–429.

March, James G. and Herbert A. Simon (1958): *Organizations.* New York: Wiley. (1993): "Organizations Revisited," *Industrial and Corporate Change* 2: 299–316.

Marcotte, Dave (1994): "Evidence of a Fall in the Wage Premium for Job Security." Working Paper, Center for Governmental Studies, Northern Illinois University, De Kalb, Illinois.

Marcusen, James R. (1995): "The Boundaries of Multinational Enterprises and the Theory of International Trade," *Journal of Economic Perspectives* 9: 169–190.

Marglin, Steven (1974): "What Do Bosses Do? The Origins and Functions of Hierarchy in Capitalist Production," *Review of Radical Political Economy* 6: 60–112.

Margo, Robert A. (1992a): "The Labor Force in the Nineteenth Century," National Bureau of Economic Research, Historical Paper 40, Cambridge, Mass. (1992b): "Employment and Unemployment in the 1930s," National Bureau of Economic Research, Working Paper 4174, Cambridge, Mass.

Marini, Margaret Mooney & Beth Anne Shelton (1993): "Measuring Household Work: Recent Experience in the United States," *Social Science Research* 22: 361–382.

Mark, Shirley (1990): "Asian-American Engineers in the Massachusetts High Technology Industry: Are Glass Ceilings a Reality?" Master of City Planning thesis, Department of Urban Studies and Planning, Massachusetts Institute of Technology, Cambridge, Mass.

Marks, Carole (1981): "Split Labor Markets and Black-White Relations, 1865–1920," *Phylon* 42: 293–308. (1983): "Lines of Communication, Recruitment Mechanisms, and the Great Migration of 1916–1918," *Social Problems* 31: 73–83.

Marsden, David (1986): *The End of Economic Man? Custom and Competition in Labour Markets*. New York: St. Martin's.

Marsden, Peter V. & Jeanne S. Hurlbert (1988): "Social Resources and Mobility Outcomes: A Replication and Extension," *Social Forces* 66: 1038–1059.

Marshall, Alfred (1925): "A Fair Rate of Wages," in A. C. Pigou, ed., *Memorials of Alfred Marshall*. New York: Macmillan.

Marwell, Gerald & Pamela Oliver (1993): *The Critical Mass in Collective Action: A Micro-Social Theory*. Cambridge: Cambridge University Press.

Marx, Karl (1958): "The Eighteenth Brumaire of Louis Bonaparte" in *Selected Works*, Volume 1. Moscow: Foreign Languages Publishing House. First published in 1852. (1964): Eric Hobsbawm, ed., *Pre-Capitalist Economic Formations*. London: Lawrence & Wishart. (1970): *Capital: A Critique of Political Economy*. 3 vols. London: Lawrence & Wishart. First published in 1867–1894. (1976): *The Poverty of Philosophy* in Karl Marx & Frederick Engels, *Collected Works*. New York: International Publishers. First published in 1847. (1978): "Wage Labour and Capital," in Robert C. Tucker, ed., *The Marx-Engels Reader*. New York: Norton. First published 1849.

Marx, Karl & Friedrich Engels (1958): "Manifesto of the Communist Party" in *Selected Works*, Volume 1. Moscow: Foreign Languages Publishing House. First published in 1848.

Massey, Douglas S., Andrew B. Gross & Kumiko Shibuya (1994): "Migration, Segregation, and the Geographic Concentration of Poverty," *American Sociological Review* 59: 425–446.

Massey, Douglas S. et al. (1994): "An Evaluation of International Migration Theory: The North American Case," *Population and Development Review* 20: 699–752.

Maurice, Marc, François Sellier & Jean-Jacques Silvestre (1984): "The Search for a Societal Effect in the Production of Company Hierarchy: A Comparison of France and Germany," in Paul Osterman, ed., *Internal Labor Markets.* Cambridge, Mass: MIT Press.

McAdam, Doug & Ronnelle Paulsen (1993): "Specifying the Relationship Between Social Ties and Activism," *American Journal of Sociology* 99: 640–667.

McCall, Nathan (1994): *Makes Me Wanna Holler: A Young Black Man in America.* New York: Vintage Books.

McGuire, Gail M. & Barbara F. Reskin (1993): "Authority Hierarchies at Work: The Impacts of Race and Sex," *Gender & Society* 7: 487–506.

McLanahan, Sara, Irwin Garfinkel & Dorothy Watson (1987): "Family Structure, Poverty, and the Underclass," Discussion Paper 823–87, Institute for Research on Poverty, University of Wisconsin-Madison.

McNall, Scott, Rhonda F. Levine & Rick Fantasia, eds. (1991): *Bringing Class Back In: Contemporary and Historical Perspectives.* Boulder: Westview Press.

Mellor, Earl & Steven Haugen (1986): "Hourly Paid Workers: Who They Are and What They Earn," *Monthly Labor Review* (February): 20–26.

Melosh, Barbara (1982): *"The Physician's Hand": Work Culture and Conflict in American Nursing.* Philadelphia: Temple University Press.

Menaghan, Elizabeth G. (1991): "Work Experiences and Family Interaction Processes: The Long Reach of the Job?" *Annual Review of Sociology* 17: 419–444.

Menger, Pierre-Michel & Marc Gurgand (1996): "Work and Compensated Unemployment in the Performing Arts: Exogenous and Endogenous Uncertainty in Artistic Labour Markets," in Victor A. Ginsburgh & Pierre-Michel Menger, eds., *Economics of the Arts: Selected Essays.* Amsterdam: Elsevier.

Metcalfe, Andrew (1988): *For Freedom and Dignity: Historical Agency and Class Structures in the Coalfields of NSW.* Sydney: Allen & Unwin Australia.

Mies, Maria (1986): *Patriarchy and Accumulation on a World Scale: Women in the International Division of Labour.* London: Zed Books.

Mikkelsen, Flemming (1992): *Arbeidskonflikter i Skandinavien 1848–1980.* Odense: Odense Universitetsforlag.

Milberg, William (1993): "Natural Order and Postmodernism in Economic Thought," *Social Research* 60: 255–278.

Miles, Robert (1987): *Capitalism and Unfree Labour: Anomaly or Necessity?* London: Tavistock.

Milkman, Ruth (1987): *Gender at Work: The Dynamics of Job Segregation by Sex During World War II.* Urbana: University of Illinois Press.

Mill, John Stuart (1929): *Principles of Political Economy.* London: Longmans, Green & Co.

Miller, Ann R. (1994): "The Industrial Affiliation of Workers: Differences by Nativity and Country of Origin," in Susan Cotts Watkins, ed., *After Ellis Island: Newcomers and Natives in the 1910 Census.* New York: Russell Sage Foundation.

Miller, Joanne (1988): "Jobs and Work," in Neil J. Smelser & Richard Swedberg, eds., *The Handbook of Sociology.* Newbury Park, Calif.: Sage Publications, 327–359.

Miller, Jon (1986): *Pathways in the Workplace: The Effects of Gender and Race on Access to Organizational Resources.* Cambridge: Cambridge University Press.

Milward, Alan S. & S. B. Saul (1973): *The Economic Development of Continental Europe, 1780–1870*. London: George Allen & Unwin.

Mincer, Jacob (1970): "The Distribution of Labor Incomes: A Survey," *Journal of Economic Literature* 8: 1–26. (1974): *Schooling, Experience, and Earnings*. New York: Columbia University Press for the National Bureau of Economic Research.

Miner, Anne S. (1985): "The Strategy of Serendipity: Ambiguity, Uncertainty, and Idiosyncratic Jobs," Ph.D. dissertation, Graduate School of Business, Stanford University, Palo Alto, Calif.

Mitchell, Daniel J. B. (1986): "Union vs. Nonunion Wage Norm Shifts," *American Economic Review* 76(2): 249–252.

Mittelman, James H. (1993): "Global Restructuring of Production and Migration," forthcoming in Yoshikazu Sakamoto, ed., *Global Transformation*. Tokyo: United Nations University Press. (1994): "Restructuring the Global Division of Labor: Old Theories and New Realities," forthcoming in Stephen Gill, ed., *Challenge and Response in Global Political Economy*.

Moch, Leslie Page (1992): *Moving Europeans: Migration in Western Europe Since 1650*. Bloomington: Indiana University Press.

Model, Suzanne (1985): "A Comparative Perspective on the Ethnic Enclave: Blacks, Italians, and Jews in New York City," *International Migration Review* 19: 64–81. (1991): "Caribbean Immigrants: A Black Success Story?" *International Migration Review* 25: 248–276. (1992): "The Ethnic Economy: Cubans and Chinese Reconsidered," *Sociological Quarterly* 33: 63–82.

Model, Suzanne, Gretchen Stiers & Eleanor Weber (1992): "Overtime and Undertime: An Analysis of Hours Worked," *Sociological Inquiry* 62: 413–436.

Mokyr, Joel (1987): "Has the Industrial Revolution Been Crowded Out? Some Reflections on Crafts and Williamson," *Explorations in Economic History* 24: 293–319. (1993): "The New Economic History and the Industrial Revolution" in Joel Mokyr, ed., *The British Industrial Revolution: An Economic Perspective*. Boulder: Westview Press.

Montgomery, David (1979): *Workers' Control in America: Studies in the History of Work, Technology, and Labor Struggles*. New York: Cambridge University Press. (1987): *The Fall of the House of Labor: The Workplace, the State, and American Labor Activism, 1865–1925*. Cambridge: Cambridge University Press. Paris: Editions de la Maison des Sciences de l'Homme. (1993): *Citizen Worker: The Experience of Workers in the United States with Democracy and the Free Market During the Nineteenth Century*. Cambridge: Cambridge University Press.

Montgomery, James D. (1991): "Social Networks and Labor Market Outcomes: Toward an Economic Analysis," *American Economic Review* 81: 1408–1418. (1992): "Job Search and Network Composition: Implications of the Strength-of-Weak-Ties Hypothesis," *American Sociological Review* 57: 586–596. (1994): "Weak Ties, Employment, and Inequality: An Equilibrium Analysis," *American Journal of Sociology* 99: 1212–1236.

Moodie, T. Dunbar (1994): *Going for Gold: Men, Mines, and Migration*. Berkeley: University of California Press.

Moody, J. Carroll & Alice Kessler-Harris, eds. (1989): *Perspectives on American Labor History: The Problems of Synthesis*. DeKalb: Northern Illinois University Press.

Morokvasic, Mirjana (1987): "Immigrants in the Parisian Garment Industry," *Work, Employment & Society* 1: 441–462.

Morris, Martina, Annette D. Bernhardt & Mark S. Handcock (1994): "Economic Inequality: New Methods for New Trends," *American Sociological Review* 59: 205–219.

Moss, Philip & Chris Tilly (1991): "Why Black Men Are Doing Worse in the Labor Market: A Review of Supply-Side and Demand-Side Explanations." Working paper, Social Science Research Council. (1992): Unpublished interview data from research project entitled "Why Aren't Employers Hiring More Black Men?" (1995): "Raised Hurdles for Black Men: Evidence from Employer Interviews." Working Paper 81, Russell Sage Foundation, New York. (1996): "Soft Skills and Race: An Investigation of Black Men's Employment Problems," *Work and Occupations* 23: 252–276.

Mottez, Bernard (1966): *Systèmes de salaire et politiques patronales. Essai sur l'évolution des pratiques et des idéologies patronales.* Paris: Editions du Centre National de la Recherche Scientifique.

Mulcahy, Susan DiGiacomo & Robert R. Faulkner (1979): "Person and Machine in a New England Factory," in Andrew Zimbalist, ed., *Case Studies on the Labor Process.* New York: Monthly Review Press.

Munger, Frank (1991): "Legal Resources of Striking Miners: Notes for a Study of Class Conflict and Law," *Social Science History* 15: 1–34.

Murphree, Mary C. (1987): "New Technology and Office Tradition: The Not-So-Changing World of the Secretary," in Heidi Hartmann, ed., *Computer Chips and Papers Clips: Technology and Women's Employment,* Volume 2. Washington, D.C.: National Academy Press.

Murray, Stephen O., Joseph H. Rankin & Dennis W. Magill (1981): "Strong Ties and Job Information," *Sociology of Work and Occupations* 8: 119–136.

Nardinelli, Clark (1980): "Child Labor and the Factory Acts," *Journal of Economic History* 40: 739–756.

Narisetti, Raju (1995): "Doctors and Teachers List Salary Woes," Work Week column, *Wall Street Journal,* November 21, A1.

Nee, Victor (1991): "Social Inequalities in Reforming State Socialism: Between Redistribution and Markets in China," *American Sociological Review* 56: 267–282.

Nee, Victor, Jimy M. Sanders & Scott Sernau (1994): "Job Transitions in an Immigrant Metropolis: Ethnic Boundaries and the Mixed Economy," *American Sociological Review* 59: 849–872.

Nelson, Daniel (1975): *Managers and Workers: Origins of the New Factory System in the United States.* Madison: University of Wisconsin Press.

Nelson, Richard (1995): "Recent Evolutionary Theorizing About Economic Change," *Journal of Economic Literature* 33: 48–90.

Newman, Katherine (1996): "Working Poor: Low Wage Employment in the Lives of Harlem Youth," in J. Graber, J. Brooks-Gunn & A. Petersen, eds., *Transitions Through Adolescence: Interpersonal Domains and Context.* Hillsdale: Lawrence Erlbaum Associates.

Nightingale, Carl Husemoller (1993): *On the Edge. A History of Poor Black Children and Their American Dreams.* New York: Basic Books.

Noble, David F. (1979): "Social Choice in Machine Design: The Case of Automatically Controlled Machine Tools," in Andrew Zimbalist, ed., *Case Studies on the Labor Process*. New York: Monthly Review Press. (1984): *Forces of Production: A Social History of Industrial Automation*. New York: Knopf.

North, Douglass C. (1981): *Structure and Change in Economic History*. New York: W. W. Norton. (1990): *Institutions, Institutional Change, and Economic Performance*. Cambridge: Cambridge University Press. (1991): "Institutions," *Journal of Economic Perspectives* 5: 97–112.

Northrup, David (1995): *Indentured Labor in the Age of Imperialism, 1834–1922*. Cambridge: Cambridge University Press.

Noyelle, Thierry (1987): *Beyond Industrial Dualism*. Boulder: Westview Press.

Numbers, Ronald L. (1985): "The Fall and Rise of the American Medical Profession," in Judith Walzer Leavitt & Ronald L. Numbers, eds., *Sickness and Health in America: Readings in the History of Medicine and Public Health*. Madison: University of Wisconsin Press, 185–196.

Olson, Mancur, Jr. (1965): *The Logic of Collective Action*. Cambridge: Harvard University Press. (1982): *The Rise and Decline of Nations: Economic Growth, Stagflation, and Social Rigidities*. New Haven: Yale University Press.

Organization for Economic Cooperation and Development (1980): *Main Economic Indicators: Historical Statistics, 1960–1979*. Paris: OECD.

Orr, Julian E. (1996): *Talking About Machines: An Ethnography of a Modern Job*. Ithaca: ILR Press.

Osterman, Paul (1975): "An Empirical Study of Labor Market Segmentation," *Industrial and Labor Relations Review* 28: 508–523. (1979): "Sex Discrimination in Professional Employment: A Case Study," *Industrial and Labor Relations Review* 32(4): 451–464. (1980): *Getting Started*. Cambridge, Mass.: M.I.T. Press. (1982): "Employment Structures Within Firms," *British Journal of Industrial Relations* 20: 349–361. (1984): ed., *Internal Labor Markets*. Cambridge, Mass.: MIT Press. (1985): "Technology and White-Collar Employment: A Research Strategy," *Proceedings of the 38th Annual Meeting of the Industrial Relations Research Association*, 52–59. (1987): "Choice of Employment Systems in Internal Labor Markets," *Industrial Relations* 26: 46–67. (1988): *Employment Futures: Reorganization, Dislocation, and Public Policy*. New York: Oxford University Press. (1993): "Why Don't 'They' Work? Employment Patterns in a High Pressure Economy," *Social Science Research* 22: 115–130.

Palmer, Phyllis (1989): *Domesticity and Dirt: Housewives and Domestic Servants in the United States, 1920–1945*. Philadelphia: Temple University Press.

Parcel, Toby L. & Charles W. Mueller (1983): *Ascription and Labor Markets: Race and Sex Differences in Earnings*. New York: Academic Press.

Parker, Robert E. (1994): *Flesh Peddlers and Warm Bodies: The Temporary Help Industry and Its Workers*. New Brunswick, N.J.: Rutgers University Press.

Parr, Joy (1990): *The Gender of Breadwinners: Women, Men, and Change in Two Industrial Towns, 1880–1950*. Toronto: University of Toronto Press.

Patrick, Steven (1995): "The Dynamic Simulation of Control and Compliance Processes in Material Organizations," *Sociological Perspectives* 38: 497–518.

Paules, Greta Foff (1991): *Dishing it Out: Power and Resistance Among Waitresses in a New Jersey Restaurant*. Philadelphia: Temple University Press.

Pelosi, Guido (1994): "Salario senza contrattazione. Le retribuzioni ad incentivo nell'industria staunitense (1890–1915)," *Passato e Presente* 12: 49–80.

Pencavel, John (1977): "Work Effort, On-the-Job Screening, and Alternative Methods of Remuneration," *Research in Labor Economics* 1: 225–258. (1986): "The Labor Supply of Men: A Survey," in Orley Ashenfelter & Richard Layard, eds., *Handbook of Labor Economics*. Amsterdam: North-Holland, 3–102.

Penn, Roger (1990): *Class, Power and Technology: Skilled Workers in Britain and America*. New York: St. Martin's.

Perlman, Selig (1928): *A Theory of the Labor Movement*. New York: MacMillan.

Perrot, Michelle (1974): *Les ouvriers en grève*, 2 vols. Paris: Mouton. (1990): ed., *A History of Private Life*. Vol. 4, *From the Fires of Revolution to the Great War*. Cambridge: Harvard University Press.

Pescarolo, Alessandra (1994): "Famiglia e impresa. Problemi di ricerca all'incrocio fra discipline," *Passato e Presente* 31: 127–142.

Petersen, Trond (1992): "Payment Systems and the Structure of Inequality: Conceptual Issues and an Analysis of Salespersons in Department Stores," *American Journal of Sociology* 98: 67–104.

Petroski, Henry (1992): *The Evolution of Useful Things*. New York: Knopf.

Pfeffer, Jeffrey (1977): "Toward an Examination of Stratification in Organizations," *Administrative Science Quarterly* 22: 553–567.

Pfeffer, Richard M. (1979): *Working for Capitali$m*. New York: Columbia University Press.

Picchio, Antonella (1992): *Social Reproduction: The Political Economy of the Labour Market*. Cambridge: Cambridge University Press.

Pierce, Jennifer L. (1995): *Gender Trials: Emotional Lives in Contemporary Law Firms*. Berkeley: University of California Press.

Pigors, Paul & Charles Myers (1981): *Personnel Administration*. McGraw-Hill.

Pinches, Michael (1987): "'All That We Have Is Our Muscle and Sweat': The Rise of Wage Labour in a Manila Squatter Community," in Michael Pinches & Salim Lakha, eds., *Wage Labour and Social Change: The Proletariat in Asia and the Pacific*. Melbourne: Centre of Southeast Asian Studies, Monash University.

Piore, Michael (1970): "Jobs and Training," in Samuel H. Beer & R. E. Barringer, eds., *The State and the Poor*. Boston: Winthrop. (1975): "Notes for a Theory of Labor Market Stratification," in Richard Edwards, Michael Reich & David Gordon, eds., *Labor Market Segmentation*. Lexington, Mass.: D. C. Heath. (1979a): "Qualitative Research in Economics," *Administrative Science Quarterly* 24: 560–569. (1979b): *Birds of Passage*. Cambridge: Cambridge University Press. (1987): "Historical Perspectives and the Interpretation of Unemployment," *Journal of Economic Literature* 25: 1834–1850.

Piore, Michael & Charles Sabel (1984): *The Second Industrial Divide: Possibilities for Prosperity*. New York: Basic Books.

Polanyi, Karl (1977): "The Economy Has No Surplus," in Harry W. Pearson, ed., *The Livelihood of Man*. New York: Academic Press.

Portes, Alejandro (1994): "By-Passing the Rules: The Dialectics of Labour Standards and Informalization in Less Developed Countries," in W. Sensenberger & D. Campbell, eds., *International Labour Standards and Economic Interdependence*. Geneva: Institute for Labour Studies. (1995): ed., *The Economic Sociology of Immi-*

gration: Essays on Networks, Ethnicity, and Entrepreneurship. New York: Russell Sage Foundation.

Portes, Alejandro & John Walton (1981): *Labor, Class, and the International System*. New York: Academic Press.

Portes, Alejandro & Julia Sensenbrenner (1993): "Embeddedness and Immigration: Notes on the Social Determinants of Economic Action," *American Journal of Sociology* 98: 1320–1350.

Portes, Alejandro & Min Zhou (1992): "Gaining the Upper Hand: Economic Mobility Among Immigrant and Domestic Minorities," *Ethnic and Racial Studies* 15: 491–522.

Portes, Alejandro & Robert D. Manning (1986): "The Immigrant Enclave: Theory and Empirical Examples," in Susan Olzak & Joane Nagel, eds., *Competitive Ethnic Relations*. Orlando, Fla.: Academic Press.

Portes, Alejandro & Rubén Rumbaut (1990): *Immigrant America: A Portrait*. Berkeley: University of California Press.

Portes, Alejandro, Manuel Castells & Lauren A. Benton, eds. (1989): *The Informal Economy: Studies in Advanced and Less Developed Countries*. Baltimore: Johns Hopkins University Press.

Powell, Walter W. (1990): "Neither Market Nor Hierarchy: Network Forms of Organization," *Research in Organizational Behavior* 12: 295–336.

Powell, Walter W. & Laurel Smith-Doerr (1994): "Networks and Economic Life," in Neil T. Smelser and Richard Swedberg, eds., *The Handbook of Economic Sociology*, 368–402. Princeton: Princeton University Press.

Powell, Walter W. & Paul J. DiMaggio, eds. (1991): *The New Institutionalism in Organizational Analysis*. Chicago: University of Chicago Press.

Prechel, Harland & Anne Gupman (1995): "Changing Economic Conditions and Their Effects on Professional Autonomy: An Analysis of Family Practitioners and Oncologists," *Sociological Forum* 10: 245–272.

Presser, Harriet B. (1994): "Employment Schedules Among Dual-Earner Spouses and the Division of Household Labor by Gender," *American Sociological Review* 59: 348–364.

Prude, Jonathan (1983): *The Coming of Industrial Order: Town and Factory Life in Rural Massachusetts*. Cambridge: Cambridge University Press.

Ramsay, R. A (1966): *Managers and Men: Adventures in Industry*. Sydney: Ure Smith.

Razin, Eran & André Langlois (1996): "Metropolitan Characteristics and Entrepreneurship Among Immigrants and Ethnic Groups in Canada," *International Migration Review* 30: 703–727.

Rebitzer, James B. (1993): "Radical Political Economy and the Economics of Labor Markets," *Journal of Economic Literature* 31: 1394–1434.

Reddy, William M. (1992): "The Concept of Class," in M. L. Bush, ed., *Social Orders and Social Classes in Europe Since 1500: Studies in Social Stratification*. London: Longman.

Redlich, Fritz (1964–65): *The German Military Enterpriser and His Work Force* [Beihefte 47 & 48 of *Vierteljahresschrift für Sozial- und Wirschaftsgeschichte*]. 2 vols. Wiesbaden: Steiner.

Reid, Douglas A. (1996): "Weddings, Weekdays, Work, and Leisure in Urban England 1791–1911: The Decline of Saint Monday Revisited," *Past & Present* 153: 135–163.

Reith, Reinhold (1992): "Conflitti salariali nella storia dell'artigianato tedesco del XVIII secolo," *Quaderni Storici* 27: 449–474.

Reitz, Jeffrey G. (1980): *The Survival of Ethnic Groups*. Toronto: McGraw-Hill Ryerson. (1990): "Ethnic Concentrations in Labour Markets and Their Implications for Ethnic Inequality," in Raymond Breton, Wsevolod W. Isajiw, Warren E. Kalbach & Jeffrey G. Reitz, *Ethnic Identity and Equality: Varieties of Experience in a Canadian City*. Toronto: University of Toronto Press.

Reskin, Barbara F., ed. (1984): *Sex Segregation in the Workplace: Trends, Explanations, Remedies*. Washington, D.C.: National Academy Press. (1993): "Sex Segregation in the Workplace," *Annual Review of Sociology* 19: 241–270.

Reskin, Barbara F. & Heidi Hartmann, eds. (1986): *Women's Work, Men's Work: Sex Segregation on the Job*. Washington, D.C.: National Academy Press.

Reskin, Barbara & Irene Padavic (1994): *Women and Men at Work*. Thousand Oaks, Calif.: Pine Forge Press.

Reskin, Barbara F. & Patricia A. Roos (1990): *Job Queues, Gender Queues: Explaining Women's Inroads into Male Occupations*. Philadelphia: Temple University Press.

Reuter, Peter, Robert MacCoun & Patrick Murphy (1990): *Money From Crime: A Study of the Economics of Drug Dealing in Washington, D.C.* Santa Monica, Calif.: Rand Corporation.

Reverby, Susan (1976): "The Sorceror's Apprentice," in David Kotelchuck, ed., *Prognosis Negative*. New York: Vintage. (1987): *Ordered to Care: The Dilemma of American Nursing, 1850–1945*. Cambridge: Cambridge University Press.

Reverby, Susan & David Rosner, eds. (1979): *Health Care in America: Essays in Social History*. Philadelphia: Temple University Press.

Reynolds, Lloyd G. (1951): *The Structure of Labor Markets: Wages and Labor Mobility in Theory and Practice*. New York: Harper & Brothers.

Reynolds, Lloyd G., Stanley H. Masters & Colletta H. Moser (1987): *Economics of Labor*. Englewood Cliffs, N.J.: Prentice Hall.

Rich, Brian L. (1995): "Explaining Feminization in the U.S. Banking Industry, 1940–1980: Human Capital, Dual Labor Markets or Gender Queuing?" *Sociological Perspectives* 38: 357–380.

Riley, Matilda White & Karyn A. Loscocco (1994): "The Changing Structure of Work Opportunities: Toward an Age-Integrated Society," in Ronald P. Abeles, Helen C. Gift & Marcia G. Ory, eds., *Aging and Quality of Life*. New York: Spring Publishing.

Robinson, Joan (1953–54): "The Production Function and the Theory of Capital," *Review of Economic Studies* 21: 81–106.

Rodgers, Daniel T. (1974): *The Work Ethic in Industrial America 1850–1920*. Chicago: University of Chicago Press.

Roos, Patricia (1985): *Gender and Work: A Comparative Analysis of Industrial Societies*. Albany, N.Y.: State University of New York Press.

Roper Starch Worldwide (1995): "The Global Work Ethic? In Few Parts of the World Does Work Take Clear Priority over Leisure," Press release. September.

Rose, Sonya O. (1986): "'Gender at Work': Sex, Class, and Industrial Capitalism," *History Workshop* 21: 113–131. (1992): *Limited Livelihoods: Gender and Class in Nineteenth-Century England*. Berkeley: University of California Press.

Rose, Stephen J. (1994): *On Shaky Ground: Rising Fears About Income and Earnings.* Research Report 94–02. Washington, D.C.: National Commission on Employment Policy. (1995): *Declining Job Security and the Professionalization of Opportunity.* Research Report 95–04. Washington, D.C.: National Commission on Employment Policy. (1996): "The Truth About Social Mobility," *Challenge* (May-June): 4–8.

Roseberry, William (1991): "La Falta de Brazos: Land and Labor in the Coffee Economies of Nineteenth-Century Latin America," *Theory and Society* 20: 351–382.

Rosen, Sherwin (1985): "Implicit Contracts: A Survey," *Journal of Economic Literature* 23 (3): 1144–1175. (1986): "The Theory of Equalizing Differences," in Orley Ashenfelter & Richard Layard, eds., *Handbook of Labor Economics,* Vol. 1. Amsterdam: North-Holland, 641–692. (1992): "Distinguished Fellow: Mincering Labor Economics," *Journal of Economic Perspectives* 6: 157–170.

Rosenbaum, James E. (1984): *Career Mobility in a Corporate Hierarchy.* New York: Academic Press.

Rosenberg, Charles E. (1987): *The Care of Strangers: The Rise of America's Hospital System.* New York: Basic Books.

Rosenbloom, Joshua L. (1994): "Employer Recruitment and the Integration of Industrial Labor Markets, 1870–1914," National Bureau of Economic Research, Working Paper Series on Historical Factors in Long-Run Growth, Historical Paper 53, Cambridge, Massachusetts.

Rosenfeld, Rachel A. (1992): "Job Mobility and Career Processes," *Annual Review of Sociology* 18: 39–61.

Rosenfeld, Rachel A. & Arne L. Kalleberg (1991): "Gender Inequality in the Labor Market: A Cross-National Perspective," *Acta Sociologica* 34: 207–226.

Rosenkrantz, Barbara Gutmann (1985): "The Search for Professional Order in 19th-Century American Medicine," in Judith Walzer Leavitt & Ronald L. Numbers, eds., *Sickness and Health in America: Readings in the History of Medicine and Public Health.* Madison: University of Wisconsin Press, 219–232.

Rosenthal, Eleanor (1997): "Senior Doctors and Nurses See Threat to Jobs," *New York Times,* January 26: 1,24.

Rosenthal, Neal H. (1989): "More Than Wages at Issue in Job Quality Debate," *Monthly Labor Review* (December): 4–8.

Rosenzweig, Mark R. (1995): "Why Are There Returns to Schooling?" *American Economic Review, Papers and Proceedings* 85: 153–158.

Ross, Arthur M. (1948): *Trade Union Wage Policy.* Berkeley & Los Angeles: University of California Press.

Ross, Ellen (1993): *Love and Toil: Motherhood in Outcast London, 1870–1918.* New York: Oxford University Press.

Rothman, David J. (1980): *Conscience and Convenience: The Asylum and Its Alternatives in Progressive America.* Boston: Little, Brown. (1991): *Strangers at the Bedside: A History of How Law and Bioethics Transformed Medical Decision Making.* New York: Basic Books.

Rothstein, Bo (1992): "Labor-Market Institutions and Working-Class Strength," in Sven Steinmo, Kathleen Thelen & Frank Longstreth, eds., *Structuring Politics: Historical Institutionalism in Comparative Analysis.* Cambridge: Cambridge University Press.

Roy, Donald (1954): "Efficiency and 'the Fix': Informal Intergroup Relations in a Piecework Machine Shop," *American Journal of Sociology* 60: 155–66.

Roy, William (1984a): "Class Conflict and Social Change in Historical Perspective," *Annual Review of Sociology* 10: 483–506. (1984b): "Institutional Governance and Social Cohesion: The Internal Organization of the American Capitalist Class, 1886–1905," *Research in Social Stratification and Mobility* 3: 147–171. (1997): *Socializing Capital: The Rise of the Large Industrial Corporation in America.* Princeton: Princeton University Press.

Rubery, Jill (1978): "Structured Labour Markets, Worker Organization and Low Pay," *Cambridge Journal of Economics* 2: 17–36.

Ruggles, Patricia (1990): *Drawing the Line: Alternative Measures and Their Implications for Public Policy.* Washington, D.C.: Urban Institute.

Rule, James & Peter Brantley (1992): "Computerized Surveillance in the Workplace: Forms and Distributions," *Sociological Forum* 7: 405–424.

Rumberger, Russell W. (1987): "The Potential Impact of Technology on the Skill Requirements of Future Jobs," in Gerald Burke & Russell Rumberger, eds., *The Future Impact of Technology on Work and Education.* Philadelphia: Falmer Press.

Rumberger, Russell & Martin Carnoy (1980): "Segmentation in the U.S. Labour Market: Its Effect on the Mobility and Earnings of Blacks and Whites," *Cambridge Journal of Economics* 4: 117–132.

Sabel, Charles F. (1982): *Work and Politics: The Division of Labor in Industry.* Cambridge: Cambridge University Press.

Sabel, Charles F. & Jonathan Zeitlin (1985): "Historical Alternatives to Mass Production: Politics, Markets, and Technology in Nineteenth-Century Industrialization," *Past & Present* 108: 133–176.

Sacks, Karen Brodkin (1984): "Computers, Ward Secretaries, and a Walkout in a Southern Hospital," in Karen Brodkin Sacks & Dorothy Remy, eds., *My Troubles Are Going to Have Trouble with Me: Everyday Trials and Triumphs of Women Workers.* New Brunswick, N.J.: Rutgers University Press.

Sah, Raaj K. (1991): "Fallibility in Human Organizations and Political Systems," *Journal of Economic Perspectives* 5: 67–88.

Sah, Raaj Kumar & Joseph E. Stiglitz (1986): "The Architecture of Economic Systems: Hierarchies and Polyarchies," *American Economic Review* 76: 716–727.

Salais, Robert, Nicolas Baverez & Benedicte Reynaud (1986): *L'Invention du chômage. Histoire et transformation d'une catégorie en France des années 1890 aux années 1980.* Paris: Presses Universitaires de France.

Salzinger, Leslie (1991): "A Maid by Any Other Name: The Transformation of 'Dirty Work' by Central American Immigrants," in Michael Burawoy et al., *Ethnography Unbound: Power and Resistance in the Modern Metropolis.* Berkeley: University of California Press.

Samuelson, Paul (1957): "Wages and Interest: A Modern Dissection of Marxian Economic Models," *American Economic Review* 47: 884–912. (1983): *Foundations of Economic Analysis.* Cambridge: Harvard University Press. First published in 1945.

Sandoval, Salvador A. M. (1993): *Social Change and Labor Unrest in Brazil Since 1945.* Boulder: Westview Press.

Sappington, David E. M. (1991): "Incentives in Principal-Agent Relationships," *Journal of Economic Perspectives* 5: 45–66.

Sassen-Koob, Saskia (1985): "Capital Mobility and Labor Migration: Their Expression in Core Cities," in Michael Timberlake, ed., *Urbanization in the World-Economy*. Orlando, Fla.: Academic Press.

Saxenian, Annalee (1994): *Regional Advantage: Culture and Competition in Silicon Valley and Route 128*. Cambridge: Harvard University Press.

Schappert, Susan M. (1995): "Office Visits to Neurologists: United States, 1991–1992." Advance Data from Vital and Health Statistics, no. 267. Hyattsville, Maryland: National Center for Health Statistics.

Scheer, Christopher (1995): "'Illegals' Made Slaves of Fashion," *Nation* 261(7): 237–238.

Schmiechen, James A. (1984): *Sweated Industries and Sweated Labor: The London Clothing Trades, 1860–1914*. Urbana: University of Illinois Press.

Schofer, Lawrence (1975): *The Formation of a Modern Labor Force: Upper Silesia 1865–1914*. Berkeley: University of California Press.

Schor, Juliet (1992): *The Overworked American*. New York: Basic Books.

Schultheiss, Katrin (1995): "'La Véritable Médecine des femmes': Anna Hamilton and the Politics of Nursing Reform in Bordeaux, 1900–1914," *French Historical Studies* 19: 183–214.

Schumpeter, Joseph (1947): "The Creative Response in Economic History," *Journal of Economic History* 7: 149–159.

Scott, Joan W. (1974): *The Glassworkers of Carmaux: French Craftsmen and Political Action in a Nineteenth-Century City*. Cambridge: Harvard University Press.

Scott, W. Richard (1987): "The Adolescence of Institutional Theory," *Administrative Science Quarterly* 32: 493–511. (1995): *Institutions and Organizations*. Thousand Oaks, Calif.: Sage.

Scranton, Philip (1983): *Proprietary Capitalism: The Textile Manufacture at Philadelphia, 1800–1885*. Cambridge: Cambridge University Press. (1989): *Figured Tapestry: Production, Markets, and Power in Philadelphia Textiles, 1885–1941*. Cambridge: Cambridge University Press.

Scull, Andrew, Charlotte Mackenzie & Nicholas Hervey (1996): *Masters of Bedlam: The Transformation of the Mad-Doctoring Trade*. Princeton: Princeton University Press.

Selanders, Louise C. (1993): *Florence Nightingale: An Environmental Adaptation Theory*. Newbury Park, Calif.: Sage Publications.

Sen, Amartya (1982): *Choice, Welfare, and Measurement*. Cambridge, Mass.: MIT Press. (1983): "Women, Technology, and Sexual Divisions," *Trade and Development* 6: 195–223. (1992): *Inequality Reexamined*. Cambridge: Harvard University Press.

Sengenberger, Werner & Duncan Campbell, eds. (1994): *International Labour Standards and Economic Interdependence*. Geneva: International Institute for Labour Studies.

Sengenberger, Werner, Gary Loveman & Michael Piore, eds. (1990): *The Re-Emergence of Small Enterprise*. Geneva: International Institute for Labor Studies.

Sennett, Richard & Jonathan Cobb (1972): *The Hidden Injuries of Class*. New York: Random House (Vintage).

Sexton, Patricia Cayo (1991): *The War on Labor and the Left: Understanding America's Unique Conservatism*. Boulder: Westview Press.

Shaiken, Harley (1985): *Work Transformed: Automation and Labor in the Computer Age*. New York: Holt, Rinehart & Winston.

Shapiro, Carl & Joseph Stiglitz (1984): "Equilibrium Unemployment as a Worker Discipline Device," *American Economic Review* 74: 433–444.

Shellenbarger, Sue (1993a): "Employers Like to Keep Things in the Family," *Wall Street Journal*, August 2, B1. (1993b): "Work-Force Study Finds Loyalty Is Weak, Divisions of Race and Gender Are Deep," *Wall Street Journal*, September 3, B1, B8. (1994): "Many Employers Flout Family and Medical Leave Law," *Wall Street Journal*, July 26, B1, B5.

Shepherd, William G. (1979): *The Economics of Industrial Organization*. Englewood Cliffs, N.J.: Prentice-Hall.

Sherer, Paul M. (1995): "Hot Thai Export to U.S.: 'Slave' Workers," *Wall Street Journal*, November 2, 12.

Shorter, Edward & Charles Tilly (1974): *Strikes in France, 1830–1968*. Cambridge: Cambridge University Press.

Shryock, Richard Harrison (1968): "Nursing Emerges as a Profession: The American Experience," *Clio Medica* 3: 131–147.

Siegel, Reva B. (1994): "Home as Work: The First Woman's Rights Claims Concerning Wives' Household Labor, 1850–1880," *Yale Law Journal* 103: 1075–1217.

Silver, Hilary (1993): "Homework and Domestic Work," *Sociological Forum* 8: 181–204.

Simmons, Colin P. & Christos Kalantaridis (1994): "Flexible Specialization in the Southern European Periphery: The Growth of Garment Manufacturing in Peonia County, Greece," *Comparative Studies in Society and History* 36: 649–675.

Simon, Curtis J. & John T. Warner (1992): "Matchmaker, Matchmaker: The Effect of Old Boy Networks on Job Match Quality, Earnings, and Tenure," *Journal of Labor Economics* 10: 306–331.

Simon, Herbert (1976): *Administrative Behavior: A Study of Decision-Making Processes in Administrative Organization*. New York: Free Press. First published in 1945. (1991): "Organizations and Markets," *Journal of Economic Perspectives* 5: 25–44.

Slichter, Sumner (1919): *The Turnover of Factory Labor*. New York: D. Appleton.

Smith, Adam (1937): *An Inquiry into the Nature and Causes of the Wealth of Nations* (Cannan Edition). New York: Random House. First published in 1776.

Smith, James P. & Michael P. Ward (1985): "Time-Series Growth in the Female Labor Force," *Journal of Labor Economics* 3: S59-S90.

Smith, Michael R. (1990): "What Is New in 'New Structuralist' Analyses of Earnings?" *American Sociological Review* 55: 827–841.

Smith, Thomas Spence (1992): *Strong Interaction*. Chicago: University of Chicago Press.

Smith, Vicki (1990): *Managing in the Corporate Interest: Control and Resistance in an American Bank*. Berkeley: University of California Press.

Smock, Pamela J. (1993): "The Economic Costs of Marital Disruption for Young Women over the Past Two Decades," *Demography* 30: 353–371.

Sobel, Richard (1994): "The Politics of the White Collar Working Class: From Structure to Action," *Research in Micropolitics* 4: 225–242.

Sokoloff, Kenneth L. (1984): "Was the Transition from the Artisanal Shop to the Nonmechanized Factory Associated with Gains in Efficiency? Evidence from the

U.S. Manufacturing Censuses of 1820 and 1850," *Explorations in Economic History* 21: 351–382.

Solow, Robert M. (1970): *Growth Theory*. New York: Oxford University Press. (1990): *The Labor Market as a Social Institution*. Oxford: Blackwell.

Solzhenitsyn, Aleksandr I. (1975): *The Gulag Archipelago 1918–1956*, Vol.2. New York: Harper and Row.

Sonenscher, Michael (1989): *Work and Wages: Natural Law, Politics, and the Eighteenth-Century Trades*. Cambridge: Cambridge University Press.

South, Scott J. & Glenna Spitze (1994): "Housework in Marital and Nonmarital Households," *American Sociological Review* 59: 327–347.

Spalding, Hobart (1992): "Peru on the Brink," *Monthly Review* January, 29–43.

Special Task Force to the Secretary of Health, Education, and Welfare (1973): *Work in America*. Cambridge: MIT Press.

Spence, A. Michael (1973): "Job Market Signalling," *Quarterly Journal of Economics* 87: 355–374.

Spenner, Kenneth I. (1988): "Technological Change, Skill Requirements, and Education: The Case for Uncertainty," in Richard M. Cyert & David C. Mowery, eds., *The Impact of Technological Change on Employment and Economic Growth: Papers Commissioned by the Panel on Technology and Employment*. Cambridge, Mass.: Harper and Row, Ballinger, 131–184.

Starr, Paul (1982): *The Social Transformation of American Medicine*. New York: Basic Books.

Steinberg, Marc (1991): "Talkin' Class: Discourse, Ideology, and Their Intersection," in Scott McNall, Rhonda Levine & Rick Fantasia, eds., *Bringing Class Back In*. Boulder: Westview Press.

Steiner, Philippe (1995): "Economic Sociology: A Historical Perspective," *European Journal of the History of Economic Thought* 2: 175–195.

Steinfeld, Robert J. (1991): *The Invention of Free Labor: The Employment Relation in English and American Law and Culture, 1350–1870*. Chapel Hill: University of North Carolina Press.

Steinmetz, George (1994): "Regulation Theory, Post-Marxism, and the New Social Movements," *Comparative Studies in Society and History* 36: 176–212.

Stephens, Evelyne Huber (1980): *The Politics of Workers' Participation: The Peruvian Approach in Comparative Perspective*. New York: Academic Press.

Stevens, Beth (1986): *Complementing the Welfare State: The Development of Private Pension, Health Insurance, and Other Employee Benefits in the United States*. Geneva: International Labour Office.

Stevens, Rosemary (1971): "Trends in Medical Specialization in the United States," *Inquiry* 8: 9–19. (1989): *In Sickness and in Wealth: American Hospitals in the Twentieth Century*. New York: Basic Books.

Stewman, Shelby (1986): "Demographic Models of Internal Labor Markets," *Administrative Science Quarterly* 31: 212–247.

Stigler, George J. & Gary S. Becker (1977): "De Gustibus non est Disputandum," *American Economic Review* 67: 76–90.

Stiglitz, Joseph (1984): "A Reformist View of Radical Economics," paper presented at the Annual Meeting of the American Economic Association, December. (1991):

"Symposium on Organizations and Economics," *Journal of Economic Perspectives* 5: 15–24.

Stinchcombe, Arthur L. (1959): "Bureaucratic and Craft Administration of Production," *Administrative Science Quarterly* 4: 168–187. (1965): "Social Structure and Organizations," in James G. March, ed., *Handbook of Organizations*. Chicago: Rand-McNally. (1972): "The Social Determinants of Success," *Science* 178: 603–604. (1978): "Generations and Cohorts in Social Mobility: Economic Development and Social Mobility in Norway," Memorandum no. 18, Institute of Applied Social Research, Oslo. (1979): "Social Mobility in Industrial Labor Markets," *Acta Sociologica* 22: 217–245. (1983): *Economic Sociology*. New York: Academic Press. (1986): "Milieu and Structure Updated," *Theory and Society* 15: 901–913. (1990a): "Work Institutions and the Sociology of Everyday Life," in Kai Erikson & Steven Peter Vallas, eds., *The Nature of Work: Sociological Perspectives*. New Haven: Yale University Press. (1990b): *Information and Organizations*. Berkeley: University of California Press. (1994): "Freedom and Oppression of Slaves in the Eighteenth-Century Caribbean," *American Sociological Review* 59: 911–929.

Stockmann, Reinhard (1985): "Gewerbliche Frauenarbeit in Deutschland 1875–1980. Zur Entwicklung der Beschäftigtenstruktur," *Geschichte und Gesellschaft* 11: 447–475.

Stone, Katherine (1974): "The Origins of Job Structures in the Steel Industry," *Review of Radical Political Economy* 6: 61–97.

Strom, Sharon Hartman (1992): *Beyond the Typewriter: Gender, Class, and the Origins of Modern American Office Work, 1900–1930*. Urbana: University of Illinois Press.

Sturdevant, Saundra Pollock & Brenda Stoltzfus (1992): *Let the Good Times Roll: Prostitution and the U.S. Military in Asia*. New York: New Press.

Sundstrom, William A. (1990): "Half a Career: Discrimination and Railroad Internal Labor Markets," *Industrial Relations* 29: 423–440.

Supple, Barry (1987): *The History of the British Coal Industry*. Volume 4, *1913–1946: The Political Economy of Decline*. Oxford: Clarendon Press.

Swedberg, Richard (1991): "Major Traditions of Economic Sociology," *Annual Review of Sociology* 17: 251–276.

Swerdlow, Marian (1990): "Rules and Compliance in the New York Subways," *Review of Radical Political Economics* 22: 1–16.

Swinnerton, Kenneth A. & Howard Wial (1995): "Is Job Stability Declining in the U.S. Economy?" *Industrial and Labor Relations Review*, 48: 293–304.

Szelényi, Szonja (1992): "Economic Subsystems and the Occupational Structure: A Comparison of Hungary and the United States," *Sociological Forum* 7: 563–586.

Szreter, Simon (1996): *Fertility, Class, and Gender in Britain, 1860–1940*. Cambridge: Cambridge University Press.

Tajfel, H. & J. C. Turner (1986): "The Social Identity Theory of Intergroup Behavior," in S. Worchel and W. G. Austin, eds., *Psychology of Intergroup Relations*. Chicago: Nelson-Hall, 7–24.

Tanner, Julian & Rhonda Cockerill (1996): "Gender, Social Change, and the Professions: The Case of Pharmacy," *Sociological Forum* 11: 643–660.

Tarrow, Sidney (1989): *Democracy and Disorder: Protest and Politics in Italy, 1965–1975*. Oxford: Clarendon Press. (1994): *Power in Movement: Social Movements, Collective Action, and Politics*. Cambridge: Cambridge University Press.

Taylor, J. Edward (1986): "Differential Migration, Networks, Information, and Risk," *Research in Human Capital and Development* 4: 147–171.

Teece, David J. (1993): "The Dynamics of Industrial Capitalism: Perspectives on Alfred Chandler's *Scale and Scope*," *Journal of Economic Literature* 31: 199–225.

Tenfelde, Klaus (1977): *Sozialgeschichte der Bergarbeiterschaft an der Ruhr im 19. Jahrhundert.* Bonn-Bad Godesberg: Verlag Neue Gesellschaft.

Tenner, Edward (1996): *Why Things Bite Back: Technology and the Revenge of Unintended Consequences.* New York: Alfred A. Knopf.

Thomas, Robert J. (1985): *Citizenship, Gender, and Work: Social Organization of Industrial Agriculture.* Berkeley: University of California Press. (1994): *What Machines Can't Do: Politics and Technology in the Industrial Enterprise.* Berkeley: University of California Press.

Thompson, E. P. (1963): *The Making of the English Working Class.* London: Gollancz. (1967): "Time, Work-Discipline, and Industrial Capitalism," *Past & Present* 38: 56–97. (1978): "Eighteenth-Century English Society: Class Struggle Without Class?" *Social History* 3: 133–165. (1991): *Customs in Common.* London: Merlin Press.

Thompson, Paul (1983): *The Nature of Work: An Introduction to Debates on the Labour Process.* London: MacMillan.

Thomson, Janice E. (1994): *Mercenaries, Pirates & Sovereigns: State-Building and Extraterritorial Violence in Early Modern Europe.* Princeton: Princeton University Press.

Thomson, Ross (1984): "The Eco-Technic Process and the Development of the Sewing Machine," in Gary Saxonhouse & Gavin Wright, eds., *Technique, Spirit, and Form in the Making of the Modern Economies: Essays in Honor of William N. Parker.* Research in Economic History, Supplement 3. Greenwich, Conn.: JAI Press. (1989): *The Path to Mechanized Shoe Production in the United States.* Chapel Hill: University of North Carolina Press. (1991): "Machine Tools as a Technological Center," unpublished paper, Department of Economics, University of Vermont.

Thurow, Lester (1975): *Generating Inequality.* New York: Basic Books. (1983): *Dangerous Currents: The State of Economics.* New York: Random House.

Tienda, Marta & Jennifer Glass (1985): "Household Structure and Labor Force Participation of Black, Hispanic, and White Mothers," *Demography* 22: 395–414.

Tilly, Charles (1978): "Migration in Modern European History," in William McNeill & Ruth Adams, eds., *Human Migration: Patterns, Implications, Policies.* Bloomington: Indiana University Press. (1983): "Flows of Capital and Forms of Industry in Europe, 1500–1900," *Theory and Society* 12: 123–143. (1984): "Demographic Origins of the European Proletariat," in David Levine, ed., *Proletarianization and Family Life.* Orlando, Flor.: Academic Press.

Tilly, Charles, Louise A. Tilly & Richard Tilly (1991): "European Economic and Social History in the 1990s," *Journal of European Economic History* 20: 645–671.

Tilly, Chris (1984): "Working in the Basement, Working on the Floor: The Restructuring of the Hospital Workforce, 1945–1980." Paper presented at the Union for Radical Political Economics Summer Conference, August 22–26. (1989a): "Half a Job: How U.S. Firms Use Part-Time Employment," Ph.D. dissertation, Departments of Economics and Urban Studies and Planning, M.I.T., Cambridge.

(1989b): Unpublished interview data gathered in connection with Tilly 1989a.
(1991): "Understanding Income Inequality," *Sociological Forum* 6: 739–755.
(1992): "Dualism in Part-Time Employment," *Industrial Relations* 31: 330–347.
(1996): *Half a Job: Bad and Good Part-Time Jobs in a Changing Labor Market.*
Philadelphia: Temple University Press.

Tilly, Chris, Barry Bluestone & Bennett Harrison (1986): "What Is Making American Wages More Unequal?" *Proceedings* of the Industrial Relations Research Association Annual Meeting, December.

Tilly, Chris & Charles Tilly (1994): "Capitalist Work and Labor Markets," in Neil J. Smelser & Richard Swedberg, eds., *Handbook of Economic Sociology.* New York: Russell Sage Foundation. Princeton: Princeton University Press.

Tilly, Louise A. (1979): "Individual Lives and Family Strategies in the French Proletariat," *Journal of Family History* 4 (2): 137–152. (1992a): *Politics and Class in Milan, 1881–1901.* New York: Oxford University Press. (1992b): "Industrialization and Gender Inequality." Working Paper 148, Center for Studies of Social Change, New School for Social Research, New York City.

Tilly, Louise A. & Joan W. Scott (1987): *Women, Work, and Family.* 2nd ed. New York: Methuen.

Tilly, Louise A. & Patricia Gurin, eds. (1990): *Women, Politics, and Change.* New York: Russell Sage Foundation.

Tilly, Richard (1990): *Vom Zollverein zum Industriestaat. Die wirtschaftlich-soziale Entwicklung Deutschlands 1834 bis 1914.* Munich: Deutscher Taschenbuch Verlag.

Tolbert, Charles, Patrick M. Horan & E. M. Beck (1980): "The Structure of Economic Segmentation: A Dual Economy Approach," *American Journal of Sociology* 85: 1095–1116.

Tomaskovic-Devey, Donald (1993a): *Gender & Racial Inequality at Work: The Sources & Consequences of Job Segregation.* Ithaca: ILR Press. (1993b): "The Gender and Race Composition of Jobs and the Male/Female, White/Black Pay Gaps," *Social Forces* 72: 45–76.

Tomlins, Christopher L. (1993): *Law, Labor, and Ideology in the Early American Republic.* Cambridge: Cambridge University Press.

Topalov, Christian (1994): *Naissance du chômeur, 1880–1910.* Paris: Albin Michel.

Topel, Robert (1991): "Specific Capital, Mobility, and Wages: Wages Rise with Job Seniority," *Journal of Political Economy* 99: 145–176.

Trager, Lillian (1988): *The City Connection: Migration and Family Interdependence in the Philippines.* Ann Arbor: University of Michigan Press.

Treiman, Donald J. & Heidi I. Hartmann, eds. (1981): *Women, Work, and Wages: Equal Pay for Jobs of Equal Value.* Washington, D.C.: National Academy Press.

Tunzelmann, G. N. von (1978): *Steam Power and British Industrialization to 1860.* Oxford: Clarendon Press.

Tuominen, Mary (1994): "The Hidden Organization of Labor: Gender, Race/Ethnicity, and Child-Care Work in the Formal and Informal Economy," *Sociological Perspectives* 37: 229–246.

Tushman, Michael L. & Lori Rosenkopf (1992): "Organizational Determinants of Technological Change: Toward a Sociology of Technological Evolution," *Research in Organizational Behavior* 14: 311–347.

U.S. Bureau of Labor Statistics (1951): *Analysis of Work Stoppages During 1950,* Bulletin 1035. (1961): *Analysis of Work Stoppages 1960,* Bulletin 1302. (1972): *Analysis of Work Stoppages, 1970,* Bulletin 1727. (1982): *Analysis of Work Stoppages, 1980,* Bulletin 2120. (1991a): *Area Wage Survey: Los Angeles-Long Beach, California, Metropolitan Area, December 1990,* Bulletin 3055–55. (1991b): *Area Wage Survey: Atlanta, Georgia, Metropolitan Area, May 1991,* Bulletin 3060–14. (1992a): *Occupational Compensation Survey: Pay and Benefits—Detroit, Michigan, Metropolitan Area, December 1991,* Bulletin 3060–60. (1992b): "Employee Tenure and Occupational Mobility in the Early 1990s," *Bureau of Labor Statistics News,* June 26.

U.S. Council of Economic Advisors (1991): *Economic Report of the President.* Washington, D.C.: U.S. Government Printing Office.

U.S. Department of Commerce (1988): *County Business Patterns, 1986.* Washington, D.C.: U.S. Government Printing Office. (1993): *Money Income of Households, Families, and Persons in the United States: 1992.* Current Population Reports, Consumer Income, Series P60–184. (1995): *Statistical Abstract of the United States, 1995.* Washington, D.C.: U.S. Government Printing Office.

U.S. Department of Health & Human Services (1993): *Trends in Hospital Personnel, 1983–1990.* Washington, D.C.: Department of Health & Human Services.

U.S. Department of Labor (1975): *Jobseeking Methods Used by American Workers.* Washington, D.C.: U.S. Government Printing Office.

Valverde, Marianna (1988): "'Giving the Female a Domestic Turn': The Social, Legal, and Moral Regulation of Women's Work in British Cotton Mills, 1820–1850," *Journal of Social History* 21: 619–634.

Van Buren, Mark E. (1992): "Organizational Size and the Use of Firm Internal Labor Markets in High Growth Establishments," *Social Science Research* 21: 311–327.

Van Maanen, John & Gideon Kunda (1989): "'Real Feelings': Emotional Expression and Organizational Culture," in B. M. Staw & L. L. Cummings, eds., *Research in Organizational Behavior,* vol. 11. Greenwich, Conn.: JAI Press, 43–103.

Vanek, Joann (1973): "Keeping Busy: Time Spent in Housework, United States, 1920–1970," Ph.D. dissertation, University of Michigan, Ann Arbor. (1974): "Time Spent in Housework," *Scientific American* 231: 116–120.

Van Haitsma, Martha (1989): "Aspects of the Underclass: Employment and Social Context of Innercity Residents." Paper presented at the Allied Social Science Associations Annual Meeting, December 28–30, Atlanta, Georgia.

van Tijn, Theo (1976): "A Contribution to the Scientific Study of the History of Trade Unions," *International Review of Social History* 21: 212–239.

van Zanden, J. L. (1993): *The Rise and Decline of Holland's Economy: Merchant Capitalism and the Labour Market.* Manchester: Manchester University Press.

Verdery, Katherine (1991): "Theorizing Socialism: A Prologue to the 'Transition'," *American Ethnologist* 18: 419–439. (1993): "What Was Socialism and Why Did It Fall?" *Contention* 3: 1–24.

Villa, Paola (1986): *The Structuring of Labor Markets: A Comparative Analysis of the Steel and Construction Industries in Italy.* Oxford: Clarendon Press.

Vincenti, Walter G. (1994): "The Retractable Airplane Landing Gear and the Northrop 'Anomaly': Variation-Selection and the Shaping of Technology," *Technology and Culture* 35: 1–33.

Visser, Jelle (1993): "Syndicalisme et désyndicalisation," *Le Mouvement Social* 162: 17–40.

Visser, Jelle & Bernhard Ebbinghaus (1992): "Making the Most of Diversity? European Integration and Transnational Organization of Labour," in Justin Greenwood, Jürgen R. Grote & Karsten Ronit, eds., *Organized Interests and the European Community*. London: Sage.

Vogel, Morris J. (1980): *The Invention of the Modern Hospital: Boston 1870–1930*. Chicago: University of Chicago Press.

Voss, Kim (1993): *The Making of American Exceptionalism: The Knights of Labor and Class Formation in the Nineteenth Century*. Ithaca: Cornell University Press.

Wadsworth, Alfred P. & Julia de Lacy Mann (1931): *The Cotton Trade and Industrial Lancashire 1600–1780*. Manchester: Manchester University Press.

Wagner, David (1980): "The Proletarianization of Nursing in the United States, 1932–1946," *International Journal of Health Services* 10: 271–290.

Walder, Andrew (1986): *Communist Neo-Traditionalism: Work and Authority in Chinese Industry*. Berkeley: University of California Press. (1992): "Property Rights and Stratification in Socialist Redistributive Economies," *American Sociological Review* 57: 524–539. (1995): "Career Mobility and the Communist Political Order," *American Sociological Review* 60: 309–328.

Waldinger, Roger D. (1986): *Through the Eye of the Needle: Immigrants and Enterprise in New York's Garment Trades*. New York: New York University Press. (1986–87): "Changing Ladders and Musical Chairs: Ethnicity and Opportunity in Post-Industrial New York," *Politics and Society* 15: 369–401. (1994): "The Making of an Immigrant Niche," *International Migration Review* 28: 3–30.

Waldinger, Roger D., Robin Ward & Howard Aldrich (1985): "Ethnic Business and Occupational Mobility in Advanced Societies," *Sociology* 19: 586–597.

Wallace, Anthony F. C. (1978): *Rockdale: The Growth of an American Village in the Early Industrial Revolution*. New York: Knopf.

Walras, Léon (1954): *Elements of Pure Economics; or the Theory of Social Wealth*. Translated by William Jaffé. Homewood, Ill.: Richard D. Irwin, for the American Economic Association. First published in 1874.

Walsh, John P. (1993): *Supermarkets Transformed: Understanding Organizational and Technological Innovations*. New Brunswick, N.J.: Rutgers University Press.

Walsh, Kenneth (1983): *Strikes in Europe and the United States: Measurement and Incidence*. New York: St. Martin's.

Walton, Richard & Robert B. McKersie (1965): *A Behavioral Theory of Labor Negotiations: An Analysis of a Social Interaction System*. New York: McGraw-Hill.

Watanabe, Shin (1987): "Job-Searching: A Comparative Study of Male Employment Relations in the United States and Japan," Unpublished Ph.D. dissertation, Department of Sociology, University of California, Los Angeles. UMI Dissertation Information Service Order No. 8727817.

Watkins, Susan Cotts, ed. (1994): *After Ellis Island: Newcomers and Natives in the 1910 Census*. New York: Russell Sage Foundation.

Way, Peter (1993): *Common Labour: Workers and the Digging of North American Canals 1780–1860*. Cambridge: Cambridge University Press.

Webb, Sidney & Beatrice Webb (1897): *Industrial Democracy*. London: Longmans.

Weber, Max (1958): *The Protestant Ethic and the Spirit of Capitalism*. New York: Scribner.

Weber, Michael P. & Ewa Morawska (1985): "East Europeans in Steel Towns: A Comparative Analysis," *Journal of Urban History* 11: 280–313.

Weisbrod, B. A. (1988): *The Nonprofit Economy*. Cambridge: Harvard University Press. (1989): "Rewarding Performance That is Hard to Measure: The Private Nonprofit Sector," *Science,* May 5, 244.

Weiss, Andrew (1995): "Human Capital vs. Signalling Explanations of Wages," *Journal of Economic Perspectives* 9: 133–154.

Wellman, Barry (1985): "Domestic Work, Paid Work, and Net Work," in Steve Duck & Daniel Perlman, eds., *Understanding Personal Relationships*. London: Sage. (1990): "The Place of Kinfolk in Personal Community Networks," *Marriage and Family Review* 15: 195–228.

Wellman, David (1995): *The Union Makes Us Strong: Radical Unionism on the San Francisco Waterfront*. Cambridge: Cambridge University Press.

Western, Bruce (1993): "Postwar Unionization in Eighteen Advanced Capitalist Countries," *American Sociological Review* 58: 266–282.

Western, Bruce & Katherine Beckett (1997): "How Unregulated Is the U.S. Labor Market? The Dynamics of Jobs and Jails, 1980–1995," unpublished paper, Princeton University.

Westwood, Sallie (1982): *All Day, Every Day: Factory and Family in the Making of Women's Lives*. Chicago: University of Illinois Press.

White, Harrison (1970): *Chains of Opportunity: System Models of Mobility in Organizations*. Cambridge: Harvard University Press. (1981): "Where Do Markets Come From?" *American Journal of Sociology* 87: 517–547. (1988): "Varieties of Markets" in Barry Wellman & Steven Berkowitz, eds., *Social Structures: A Network Approach*. Cambridge: Cambridge University Press. (1992): *Identity and Control: A Structural Theory of Social Action*. Princeton: Princeton University Press. (1993): *Careers & Creativity: Social Forces in the Arts*. Boulder: Westview Press.

Whitley, Richard (1984): *The Intellectual and Social Organization of the Sciences*. Oxford: Clarendon Press.

Wial, Howard (1991): "Getting a Good Job: Mobility in a Segmented Labor Market," *Industrial Relations* 30: 396–416.

Wilentz, Sean (1981): "Artisanal Origins of the American Working Class," *International Labor and Working Class History* 19: 1–22.

Williams, Christine L. (1989): *Gender Differences at Work: Women and Men in Nontraditional Occupations*. Berkeley: University of California Press.

Williamson, Oliver (1975): *Markets and Hierarchies, Analysis and Antitrust Implications: A Study in the Economics of Internal Organization*. New York: Free Press. (1985): *The Economic Institutions of Capitalism*. New York: Free Press. (1991): "Comparative Economic Organization: The Analysis of Discrete Structural Alternatives," *Administrative Science Quarterly* 36: 269–296.

Willis, Robert J. (1986): "Wage Determinants: A Survey and Reinterpretation of Human Capital Earnings Functions," in Orley Ashenfelter & Richard Layard, eds., *Handbook of Labor Economics,* Vol. 1. Amsterdam: North-Holland, 525–602.

Winter, Sidney (1964): "Economic 'Natural Selection' and the Theory of the Firm," *Yale Economic Essays* 4: 225–272. (1980): "An Essay on the Theory of Production," Proceedings of the Centennial Symposium of the University of Michigan. Department of Economics.

Wolfe, Samuel, ed. (1978): *Organization of Health Workers and Labor Conflict.* Farmingdale, N.Y.: Baywood.

Wolinsky, Fredric D. (1993): "The Professional Dominance, Deprofessionalization, Proletarianization, and Corporatization Perspectives: An Overview and Synthesis," in Frederic W. Hafferty & John B. McKinlay, eds., *The Changing Medical Profession: An International Perspective.* New York: Oxford University Press.

Wood, Stephen, ed. (1982): *The Degradation of Work? Skill, Deskilling, and the Labour Process.* London: Hutchinson.

Woods, James D. (1993): *The Corporate Closet: The Professional Lives of Gay Men in America.* New York: Free Press.

Worsley, Peter (1986): *The Three Worlds: Culture and World Development.* London: Weidenfeld & Nicolson.

Wright, Erik Olin (1979): *Class Structure and Income Determination.* New York: Academic Press. (1985): *Classes.* London: Verso.

Wright, Gavin (1978): *The Political Economy of the Cotton South: Households, Markets, and Wealth in the Nineteenth Century.* New York: Norton. (1990): "The Origins of American Industrial Success, 1879–1940," *American Economic Review* 80: 651–668.

Wright, Rosemary & Jerry A. Jacobs (1994): "Male Flight from Computer Work: A New Look at Occupational Resegregation and Ghettoization," *American Sociological Review* 59: 511–536.

Wuthnow, Robert (1991): *Acts of Compassion: Caring for Others and Helping Ourselves.* Princeton: Princeton University Press.

Yankelovich, Daniel (1993): "How Changes in the Economy Are Reshaping American Values," in Henry J. Aaron, Thomas E. Mann & Timothy Taylor, eds., *Values and Public Policy.* Washington, D.C.: Brookings Institution.

Yankelovich, Daniel et al. (1985): *The World at Work: An International Report on Jobs, Productivity, and Human Values: A Joint Report of the Public Agenda Foundation and the Aspen Institute for Humanistic Studies.* New York: Octagon Books.

Yans-McLaughlin, Virginia, ed. (1990): *Immigration Reconsidered: History, Sociology, and Politics.* New York: Oxford University Press.

Young, H. Peyton (1993): "The Evolution of Conventions," *Econometrica* 61: 57–84.

Zelizer, Viviana (1985): *Pricing the Priceless Child: The Changing Social Value of Children.* New York: Basic Books. (1988): "Beyond the Polemics on the Market: Establishing a Theoretical and Empirical Agenda," *Sociological Forum* 3: 614–634. (1994a): "The Creation of Domestic Currencies," *American Economic Review, Papers and Proceedings* 84: 138–142. (1994b): *The Social Meaning of Money.* New York: Basic Books.

Zimbalist, Andrew, ed. (1979): *Case Studies on the Labor Process.* New York: Monthly Review Press.

Zolberg, Aristide (1986): "How Many Exceptionalisms?" in Ira Katznelson & Aristide R. Zolberg, eds., *Working-Class Formation: Nineteenth-Century Patterns in Western Europe and the United States.* Princeton: Princeton University Press.

Zuboff, Shoshana (1988): *In the Age of the Smart Machine: The Future of Work and Power.* New York: Basic Books.

Zunz, Olivier (1982): *The Changing Face of Inequality: Urbanization, Industrial Development, and Immigrants in Detroit, 1880–1920*. Chicago: University of Chicago Press. (1990): *Making America Corporate, 1870–1920*. Chicago: University of Chicago Press.

Index